Academic Entrepreneurship

NEW HORIZONS IN ENTREPRENEURSHIP

Series Editor: Sankaran Venkataraman
*Darden Graduate School of Business
Administration, University of Virginia*

This important series is designed to make a significant contribution to the development of Entrepreneurship Studies. As this field has expanded dramatically in recent years, the series will provide an invaluable forum for the publication of high-quality works of scholarship and show the diversity of issues and practices around the world.

The main emphasis of the series is on the development and application of new and original ideas in Entrepreneurship. Global in its approach, it includes some of the best theoretical and empirical work with contributions to fundamental principles, rigorous evaluations of existing concepts and competing theories, historical surveys and future visions. Titles include original monographs, edited collections, and texts.

Titles in the series include:

A General Theory of Entrepreneurship
The Individual–Opportunity Nexus
Scott Shane

Academic Entrepreneurship

University Spinoffs and Wealth Creation

Scott Shane

Case Western Reserve University

NEW HORIZONS IN ENTREPRENEURSHIP

Edward Elgar
Cheltenham, UK • Northampton, MA, USA

Published by
Edward Elgar Publishing Limited
Glensanda House
Montpellier Parade
Cheltenham
Glos GL50 1UA
UK

Edward Elgar Publishing, Inc.
136 West Street
Suite 202
Northampton
Massachusetts 01060
USA

A catalogue record for this book
is available from the British Library

Library of Congress Cataloguing in Publication Data
Shane, Scott Andrew, 1964–
    Academic entrepreneurship : university spinoffs and wealth creation / Scott Shane.
    p. cm. — (New horizons in entrepreneurship)
    1. High technology industries—United States. 2. University-based new business
    enterprises—United States. 3. Academic-industrial collaboration—United States.
    4. Research, Industrial—United States. 5. Technology transfer—United States.
    6. Entrepreneurship—United States. I. Title: University spinoffs and wealth
    creation. II. Title. III. New horizons in entrepreneurship series

HC110.H53S513 2004
338′.04′0973—dc22

ISBN 1 84376 454 7 (cased)   2003062357

Typeset by Cambrian Typesetters, Frimley, Surrey
Printed and bound in Great Britain by MPG Books Ltd, Bodmin, Cornwall

To Lynne, for making my accomplishments possible through everything she does.

Contents

Foreword

There is worldwide interest in translating the technology arising from university research into economic development through entrepreneurship. Representatives have visited the Technology Licensing Office at the Massachusetts Institute of Technology from Finland to Brazil, and from South Africa to Malaysia, asking how to do it.

The reasons for this interest are evident. As economies progress from agricultural foundations to technological ones, it becomes increasingly important for countries to reach and remain at the state of the technological art through their universities' research, but then also to translate their technological findings into industrial development. Yet, as multinationals and other large firms are driven more and more by stock markets that value primarily short-term earnings, investment by these firms in basic research and even in longer-term development is decreasing. Such bastions of research as Bell Labs, IBM's basic research facilities and Xerox Park have all been closed down or converted to near-term development laboratories. Even pharmaceutical companies now proclaim that they are not looking for basic research developments in their technology acquisition, but only for drugs in late-stage clinical testing, whose efficacy has been largely proven.

Thus, there remains a 'development gap' between university research findings and investment in developing these findings into new products and processing. Entrepreneurial ventures are beginning to fill this gap using high-risk venture capital and, in some cases, supplementing it with government support for small businesses, to invest in new technologies from universities. The universities' increasing sophistication in intellectual property and licensing enable the new ventures to protect themselves from later competition from larger firms through exclusive licenses to university patents. Then, when the entrepreneurial spinoffs have stepped up the technology to a point of evident commercial utility, they may either bring the product to market themselves, or form alliances with large firms to develop further and market the technology.

The process is a 'food chain'. It begins with government support of basic research in universities, then goes on to identification of inventions arising from the research to be protected with intellectual property. Then comes 'technology licensing', the process of licensing the inventions to a company to develop it. In the case of new ventures, this part itself involves many steps:

conceiving and developing the idea of a new company, commitment to its formation by the founders, identifying critical staff, finding funding, and negotiating the license agreement with the university. Putting together this agreement is complex: on one side it must give the new venture sufficient latitude to operate and provide incentive for investors, and on the other side provide the university with (a) assurance that sufficient investment will be made in developing the technology, (b) protection from liability and (c) financial return. Next in the 'food chain' is development of the technology (often including the critical step of identification of the best uses for platform technologies) and finally comes the marketing of the product, alone or through strategic alliances with large companies.

Finally, the 'food chain' may loop back on itself, with both positive and negative consequences. Positive consequences include more university partnerships with industry, increasing sophistication on both sides and education of both faculty and students in entrepreneurship. On the other side universities worry about distortion of the direction of research, conflicts of commitment by faculty and the prospect of both the appearance and the actuality of conflicts of interest. Caution about these negative consequences is well warranted.

MIT has been engaged in spinning out technology from its laboratories into entrepreneurial ventures for over half a century – since shortly after World War II. More recently, beginning in the late 1980s, the process has been formalized through technology licensing to new ventures. Since then, more than 250 new companies have spun out of the MIT Technology-Licensing Office. Their effect on the region has been notable: creating new jobs, increasing the value of local real estate, introducing new products to the market, and helping to feed the entrepreneurial spirit of the New England region.

Scott Shane spent many months in our office, combing through a complex database that was never designed to yield with ease the information he sought. He spent much more time coming to understand the non-quantitative aspects that lead to successful technology transfer, through intensive conversations with our staff and extensive interviews with company founders. His enquiring mind and hard work led to insights of value to all of us. This book describes what he learned, and couples it with analysis of the literature on university technology licensing and spinouts, resulting in a valuable roadmap for university administrators and governments interested in economic development through technology transfer from universities.

Lita Nelsen
Cambridge, Massachusetts
June 2003

Acknowledgments

Like many sole authored books, this volume was the product of the efforts of many people. The most important contributor to my efforts to write this book is Lita Nelsen, Director of the MIT Technology-Licensing Office. For three years, from 1996 to 1999, Lita allowed me access to her office files, answered numerous questions about technology transfer and educated me about university spinoffs. If it were not for Lita's willingness to allow an assistant professor at the Sloan School of Management to learn about MIT spinoffs, this book would never have been written.

Other members of the MIT Technology-Licensing Office also provided me with a great deal of help in writing this book. Don Kaiser provided me with numerous tables and runs of data. Lori Pressman provided me with access to a vide variety of data, answered numerous questions and turned over to me large amounts of her own research on MIT spinoffs. I am very thankful for the assistance that both of these licensing officers gave me.

This book is also the result of efforts by Ed Roberts to convince me to change my focus of research to technology entrepreneurship. Ed's blunt advice to study something fitting a high technology university, though somewhat painful to hear at the time, proved to be among the most valuable pieces of advice I have been given in my academic career. Because of Ed's advice, I have learned a great deal about a truly important economic phenomenon. Moreover, his help in putting me in touch with his vast array of Boston area contacts opened doors for me so that I could conduct interviews for this book. For both of those efforts, I am truly grateful.

Over the past several years, I also have been fortunate to have several collaborators who have taught me a great deal about technology transfer and entrepreneurship through joint efforts to write scholarly articles. Although there have been many, five have been particularly important in helping to shape the ideas in this book. Dan Cable and I have collaborated on several papers on new venture finance over the past six years. Chapter 11 of this book would not have been possible without my work with him. Rakesh Khurana and I collaborated on a study of the effects of career experiences of firm founders on the formation of university spinoffs. Many of the ideas discussed in Chapter 9 originated in my work with Rakesh. Riitta Katila and I collaborated on a study of the effects of industry on the commercialization of university technology by spinoff companies. My work with Riitta was the foundation for many of the ideas and data presented in Chapter 7. Dante DiGregorio and I jointly conducted a study of differences in rates of spinoff company formation across universities. The ideas that came out of my work with Dante shaped many of the arguments and much of the evidence presented in Chapter 4. Toby Stuart and I conducted a study of the life histories of the MIT spinoffs. That research project contributed significantly to the ideas presented in both Chapters 11 and 12.

Several other colleagues also need to be acknowledged, as discussions with them led to many of the ideas and much of the research in this book: Maryann Feldman, Brent Goldfarb, Rob Lowe, Atul Nerkar, Wes Sine, Scott Stern, Marie Thursby and Eric Von Hippel. Having great colleagues, such as these, helped me to develop a deeper and richer understanding of university spinoffs both theoretically and empirically. Their generosity with time helped me to write a better book than I would have written had I never interacted with them.

Mark Coticchia, Rob Lowe, Lita Nelsen, Nicos Nicolaou and Mike Wright not only read the book, but also gave me detailed and extensive comments that allowed me to greatly improve the final version of the manuscript before publication.

Lastly, I have to thank two people whose consistent support and love made it possible for me to write this book. My daughter, Hannah, is such a good child that I always had the time for serious writing, and always had someone to play with when I was stopped by writer's block. I also have to thank my wife, Lynne, for encouraging me to write this book, and then supporting me in that effort even when it meant that she had to take over other activities so that I could complete the project.

1. Introduction

What do Cirrus Logic, the semiconductor company, Lycos, the Internet search engine, and Genentech, the biotechnology firm, have in common? All were firms founded to exploit technological inventions made by faculty, staff or students of American universities. Throughout the history of the modern university, but particularly in the United States since the passage of the Bayh–Dole Act in 1980, these types of firms, called university spinoffs, have become important parts of the economic landscape.

Moreover, university spinoffs are becoming a significant global phenomenon. In the United Kingdom, university technology commercialization activities accelerated in the late 1990s, a period when many UK institutions established university technology transfer offices (Wright *et al.*, 2002). Charles and Conway (2001) report that United Kingdom universities have generated 338 spinoffs over the past five years. In fact, in the United Kingdom, 175 spinoff companies were incorporated in 2001, a figure equal to approximately 31 percent of the 554 university spinoffs formed in the 1996 to 2001 period (Wright *et al.*, 2002).

Other countries are also seeing significant growth and interest in spinoff activity. Governments in continental Europe are devoting increasing amounts of money to universities, with the goal of turning them into engines of economic growth through spinoff company formation. Asian universities are increasing their production of university spinoffs by adopting new policies that favor the formation of these companies. For instance, the Japanese government recently changed its intellectual property laws to favor spinoff company formation, and universities in other Asian countries are reporting significant increases in the formation of these entities.

University spinoffs are an important class of firms because they are an economically powerful subset of high technology start-ups. Although only 3376 university spinoffs were founded in the United States between 1980 and 2000 (Pressman, 2001), on average, these companies are extremely successful firms. Not only can we count several billion dollar public companies among them, but research also shows that they are significantly more likely than the average firm to go public. For example, Shane and Stuart (2002) report that, from 1980 to 1986, 18 percent of all spinoffs from the Massachusetts Institute of Technology (MIT) went public, a rate of initial public offering over 257 times higher than that of the average firm. Moreover, in some industries, like biotechnology, university spinoffs are the dominant form of technology start-up, with as many, if not more, biotechnology start-ups emerging from university research laboratories than out of corporate research laboratories.

Perhaps because of the economic importance of university spinoffs, many university administrators, policy makers, and would-be entrepreneurs both inside and outside academia have become very interested in these firms. As a result of this interest, many universities have begun to invest significant resources in their development. Many, if not all, the major research universities in the United States, Canada and the United Kingdom have technology transfer operations with professionals who track faculty, staff and student inventions, seek intellectual property protection for those inventions and then license those inventions to private sector firms that commercialize them. Not only has the number of US universities with these offices grown rapidly over the past 20 years, but also the volume of patenting and licensing of university inventions and the employment levels of university licensing offices have grown dramatically over the same time period.

Moreover, many of these institutions focus significant attention on the spin-off company licensees of university intellectual property by establishing incubators, venture capital funds, business plan competitions and support systems to help entrepreneurs to start new companies to commercialize university inventions. Policy makers, seeing the positive effect of these new companies on local economic development, have been supportive of these efforts, particularly at US state universities, which are viewed as having a mission to promote local economic development. As a result of this interest in spinoffs, many US state universities have made their creation a central activity, with some universities, like Iowa State University, even putting the creation of spinoff companies into their strategic plans.

In parallel with this growth in interest in spinoff companies, there has been a significant growth in the creation of these companies in the United States over the past 20 years. The Association of University Technology Managers (Pressman, 2002) reports that the proportion of university technology in the United States that is licensed to spin off companies has grown every year since 1980, with the proportion of spinoff company licenses reaching a high of 14 percent in 2002.

Given the level of interest in university spinoffs among university administrators, policy makers, and would-be entrepreneurs both on and off academic campuses, one would expect that the topic would be the subject of significant academic inquiry. However, scholarly investigation of this phenomenon is virtually non-existent. Only a handful of books and scholarly articles that discuss any aspect of university spinoffs have ever been written. Moreover, the focus of these books and articles has often been on a particular dimension of spinoff activity, such as the specific case of biotechnology, or the effect of spinoff companies on the academic mission of universities, leaving the general topic of spinoffs largely unexplored.

As a result, to date, we have no comprehensive study of university spinoffs. We lack systematic explanations for and evidence of the importance of spinoff companies, the historical evolution of spinoff activity, the factors that explain the formation of spinoffs, the process of spinoff creation and development, the factors that influence the performance of university spinoffs or the effect of spinoffs on the universities that create them. Simply put, we have very little information about many aspects of spinoff activity, and no systematic effort has been made to assemble in one place the pieces of knowledge that we do have. Our knowledge of spinoff companies and their links to universities and society at large is fragmentary and quite limited.

THE PURPOSE OF THE BOOK

The purpose of this book is to describe and explain the formation of university spinoff companies and account for their role in the commercialization of university technology and wealth creation in the United States and elsewhere. Specifically the book has six goals. First, it seeks to explain why university spinoff activity is an important subject of scholarly investigation. Second, it traces the historical development of university spinoff activity. Third, the book aims to describe how four major factors – the university and societal environment, the nature of technology, the industries in which spinoffs operate, and the people involved in the spinoff process – jointly influence spinoff activity. Fourth, the book seeks to explain the process of spinoff company creation, focusing on the development of university technology into new products and services, the identification and exploitation of markets for these new products and services, and the acquisition of financial resources for the new organizations that exploit university technologies. Fifth, the book aims to examine the factors that enhance the performance of university spinoffs, hoping to differentiate successful and unsuccessful companies. Sixth, it seeks to discuss the effect that university spinoffs have on the institutions that spawn them.

To achieve these goals, this book provides conceptual arguments, reviews existing work by academic researchers and informed observers, and offers new primary data collected from my studies of spinoffs from a range of US academic institutions, and my in-depth investigation of spinoffs from the Massachusetts Institute of Technology founded between 1980 and 1996. For each topic presented, the book provides both conceptual arguments and either primary or secondary empirical evidence. Some of this evidence is based on large sample, quantitative studies, while the rest is based on small sample, qualitative evidence. Some of this evidence comes from my own primary empirical research (which will be described in more detail below), while the remainder comes from the work of other scholars.

To develop a systematic explanation for university spinoffs, the book weaves the explanations for the different aspects of university spinoffs into a general framework. In doing so, it adheres to the same definition of a university spinoff (to be explained below) when discussing all dimensions of spinoff activity, and seeks to adhere to the same basic assumptions about spinoffs throughout the chapters. The book also outlines the relationships between the different parts of the university spinoff story so that readers can see the phenomenon as a related whole, rather than as unrelated fragments of information.

THE DEFINITION OF A UNIVERSITY SPINOFF

To investigate a topic, researchers must first define it. This book defines a university spinoff as a new company founded to exploit a piece of intellectual property created in an academic institution. Companies established by current or former members of a university, which do not commercialize intellectual property created in academic institutions, are not included in the definition of a spinoff employed here. Thus university spinoffs are a subset of all start-up companies created by the students and employees of academic institutions.

Sometimes patents, copyrights and other legal mechanisms are used to protect the intellectual property that leads to spinoffs, while at other times the intellectual property that leads to spinoff company formation takes the form of knowhow or trade secrets. Moreover, sometimes entrepreneurs create university spinoffs by licensing university inventions, while at other times the spinoffs are created without the intellectual property being formally licensed from the institution in which it was created.

These distinctions are important for two reasons. First, it is far harder for researchers to measure the formation of spinoff companies created to exploit intellectual property that is not protected by legal mechanisms or that has not been disclosed by inventors to university administrators. As a result, this book likely underestimates the spinoff activity that occurs to exploit inventions that are neither patented nor protected by copyrights. This book also underestimates the spinoff activity that occurs 'through the back door': that is, companies founded to exploit technologies that inventors fail to disclose to university administrators.

Second, universities are much more likely to manage the intellectual property created on their campuses now than they were in earlier periods in their histories. As a result, this book likely underestimates the spinoff activity that occurred in previous periods, when university inventors were more likely to patent their inventions directly and did not need to license back their inventions to found spinoff companies. Moreover, many of the historical examples of university spinoffs described in this book are companies that successfully exploited university knowhow or trade secrets, rather than licensed inventions.

In the current institutional environment, the faculty, staff and students of most universities in the United States, Canada and the United Kingdom are required to assign to the university where they work or study the rights to any inventions that they make while at the university. However, universities differ as to whether student inventions made in the normal course of their studies are included in this requirement.[1] They also differ as to how much of the university's resources inventors are allowed to use without triggering institutional ownership of the invention. Furthermore, universities differ as to how vigorously they enforce their intellectual property rights, and how much effort they put into enforcing inventor disclosure of potential inventions. Nevertheless, one can say that, on average, when faculty, staff or students invent new technologies in universities in the United States, Canada and the United Kingdom, the institutions in which the inventors are located typically assert their rights to the inventions, and seek to make decisions about their disposition. In some cases, entrepreneurs found new companies to exploit that intellectual property, creating university spinoffs.

It is important to note that the definition of university spinoff used in this book differs from definitions used by other researchers. For example, some authors (such as Roberts, 1991a) have defined spinoffs as companies founded by anyone who has studied or worked at a university. Other researchers view spinoffs as companies where academic scientists serve on scientific advisory boards in return for equity compensation. This book does not employ these alternative definitions, for four reasons. First, to define university spinoffs as companies that are founded by anyone who has ever studied or worked at a university would require the discussion of such a wide range of new companies as to be theoretically meaningless. For example, including the real estate side businesses of university faculty members as university spinoffs would seem to be inconsistent with the idea of understanding the creation of new companies based on intellectual property created in universities. Second, comparing companies founded by people who attended or worked at a university many years earlier means that the factors leading to the formation and development of the new companies are distantly related to the university, at best. Third, it is not clear that focusing on the people who found companies rather than the opportunities that they exploit is the best lens through which to view entrepreneurial activity (Shane and Venkataraman, 2000). Fourth, many of the companies that give equity ownership to faculty members who serve on their scientific advisory boards are not new companies, but instead are small, established firms. As a result, including companies that offer equity to scientific advisors with new companies founded to exploit university inventions confounds new firm creation with ownership-based definitions of entrepreneurial activity.

Because of the differences between the definition of a university spinoff used in this book and those used in previous books and articles, the findings in this book are not directly comparable to the findings of many prior researchers. As a result, this book discusses in greatest detail the findings of those authors who use the same definition of a university spinoff as this book, and makes more sparing use of the findings of authors who have different definitions. Astute readers of the British literature on university technology transfer will note that this book's definition of spinoffs is most closely related to the definition of 'spinout' companies as discussed in that literature. Therefore British studies of spinout companies are discussed in great detail in this book.

While most university spinoffs exploit patented inventions, not all do. Many software spinoffs also exploit technologies that are protected by copyrights. Other spinoffs exploit university intellectual property that is protected neither by patents nor by copyrights. For example, the Wharton Economic Forecasting Association was a spinoff founded by Nobel Prize-winning University of Pennsylvania economist Lawrence Klein, who contracted with the University of Pennsylvania to license the Wharton name for his financial forecasting firm (Matkin, 1990). Nevertheless, almost all of the academic research on this topic focuses on patented inventions. Therefore most of what will be discussed in subsequent chapters examines the formation of new companies to exploit university-assigned patented inventions.

Faculty, staff or students can found university spinoffs, as all three of these groups develop new technologies on university campuses. While the distribution of inventors who create spinoff technologies across the categories of faculty, staff and students differs by type of technology, on average, university faculty members create most of the intellectual property that leads to university spinoffs.

While the inventors of the technology that leads to university spinoffs are, by definition, faculty, staff and students of academic institutions, the entrepreneurs that lead the efforts to found these companies need not be members of the university community. University spinoffs can be, and often are, created by entrepreneurs who come from outside the academic institution to lead the effort to exploit university technologies to create new firms. Similarly, investors who bring together external entrepreneurs and university technologies to establish new companies are another category of lead founders of university spinoffs. Empirical data on the spinoffs founded to exploit MIT-assigned intellectual property between 1980 and 1996 indicate that university inventors were the lead entrepreneurs in approximately one-third of the spin-offs, with the other two groups each driving the formation of approximately one-third of the new companies as well.[2]

AN INTERDISCIPLINARY APPROACH

This book takes a phenomenon-oriented, rather than disciplinary, perspective on university spinoffs. While many scholars in business schools focus on artic-ulating a particular disciplinary perspective, using a phenomenon as a setting in which to test the theories of that discipline, this book focuses on explaining the spinoff phenomenon, using a variety of theoretical frameworks to under-stand it. As a result, the approach of this book differs from the approach that would be taken by economists, historians, political scientists, psychologists or sociologists who might seek to examine spinoffs through the theoretical lens of their fields.

The present approach is undertaken because understanding university spin-offs seems to require an interdisciplinary investigation. While the fields of economics, law, psychology, public policy and sociology all illuminate some dimensions of spinoff activity, none of these perspectives appears to illuminate all dimensions. Moreover, in the absence of a broad and deep empirical liter-ature on university spinoffs, consideration of disciplinary disagreements about university spinoffs seems premature. Rather, an effort to provide a straightfor-ward and logical explanation for university spinoffs, coupled with an effort to organize the empirical findings on university spinoffs in a coherent manner, seems to be a promising way to advance our understanding of this phenome-non. Furthermore, each of these lenses appears to be a complement to, rather than a substitute for, the alternative perspectives. As a result, the examination of university spinoffs through multiple perspectives provides a much richer understanding of the phenomenon than each of these perspectives provides on its own.

THE STRUCTURE OF THE BOOK

This book has a very simple structure. The first section, encompassing the next two chapters, focuses on explaining why university spinoffs are important economic entities, and on describing the history of university spinoff activity. The second section of the book, incorporating the subsequent five chapters, discusses the set of factors that affect the creation of university spinoffs, including the university environment, the societal context in which the univer-sity and the spinoffs operate, the technology that would be exploited by the new company, the industry in which the spinoff would operate, and the people involved in founding spinoff companies. The third section of the book, including Chapters 9, 10, and 11, discusses the process of creating university spinoffs. The first of these chapters discusses the process by which university technologies are created from scholarly research, resulting in inventions that are sometimes patented and licensed, and sometimes lead to the formation of new firms. The second of these chapters focuses on the transformation of the university invention into a product or service and the development of a market, whereas the third of these chapters focuses on the acquisition of financial capital by the new company. The final section of the book consists of three chapters devoted to discussing the implications of spinoff activity: the first discusses the factors that influence the performance of university spinoffs; the second discusses the downside of spinoff activity for universities; and the third provides general conclusions for the book. Below, I provide a brief introduction to each of the chapters.

Chapter 2 explains why university spinoffs are an important topic of investigation, pointing to their economic impact, and the impact that they have on the universities that spawn them. Specifically, this chapter discusses a variety of ways in which university spinoffs benefit society and universities, including their effects on local economic development, their ability to produce income for universities, their tendency to commercialize technology that otherwise would be undeveloped, and their usefulness in helping universities with their core missions of research and teaching.

Chapter 3 discusses the history of university spinoffs. Starting with a brief description of spinoff companies in 19th-century Germany, where the modern university was born, this chapter traces the involvement of universities in the creation of new technology companies over time. The chapter discusses university spinoff activity in the United States since the passage of the Hatch Act in 1887, which established the land grant university, and introduced the linkage between universities and commercial economic activity in the United States. Chapter 3 also explains how changes generated by the two world wars and the Cold War influenced spinoff activity. The chapter focuses attention on the key watershed event in the history of university spinoffs in the United States: the passage of the Bayh–Dole Act in 1980, which gave universities the property rights to federally funded inventions. In particular, it describes the meteoric rise in the number of university spinoff companies since the passage of the Bayh–Dole Act, from fewer than 90 per year in the 1980s to over 500 in 2000, and explains why four central forces (the birth and growth of biotechnology; changes in university patent rights; changes in patent laws; and changes in the spinoff financing process) have led to this dramatic growth.

Chapter 4 discusses the variance across universities in their tendency to produce spinoff companies. This chapter explains why some universities, like

Arizona State University and Harvard University, produce virtually no new companies, despite generating a large number of technological inventions, whereas other universities, like Carnegie Mellon University and Massachusetts Institute of Technology, produce a much higher number of spinoff companies, given their level of technological invention. This chapter explains why university policies toward exclusive licensing, the distribution of royalties to inventors, holding equity in spinoff companies, faculty leaves of absence, the use of university resources to develop spinoff company technologies and pre-seed stage investment funds all influence the rate of university spinoff activity. Chapter 4 also explains how three characteristics of university technology transfer offices – resource richness, start-up company expertise, and network ties to investors and other spinoff company stakeholders – influence rates of spinoff company formation across academic institutions. Finally, this chapter explains how university cultures that reinforce entrepreneurial activity, the presence of entrepreneurial role models, the tendency of university researchers to obtain industry rather than government funding, and academic prestige also influence the variance in spinoff rates across universities.

Chapter 5 examines the effect of the institutional environment on university spinoff rates. The chapter documents differences in rates of university spinoff activity that exist across different geographic locations. It also explains why and how four environmental factors affect the level of spinoff activity in a particular location: access to capital, locus of property rights, rigidity of the academic labor market and the industrial composition of the area.

Chapter 6 explores the types of technologies that tend to be used to generate spinoff companies. Because established firms have a variety of advantages in commercializing technology, including complementary assets in manufacturing, marketing and distribution, only some university inventions are appropriate for creating spinoffs. This chapter explains why radical, tacit, early stage and general-purpose technologies, which provide significant value to customers, represent major technical advances and have strong intellectual property protection, are more likely than other technologies to provide the basis for spinoffs.

Chapter 7 examines the widespread variation across industries in the creation of university spinoffs. The chapter explains why university spinoffs are most common in biomedical industries, focusing on the effects of the collapsed discovery process in biotechnology, the long commercialization time horizon in the life sciences, the increasing production of biomedical inventions at universities, the locus of life science expertise in universities, the limited cost sensitivity of customers for biomedical products and services, and the discreteness of biomedical inventions. In addition, Chapter 7 identifies specific industry characteristics that prior research has found are associated with spinoff company formation, including the effectiveness of patents, the importance of complementary assets in manufacturing, marketing and distribution, the age of the industry's technology base, the degree of market segmentation, and average firm size. Finally, this chapter discusses the industry conditions that make university spinoffs more effective than established firms at commercializing university inventions, and explains why industries with a large number of firms, with less value added generated from manufacturing, and smaller markets are more amenable than other industries to spinoff company efforts to commercialize university technology.

Chapter 8 explores the role of people in the process of creating university spinoffs. The chapter discusses the central role that university inventors play in the formation of these companies. In addition, it describes the three types of entrepreneurs that lead the efforts to found university spinoffs: the inventors of the technologies (inventor-led spinoffs), external entrepreneurs who license university inventions (external entrepreneur-led spinoffs) and investors who bring together inventors and entrepreneurs to create new companies (investor-led spinoffs). Chapter 8 also explains the differences in the spinoffs founded by these three types of lead entrepreneurs and discusses the reasons why inventors found spinoffs, focusing on the effect of psychological attributes and career-related factors, the two dominant explanations in the literature to date.

Chapter 9 describes formation of university spinoffs. Beginning with research funding, this chapter traces the creation and disclosure of technological inventions, and the patenting and marketing of those technologies. It also explains the process of spinoff company formation, providing an explanation for how entrepreneurs discover commercial opportunities in university technologies.

Chapter 10 discusses the development of university technologies by spinoff companies. In particular, it explains why and how spinoff company founders transform their technologies into new products and services. Chapter 10 also explains how the founders of spinoff companies evaluate their markets, identify customer needs, gather feedback from customers, choose applications and sell their new products and services.

Chapter 11 discusses the acquisition of financial resources by university spinoffs. The chapter explains why spinoffs require large amounts of external capital and why, outside of biotechnology, this initial capital generally comes from the public sector, rather than from private investors. Chapter 11 also explains how the information asymmetry and uncertainty generated by university spinoffs necessitate two very important processes in private sector financing: the founders' use of information to demonstrate the value of their ventures to potential investors, and the exploitation of social ties between investors and entrepreneurs. Finally, this chapter discusses the matching of spinoff ventures to the right types of investors, such as business angels and venture capitalists.

Chapter 12 describes the performance of university spinoffs and identifies the factors that differentiate more successful spinoffs from less successful ones. The chapter explains how the human capital of founders, the amounts of financial capital raised by the new ventures, the founders' efforts to meet customer needs, the new ventures' technological base, the new firms' strategy and the support provided by the university from which the spinoff emerges all influence the performance of university spinoffs.

Chapter 13 discusses the disadvantages of university spinoffs. First, it explains how university spinoffs create several problems for the traditional model of universities as a source of knowledge creation for the good of society, including exacerbating the conflict between applied and commercially oriented fields, like engineering and business, and less applied and commercially oriented fields like the arts and humanities; reorienting faculty and staff effort toward commercial goals and away from the scholarly goal of knowledge creation; and creating conflicts of interest between the faculty and the institution at large. Second, the chapter explains how spinoff companies generate problems for the management of technology transfer in universities by raising the cost and difficulty of technology transfer and by imposing greater risks on the university than does licensing to established firms.

The final chapter of this book summarizes the key ideas discussed in the other chapters and links them together to create an overall picture of university spinoffs. This chapter also points out additional dimensions of university spinoffs not covered in depth in this book, so that readers may consider them, and highlights those topics most in need of additional scholarly research and policy discussion.

THE RESEARCH UNDERLYING THE BOOK

This book is the result of over seven years of scholarly research on university spinoffs that began when I first started to teach at the Sloan School of Management at the Massachusetts Institute of Technology in the summer of 1996. This research continued during my tenure at the Robert H. Smith School of Business at the University of Maryland and the Weatherhead School of Management at Case Western Reserve University. While this research initially began with in-depth qualitative studies of the technologies and companies that spun out of MIT, it has also included surveys of investors, statistical analyses of MIT inventions, and quantitative comparisons of different universities' technology licensing activities. The arguments and evidence described in the chapters that follow are based on a variety of different research projects conducted with many co-authors.

One of these projects, conducted with Dan Cable of the University of North

Carolina at Chapel Hill, surveyed 202 seed stage venture capitalists and business angels, and conducted in-depth interviews with the entrepreneurs and financiers of 50 spinoffs from the Massachusetts Institute of Technology. Published in the journal *Management Science*, in 2002, in an article entitled 'Network ties, reputation, and the financing of new ventures', this effort sought to understand the venture finance decisions of early stage investors in new firms.

Another project, conducted alone, examined in-depth case studies of eight new ventures founded to exploit a single invention assigned to the Massachusetts Institute of Technology. Published in the journal, *Organization Science*, in the summer of 2000, this study, entitled 'Prior knowledge and the discovery of entrepreneurial opportunities', sought to understand how entrepreneurs discover business opportunities in new technologies.

A third project, also conducted alone, explored the firm-founding patents among the population of 1397 inventions assigned to the Massachusetts Institute of Technology between 1980 and 1996. The goal of this project, which was published in the journal, *Management Science*, in 2001 under the title 'Technology opportunities and new firm creation', was to identify the dimensions of university technology that make some inventions more likely than other inventions to be exploited by spinoffs.

A fourth project, conducted alone as well, explored the firm-founding patents among the population of 1397 inventions assigned to the Massachusetts Institute of Technology between 1980 and 1996. Also published in the journal, *Management Science*, this project, entitled 'Technology regimes and new firm formation', sought to identify the industry characteristics that encouraged the formation of spinoff companies as a mode of technology exploitation.

A fifth project, conducted with Rakesh Khurana of Harvard University, also explored the firm-founding patents among the population of 1397 inventions assigned to the Massachusetts Institute of Technology between 1980 and 1996. Published in the journal, *Industrial and Corporate Change*, in 2003 under the title 'Bringing individuals back in: The effects of career experience on new firm founding', this study sought to identify the characteristics of university inventors that encourage the formation of spinoff companies as a vehicle for technology commercialization.

A sixth project, conducted with Toby Stuart of Columbia University, examined the life histories of the 134 companies founded to exploit inventions assigned to the Massachusetts Institute of Technology from 1980 to 1997. Published in the journal *Management Science*, under the title 'Organisational endowments and the performance of university start-ups', this study had as its goal the examination of the effect of social relationships and business strategy on new venture finance and development.

A seventh project, conducted with Atul Nerkar of Columbia University, also examined the life histories of 134 companies founded to exploit inventions assigned to the Massachusetts Institute of Technology from 1980 to 1997. The purpose of this research project, published in the *International Journal of Industrial Organization*, under the title 'When do startups that exploit academic knowledge survive?', was to identify the effect of the relationship between industry conditions and technology characteristics on the survival of university spinoffs over time.

An eighth project, conducted with Riitta Katila of Stanford University, examined efforts by new and established firms to commercialize the 966 inventions licensed by the Massachusetts Institute of Technology from 1980 to 1996. The purpose of this study, entitled 'When are new firms more innovative than established firms?', was to investigate the effect of industry conditions on the exploitation of commercialization of university inventions by new and established firms.

A ninth project, conducted with Dante DiGregorio of the University of New Mexico, examined the formation of spinoff companies out of the university technology licensing offices of 101 US universities from 1994 to 1998. The purpose of this study, which was published in the journal, *Research Policy*, under the title 'Why do some universities generate more start-ups than others?', was to identify the university characteristics that enhance and inhibit spinoff activity.

This book also provides primary data not previously published in scholarly articles. In particular, it includes a great deal of material from field interviews conducted with people involved in the formation and development of MIT spinoffs. These interviews were semi-structured and ranged in length from 30 minutes to two hours. In conducting the interviews, I sought to obtain information from several parties involved with each new venture. Interviewees included inventors, entrepreneurs, investors, licensing officers and other stakeholders of the new ventures. While the data from these interviews are used to support many of the arguments presented throughout the book, this information provides the bulk of the evidence behind the arguments made in Chapters 9 and 10 about the process through which university spinoffs are formed and develop their technologies and markets.

This book also takes advantage of the wealth of data collected by the Association of University Technology Managers on trends in university technology transfer and spinoff activity in the United States over the past 20 plus years. I use these data to document the dramatic increase in spinoff companies from US research universities in recent years.

The book also draws heavily on the work of other scholars who have studied university spinoffs. While the group of scholars investigating this subject is not large, many of them have made important contributions to our understanding of this topic. Because many of my arguments would be incomplete or unsupported without reference to the contributions of other scholars, I make use of published papers on university spinoffs and technology transfer that I have read in scholarly journals or conference proceedings, as well as unpublished research that I have seen presented at conferences. In particular, I draw heavily upon the research of Sue Birley and Nicos Nicolaou of Imperial College of Science, Technology and Medicine; Maryann Feldman of the Univeristy of Toronto; David Hsu of the University of Pennsylvania; Rob Lowe of Carnegie Mellon University; David Mowery of the University of California at Berkeley; Bhaven Sampat and Marie Thursby of Georgia Institute of Technology; Mike Wright of the University of Nottingham; Arvids Ziedonis of the University of Michigan; and Lynne Zucker and Michael Darby of the University of California at Los Angeles.

Lastly, there is no doubt that the ideas in this book were influenced by my discussions with many venture capitalists, business angels, technology transfer officers and entrepreneurs. In many cases, these practitioners provided the core insights into a dimension of university spinoffs that allowed me to formulate and empirically investigate the propositions offered in this book. While these contributions are not directly referenced, they are no doubt important in developing the arguments and evidence presented here.

I now turn to the second chapter of the book, where I begin to explore the puzzle of university spinoffs. In that chapter, I explain why university spinoffs are an important subject of scholarly inquiry.

NOTES

1. Some universities, such as Imperial College of Science, Technology and Medicine (in the United Kingdom) exempt students who are not working on sponsored research projects from the assignment rule.
2. Even when inventors are not the lead entrepreneurs in the formation of spinoff companies, as is the case when the lead entrepreneurs are investors or external entrepreneurs, inventors are usually founders of those companies in a legal sense. Typically, the inventors of university technology that leads to the formation of spinoff companies hold founders' stock, even if they do not assume a management role.

2. Why do university spinoffs matter?

For researchers to justify devoting scarce resources of time and effort to explaining an economic or business phenomenon, that phenomenon should be important. The first chapter alluded to the importance of university spinoffs by identifying three major technology companies that began as university spinoffs (Cirrus Logic, Genentech and Lycos) and by showing the high level of performance of spinoffs created at MIT between 1980 and 1996. This chapter builds on that initial introduction and explains why university spinoffs are an important topic of scholarly investigation, pointing to their economic impact and the impact that they have on the universities that spawn them.

The chapter is divided into two sections. The first section identifies several examples of important technology companies that began as university spinoffs to show that a fair number of high technology companies can trace their origins back to university research. While this effort is by no means comprehensive (we have no systematic data on which companies are university spinoffs and which are not), the data are illustrative of the successful high technology companies that were once university spinoffs. The second section summarizes the evidence in support of several different arguments for why university spinoffs are valuable entities for the overall economy and for the universities that spawn them.

EXAMPLES OF UNIVERSITY SPINOFFS

Even the most casual observation of the spinoff phenomenon demonstrates that some of the most important technology companies ever created were originally university spinoffs. For example, Digital Equipment Corporation was founded by Kenneth Olson to exploit intellectual property that he developed while working at Lincoln Laboratory at the Massachusetts Institute of Technology (Roberts, 1991a). Similarly, An Wang founded the computer firm that bore his name to commercialize technology that had been developed at Harvard University's Computer Laboratory. Norman Alpert, a University of Vermont faculty member, founded BioTek Instruments, a medical instrumentation company (Samson and Gurdon, 1993). Additional university spinoffs include Tracor, which emerged from the University of Texas at Austin, and the medical device company, Medtronic, which was based on University of Minnesota technology (Chrisman *et al.*, 1995). More recently, the computer software start-ups, Inktomi and Akamai, were university spinoffs, as was the Internet search engine Google, which was founded by Stanford University doctoral students (Pressman, 2002).

Examples of important university spinoffs are not limited to the United States. Connaught Laboratories, MacDonald Dettwiler, Develcon and SED Systems are examples of successful Canadian University spinoffs (Doutriaux and Barker, 1995). Moreover, TurboGenset, a university spinoff from Imperial College in the United Kingdom, that makes high-speed magnetic systems for power production, was worth over $1 billion in 2000 (Charles and Conway, 2001).

Sometimes university technologies do not lead to world-famous spinoff companies, but lead instead to the founding of companies that generate world-famous technologies, which are then transferred to larger, more established companies when the spinoffs are acquired or merge. For example, Perry Rosenthal founded Polymer Technology Corporation to exploit contact lens technology he developed while a faculty member at Harvard University and later sold the company to Bausch and Lomb.

In some industries, like biotechnology, the university spinoff is the dominant type of firm on the industrial landscape, and many of the companies founded in this industry were originally university spinoffs. For instance, the first biotechnology firm, Cetus, was a spinoff from the University of California at Berkeley. The most famous university biotechnology spinoff, Genentech, emerged from the University of California at San Francisco and Stanford University to exploit the Cohen–Boyer genetic engineering patent (Parker and Zilberman, 1993). In addition, many other important biotechnology firms, including Amgen, Biogen, Chiron, Genta and Regeneron, were also university spinoffs.

While many observers think of university spinoffs as new companies that develop cutting edge technology for sale to large industrial firms, university spinoffs actually take a wide variety of forms. Some even aim at consumer markets. For example, Hangers Cleaners, a spinoff from the University of North Carolina at Chapel Hill and North Carolina State University, is using a patented technology to transform the dry cleaning industry (Pressman, 2002). With 51 franchisees in 23 US states, this company uses liquid carbon dioxide instead of perchloroethylene to clean clothes, providing a way to avoid the use of dangerous byproducts and chemicals in the dry cleaning process, and thus minimizing the cost of insurance, hazardous waste disposal and regulatory compliance in that industry (Pressman, 2002).

University spinoffs exploit a wide variety of different technologies, from software to medical devices, to communications equipment, to biotechnology.

However, university spinoffs are not evenly distributed across all university technologies (for reasons that will be discussed further in Chapters 6 and 7). To illustrate the distribution of technologies that university spinoff companies exploit, Table 2.1 summarizes the technologies exploited by spinoffs from MIT from 1980 to 1996, the period that I studied in my research.[1] While MIT is not representative of all universities (in fact, it is exemplary in its generation of spinoffs), this table is illustrative of the range of technologies that lead to spinoffs.

THE IMPORTANCE OF UNIVERSITY SPINOFFS

University spinoffs are rare entities. From the passage of the Bayh–Dole Act in 1980 until 2000, only 3376 academic spinoff companies were established in the United States (Pressman, 2002). Given the relatively large number of faculty, staff and students at academic institutions in the United States, this number of spinoffs is quite small. In fact, DiGregorio and Shane (2003) report that, from 1993 to 1998, the average American research university created just over two spinoffs per year.

Not only are these numbers small in an absolute sense, they are also small in comparison to the level of entrepreneurial activity taking place at American universities. While data on other types of university entrepreneurial activity directly comparable to Pressman's (2002) data on spinoffs are not available, most indirect data suggest that spinoff activity is small in portion to the total amount of start-up activity taking place at American academic institutions. For example, Richter (1986) estimated that 3.3 percent of full-time science and engineering faculty at four-year academic institutions, or roughly 3000 faculty members, also work for their own businesses. This estimate, taken at a time when American academic institutions generated fewer than 100 spinoffs per year, indicates the rarity of spinoff activity relative to general entrepreneurial activity in science and engineering.

In a somewhat more recent study that compares university entrepreneurial activity to university spinoff activity, Allen and Norling (1991) surveyed 912 faculty members in science, engineering, business and medicine at 40 educational institutions in the United States and asked them about their entrepreneurial activity. The authors found that 16.2 percent of the academics engaged in firm formation, but only 4.4 percent did so on the basis of their academic research. At best, these data suggest that university spinoff activity, which depends on intellectual property created from scholarly research, might occur about one fourth as often as academic entrepreneurship in general.[2]

While university spinoffs are rare entities, they are, nonetheless, quite important. University spinoffs are valuable in at least five ways: they enhance

Table 2.1   The MIT spinoffs from 1980 to 1996

Name of the company	Year founded	Technology exploited
Active Control Experts	1992	Software
Active Impulse Systems	1996	Optics/lasers
Acusphere, Inc.	1994	Biotech
Adrenaline, Inc.	1995	Mechanical devices
AESOP	1994	Mechanical devices
Algos Pharmaceuticals	1993	Biotech
Alpha-Beta Technologies	1988	Biotech
American Superconductor	1987	Semiconductors
Amira	1989	Biotech
Applied Biotechnology	1987	Biotech
Applied Language Technologies	1994	Software
Ariad Pharmaceuticals, Inc.	1990	Biotech
Arris Pharmaceuticals	1990	Biotech
Aspen Technologies	1982	Software
Aware, Inc.	1991	Software
Barrett Technologies, Inc.	1990	Robotics
Beyond Inc.	1989	Software
Biomat Corporation	1988	Medical devices
Biosurface Technology	1987	Biotech
Boreas, Inc	1989	Mechanical devices
Boston Biomotion, Inc.	1993	Medical devices
Boston Dynamics, Inc.	1992	Software
Botticelli Interactive, Inc.	1996	Software
Cambridge Heart	1992	Medical devices
Celadon	1988	Software
Chemgenics Pharmaceuticals	1992	Biotech
Cirrus Logic	1983	Semiconductors
Clean Combustion	1995	Mechanical devices
Coastal Partners	1991	Semiconductors
Comtech Labs	1990	Medical devices
Continental Divide Robotics	1994	Robotics
Convolve, Inc.	1989	Software
Cubist Pharmaceuticals, Inc,	1992	Biotech
Cyra Technologies	1994	Hardware
Dataflow Computer	1985	Hardware
Diamond Materials, Inc.	1988	Materials
Digital Optics Corporations	1994	Optics/lasers
Diva	1993	Software
Eidak	1988	Software
Electronics for Imaging	1990	Software
Enzytech	1987	Biotech
EQB	1980	Medical devices
Exa Corporation	1991	Hardware
Facia Reco Associates	1994	Software
Faradaics	1989	Materials
Firefly Network	1995	Software
Gel Sciences	1993	Materials
GelTex Pharmaceuticals	1992	Biotech
Genetix Pharmaceuticals	1996	Biotech
Genometrix Inc.	1994	Medical devices
Gentest	1982	Medical devices
Gnat Robotics	1990	Robotics
HPJ	1993	Biotech
Hydrogen Microsystems	1996	Mechanical devices
IDUN Pharmaceuticals	1994	Biotech
Immulogic Pharmaceuticals	1987	Biotech
Ingenex	1992	Biotech
Instrumar	1989	Materials
Integra Life Sciences	1991	Biotech
Integrated Computing Engines	1994	Hardware
Integrated Environmental	1996	Mechanical devices
Inteletech	1992	Software
Interneuron	1989	Biotech
Intersense	1995	Software
Jentek Sensors	1993	Materials
Kinematix	1994	Software
Kopin	1985	Hardware

Name of the company	Year founded	Technology exploited
Lab Connections	1990	Materials
Lasertron	1980	Semiconductors
Lightpath Computer	1991	Hardware
Lightspeed Semiconductor	1995	Semiconductors
Low Entropy Systems	1993	Semiconductors
Manufacturing Software	1988	Software
Matritech	1987	Biotech
Mattek	1986	Biotech
Medic Monitor	1986	Medical devices
Metabolix	1993	Biotech
Metal Matrix Cast Composites	1993	Materials
Micracor	1989	Optics/lasers
Microgravity Research	1983	Materials
Micromet Instruments	1983	Materials
Molecular Displays	1990	Hardware
Morphogen Pharmaceuticals	1995	Biotech
Mosaic Technologies	1994	Biotech
Naxcor	1984	Biotech
Nemapharm	1995	Biotech
Neomorphics	1988	Biotech
Neurometrix	1996	Medical devices
New Technologies	1994	Software
Newton Laboratories	1995	Medical devices
NBX Corporation	1996	Software
NFX Corporation	1993	Software
Oculon Corporation	1988	Biotech
One Cell Systems	1991	Biotech
Open Market	1994	Software
OPUS Technologies	1995	Software
Organogenesis	1985	Biotech
Osteo-Technology	1986	Medical devices
Paranormics	1988	Materials
Praecis Pharmaceuticals	1993	Biotech
Proteinix	1989	Biotech
Quantum Energy Technologies	1995	Materials
Queues Limited	1990	Software
Reprogenesis	1993	Biotech
RSA Data Security	1983	Software
Sangamo Biosciences	1996	Biotech
Sensable Technologies	1993	Robotics
Silicon Process Corporation	1995	Optics/lasers
Soligen	1991	Mechanical devices
Somatix	1988	Biotech
Sontra Medical	1995	Biotech
Specific Surface Corporation	1995	Mechanical devices
Spectra Science	1990	Medical devices
Step Research	1995	Software
Stressgen Biotechnologies	1992	Biotech
Sutek Corporation	1982	Materials
Technodata Software	1994	Software
Teratech Corporation	1994	Medical devices
Therics Inc.	1994	Medical devices
Thermal Technologies	1987	Biotech
Thinking Machines Corporation	1986	Hardware
Three Space Motion	1982	Robotics
Time and Light	1996	Software
Tonyan Composites	1992	Materials
Transgenic Sciences	1988	Biotech
Trexel Inc	1982	Materials
Turbovision	1993	Mechanical devices
USAnimation	1991	Software
Vazo Rx	1992	Biotech
Virtual Machine Works	1993	Software
Volumetric Imaging	1990	Software
Xenos Medical Systems	1987	Medical devices
Xsirius Superconductivity	1989	Materials
Z Corporation	1994	Mechanical devices

Source: The records of the MIT Technology Licensing Office.

local economic development; they are useful for commercializing university technologies; they help universities with their major missions of research and teaching; they are disproportionately high performing companies; and they generate more income for universities than licensing to established companies. The remainder of this chapter discusses these arguments for the importance of university spinoffs.

Spinoffs Encourage Economic Development

University spinoffs are important entities for encouraging local economic development. Researchers have proposed four ways in which spinoffs encourage local economic activity. First, they generate significant economic value by producing innovative products that satisfy customer wants and needs. Second, they generate jobs, particularly for highly educated people. Third, they induce investment in the development of university technology, furthering the advance of that technology. Fourth, they have highly localized economic impact.

Spinoffs generate significant economic value

Researchers estimate that the economic impact of American academic spinoffs, measured by the amount of financial value added they generate, is relatively large. According to the Association of University Technology Managers, from 1980 to 1999, American university spinoffs generated $33.5 billion in economic value added (Cohen, 2000). That is, the average American university spinoff generated approximately $10 million in economic value, though this impact was highly skewed across the different spinoffs.

Moreover, the indirect effects of the economic impact of university spinoffs may even be larger than the direct effects. While we do not have any research that estimates the indirect effects of university spinoffs on local economic development, we do have some case study evidence. For example, Goldman (1984) found that 72 percent of the high technology companies in the Boston area in the early 1980s were based on technologies originally developed at MIT laboratories. As a result, the Route 128 economic infrastructure might not have existed in the absence of MIT and its spinoffs, even though most of these spinoff companies were not based on technologies formally licensed from MIT. Similarly, Mustar (1997) estimated that 40 percent of all high technology companies founded in France between 1987 and 1997 were university spinoffs, suggesting that the French high technology industries are highly dependent on university spinoffs. Wickstead (1985) found that 17 percent of the new technology companies founded in the Cambridge area of the United Kingdom were university spinoffs, while Dahlstrand (1999) found that 5 percent of all high technology companies in the Gothenburg region of Sweden had spun directly out of universities.[3]

In addition, university spinoffs have positive economic impact in ways that are difficult to quantify, but are valuable nonetheless. For instance, university spinoffs increase the economic diversification of localities, making economies less dependent on old industries. McQueen and Wallmark (1991) found that the formation of spinoff companies in Gothenburg, Sweden led to economic diversification of the area, making the economy less dependent on individual companies or particular industries, such as shipbuilding, thereby enhancing economic stability.

University spinoffs are also beneficial entities because they are very effective generators of novel products and services, creating more new innovative products and services than other technology start-ups (Blair and Hitchens, 1998). Because firms that develop more innovative products and services satisfy important customer wants and needs, university spinoffs can be seen as useful entities in finding high technology solutions to unsatisfied customer demand.

Several studies support this proposition. For example, Dahlstrand (1997) found that, on average, spinoffs from Chalmers Institute of Technology produced more patents than other Swedish technology firms. Similarly, Blair and Hitchens (1998) found that university spinoffs in the United Kingdom produce more new products and services than non-university new high technology firms.

Moreover, many of the products and services that university spinoffs produce, particularly those in the life sciences, enhance the quality of human life. While researchers find it difficult to estimate directly how much it is worth for people to have a drug that allows them a year of pain-free life or the ability to do something that they otherwise would have been unable to do, those contributions have significant value. For instance, Integra Life Sciences, an MIT spinoff, produces artificial skin that helps burn victims regenerate skin. How much economic impact is generated by helping burn victims have improved quality of life may be difficult to estimate, but it is clear that artificial skin has a value to burn victims and to the society in which they live and work.

Spinoffs create jobs

University spinoffs are also important economic entities because they create jobs, particularly for highly educated people. According to the Association of University Technology Managers, from 1980 to 1999, spinoffs from American academic institutions generated 280 000 jobs (Cohen, 2000). At an average of 83 jobs per spinoff, this rate of job creation shows that the average university spinoff creates more jobs than the average small business founded in the United States.[4]

University spinoffs appear to have relatively high average rates of job creation in other countries as well. The Scottish Enterprise, an agency devoted to supporting spinoff activity in Scotland, estimates that each university spinoff company in the United Kingdom generates an average of 44 jobs (Charles and Conway, 2001), a number that is larger than the rate of job creation by the average small business founded in the United Kingdom. Blair and Hitchens (1998) found that, up to 1992, the University of Linkoping in Sweden had 53 spinoff companies that generated 650 full-time jobs. Kobus (1992) reports that the University of Twente, in the Netherlands, created 92 spinoff companies from 1984 to 1992 and that these companies generated 445 jobs. Blair and Hitchens (1998) report that the University of Liège, Belgium created 25 spinouts between 1986 and 1994 and that these companies generated 250 jobs by 1994. Queen's University in Northern Ireland formed 17 spinoffs from 1984 to 1995, which generated 180 jobs (Blair and Hitchens, 1998). Many of these ratios of jobs created to spinoffs formed exceed the number of jobs created by the average start-up company in each of these countries.

Perhaps a more important measure of the job-creating value of spinoffs than the number of jobs created per spinoff company is the relative advantage that spinoffs have over established firm licensees of university technologies in creating jobs. Researchers have shown that university spinoffs are better at creating jobs than established company licensees of university technologies. For instance, Pressman *et al.* (1995) evaluated the economic impact of MIT technology licenses and found that 70 percent of the job creation was accounted for by spinoff companies, which made up only 35 percent of the licensees, demonstrating the superior job creation capability of university spinoffs relative to established company licensees.

Moreover, the jobs that spinoffs create are very knowledge-intensive jobs. Research has shown that university spinoffs create jobs for highly educated people at a higher rate than other technology start-ups. For example, Blair and Hitchens (1998) found that university spinoffs in the United Kingdom and Ireland had three times the level of university graduates as non-spinoff high technology companies in the United Kingdom and Ireland.

Spinoffs induce investment in university technologies
Inducing the private sector to invest in the commercialization of university technologies was one of the goals of the Bayh–Dole Act. Therefore the level of investment in university technology development that results from the creation of university spinoffs is an important measure of the value of university spinoffs. Although comprehensive data on the level of investment in the development of university technology belonging to spinoff companies are not available, data from specific academic institutions suggest that university spinoffs are effective at encouraging investment in university technology development. For example, Golub (2003) found that Columbia University's 46

spinoff companies raised $211 million in private sector financing (a figure averaging $4.6 for each spinoff created which is 23.4 times the $9 million dollars in royalties that Columbia University received from licensing. Similarly, Pressman *et al.* (1995) estimate that the amount of induced investment in MIT spinoffs was 41 times the amount of money generated by royalties from licenses.

The best test of the value of university spinoffs in encouraging investment in university technologies lies in the relative performance of university spinoffs and established company licensees in inducing investment in university technology. One piece of research shows that university spinoffs, in fact, do a better job than established companies in attracting investment in the development and commercialization of university technologies. Pressman *et al.* (1995) found that MIT spinoffs received 77 percent of the subsequent investment in technology development by MIT licensees, but made up only 35 percent of the licensees, demonstrating the superior effect of spinoffs relative to established firm licensees in inducing investment in the development of university technology.

Another measure of the value of university spinoffs in generating investment in technology development lies in their tendency to invest in research and development. Studies have shown that university spinoffs are much more research and development (R&D)-intensive than the typical start-up company, with R&D intensity exceeding 20 percent of sales in many cases (Mustar, 1997). Similarly, Blair and Hitchens (1998) report that the R&D expenditures of spinoffs from universities in the United Kingdom are more than twice those of other new high technology firms. The greater R&D intensity of university spinoffs relative to other start-up companies indicates the value of these firms in generating further technical advance in industry.

Spinoffs promote local economic development
University spinoffs are also valuable entities because they are important contributors to local economic development. University spinoffs enhance economic growth by transforming university technology into business opportunities. Because most of the economic activity that the spinoffs undertake – their hiring, sourcing of supply, production, and so on – is local, they have significant multiplier effects on local economic activity.

Moreover, because new technology companies tend to cluster, the economic impact of university spinoffs is often magnified. Spinoffs frequently serve as catalysts for the formation of geographic clusters of new firms in particular technologies. For example, university spinoffs like Chiron and Genentech led to the formation of a biotechnology cluster in the San Francisco Bay Area (Lowe, 2002).

University spinoffs are more likely than established firm licensees to contribute to local economic development because they are more likely to locate close to the laboratories from which their technologies emerge. Researchers have offered three explanations for the greater geographic localization of spinoffs relative to established firm licensees. First, when institutional conflict of interest policies allow it, the university researchers who found spinoffs often make use of the laboratories where their inventions are created to conduct additional contract research that keeps the inventor involved (Wilson and Szygenda, 1991). The ability to conduct additional research is, of course, facilitated by physical proximity. Second, geographic localization permits inventor–entrepreneurs to remain affiliated with the universities in which they work after establishing their companies. For instance, Zucker, Darby and Armstrong (1998) found that the university star scientists in biotechnology who tended to found new biotechnology firms often established them near their universities so that they could commercialize their inventions while retaining employment at their academic institutions. Third, established firm licensees already have a geographic base of operations. Changing the location of a firm is much more difficult than selecting a location for the firm in the first place. Because new firms are much more likely to locate near universities that spawn them than established firms are to relocate to the area near a university that licenses to them, spinoffs tend to be more geographically localized than established firm licensees.

The empirical evidence on university spinoffs shows that they tend to locate very close to the universities that spawn them, while other licensees of university technologies are less geographically proximate. For instance, Pressman (2002) reports that, in the United States, 80 percent of all spinoffs operate in the same state as the institution that they came from, whereas Tornatzky *et al.* (1995) report that 71 percent of all licensees of university technology come from outside the state where the university is located.

Similar results have been found outside the United States. In Canada, 98 percent of spinoff companies operate in the same province as the university from which they emerged (Pressman, 2002); in the United Kingdom, 74 percent of all spinoffs created since 1996 are located in the same region as their spawning university (Wright *et al.*, 2002). At a more micro level, Wallmark (1997) found that 30 out of 38 spinoffs from Chalmers Institute of Technology were located in the same city as the university, Gothenburg, Sweden.

The best evidence for the geographic localization of university spinoffs is that provided by Roberts (1991a). He observed that spinoffs not only tend to be founded in the same city and state as the university from which they emerged, but are often established in locations geographically very proximate to the laboratories in which they were born. For example, MIT's Lincoln Laboratory is located in a different town, Lexington, Massachusetts, from the

Institute itself, which is located in Cambridge, Massachusetts. Roberts (1991a) found that Lincoln Laboratory spinoffs tended to be established in Lexington, whereas Institute spinoffs tended to be founded in Cambridge.

In addition to the direct effect of spinoffs on local economic development, there is also an indirect effect. Because inventor–entrepreneurs often want to retain employment at their universities while establishing their companies, the creation of university spinoffs also encourages venture capitalists and other supporting institutions to locate in geographical areas where universities are found. As a result, university spinoffs serve as magnets for the creation of an infrastructure to support the creation of new technology companies in general. For example, in a study of new biotechnology companies, Audretsch and Stephan (1996) found that venture capitalists were attracted to areas where leading university scientists were employed, as a way to increase the probability of financing the scientists' new biotechnology firms. As a result, geographic locations with a larger number of university spinoffs in biotechnology tended to attract more new firm investors, which, in turn, facilitated the development of new technology companies in general, further enhancing local economic growth.

Spinoffs Enhance the Commercialization of University Technologies

University spinoffs are also valuable entities because they enhance the commercialization of university technologies that would otherwise go undeveloped. Researchers have identified two ways that spinoffs enhance the development of technology. First, they provide a mechanism for firms to commercialize inventions that are too uncertain for established companies to pursue. Second, they provide a way to ensure inventor involvement in the subsequent development of university technologies, which is crucial when technologies are based on tacit knowledge.

Spinoffs are an effective commercialization vehicle for uncertain technologies

University spinoffs are an effective vehicle for commercializing uncertain, early stage university technologies that otherwise would remain unlicensed because large, established firms are unwilling to invest in the development of these types of inventions. Thursby and Thursby (2000) conducted a survey of licensees of university technologies and found that one of the two most important reasons why established companies do not license university technology is the early stage of development of the invention. Moreover, Thursby *et al.* (2001) surveyed licensing officers at 62 universities and found that, when established firms do license university inventions, they tend to license later stage university inventions.

Research also has shown that university spinoffs often invest in the uncertain early stage technologies that large, established firms fail to license. Thursby *et al.*'s (2001) survey of licensing officers at 62 universities found that new and small companies tend to license early stage inventions. Matkin (1990) found that the most common reason for university researchers founding their spinoff companies was that existing firms would not license and develop their inventions, and they wanted their technologies to be commercialized. Lowe (2002) found that most of the spinoffs at the University of California were founded either because established firms were unwilling to license these technologies or because established firm efforts to commercialize them had failed. Hsu and Bernstein (1997) examined several case studies of technology transfer at Harvard University and MIT and found that half of the licensed inventions would have been unlicensed in the absence of the formation of a spinoff.

Spinoffs are an effective vehicle for encouraging inventor involvement
University spinoffs are also valuable entities because they are effective mechanisms for getting inventors involved in the process of technology commercialization, a necessary condition for the development of products or services from university technology. University inventions often require additional development to be commercialized, with the knowledge necessary to undertake this additional development being tacit. Because the inventor is often the only party who has the knowledge necessary to develop the technology further, inventor involvement is a necessary condition of technology commercialization (Lowe, 2002; Jensen and Thursby, 2001).[5]

Inventor involvement is easier to achieve through the formation of a spinoff company than through licensing to an established company, for several reasons. First, many scientists perceive that start-ups are more desirable places to work than established companies because they believe that start-ups undertake more interesting and more challenging projects than established firms, and tend to have smarter employees (Kenney, 1986). As a result, inventors are more inclined to work with new companies seeking to commercialize their university inventions than they are to work with established companies seeking to commercialize their inventions.

Second, start-up firms focus more of their attention on technology development as opposed to other aspects of business, and university researchers are more interested in technology development than in other aspects of business. Consequently, university inventors generally believe that they fit in better with spinoff companies and can contribute more to their development of technologies than they can to the development of technologies by established firms.

Third, equity is a more effective tool to ensure inventor involvement in spinoffs than other forms of compensation (Jensen and Thursby, 2001). Spinoffs can provide inventors with equity holdings more easily than established firms because the distribution of equity at the time of firm founding does not involve the transfer of equity from someone who has it to someone else, as is the case when equity is distributed after founding. This latter condition makes it difficult to give proper incentives to ensure inventor involvement when university technology is licensed to established firms.

Some qualitative research provides evidence in support of the proposition that equity is an important tool to encourage inventor involvement in the development and commercialization of university technology, and that spinoffs are a valuable vehicle for providing those equity incentives. For instance, Lowe (2002:54) quotes one University of California inventor who explains why he was more interested in developing technology through a spinoff than through license to an established company. The inventor says,

> The obvious question is 'why didn't UC license it directly?' Of course Pangenix wouldn't exist. But what do the companies get when they license from UC? When they license from [Pangenix], companies are guaranteed access to my experience . . . If the university was licensing it around, we would be getting phone calls from people asking about problems. I wouldn't be as sympathetic.

Spinoffs Help Universities with their Mission

University spinoffs are also valuable entities because they help universities achieve their primary missions of scholarly research and teaching. Research has shown that spinoffs help universities with their core mission in three fundamental ways: they provide financial support for university research, help to attract and retain faculty, and facilitate the training of students.

Spinoffs support additional research

University spinoffs enhance scholarly research at universities. Researchers have observed that faculty research productivity is positively correlated with their entrepreneurial activity. For instance, Louis *et al.* (2001) examined the activity of life scientists and found that engaging in entrepreneurial activities, such as holding equity in a spinoff company, enhanced faculty research productivity. Similarly, Doutriaux and Barker (1995) studied Canadian researchers who started spinoff companies and found that their research funding increased by an average of 57 percent from two to three years before founding a company to two to three years after founding a company.

Moreover, spinoffs often provide funding for scholarly research at universities, as the qualitative evidence on MIT spinoffs suggests. For instance, Hsu and Bernstein (1997) report that several MIT spinoffs used Small Business Innovation Research (SBIR) grants to fund sponsored research at the Institute.

Other spinoffs financed the development of laboratories and donated equipment to the Institute. Still other spinoffs paid for the education of PhD students whose thesis research involved working at the companies on research projects.[6]

Several researchers have even observed that many academic entrepreneurs view university spinoffs as a vehicle to obtain research funding. For instance, Blair and Hitchens (1998) report that, in the United Kingdom, many academics form companies because new companies are more likely to receive additional research funding than research groups or laboratories are to obtain grant money. The faculty entrepreneurs at MIT that I interviewed corroborate this argument.[7] For example, the inventor–founder of one MIT computer spinoff explains that he created his spinoff because he was unable to obtain adequate funding to develop his technology further in the university. He states, 'It was easy to say keep it in the university, it needs more funding. But there was no way to cook it. I couldn't get the funds I needed.'

Similarly, the founder of several MIT biotechnology spinoffs explains that founding companies is often a more effective way of obtaining research funding than writing a proposal to a granting agency. Therefore he says that he and many other MIT entrepreneurs use spinoffs as a vehicle to raise money for research. Describing one of his spinoffs, the entrepreneur says,

> It was a great idea from a science point of view. It gave my lab over $10 million for ten years. It's hard to get that kind of money from any source. I would say that raising funds for research was probably our primary objective for founding a company in that case.

Another MIT inventor–founder provides a similar argument, stating that, under certain circumstances, starting a company is a more effective fund raising strategy than seeking money from a granting agency. He says,

> I'm going to go to a source of funds that allows me to efficiently and effectively convert this idea into something useful and starting a company was a vehicle whereby a lab could be built and financed in order to carry on the work in a very effective way. The amount of money needed to do this on a commercial scale far exceeds what you're likely to get from granting agencies or by gifts or grants from industry to do it.

Part of the reason why founding a university spinoff is an effective way to raise money for the development of a technology, particularly in the biological sciences, is that the process of obtaining a large sum of money for research by founding a company is quite similar to the process for obtaining a large sum of money for research from a granting agency. One of the MIT inventor–founders illustrates this point. He says,

If I stayed at the Institute to develop the technology, I would have had to go to some granting agency or some company and get money. I would have had to provide, effectively, a technology business plan to someone whether that be the NIH, the NSF, the American Cancer Society or Howard Hughes, and basically ask someone for money to do this. I see the element of starting a company as changing the granting agency from NIH to Wall Street and I don't really care who pays the freight to get the job done.

Spinoffs attract and retain faculty

Spinoffs are also useful to universities because they help to attract and retain productive science and engineering faculty. By allowing faculty to supplement their salaries with equity in their own companies, universities provide a financial mechanism to retain and recruit faculty, particularly in the biomedical areas, that is similar to the use of practice plans common with clinical faculty in medical schools (Matkin, 1990). At least in the biological sciences, researchers have observed that allowing faculty to found spinoffs has been an effective mechanism to deter faculty from taking higher paying industry jobs (Powell and Owen-Smith, 1998).

Spinoffs help to train students

A final way in which spinoffs benefit universities is through the contribution that they provide to the education and training of students. Interaction with university spinoffs provides faculty with knowledge about starting companies that is useful in educating students for a world in which entrepreneurial activity is increasingly common among scientifically trained people (Richter, 1986). In particular, McQueen and Wallmark (1991) explain that spinoff companies help faculty to learn about commercial uses for new technology, rather than just scholarly uses for academic inventions. Because university students are more likely to work in the private sector than to become university researchers, making academic researchers cognizant of the commercial uses for new technology is important in training students to understand the practical value of research (Etzkowitz, 2003). This is particularly important in many fields of science and engineering where there are few academic positions available. In these fields, assigning doctoral students to work on more commercial aspects of technology development offers those students career opportunities that they otherwise would not have.

My interviews with the founders of MIT spinoffs provide qualitative evidence in support of the proposition that spinoffs help faculty to prepare science and engineering students for the commercial world in which they are likely to work. For example, the inventor–founder of two MIT materials spinoffs explains, 'The fact that I had so much industrial experience working with my companies was a very important element in terms of my professional growth. I became a better professor because I had a much better idea than many people about what's going on in the world.'

Spinoffs are High Performing Companies

On average, university spinoffs are very high performing companies. Take, for example, the 134 new companies founded to exploit inventions assigned to the Massachusetts Institute of Technology (MIT) between 1980 and 1996. Table 2.2 identifies the MIT spinoffs founded between 1980 and 1996 that went public during that time period. As the table shows, 24 of the new companies, or 18 percent, experienced an initial public offering (IPO). As alluded to in the previous chapter, these rates of initial public offering are over 257 times the rate of initial public offering for the typical start-up company in the United States.[8]

Table 2.2   The MIT spinoffs founded between 1980 and 1996 that went public

Name of company	Year of initial public offering
Algos Pharmaceuticals	1996
Alpha-Beta Pharmaceuticals	1992
American Superconductor	1991
Ariad Pharmaceuticals	1994
Arris Pharmaceuticals	1993
Aspen Technologies	1995
Aware Inc.	1996
Biosurface Technology	1993
Cambridge Heart	1995
Cirrus Logic	1989
Cubist Pharmaceuticals	1996
Electronics for Imaging	1992
Geltex Pharmaceuticals	1995
Immulogic	1991
Integra Life Sciences	1996
Interneuron	1990
Kopin	1992
Matritech	1992
Open Market	1996
Organogenesis	1984
Soligen	1994
Somatix	1992
Spectrascience	1995
Stressgen Biologics	1996

Source: Author's compilation.

MIT is admittedly an extreme case of an American university. However, even at the more typical educational institution, university spinoffs are much more likely to go public than the average new firm. For example, Goldfarb and Henrekson (2003) estimate that the percentage of university spinoffs in the United States that have gone public exceeds 8 percent, a figure that is still 114 times the average for a new company in the United States.

University spinoffs also show disproportionately positive performance when measured by metrics other than the tendency to go public. For instance, they are significantly more likely than the average new firm to receive venture capital or business angel financing. For instance, Wright *et al.* (2002) report that, in the United Kingdom, 25 percent of the university spinoff companies founded between 1996 and 2001 received financing from venture capital firms, and another 17 percent received external financing from business angels, while less than 1 percent of all start-ups in the United Kingdom received venture capital financing during this period.

The survival rate of university spinoff companies is also extremely high. Of the 3376 university spinoffs founded between 1980 and 2000, 68 percent remained operational in 2001 (Pressman, 2002).[9] This number is much higher than the average survival rate of new firms in the United States. For spinoffs from the best universities, this survival rate is even higher. Of the 134 spinoffs from MIT founded from 1980 to 1996, only 20 percent had failed by 1997. Lowe (2002) reports that only 6 percent of the spinoffs from the University of California system have ever declared bankruptcy, while Golub (2003) writes that, in the 1990s, New York University spun off 13 companies, of which 11 are still alive.

Similar results have been found in other countries. Mustar (1997) found that only 16 percent of the French spinoffs he studied had failed over the six-year period that he tracked them. Dahlstrand (1997) found that only 13 percent of the spinoffs from Chalmers Institute of Technology in Sweden founded between 1960 and 1993 had failed by 1993. Kobus (1992) reports that the University of Twente in the Netherlands created 92 spinoff companies from 1984 to 1992, and that only 16 had failed by 1992. Blair and Hitchens (1998) found that Queen's University in Northern Ireland created 17 spinoffs from 1984 to 1995, and only one had failed by 1997.

University spinoffs are also highly profitable companies, producing more value than the average technology start-up. Using a comparison of 16 new high technology firms that were not university spinoffs and 29 university spinoffs, Blair and Hitchens (1998) found that university spinoffs have a higher level of value-added as a percentage of sales than other new high technology firms.

In short, university spinoffs are valuable companies. They are more likely than the average start-up to raise funds from venture capitalists and business angels and to go public. They are also less likely than the average start-up to fail. Moreover, university spinoffs are more profitable, on average, than the typical high technology start-up.

Creating Spinoffs is More Profitable than Licensing to Established Companies

Not only are university spinoffs better performing companies than typical start-ups, but universities make more money through the creation of spinoff companies than by licensing to established companies. Previous research has offered several reasons for the greater profitability of spinoffs than licensing to established companies. First, as part of the payment for their intellectual property, universities can more easily take equity in spinoffs than they can in established company licensees; and equity ownership is superior to royalties on sales of products resulting from the invention as a way to profit from university technology.

Royalties can only be earned if a licensee successfully commercializes a university invention; however, researchers have found that the commercialization of university inventions is highly uncertain, with only about 20 percent of university inventions being successfully commercialized (Shane and Katila, 2003). Moreover, many licensees of university inventions successfully develop new products and services that do not make use of the university technology that the company licensed. For instance, Lowe (2002) found that several University of California spinoffs dramatically changed the technologies with which they were working before they reached the commercialization stage, making the patents that they licensed irrelevant to their products, and making it unnecessary for them to pay royalties to the University of California.[10] Similarly, several MIT spinoffs, including Aware, Integrated Computing Engines and Lightspeed Semiconductors, changed their technology during their development, abandoning their original MIT patents, and allowing them to create value for their shareholders without having to pay royalties to MIT.

By holding equity, the university can capture value from the creation of a spinoff even if the spinoff does not commercialize the licensed university technology because the value of the equity is linked to the overall success of the firm, not to the success of a particular piece of intellectual property, as is the case with royalties (Matkin, 1990). Therefore, when universities hold equity, they benefit from any activities undertaken by the spinoff rather than realizing a return only if the licensee commercializes a technology that uses the university's intellectual property.[11]

Second, by holding equity in a spinoff, universities can obtain financial returns from their technology earlier than they can if they rely on royalties. Because university inventions often require additional development after the technologies are licensed, but before those inventions can be commercialized, the time period from the signing of a license agreement to the receipt of revenue from licensed university inventions is relatively long. For biomedical inventions that need Food and Drug Administration (FDA) approval, eight to 12 years of development is not uncommon. Because start-up companies often go public before they have introduced products into the market, a university can cash out of equity holdings in a spinoff well before the licensee commercializes its invention. In fact, Bray and Lee (2000) explain that the sale of equity at an initial public offering allows a university to earn a financial return on its technology within three to four years after licensing, rather than the eight to 12 that it often takes to commercialize university technologies and earn royalties on licenses.

Third, established companies will not pay very much to license university inventions. In general, universities can charge licensees only small milestone payments, measured in the thousands of dollars, and royalties as a small percentage of sales from successfully commercialized inventions. In part, the low prices for university inventions reflect the fact that few university inventions attract multiple bidders (Jansen and Dillon, 1999), leaving universities to take the offers that they receive, or fail to license their technologies.

The low prices also reflect the fact that these inventions are at such an early stage that they have very little value in the absence of additional development being undertaken by the licensor. Therefore earning a reasonable compensation from university inventions requires making an investment that will grow in value along with the value of the licensing organization. An equity holding in a spinoff company is this type of investment.

The data that I collected on the MIT spinoffs support the proposition that universities will not earn very much money through royalties on licensed inventions. For instance, the inventor–founder of one biotechnology spinoff explains,

> Most companies will not pay very much for early stage technology. Industry is being asked to bear most of the risk of the conversion of that technology into something tangibly valuable and, as a result of that, the Institute has residuals to that intellectual property that are not worth a whole lot.

Fourth, universities, like other licensors, often find it difficult to ensure that they receive royalties from licensed inventions because the licensees of most technologies can invent around or improve upon licensed intellectual property (Levin *et al.*, 1987), thereby avoiding the payment of royalties on those inventions. As a result, universities often can more effectively earn financial returns on their equity holdings, which do not require verification that licensees are actually employing university intellectual property in the products or services that they develop, than they can from licensing their intellectual property.

The experience of the University of Illinois and Netscape is instructive in this regard. According to Reid (1997), when Jim Clark became the CEO of Netscape, he told the company's software engineers to build a new web browser from scratch so as to avoid any violation of the University of Illinois' intellectual property rights to the Mosaic web browser. As Reid (1997:23) explains,

> At Clark's wise insistence, they [Netscape] had already burned, deleted, and otherwise eradicated everything that they ever had owned pertaining to the original Mosaic code. This was important because Mosaic had been developed on university time and equipment. As such it belonged to the university. . . . By then a number of companies had already started licensing and bundling Mosaic into Internet connectivity kits that were becoming hot items in software stores. But [Netscape] had no intention of signing a licensing agreement, and as a result its products had to be wholly original implementations.

Because software code often can be rewritten to accomplish a given objective in a different way, inventing around existing intellectual property protection in software is relatively easy, and Netscape was successful in avoiding any violation of the University of Illinois patents on Mosaic.[12]

Fifth, to earn a return from licensing, the university needs to ensure that its licensees put sufficient effort into developing the technologies that it licenses, otherwise commercialization will not be possible. The founders of university spinoffs put more effort into developing and commercializing university inventions than do managers in established firms. Because the survival and financial performance of university spinoffs depend more on the successful commercialization of the spinoff's licensed university inventions than does the survival and financial performance of established firm licensees, the founders of university spinoffs have a much greater incentive than managers in established firms to commercialize university inventions.

My interviews with MIT inventors provide empirical support for the proposition that commercialization is more likely when spinoffs license university inventions than when established companies license them. For instance, the inventor–founder of one biotechnology spinoff explains why managers in established firms do not put much effort into developing and commercializing university inventions:

> You have to have a champion in the company doing the licensing which in and of itself is fairly rare since people in large companies often do not champion outside technology. Moreover, even if the new piece of technology captures the imagination of someone in research, and they encourage the company to license it, the ability of that company to realize potential benefit of that through conversion of the early stages of intellectual property into a potential product is fraught with all sorts of obstacles. A lot of these licenses wind up going down the drain because the champion leaves the company. Or the champion who wants to license the product doesn't have the clout to force it through the company.

Lastly, this inventor–founder adds, even if the potential champion can get the technology licensed and does not leave the company, that person might not 'have the vision, resources, and commitment to elaborate the technology so that it will see the light of day'.

Some large sample empirical evidence also suggests that universities earn greater returns from creating spinoffs than they do from licensing to established companies. The best data on university returns from taking equity in spinoffs and from royalties from licensing to established companies come from the United Kingdom. While not direct evidence that spinoffs generate higher returns than established firm licenses, the UK data are suggestive.

In 2001, UK universities reported licensing income of £16 251 917, but an equity position equal to £180 242 438, or over 11 years of royalty income (Wright *et al.*, 2002). Because universities rarely take equity positions in established companies,[13] almost all of the returns from equity investments represent returns from investments in spinoff companies. In contrast, licensing income represents royalties from licensing both to spinoffs and to established company licensees because both types of entities pay royalties on licensed university inventions.

Moreover, licensees of university inventions typically pay royalties only for the time remaining on a university patent, and only on those inventions that are commercialized. Because patents last only 20 years, and because university inventions, on average, are licensed when university patents are four years old and commercialized when they are seven years old, university inventions on commercialized inventions yield royalties for an average of only 13 years. Only about one-third of university inventions are ever commercialized, suggesting that the average university invention pays royalties for four and one-third years, significantly less time than the 11 years of royalty income that the equity positions represent.

Some fragmentary evidence from the United States also supports the proposition that universities make more money by taking equity in their spinoffs than from licensing their inventions to established companies. For instance, Carnegie Mellon's agreement with its spinoff, Lycos, gave the university 10 percent of Lycos' stock, a 1.5 percent royalty for the use of the Lycos trademark for anything other than on-line search, and $2 million in upfront fees (Zuckoff, 1998). The Carnegie Mellon administration's share of divested equity in Lycos was $20 120 000, whereas the royalties that it earned from the license totaled only $1 060 000. Moreover, after Lycos' initial public offering in 1996, this arrangement made Carnegie Mellon's equity holding in Lycos worth $60 million, about 30 times the annual royalty income for all its university licensees. Furthermore, Carnegie Mellon's return from its divested equity in Lycos exceeded the total amount of royalties from licensing technology to all other licensees combined.

Data reported by other researchers also suggest that several other universities have earned more money from creating spinoffs than from licensing their
inventions to established companies. For example, Feldman (2001) reports
that, in 2000, Johns Hopkins University had a capital gain from the sale of
equity in two spinoffs equal to all its other licensing income combined.
Similarly, Matkin (1990) reports that, in 1988, MIT invested in eight licensees
of its technology and that its equity stake was valued at $3.5 million, a figure
larger than the royalty income it received in that year.

A few studies have tried to compare directly the returns to universities of
equity positions in spinoffs with licenses to established companies. For
instance, Gregory and Sheahen (1991) compared 248 licenses to established
firms with seven university spinoffs and found that the spinoffs produced more
than three times as much income for universities as the licenses. Bray and Lee
(2000) found that spinoffs generate more income than established firm
licensees using a different methodology from Gregory and Sheahen (1991).
Arguing that the value of equity holdings in spinoffs should be compared, not
to ongoing royalties from licensing, but to the license issue fee (because equity
is generally used to capitalize that fee), Bray and Lee (2000) estimated the
mean level of university equity holdings in 16 spinoffs that experienced an
initial public offering. They found that the mean value of university equity
holdings in spinoffs that went public was $1 284 242, a figure 20 times that of
the initial licensing issue fee. Bray and Lee (2000) also examined the returns
from 12 companies that the University of Washington held equity in between
1984 and 1996. The authors found that half of the companies failed and so
provided no return, while the university sold $8.26 million in equity in the
remaining six firms when they went public. As a result, the authors estimated
that the average income produced by the sale of equity in the spinoff companies was $688 000, a significantly larger number than the initial license fees
charged to establish firm licensees (Bray and Lee, 2000).

In short, prior research has offered a variety of reasons why forming spinoffs should generate greater returns to universities than licensing to established firms. Some empirical evidence, assembled in a variety of different
ways, provides support for these arguments.

SUMMARY

This chapter has explained why university spinoffs are an important subject
for scholarly inquiry. The first part of the chapter identified several important
examples of university spinoffs, including Google in Internet search engines,
Cirrus Logic in semiconductors and Genentech in biotechnology.

The second part of the chapter offered several different explanations for why university spinoffs are valuable. First, university spinoffs enhance local economic development. Research has shown that spinoffs generate high levels of economic value-added, provide an important source of jobs, particularly for highly educated people, induce the additional private sector investment in university inventions that is necessary to commercialize technology; and tend to locate close to the universities that spawn them.

Second, spinoffs enhance the commercialization of university technologies that would otherwise go undeveloped because they are too uncertain for established companies to pursue or because they involve tacit knowledge and require additional inventor involvement to be commercialized successfully.

Third, spinoffs help universities with their primary missions of research and teaching. University spinoffs enhance the scholarly productivity of academic researchers, providing additional funding for research. University spinoffs also help universities to attract and retain faculty by supplementing faculty compensation. Furthermore, spinoffs facilitate the training of students by providing professors with knowledge of the commercial development of technology, which is valuable to students who are more likely to make commercial use of technology than to make academic use of it.

Fourth, university spinoffs are high performing companies. Research has shown that that university spinoffs are more likely than the average start-up to experience an initial public offering, to raise venture capital and to survive over time. Moreover, university spinoffs are more effective at generating income for universities than licensing to established companies because spinoffs permit universities to obtain equity in licensees, and equity allows universities to profit from the success of licensees in general rather than from the commercialization of specific pieces of technology. Spinoffs also overcome problems in appropriating the value of intellectual property through the exercise of legal rights, provide a greater incentive for licensees to expend effort to further develop university technologies, and allow universities to obtain financial returns from their technologies prior to the successful commercialization of the technology through the sale of equity in an initial public offering.

Having explained why university spinoffs are important economic entities, I now turn to a discussion of the history of university technology commercialization and spinoff activity, the subject of Chapter 3.

NOTES

1. Lowe (2002) points out that the University of California system generates more spinoffs than MIT. However, the University of California is a collection of universities (for example, University of California at Berkeley, University of California Los Angeles, University of California at San Diego, and so on), whereas MIT is a single university.

2. However, this number might also vary by technical field. For instance, Louis *et al.* (1989) surveyed life science faculty at US universities and found that 7 percent held equity in a company based on their research. This is almost double Allen and Norling's (1991) estimate of the number of firms that science and engineering faculty founded to exploit their academic research.

3. However, much like the MIT case described above, most of the spinoff companies described in the studies by Wickstead (1985) and Dahlstrand (1999) did not formally license university technologies. Rather, either they were founded to exploit technologies without legal forms of intellectual property protection, or based on patents and copyrights assigned to the inventors of the technologies, not their institutions.

4. However, this job creation is unevenly distributed across universities. MIT estimates that its roughly 100 spinoffs founded from 1980 to 1997 created 8721 jobs by 1997, whereas Columbia University's 46 spinoff companies, none of which was founded before the mid-1990s, have created only 300 jobs (Golub, 2003).

5. Inventor involvement in technology development by the spinoff may be most effective if the inventor takes on the role of chief technology officer rather than the role of chief executive officer. As will be discussed in greater detail in Chapter 12, the performance of university spinoffs is enhanced by the involvement on the founding team of an experienced manager, who often takes on the role of chief executive officer.

6. The ability to obtain additional research funding from university spinoffs does depend on the university building a positive relationship with those companies. Take, for example, the case of Netscape. The University of Illinois fought hard to assert its intellectual property rights to the Mosaic web browser and, as a result, ended up in conflict with Netscape. Netscape settled with the university for an amount estimated at $2 million, but only after the university rejected Netscape stock as compensation. Not only did the university give up the value of the stock allotment, which was ultimately worth $17 million, but it ended up with a public relations nightmare. Marc Andreessen, the alumnus whose technology led to the founding of Netscape, publicly stated that he would never give money to the school, and the university lost the value of any future gifts (Reid, 1997).

7. Readers should note that the decision to found a spinoff company as a way to raise research money is a major decision for inventor–founders. At many universities, including MIT, conflict of interest policies forbid faculty and staff taking sponsored research from a company in which they hold equity. As a result, the founders of spinoffs must either resign from the university to obtain funding from an outside agency while taking equity in the spinoff, or form a spinoff, but not hold any equity in it. In the examples from MIT described below, the first and third examples are inventor–entrepreneurs who chose to leave the Institute so that they could obtain funding for the further development of their technologies, while the second example is an inventor–entrepreneur who did not own equity in the spinoff. These examples indicate that some inventor–entrepreneurs believe that the benefits of a spinoff as a mechanism for raising money to develop promising technology are so great that they are willing to incur significant personal cost – giving up either equity or tenure – to obtain research funding, while adhering to the conflict of interest rules of their institutions.

8. During the 1980 to 1996 period, 111 274 000 companies were founded in the United States, and 7456 companies went public, or 7/100ths of 1 percent of the number of companies founded. A comparison of the proportion of companies that were founded to exploit MIT-assigned inventions between 1980 and 1996 that went public with the proportion of all companies founded during the same period that went public indicates that the ratio is 257 to 1; that is, companies founded to commercialize MIT inventions are 257 times more likely than the average company to go public. Unfortunately, no information is available on the average level of capital gain on MIT spinoffs that go public, so it is not possible to compare this level of gain to the average level of capital gain on an IPO.

9. However, many of the surviving firms may be dormant companies that have not legally dissolved, understating the failure rate of university spinoffs.

10. However, some firms still paid royalties to avoid any legal complications.

11. To earn significant amounts of royalties, the sales of commercialized technologies also have to be quite substantial. Royalties are often a small percentage of sales (for example, 2

percent) and most university spinoffs do not create a high volume of sales. As a result, less than 0.6 percent of all active licenses have produced royalty income in excess of $1 000 000 (Pressman, 2002).

12. Moreover, universities find themselves in a delicate position if they try to enforce their intellectual property rights. The main mechanism for enforcing intellectual property rights is the patent court system. However, universities find it difficult to sue companies that hire their graduates and make financial contributions to support their research, and lawsuits to enforce property rights that do not generate very large sums of money often seem foolish because the risk of alienating licensees often greatly exceeds any financial benefit that could be gained from enforcing the property rights.

13. Universities rarely take equity when they license technology to public companies because universities can invest their endowment in public companies whenever they like. As a result, the only established companies in which universities take equity are small, established private firms.

3. University spinoffs in historical perspective

This chapter explores the history of university spinoffs. Starting from the beginning of the modern university in 19th-century Germany and continuing to the present day, university spinoffs have been a part of the university technology commercialization landscape. The first section of the chapter discusses the evolution of efforts by universities to commercialize technologies created by their faculty, staff and students through the creation of new companies from the earliest efforts to the present day. In addition to providing an overview of the development of technology commercialization and spinoff activity in the United States since the beginning of the 20th century, this section describes the birth of the modern era of spinoff activity – the period since the passage of the Bayh–Dole Act in 1980 – and the tremendous increases in technology commercialization and spinoff activity that have occurred since 1980.

The second section of the chapter seeks to explain the rapid growth of spinoffs from academic institutions in the United States over the past 20 years, focusing on the central forces that have led to the dramatic rise in spinoff activity: the passage of the Bayh–Dole Act, the birth and growth of biotechnology, changes in US patent laws, contagion effects, the growth in the use of equity, the shortening of the product life cycle in many industries, and changes in the new firm financing process.

THE HISTORY OF UNIVERSITY TECHNOLOGY COMMERCIALIZATION AND SPINOFF ACTIVITY

Universities have been involved in the commercialization of technology ever since they were first established. Academic research in science and engineering has always had a practical side, which has led academics to make commercial use of the technologies that they have developed. However, the level of university technology commercialization and spinoff activity has changed over time. This section explores the evolution of university technology commercialization and spinoff activity from the 19th century to the present day. As the section shows, the creation of spinoffs has always been part of university activity, perhaps because of the practical orientation of many fields of engineering and science, but has also increased over time as the institutional environment has become more supporting of spinoff activity. For the purposes of analysis, the discussion of the history of university technology commercialization and spinoff activity is divided into five periods: the 19th century, the first half of the 20th century, the period from 1945 to 1980, the 1980s and the 1990s.

The 19th Century

The modern university was established in Germany in the 19th century. Therefore it is not surprising that the earliest examples of university spinoffs should be found in 19th-century German universities. For instance, Gustin (1975) identifies several chemistry professors in 19th-century Germany who founded companies on the basis of their technological developments and knowledge. He explains that one of the most famous of these efforts was that of Professor Johann Pickel, who produced salts, potash, and acetic acid on the basis of his scientific discoveries, and that another well-known effort was a company founded by Justus von Liebig to manufacture chemical fertilizers.

The United States, like many countries, modeled its university system on that established in Germany, so it is not surprising that the United States also saw its share of technology commercialization through spinoffs by university professors throughout the 19th century. However, early efforts to commercialize university technologies in the United States were rather limited, both because of the relatively limited level of technology production at universities at this time and because of the relatively small size of universities prior to the 20th century.

One of the unique features of the American university system in the 19th century was the creation of land grant universities, which had effects on spurring the development of spinoff companies to exploit university inventions. The Hatch Act of 1887, which established the land grant system of state universities, was based on the principle of technology commercialization (Golub, 2003). Specifically, this Act called on universities to develop and disseminate knowledge that resulted from academic research for the development of both industry and agriculture (Rosenberg and Nelson, 1994). Several entrepreneurial efforts were undertaken by academics in the late 19th and early 20th century as a way to take university knowledge and use it to help farmers and manufacturers through extension services.

The Early 20th Century

While university technology commercialization efforts in the United States were relatively small in the 19th century, they began to grow at the beginning of the

20th century (Mowery and Sampat, 2001b). In fact, the 20th century marked the beginning of several organized efforts by American universities to work with new companies to commercialize university technologies as a way to develop local economies. For instance, in 1925, MIT helped to found the Northeast Council, an organization that sought to use the Institute's research to help develop local businesses both through translation of the research into a form useful for private firms and through the creation of spinoff companies (Golub, 2003).

However, at the turn of the 20th century, many academics and university administrators took a negative view of efforts by faculty members to patent and license their inventions. For instance, Johns Hopkins University would not offer T. Brailsford Robertson a chair in Physiology because he tried to patent the invention of tethalin (Bok, 2003). Similarly, the Rockefeller Foundation tried to cut off funding for Herbert Evans, a faculty member of the University of California at Berkeley, because he applied for a patent on a Foundation funded invention (Bok, 2003).

As a result of this largely negative view of technology commercialization from the beginning of the 20th century to the early 1970s, universities' efforts to support technology commercialization and spinoff activity were more indirect than direct (Mowery *et al.*, 2001). In general, during this period, most university researchers did not involve their institutions formally in their efforts to commercialize their inventions through the formation of new companies (Mowery and Sampat, 2001a). For instance, in 1907, Frederick Cottrell, a professor at the University of California at Berkeley, patented his invention of the electrostatic precipitator, a device that helped to reduce industrial air pollution, and started a company to exploit this invention (Matkin, 1990). As reflected the thinking of many academics at the time, Cottrell decided to found this company without involving his university, believing that university involvement with spinoff companies was inappropriate to the academic mission (Matkin, 1990; Mowery *et al.*, 2001).

To accommodate his view that the commercialization of university technology was valuable, but that universities should not be directly involved in this activity, Cottrell founded an organization called the Research Corporation, an independent entity designed to commercialize university inventions (Mowery and Sampat, 2001a). The Research Corporation did this by taking assignment of university patents, and then licensing those patents to private sector firms (Mowery and Sampat, 2001b). In the early part of the 20th century, most technology commercialization of university inventions was conducted through the Research Corporation, which grew to be the dominant entity in this activity (Mowery and Sampat, 2001a).

University patenting and technology commercialization activity increased after World War I, a fact that can be attributed, at least in part, to the acceleration of technological development in the 1920s, as well as to the increased involvement of industry in university research (Mowery and Sampat, 2001b). However, the volume of the commercialization effort in the first part of the 20th century was still relatively low. During this period, universities produced much less technology for commercial purposes than they do today, in both absolute and relative terms. This time period also saw no appreciable change of formation of new companies to exploit intellectual property created at American universities, which remained relatively low in volume and was conducted by academics largely independently of the academic institutions that employed them.

In the pre-World War II period, most American universities were quite ambivalent about efforts to make commercial use of their intellectual property. On the one hand, American universities, particularly public institutions, undertook a relatively large volume of research in conjunction with industry, leading some universities to produce technology that was valuable to the private sector (Mowery *et al.*, 2001). On the other hand, many academics, as well as other important university stakeholders, maintained the view that universities should not be directly involved in technology commercialization efforts (Mowery and Sampat, 2001a). This ambivalence led universities to become more involved in technology commercialization efforts between the two world wars than before World War I, but in less direct ways than are common today (Mowery *et al.*, 2001).

The University of Wisconsin's involvement with the invention of irradiation to improve vitamin content of foods is a prototypical example of the between-war approach of American universities to technology commercialization. In 1924, Harry Steenbok, a professor at the University of Wisconsin at Madison, invented a way to enhance the Vitamin D content of foods, beverages and medicines through irradiation (Mowery and Sampat, 2001b). Unlike many academics at the time, Professor Steenbok decided to patent his invention, resulting in severe criticism from his academic colleagues, and many members of the American medical profession, who felt that universities should put any inventions that they produced into the public domain (Mowery and Sampat, 2001a). Because of this criticism, the University of Wisconsin was unwilling to take assignment, or manage the disposition, of Professor Steenbok's patents (Mowery *et al.*, 2001). To facilitate the commercialization of his invention under these conditions, Professor Steenbok persuaded several prominent University of Wisconsin alumni to support the creation of the Wisconsin Alumni Research Foundation (WARF), a legally independent organization that would receive patents assigned to University of Wisconsin faculty and then license them, as a way to provide income for the faculty inventors and the university (Mowery and Sampat, 2001b).

During the 1920s and 1930s, other universities, particularly leading public research institutions, followed the University of Wisconsin example and began to institute policies and systems to manage and commercialize university-generated intellectual property (Mowery and Sampat, 2001a). This growth in formalized university technology commercialization processes was spurred by the creation of commercializable intellectual property as a byproduct of research interactions with private industry, the severe financial squeeze that many universities felt during the economic depression of the 1930s and the success of pioneering institutions, like the University of Wisconsin, in generating income from technology licensing (Mowery and Sampat, 2001b).

One part of the new, more formal, commercialization process at American universities that grew out of these efforts was the establishment of policies that required university employees to disclose their inventions to university administrators (Mowery and Sampat, 2001a). Beginning with the University of California, which instituted the first policy in 1926, several public universities began to require employees to disclose their inventions to the institution as a matter of policy (Mowery et al., 2001). In 1932, the Massachusetts Institute of Technology became the first private university in the United States to institute an invention disclosure policy (Mowery and Sampat, 2001b).

A second part of the more formal commercialization process at American universities that emerged in the interwar period was the creation of formal university technology transfer units (Mowery et al., 2001). During the 1930s, several universities, such as the Massachusetts Institute of Technology, Purdue University and the University of Cincinnati, followed the University of Wisconsin's lead in developing administrative units and foundations to manage the process of patenting and licensing inventions that were made as a result of research conducted on their campuses (Mowery and Sampat, 2001b). The formation of administrative units for technology transfer allowed universities to organize their intellectual property and manage it for the benefit of the university as a whole. This change meant that university intellectual property could be made available to a variety of firms through the central administration rather than just to private firms that had funded specific research projects. Etzkowitz (2003) reports that this reorganization was what enabled Stanford University to make available to a variety of private firms inventions developed in physics and electrical engineering in the period before the passage of the Bayh–Dole Act in 1980.

Despite these pioneering efforts, most university technology commercialization activities were still indirect in the pre-World War II period. Most universities remained uninterested in direct commercialization of their intellectual property, and many of them signed contracts with the Research Corporation to manage their intellectual property for them (Mowery and Sampat, 2001a). For instance, in 1937, even MIT, one of the larger academic producers of inventions at the time, and an institution with its own technology transfer office, contracted with the Research Corporation to manage and license its patented inventions (Mowery and Sampat, 2001a).

In addition, by current standards, the volume of university technology commercialization activity at this time was quite small, with universities producing very few patents, and even fewer university spinoffs. Almost no university spinoffs established during the between war period became firms of any size or substance. In fact, one of the few east coast university spinoffs from the between-war period that achieved any level of success at all was Kenneth Germeshausen and Harold Edgerton's consulting firm, founded in 1931 to exploit the invention of stroboscopic photography at MIT (Roberts, 1991a). On the west coast, Hewlett Packard, which came out of Stanford University, was perhaps the most important university spinoff of this period (Saxenian, 1994).

From 1945 to 1980

World War II transformed the American research university. During World War II, the federal government provided to academic departments, particularly those in engineering, with large amounts of money to support research to aid the war effort. This acceleration in funding meant that American public universities, which were once funded largely by their state governments and, in some cases, the federal government's Department of Agriculture, began to see a significant amount of direct federal government funding of research, particularly in academic departments that had previously not received large amounts of external funding (Mowery and Sampat, 2001b). This funding, established with very pragmatic goals in mind, led to a significant increase in the creation of commercializable technology at American universities (Mowery *et al.*, 2001).

The rise in inventions that resulted from federal funding of research during World War II led universities to become more deeply involved in the management of their patents and licensing (Mowery and Sampat, 2001b). One important change in the management of university technology commercialization in the post-World War II period was a significant increase in the number of universities with explicit policies to cover the disclosure and management of inventions by faculty, staff and students. During the 1940 to 1955 period, for example, 64 universities adopted patent policies for the first time and 21 universities revised their policies (Mowery and Sampat, 2001a).

However, these policies often reflected a continuing ambivalence of universities toward technology commercialization. While universities increased their management of intellectual property during the immediate post-World War II period, it was far from clear that they did so to advance technology commercialization. As many observers have pointed out, the policies established during this period were often not very supportive of technology commercialization, and often discouraged or prohibited patenting of inventions (Mowery and Sampat, 2001b).

A second important change in technology commercialization that resulted from World War II was the formation of spinoffs, which for the first time became something that could be seen as a regular activity at some universities. As a byproduct of the war effort, which had generated a sizable amount of commercializable technology, several leading research universities, like MIT, which had received significant wartime research funding, began to see the formation of spinoff companies to commercialize this technology by academic entrepreneurs who believed in the commercial potential of the inventions made at the universities (Roberts, 1991a). For example, in the post-World War II period, a variety of spinoff companies were founded to exploit wartime developments in computer hardware and software, precision machinery, electronic components, machine tools and other devices made at MIT's Lincoln Laboratory (Wainer, 1965). Specifically, Roberts (1991a) reports that, at MIT, Robert Van de Graaff and John Trump formed the High Voltage Engineering Corporation in 1946 to use atomic accelerators developed at the Institute, and Richard Bolt, Leo Beranek and Robert Newman founded BBN, Inc. in 1948 to take advantage of MIT technology in acoustics and noise control, both of which were funded by federal government research projects during World War II.

In conjunction with this effort of entrepreneurs to create spinoff companies to exploit technologies developed at MIT, the first modern venture capital organization, American Research and Development Corporation (ARD), was founded in Boston at the end of World War II (Lerner, 1998), with the explicit goal of commercializing the military technologies invented at MIT (Roberts, 1991a). ARD provided a great deal of assistance to the formation of companies to commercialize university inventions. As Roberts (1991a) explains, ARD's charter called for it to invest in technologies developed at MIT, and the firm invested primarily in businesses and technologies developed by MIT faculty. Moreover, ARD arranged to house the spinoff companies that it financed in MIT facilities through a cost-sharing arrangement, which minimized the total cost outlay for the new companies (Roberts, 1991a). Among the MIT spinoffs that ARD invested in were High Voltage Engineering, which produced electrostatic generators, and Ionics, which engaged in a membrane–ion exchange process (Roberts, 1991a).

However, none of the ARD-funded university spinoffs were more famous than the MIT spinoff, Digital Equipment Corporation, which was the first successful venture capital-backed university spinoff. That company, which Kenneth Olson founded to take advantage of technology he had developed at Lincoln Laboratory (Roberts, 1991a), was the first of what would prove to be many venture capital-backed university spinoffs to go public. As was typical of the spinoffs formed during this period, MIT received no royalties from the commercialization of technology by Digitial Equipment Corporation, and had no equity stake in the company.

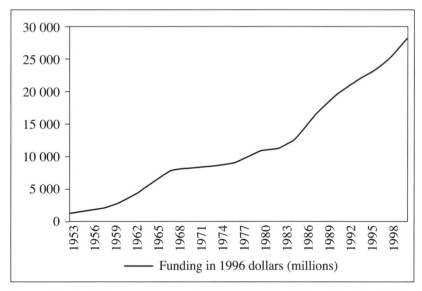

Source: Based on data contained in appendix Table 5.2, National Science Foundation (2002), *Science and Engineering Indicators*, Washington, DC: US Government Printing Office.

Figure 3.1 Real university research and development expenditure from 1953 to 2000

The post-World War II period was also marked by a dramatic rise in university research and development activity that has continued largely unabated until today. Figure 3.1 shows the real (1996 dollars) value of university research and development expenditures since 1953.

The level of this increase in university research and development expenditure over the past 40 years has made universities much more important to overall research and development activity in the United States than they once were. For instance, in 1960, universities accounted for only 7.4 percent of all research and development expenditure in the United States, a figure that has grown steadily across the ensuing years to almost double by 1997, when the figure reached 14.5 percent (Mowery *et al*., 2001).

Much of the rise in university research and development and corresponding focus on technology commercialization in the 1950s and 1960s can be attributed to a dramatic increase in federal funding of research and development at American universities (Mowery and Sampat, 2001a). Federal funding as a percentage of university research and development activity increased from 54.6 percent in 1960 to a high of 73.4 percent in 1966 (Mowery, 2001). This increase in federal funding of research at American universities led to an increase in university patenting and technology commercialization activity through a standard input–output relationship.

The heavy federal funding of American universities during the Cold War also had an affect on the creation of spinoff companies. During the 1950s and 1960s, entrepreneurs at many of the major universities began to create new spinoff companies to exploit technologies developed with federal funds (Leslie, 1993). Moreover, the development of these companies was supported by a mechanism that had not operated to a very large degree with previous generations of university spinoffs – the use of direct contracts with government agencies or indirect government funding through contracts with aerospace or other defense-related companies that were themselves heavy recipients of federal government military contracts (Feldman, 1994). For instance, during the Cold War, entrepreneurs spinning out of MIT's research laboratories and engineering departments created many new companies funded by contracts with the US military and major aerospace companies (Saxenian, 1994; Leslie, 1993). However, as was the standard institutional arrangement at the time, MIT received no royalties from the commercialization of Institute-originated technologies by these companies, nor did it have an equity stake in them.

The rise in federal funding of American university research also led many of the largest research universities to further develop their technology commercialization policies and procedures, largely in response to demands from their federal funding sources to develop formal policies towards patents and other intellectual property (Mowery and Sampat, 2001a). For instance, the 1960s marked a change in the policies of the Department of Defense, which began to permit any university with an approved patent policy to keep title to patented inventions that were the outcome of research that the department had financed, leading many universities to seek and obtain Department of Defense-approved patent policies (Mowery et al., 2001). In addition, in the 1960s and 1970s, the Department of Health, Education and Welfare and the National Science Foundation established Institutional Patent Agreements (Mowery and Sampat, 2001b), which were negotiated bilaterally between individual universities and the federal departments, and which permitted the universities to patent and license department-funded university research (Mowery et al., 2001).

Along with the changes in university patent policies came a change in institutional arrangements to manage patents. Although some institutions, such as the University of California and the University of Florida, managed their own patents in the 1950s, most institutions still assigned their patents to the Research Corporation or other external entities (Mowery and Sampat, 2001b). However, in the 1960s, several universities began to enter into the management of their own patent portfolios through the establishment of technology licensing offices, increasing the number of such offices from 6 in 1960 to 25 by 1980 (Mowery and Sampat, 2001a).

Moreover, the 1960s saw the introduction of a larger number of private universities into the patent management game. Prior to 1960, public universities were much more likely than their private counterparts to have patent policies and to engage in active management of patenting and licensing of inventions that were developed on campus (Mowery and Sampat, 2001a). However, during the 1960s, private universities significantly increased their efforts to patent and license their technologies (Mowery, 2001). In particular, they began to manage technology commercialization efforts directly, taking over their own patent management (Mowery and Sampat, 2001b).

The 1970s were another decade of profound change in university technology commercialization and spinoff activity. Beginning in 1970, university patenting began to accelerate, initiating the rise in university patenting activity that continues to this day (Mowery, 2001). This increase in university patenting activity is significantly higher than the increase in the academic share of research and development in the United States, which means that, since the 1970s, universities have seen a large increase in their patent productivity (Mowery, 2001).

In addition, in the 1970s, several universities began to experiment with policies to promote spinoff activity. For instance, in 1972, using a grant from the MIT Corporation and private gifts, Richard Morse, a founder of National Research Corporation and the inventor of frozen orange juice, established the MIT Development Foundation (MITDF), an organization designed to facilitate MIT spinoffs by providing faculty, staff and students with business planning, market forecasting, seed capital and education on firm formation and technology transfer (Roberts, 1991a). In return for providing assistance, the MITDF was to take equity in the spinoff companies and use the proceeds of that equity for the benefit of the institution (Matkin, 1990).

However, the MITDF proved to be an experiment, not a long-lasting organization. It went out of business in 1977, having funded only three companies: Rheocast, Sala Magnetics and Surftech Corporation (Matkin, 1990).

Other university experiments to support university spinoff activity initiated in the 1970s proved to be more long-lasting. Perhaps the most important of these experiments was the creation of university-linked venture capital funds. The first of these was founded in 1974 when Boston University established the Community Technology Fund to invest in Boston University spinoff companies (Roberts and Malone, 1996). Throughout the 1970s, other universities began to follow Boston University's example, establishing their own directly managed venture capital funds.

The 1970s also saw the creation of an important industry for university spinoffs, biotechnology. As will be described in greater detail later, biotechnology has proved to be the industry in which university spinoffs are most important. This industry traces its origins back to the early 1970s, when researchers from Stanford and the University of California at Berkeley founded the first biotechnology firm, Cetus, in 1971 (Kenney, 1986). Moreover, the first commercial application of genetic engineering occurred a couple of years later, in 1974, when venture capitalist Robert Swanson persuaded Herbert Boyer, the co-inventor of the Cohen–Boyer gene splicing process, to form a company to commercialize this new technology (Kenney, 1986).

The 1970s also marked a change in the role of the federal government in the funding of university research and the commercialization of university technology, an important trend that accounts for the watershed event of the passage of the Bayh–Dole Act in 1980 (about which, more below). The 1970s witnessed the reversal of a decline in the share of industry funding of academic research that occurred in the 1950s and 1960s as a result of the Cold War (Mowery and Sampat, 2001b). In 1970, the federal government funded 70.5 percent of all university research and development, with the private sector funding just 2.6 percent. (By way of comparison, by 1997, the federal government share had declined to 59.6 percent, while private sector funding had increased to 7.1 percent) (Mowery *et al.*, 2001).

Moreover, by the late 1970s, the federal government policies to promote commercialization of university technology had become less supportive than they had been in the previous decade. In the 1960s, universities that had negotiated Institutional Patent Agreements with the Department of Health, Education and Welfare were allowed to license technology exclusively under those agreements (Mowery and Sampat, 2001b). By the 1970s, however, the Department had begun to challenge the use of exclusive licenses under these agreements (Mowery *et al.*, 2001). The threat that the Department might limit the use of exclusive licenses dampened university efforts to make use of the patent and license rights under these agreements (Mowery et al, 2001; Mowery and Sampat, 2001b). The declining federal funding of university research, combined with the difficulties of exploiting federally funded university inventions under the existing institutional regime, led many policy makers to call for a change in the arrangements to govern university technology commercialization.

The 1980s

The watershed event in university technology commercialization in the United States was the passage of the Bayh–Dole Act in 1980, which gave academic institutions the property rights to federally funded inventions.[1] Specifically, the Bayh–Dole Act put in place a common policy for universities seeking to commercialize federally funded inventions, and removed the need to operate through a complex set of bilateral Institutional Patent Agreements negotiated between individual universities and government agencies (Mowery, 2001). In short, the Act gave universities greater incentives to license their technologies and made the process easier to undertake.

As a result, Bayh–Dole ushered in a period of intense growth in university technology production and patenting. Since 1980, university patenting has grown fivefold. Moreover, research productivity at American universities has increased dramatically, with patents per million dollars of research expenditures increasing from 0.03 in 1980 to 0.11 in 1997 (Mowery, 2001). Because of this dramatic growth of university patents, academic institutions have begun to account for an increasing portion of patents in the United States. As Figure 3.2 shows, universities' share of patents issued in the United States has risen significantly since 1980.

The Bayh–Dole Act also led dramatic growth in the infrastructure for technology transfer and commercialization at a wide range of universities. Many universities that previously did not engage in technology commercialization began patenting, licensing and generating spinoffs after the passage of the Act

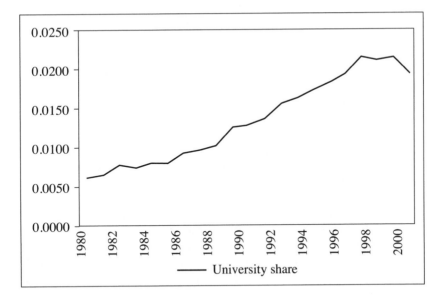

Source: Based on data provided by the United States Patent and Trademark Office.

Figure 3.2   The university share of US patents granted, 1980 to 2000

(Mowery, 2001). In fact, the count of university technology transfer offices grew from 25 in 1980 to over 200 by 1995 (Mowery and Sampat, 2001a).

Moreover, during the 1980s, a variety of institutions were established to support the commercialization of university technology, with a particular emphasis on mechanisms to create spinoff companies. For instance, in 1983, Texas A&M University established the Institute for Ventures in New Technology, an organization designed to aid small businesses with the transfer of university technology (Wilson and Szygenda, 1991). In 1987, the trustees of Pennsylvania State University incorporated economic development as part of the university mission, leading the university to develop a wide variety of supporting institutions for technology commercialization, including the development of a science park, business incubators, a plan to make venture capital and equity investments in new firms, and a program to help faculty, staff and students exploit university technology in entrepreneurial ways (Matkin, 1990). In 1987, the University of Texas at Austin established the Center for Technology Development and Transfer to commercialize university research (Smilor *et al.*, 1990). The efforts of this center were supported by the Texas state legislature, which passed an equity ownership bill that allowed that university to take equity in university spinoffs for the first time.

The 1980s were also a period during which supporting institutions to finance spinoffs were developed at many American universities. Some of these institutions took the form of venture capital firms. For example, the University of Rochester established a venture capital subsidiary in 1981, capitalized with $67 million of the university's endowment (Matkin, 1990). Baylor College of Medicine established BCM Technologies in 1983 to invest in spinoffs from that institution. In 1985, University of Texas–Southwestern Medical Center created Dallas Biomedical Corporation with the same purpose (Lerner, 1998). In 1987, Penn State University invested $250 000 of its endowment to establish a venture capital fund to invest in university technology companies to be managed by Zero Stage Capital, a Massachusetts-based venture capital firm, which then raised $10 million for a fund to commercialize the university's inventions (Matkin, 1990).

Other financing institutions took the form of centers for the funding of technology commercialization. These organizations provided pre-seed stage funding for technology development, either alone or in conjunction with venture capital. Examples of such organizations founded in the 1980s include the Center for Biotechnology Research, which was created by Stanford University and the University of California in 1982 to invest in university spinoffs in biotechnology (Lerner, 1998). Similarly, in 1986, the University of Chicago founded ARCH Development Corporation, an organization designed to create and finance new companies to commercialize inventions out of the University of Chicago and Argone National Laboratory (Roberts and Malone, 1996). In

1988, using private investor funds, Johns Hopkins University founded an organization called Triad Investors Corporation to commercialize technology from the university and the university health system, and to assist inventors with intellectual property management, firm creation and financing (Matkin, 1990).

The 1980s also witnessed a dramatic shift in attitudes toward spinoff activity at American universities. This attitude change is best exemplified by a reversal of Harvard University's policy toward university spinoffs. At the beginning of the 1980s, most academic institutions were still quite resistant to the idea of establishing university spinoffs, thinking that such an activity ran counter to the university mission. As a result, in 1980, when Harvard University considered launching a biotechnology company to commercialize the research of faculty member Mark Ptashne with the support of venture capital firms, the effort raised a firestorm of opposition (Kenney, 1996). The *New York Times* (1980:34) wrote a blistering editorial, arguing that universities should not be in the business of establishing companies, lest they lose sight of their proper role in society. The editorial stated,

> Consider the risks as well. Where would the search for commercial success end? Why shouldn't a university's law school establish a prosperous law firm, the business school a consulting company, the engineering school a construction company? Universities that seek a legitimate return from the ideas and inventions of their faculties must be careful not to lose their academic souls.

As a result of the opposition it faced to the idea of establishing a new firm to exploit the research of a faculty member, Harvard University backed out of the effort. In explaining the university's decision, Derek Bok, then President of Harvard, wrote (1981:35):

> In such enterprises [efforts to join the university with its professors to launch new companies] the risks are much harder to control, and there are few benefits to society or the academy that cannot be achieved in other ways. Instead of helping its professors to launch new companies, therefore, the university would do better to seize the initiative by asking the faculty to consider this new phenomenon in order to fashion appropriate safeguards that will maintain its academic standards and preserve its intellectual values.

However, less than a decade later, Harvard University reversed this decision. In 1988, the university established Medical Science Partners, a venture capital entity to invest in companies that would commercialize technology developed at the university (Matkin, 1990). Not only was there no outcry of opposition to the effort to create Medical Science Partners, but also many important university stakeholders felt that Harvard University had already fallen behind other universities in the technology commercialization game and would need to adopt other policy changes, in conjunction with the establishment of a venture capital fund, to catch up (Matkin, 1990).

The 1990s: Recent Trends in Technology Commercialization

The decade of the 1990s showed a marked increase in university technology production and commercialization activity at US universities and hospitals. As Figure 3.3 shows, invention disclosures, patent applications, issued patents, and licenses and options executed have all increased dramatically over the past decade. For those respondents to all ten years of the Association of University Technology Managers' survey of academic patenting, licensing and technology transfer activity, invention disclosures have increased by 79 percent over

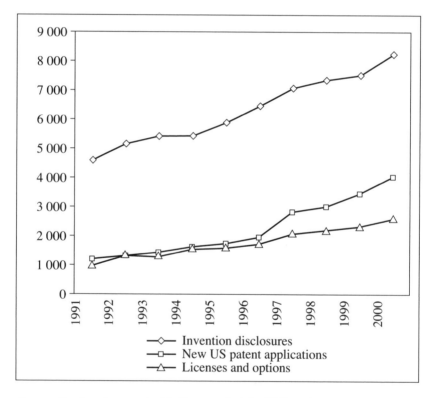

Source: Based on data contained in Pressman, L. (ed.) (2002), *AUTM Licensing Survey: FY 2001*, Northbrook, IL: Association of University Technology Managers.

Figure 3.3   Ten-year trends in commercialization activities at US academic institutions

the past ten years (Pressman, 2002). Moreover, new US patent applications from these institutions have increased by 230 percent, and licenses and options executed have increased by 159 percent even though the total research budgets (in 1991 dollars) of American academic institutions increased only by 43 percent during the same time period (Pressman, 2002). As a result, the R&D cost of each license or option created has fallen to $5.88 million from $10.68 million (1991 dollars) over the last decade.

The growth in the technology production and commercialization activity at American universities has led to a significant increase in the economic returns earned from licensing by American academic institutions over the past ten years (Pressman, 2002). As Figure 3.4 shows, the number of income-generating licensing agreements and the dollar value of royalties have both increased dramatically over the decade. However, as Feldman (2001) correctly points out, the average revenue per license has not increased. Almost all of the increased licensing income that has occurred over the past ten years can be attributed to an increase in the total number of licenses in existence.

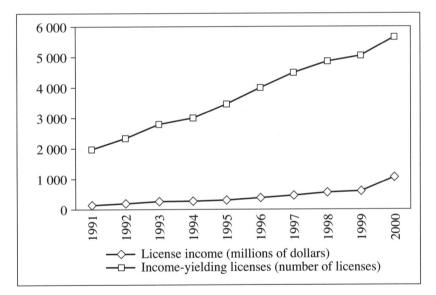

Source: Based on data contained in Pressman, L. (ed.) (2002), *AUTM Licensing Survey: FY 2001*, Northbook, IL: Association of University Technology Managers.

Figure 3.4   Ten-year trends in income from university licensing

Over the past decade, universities also have become increasingly likely to generate spinoff companies. For instance, Lowe (2002) reports that one-quarter of licensees of technology at the University of California are now spinoff companies, while Golub (2003) reports that two-thirds of the 46 Columbia University spinoffs have been founded since 1997.

More systematic investigations of university spinoff activity also demonstrate this increasing trend in spinoff activity. For example, Shane (2001b) examined the founding of spinoff companies to exploit MIT-assigned inventions and observed an increasing trend from 1980 to 1996, with a sharp increase in the rate occurring in the late 1980s and continuing through the 1990s. For instance, as Table 3.1 shows, in 1980, MIT licensed 13 patents to spinoff companies but, in 1996, it licensed 38.

Data from the Association of University Technology Managers shows a similar increase in spinoff activity across American academic institutions. As Figure 3.5 shows, from 1980 to 1993, American academic institutions generated an average of 83.5 spinoffs per year, but, by 2000, these same institutions

*Table 3.1   The distribution of MIT spinoff patents by
year of patent issue, 1980 to 1996*

Year	Number of spinoff patents
1980	13
1981	14
1982	13
1983	14
1984	15
1985	9
1986	12
1987	13
1988	17
1989	31
1990	29
1991	26
1992	35
1993	32
1994	28
1995	25
1996	38

Source: Reprinted by permission, Shane, S. 'Technology opportunities and new firm creation' *Management Science*, **47**(2), 2001, 205–20. Copyright 2001, the Institute for Operations Research and the Management Science, 901 Elkridge Landing Road, Suite 400, Linthicum, MD 21090 USA.

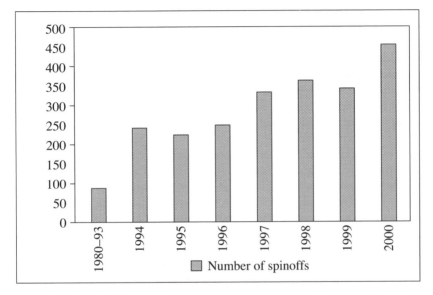

Note: The figure for 1980–93 is the average annual number of spinoffs per year; for all other years, the figure is the actual number of spinoffs per year.

Source: Based on data contained in Pressman, L. (ed.) (2002), *AUTM Licensing Survey: FY 2000*, Northbook, IL: Association of University Technology Managers.

Figure 3.5   The number of spinoffs from American academic institutions, 1980 to 2000

were generating 454 spinoffs per year, an increase of 444 percent (Pressman, 2002). In addition, from 1995 until 2000, the number of institutions producing spinoffs in a given year rose to 64 percent of the total, from 53 percent (Pressman, 2002).

WHAT EXPLAINS THE TREND TOWARD SPINOFFS?

The data show that, in the United States, there has been a dramatic increase in the number of university spinoff companies since 1980. So why has this trend occurred? A variety of explanations can be offered, including the birth and growth of biomedical technology, the passage of the Bayh–Dole Act, changes in patent laws, contagion effects, changes in the financing process, and the growth in the use of equity holdings by universities. These different explanations are discussed in the subsections below.

The Growth of Biomedical Technology

One explanation for the trend toward spinoffs from academic institutions has been the significant rise in the importance of biomedical technology at American educational institutions. Starting in the early 1970s, and continuing since then, federal support for biomedical research at universities has grown dramatically (Mowery and Sampat, 2001b). In particular, through the National Institutes of Health, the federal government began an effort to fund molecular biology research in the 1970s that has led to many basic scientific developments with significant commercial potential (Mowery and Sampat, 2001b).

Perhaps as a result of the dramatic rise in federal funding for biomedical research at universities, university technology production has shifted significantly toward the creation of biomedical inventions. Since the 1970s, university patents have become increasingly concentrated in biomedical fields (Shane, forthcoming), with biomedical inventions rising from 11 percent of university patenting in 1971 to a remarkable 48 percent by 1997 (Mowery, 2001). As Figure 3.6 shows, the growth in the university share of inventions in the biomedical fields has outstripped the growth in the university share of inventions in other domains.

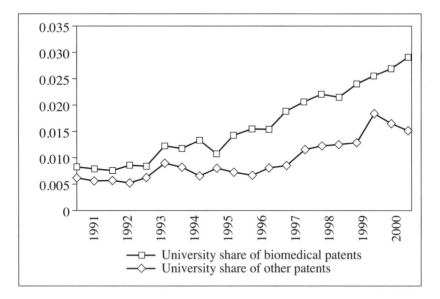

Source: Based on data contained in National Science Foundation, *Science and Engineering Indicators*, various years.

Figure 3.6   Growth in the university share of patents over time

The shift of universities toward biomedical technology production may be an important factor behind the rise in spinoff activity from academic institutions because biomedical inventions are more likely than physical science inventions to provide the basis for the creation of new companies. As will be explained in greater detail in Chapter 7, researchers have offered several reasons for biomedical inventions being disproportionately likely to lead to the formation of university spinoffs. First, patent protection for biomedical inventions is stronger than for other types of inventions (Levin *et al.*, 1987). Second, customers of biomedical inventions tend to support innovation without trading off value for price. Third, biomedical technologies are often discrete inventions that can be used independently of other pieces of technology. Fourth, the scientific advances made in universities in biomedical fields tend to be more directly related to commercial activity than is the case in other technical fields.

The Passage of the Bayh–Dole Act

A second explanation for the rise in university spinoffs in the United States over the past two decades is the passage of the Bayh–Dole Act in 1980, and the provision of follow-on rights in 1984. The Act and follow-on laws made it significantly easier for universities to license and commercialize federally funded inventions, facilitating the formation of spinoff companies interested in licensing and developing these technologies. Because federally funded inventions account for more than two-thirds of all university inventions, the simplification of the procedures necessary to exploit federally funded technologies has had a dramatic effect on the willingness of universities to get into the patent and licensing game, particularly at smaller institutions that previously could not justify the cost of negotiating Institutional Patent Agreements or setting up technology transfer offices (Mowery and Sampat, 2001b).

Moreover, the Bayh–Dole Act legitimated spinoff activity at US universities. The Act states that one of its goals is 'to encourage maximum participation of small business firms in federally supported research and development efforts'. As a result, the Act encouraged a bias at academic institutions toward licensing to new and small firms (Lowe, 2002). This change in orientation was important in altering thinking at universities, which had long-established beliefs about the inappropriateness of direct university involvement in technology commercialization and spinoff activity (Mowery *et al.*, 2001). By encouraging universities to focus directly on technology commercialization and spinoff activity, the Act helped to reduce the opposition to spinoff activities within universities, and led many university administrators to believe that founding companies to exploit technology, an activity once thought of as inappropriate, was legitimate and even desirable.

Furthermore, the Act increased the incentives for universities to market their technologies to private sector firms (Golub, 2003). As Chapter 9 will discuss in greater detail, universities must make significant efforts to market their technologies if they seek to license them. As a result, university technology commercialization and spinoff activity requires the allocation of university resources to efforts to find licensees. Without the passage of the Bayh–Dole Act, universities would have seen little reason to search out licensees for their technologies and would have had a hard time finding external entrepreneur licensees, a group that has led the efforts to found a significant portion of university spinoffs.

Finally, the Act encouraged spinoff activity by facilitating exclusive licensing. Specifically, the Act provided the federal government's direct support of exclusive licensing of federally funded research (Mowery *et al.*, 2001). As a result, exclusive licensing, something that several federal agencies opposed under the previous Institutional Patent Agreement regime, became easy to do (Pressman *et al.*, 1995). Exclusive licensing is extremely important in encouraging spinoff activity because new firms have very few competitive advantages, and often are unwilling to bear the risks of developing new technology, unless they have some assurance that they will be able to have exclusive rights to that technology once it has been developed. As a result, the Bayh–Dole Act's support for exclusive licensing was an important factor in encouraging the growth in university spinoff activity since 1980.

Changes in Patent Laws

Changes in patent laws provide a third explanation for the rise in university spinoff activity over the past two decades. Starting with the *Diamond* v. *Chakrabarthy* case in 1980, which made biological life forms patentable, the *Diamond* v. *Diehr* case in 1981, which strengthened software patents, and the creation of the Court of Appeals for the Federal Circuit in 1982, which made it easier for people to sue to protect their intellectual property, the federal government has engaged in a series of actions over the past 20 years that have strengthened intellectual property rights in the United States. Because university spinoffs are often founded to exploit patented university inventions and have few other sources of competitive advantage initially, stronger intellectual property laws enhance spinoff activity.

Thus one might attribute to the *Diamond* v. *Chakrabarthy* decision the growth of spinoffs based on basic research outputs, which universities are effective at generating. Similarly, one might attribute to the *Diamond* v. *Diehr* decision the growth of software spinoffs based on patents. One might also attribute the growth of spinoff companies to the ability of university inventors and university spinoffs to use the Court of Appeals for the Federal Circuit to protect the intellectual property belonging to university spinoffs.

Contagion Effect

A fourth explanation for the rise in spinoff activity over the past two decades is a contagion effect. The exploitation of entrepreneurial opportunities involves making decisions under uncertainty and limited information about products, markets, ways of organizing, strategy and the acquisition of resources (Shane, 2003). The skills and information necessary to make these decisions are often unavailable in codified form, but often can be learned through observation of others (Busenitz and Lau, 1996). Consequently, the presence of entrepreneurial role models may be quite instrumental in leading to the formation of university spinoffs.

Several researchers have observed that the growth of spinoff activity is consistent with contagion effects. For instance, Feldman (1999) found that, when spinoff activity began to grow, the growth itself led to further increases through an endogenous process. She argued that faculty members' decisions to start companies are socially conditioned. Thus the efforts by pioneering faculty members to found companies have led other faculty members to found companies as well, because it led the followers to believe that firm formation was an easy and desirable activity (Feldman *et al.*, 2000).

Moreover, the growth of interest of senior faculty members in scientific fields in firm formation appears to have been stimulated by activities of highly prestigious colleagues, whom other scientists view as role models. As Etzkowitz (1989) explained, senior faculty members in biological sciences at many universities viewed the formation of new companies to develop and sell such things as a cell line, as a new type of professional achievement. He quotes one professor as saying, 'Nowadays, it is understood if someone like [Walter] Gilbert quits Harvard [to found a firm], being in a company does not imply mediocrity' (Etzkowitz, 1989:22). In a larger sample study, Audretsch *et al.* (2000) provides similar results, showing that science-based firm formation is, in fact, influenced by a demonstration effect of prior start-up efforts by other scientists.

Furthermore, once a university has generated several successful companies, faculty members can offer tangible support to their colleagues interested in going down the entrepreneurial route. The first generation of entrepreneurial faculty train subsequent generations of doctoral students in laboratories that are directly connected to the spinoff process, and in which spinoffs are seen as a natural and supported activity (Tornatzky *et al.*, 1997). As a result, the directors of these laboratories teach more junior colleagues to create scientific discoveries that are effectively exploited through the formation of spinoff companies.

The first generation of scientist–entrepreneurs also directly help students and junior faculty to found companies based on their research. For instance, on campuses such as MIT's, where more than one generation of academic entrepreneurs can be found, the first generation often offers the second generation specific advice on the firm formation process, connects would-be entrepreneurs with the investors, suppliers and employees that they will need to found their companies, and even serves as a pool of business angels who finance the firm formation process (Etzkowitz, 1998).

The Financing System

A fifth explanation for the development of university spinoffs has been the set of changes that have occurred in capital markets over the past two decades. The past 20 years have witnessed a dramatic rise in the availability of venture capital and business angel financing (Gompers and Lerner, 1999), providing a source of external financing to university spinoffs that could not be tapped easily in prior periods. While the vast majority of this financing does not get invested in seed-stage companies, the amount of seed-stage financing available to start-up companies has increased over the past 20 years. The growth in seed-stage capital has increased the capital pool available for the founders of university spinoffs to tap.

In addition, since 1980, several public sector programs that finance the development of university spinoffs have been established. These programs reduce a funding gap that exists from the time when university inventions are created and spinoffs are often founded until the time when the private sector becomes interested in financing spinoff companies. Two of the most important public sector programs for mitigating the funding gap in the United States are the Small Business Innovation Research (SBIR) Program, which was founded in 1982, and the Advanced Technology Program (ATP), which was founded in 1990. The SBIR program requires all federal government agencies to set aside 2 percent of their budgets for funding projects proposed by small businesses. The ATP program provides funding for the development of high-risk technologies, approximately 60 percent of which goes to new and small businesses.[2] As will be discussed in greater detail in Chapter 10, many university spinoffs make significant use of government programs to develop their technologies in the pre-commercialization stage. As a result, the presence of these institutions makes the financing of university spinoffs easier, and thus facilitates their formation.

The provision of financing from government agencies also encourages private sector financing of start-up firms. For example, Lerner (1999) compared SBIR grant awardees with a matched sample of firms. He found that the SBIR grant recipients were no more likely to receive venture capital than the matched sample before receiving an SBIR award, but were significantly more likely to receive venture capital afterwards. Lerner (1999) attributed the recipients' superior ability to garner outside capital after receipt of the awards to the certification effect of receiving the government grants.

Furthermore, capital markets have become increasingly willing to finance firms before they have a commercial product, which enhances the formation of university spinoffs. During the 1980s, investment banks began to take public biotechnology firms that were far from having a commercial product, something that the initial public offering market had previously been unwilling to do (Stephan and Levin, 1996). This capital market shift made it possible for university entrepreneurs in capital-intensive fields like biotechnology to raise enough money to develop new products in the context of new firms. Moreover, because university spinoffs often have products that are relatively far from commercialization, the ability of founders and investors to liquidate their investments before products have been launched has made it easier for people to start these types of companies (Bray and Lee, 2000).[3]

University Equity Policies

A final explanation for the growth in university spinoff activity over the past two decades has been the shift in universities toward a policy of taking equity in licensees of university technology. Universities take equity in licensees in two ways: first, they take equity in return for intellectual property or some other consideration; second, they make cash investments in licensees, often alongside venture capitalists and angel investors, in return for equity. Whether in return for providing intellectual property or in return for the investment of the universities' capital, research has shown that equity ownership in licensees by universities has been increasing over the past 20 years (Feldman, 2001). Figure 3.7 shows the recent trend toward the use of equity.

Holding equity in spinoff companies is even more widespread than holding equity in licensees overall. The Association of University Technology Managers (1996) reported that universities held equity in 37 percent of their spinoffs from 1980 to 1995. By 2000, the universities from which the spinoff's technology was licensed held equity in more than half (56 percent) of university spinoffs (Pressman, 2002). DiGregorio and Shane (2003) report that, over the 1993 to 1998 period, 80 percent of US universities were permitted to take equity in spinoffs, and 74 percent had done so.[4]

The use of equity is associated with an increase in spinoff activity for several reasons. First, taking equity in lieu of patent costs allows new companies to minimize cash outlays (DiGregorio and Shane, 2003).[5] Because the use of equity to capitalize patent costs allows the spinoffs to preserve capital for other organizing activities, many entrepreneurs favor equity deals, so taking equity encourages spinoff formation at the margin.

Second, the use of equity enhances the ability of universities to benefit

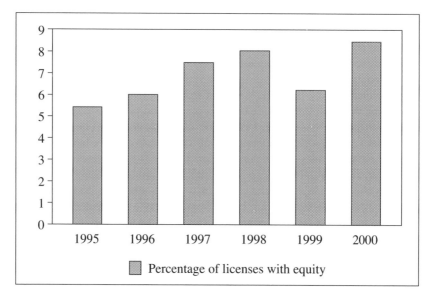

Source: Based on data contained in Pressman, L. (ed.), Association of University Technology Managers, *AUTM Licensing Survey*, various years.

Figure 3.7   Percentage of licenses with equity, 1995 to 2000

from the commercialization of uncertain technology (DiGregorio and Shane, 2003). As Chapter 2 explained, making an equity investment allows the university to gain from technology transfer, even if the spinoff moves away from the initially licensed technology (Bray and Lee, 2000).

SUMMARY

Universities have long been involved in the commercialization of technology and the formation of spinoff companies. Several 19th-century German chemistry professors founded companies to produce salts, potash, acetic acid and chemical fertilizer. In the United States, the Hatch Act of 1887, which established the land grant system, was based on the idea of making university research useful to industry and agriculture. The creation of land grant institutions led many American universities to have a commercial orientation that facilitated the development of spinoff companies from their earliest days.

In the early 20th century, entrepreneurs at and around universities began to experiment for the first time with spinning off companies as a way to use university inventions to develop local economies. However, universities were largely ambivalent about technology commercialization at this time, and most university technology commercialization prior to World War II was conducted indirectly through buffering institutions like the Research Corporation.

Between World War I and World War II, universities became more involved in technology commercialization as a result of increased involvement with industry. This increased technology commercialization led to the development of invention disclosure policies and technology transfer units at several universities, particularly public ones.

World War II transformed the American research university by increasing both the total amount of university research funding and the federal government's share of that research funding. This transformation continued through the Cold War, during which time American university research was seen as important to the defense effort. This increase in federal research funding led to the creation of a generation of spinoff companies from universities to commercialize the outputs of federally funded research. The effort to found spinoff companies was helped along by the creation of ARD, the first venture capital firm, which was founded in Boston with the explicit goal of helping to commercialize MIT inventions.

The 1970s were a period of profound change in university technology commercialization. Beginning in 1970, university patenting began to increase both in absolute terms and in terms of inventions per dollar of research. Universities began to develop policies to support spinoffs both through direct assistance and through venture capital funds. The 1970s also saw the origins of the most important industry for university spinoffs, biotechnology. However, the 1970s also witnessed some negative changes that set the stage for the formation of a new institutional arrangement for university technology commercialization in the 1980s. First, federal funding of university research began to decline during this period. Second, federal agencies began to develop policies that hindered efforts of universities to commercialize federally funded inventions under the terms of the institutional regime of the time.

In 1980, the US Congress passed the Bayh–Dole Act, which gave universities the property rights to federally funded inventions, marking a watershed in the development of university spinoffs. The Act led to a dramatic increase in university invention disclosures, patent production, patent productivity, licensing office creation and licensing activity. The 1980s also marked a period of intense creation of mechanisms to support university spinoffs, including the formation of incubators and the establishment of venture capital funds. Perhaps because of these widespread changes, the 1980s marked a shift in attitudes of university administrators toward support for the formation of spinoff companies.

The 1990s showed marked increases in university technology creation and commercialization at American academic institutions, with invention disclosures, patent applications, licenses executed, licensing income and spinoff company formation, all rising significantly during this decade. Researchers have offered several explanations for the dramatic growth in spinoff activity over the past two decades. Observers have attributed this growth to the rise of biomedical research at universities, the Bayh–Dole Act, changes in patent laws, a contagion effect, and changes in the financing system.

Having described the history of technology commercialization and spinoff activity at academic institutions, I now turn to a discussion of variation in spinoff activity across universities, the subject of Chapter 4.

NOTES

1. Similar changes were occurring elsewhere in the world at the same time. For example, in the United Kingdom, the 1977 Patents Act gave universities the rights to intellectual property produced by their employees in the course of their employment.
2. In the United Kingdom, the University Challenge Fund, established in 1998 to provide seed stage financing to university spinoffs, plays a similar role to that played by the ATP and SBIR funds in the United States. Although the University Challenge Fund provides universities with money to make seed-stage investments in spinoff companies directly, and the ATP and SBIR programs fund spinoff companies indirectly, all three agencies provide funds to spinoff companies during the earliest stages in their lives, when technical and market risks are often too high for private sector investors and a funding gap is therefore thought to exist.
3. At the same time that capital markets have been making it easier for university researchers to finance spinoffs, the government has been making it harder for researchers to obtain grants (Stephan and Levin, 1996). This shift also encouraged the creation of spinoffs by making start-up company funding a relatively effective way to finance technology development.
4. Charles and Conway (2001) report that, in the United Kingdom, 32 percent of academic institutions had equity holdings in spinoff companies, which totaled just under $308 million. Moreover, most of the UK institutions making equity investments tend to hold on to their equity investments, rather than liquidate them. Less than 8 percent of institutions in the United Kingdom sold their equity investments in 2000, with those sales raising approximately $61 million (Charles and Conway, 2001).
5. The university share of equity is generally negotiated, but licensing officers at Carnegie Mellon University seek 5 percent (Anonymous, 2001).

4. Variation in spinoff activities across institutions

This chapter discusses an important empirical observation about university spinoffs: the wide variance across universities in their tendency to produce spinoff companies. This chapter will explain why some universities, like Arizona State University and Harvard University, produce virtually no new companies, despite generating a large number of technological inventions, whereas other universities, like Carnegie Mellon University and Emory University, produce a large number of spinoffs, given their level of technological production. As this chapter explains, three key factors appear to explain cross-university variation in spinoff activity: university policies, technology licensing office expertise, and university goals and culture. Each of these explanations will be explored in turn, but first some evidence of the concentration in spinoff activity in a relatively small set of universities is provided.

THE CONCENTRATION OF SPINOFF ACTIVITY

Many observers have noted that university spinoff activity is concentrated in a small number of academic institutions. Describing her interactions with 70 different academic institutions as a representative of the Howard Hughes Medical Institute, Leonard (2001) points out strong variance across the institutions in their interest in, and support of, spinoffs. In a more quantitative observation, Pressman (2002) reported that, in 2000, 121 academic institutions in the United States generated spinoff companies, while 69 institutions (36 percent) did not.[1]

The variance across universities in the rate of spinoff company formation is not limited to the United States. Charles and Conway (2001) reported that, in 2000, 24 universities accounted for 75 percent of all spinoffs in the United Kingdom. In fact, over the 1996 to 2001 period, approximately one-fourth of all UK universities generating intellectual property created no spinoff companies, whereas 27 percent generated more than ten spinoff companies during the same period (Wright et al., 2002). Similarly, Dahlstrand (1999) points out that almost all of the university spinoffs in the Gothenburg area of Sweden were spinoffs from Chalmers Institute of Technology; almost none were spinoffs from Gothenburg University.

Moreover, the tendency to generate spinoffs is not just a function of the amount of technology created at a university. Tornatzky *et al.* (1997) found that the proportion of licenses to spinoff companies ranged from 0 to 71 percent between 1994 and 1996 for universities in the Southern United States. Moreover, Table 4.1 shows the proportion of university spinoffs per invention disclosure for selected universities. The table indicates that some universities, like the University of Maryland and Northwestern University, produce virtually no spinoffs, despite generating a large number of technological inventions, whereas other universities, like the Massachusetts Institute of Technology and the University of Virginia, produce a much higher number of spinoff companies, given their level of technology creation.

Table 4.1   Spinoffs per invention disclosure in 2000, selected universities

University	Disclosures	Spinoffs	Ratio
University of Miami	32	0	0.00
University of Maryland, College Park	122	2	0.02
Northwestern University	115	2	0.02
Ohio State University	106	2	0.02
SUNY Research Foundation	186	4	0.02
W.A.R.F./University of Wisconsin Madison	277	6	0.02
University of Pennsylvania	223	6	0.03
Johns Hopkins University	355	10	0.03
Rutgers, the State University of NJ	141	4	0.03
University of Rochester	67	2	0.03
Stanford University	252	8	0.03
Georgia Institute of Technology	170	6	0.04
University of North Carolina, Chapel Hill	113	4	0.04
Columbia University	194	7	0.04
University of Florida	166	6	0.04
Purdue Research Foundation	118	5	0.04
Iowa State University	111	5	0.05
University of Pittsburgh	110	5	0.05
University of Michigan	168	8	0.05
University of Southern California	146	7	0.05
Univeristy of Texas, Austin	87	5	0.06
Boston University	69	5	0.07
Massachusetts Institute of Technology (MIT)	425	31	0.07
University of Virginia Patent Foundation	124	10	0.08
University of Georgia	73	7	0.10
New York University	17	7	0.41

Source: Based on data contained in Pressman, L. (ed.) (2002), *AUTM Licensing Survey: FY2000*, Northbrook, IL: Association of University Technology Managers.

If the variation across universities in the rate of spinoff formation is not explained by the university's overall level of technology creation, then why do some universities generate more spinoffs than others? The answer to this question is the subject of the next section.

WHY DO SOME UNIVERSITIES GENERATE MORE SPINOFFS THAN OTHERS?

The evidence gathered to date suggests three main reasons for some universities generating more spinoffs than others: differences in university policies, differences in university licensing offices and differences in other characteristics of universities. Each of these factors is discussed in turn.

University Policies

Universities adopt very different policies toward technology transfer. Some universities are more likely than others to adopt policies designed to support creation of spinoffs, perhaps because they have a goal of supporting economic development (Tornatzky *et al.*, 1997). Researchers have identified several policies that enhance the amount of spinoff activity, including offering exclusive licenses, taking equity in spinoffs, allowing faculty inventors leave of absence to found companies to exploit their inventions, permitting the use of university resources to develop the technology, permitting inventors to keep a lower share of royalties from the licensing of technology, and providing access to pre-seed stage capital.

Exclusive licenses

One policy that influences the rate of spinoff activity out of universities is exclusive licensing. Permitting exclusive licenses encourages spinoff activity for several reasons. As described in the previous chapter, entrepreneurs are unwilling to found companies and bear the risks of developing new technology, and investors are unwilling to finance them, unless they have some assurance that they will have exclusive right to that technology once it has been developed, because the first application that they select for the technology may prove to be less valuable than subsequent applications. Moreover, non-exclusive licensing allows potential competitors to gain access to the technology, making it harder for the spinoff to appropriate the returns to technology development.

My investigations of the MIT spinoffs provide qualitative evidence in support of the proposition that the founders of university spinoffs seek exclusive licenses and that the ability to offer exclusive licenses to university technology is an important characteristic in enhancing the rate of spinoff activity from a university. Take one MIT semiconductor spinoff as a case in point. In a letter to the MIT Technology Licensing Office dated 18 September 1980, the founder of that company wrote,

> I feel that the research on storage/logic arrays is now sufficiently mature for commercial utilization and I am formulating plans for the creation of a new company to commercially use this technology for the design of integrated circuits and to make this technology available to others. *In order to proceed further with my plans, I need a commitment from M.I.T. that I shall be granted an exclusive license* for the use and sublicensing of the patents on SLAs owned by M.I.T. for a suitable period of time and at mutually agreeable terms and conditions that could be negotiated as I proceed with my plans.

Non-exclusive licensing also hinders the ability to create university spin-offs because it reduces the amount of capital that investors will put behind the development of the companies. One of the venture capitalists that has invested in several MIT spinoffs explains that university laboratories that allow corporate sponsors a non-exclusive license to the intellectual property produced by the lab are a poor source of university spinoffs. Speaking about MIT's Media Lab in particular, he says, 'From a commercial point of view, intellectual property to which you cannot get an exclusive license is not the basis for an investment. So basically anything that comes out of the Media Lab is not useful for a venture capitalist.'

Several pieces of quantitative evidence also support the proposition that universities that are willing to provide exclusive licenses are more likely than other universities to generate spinoffs. First, Pressman (2002) reports that, in 2000, 90 percent of all licenses offered to spinoffs were exclusive licenses, as compared with only 37 percent of licenses offered to large, established companies, suggesting that offering exclusive licenses is more important to entrepreneurs than to large established firms. Second, Roberts and Malone (1996) compare several major research universities and report that Stanford University had fewer spinoffs than it otherwise would have had in the early 1990s because of the university's policy of not signing exclusive licenses. Third, Hsu and Bernstein (1997) interviewed founders of spinoffs from Harvard University and MIT. They reported that, in most cases, the founders of the spinoffs would not have established their firms in the absence of exclusive licenses.

Taking equity

A second important policy that leads some universities to produce more spinoffs than others is the willingness to take equity in lieu or partial lieu of royalties and fees for their intellectual property.[2] In many institutions, licensing offices capitalize royalties and fees and take equity in the spinoff company rather than demanding payment in cash. As explained in Chapter 3, new firms are cash constrained. A university's willingness to take equity in return for paying patent and other upfront costs facilitates spinoff formation by allowing the spinoff to conserve cash (DiGregorio and Shane, 2003; Hsu and Bernstein, 1997). Moreover, a university's equity position provides the spinoff with legitimacy. By demonstrating that a research institution supports the spinoff, a university's equity holding often facilitates the spinoff's ability to raise resources from external stakeholders (Feldman, 2001).[3]

Several pieces of evidence support the proposition that a willingness to hold equity in spinoffs enhances a university's rate of spinoff creation. DiGregorio and Shane (2003) examined the rate of spinoff formation from 101 American universities from 1993 to 1998. They found that universities permitted to take an equity stake in licensees have a spinoff rate 1.69 times the rate of those not permitted to take equity, and that universities that have taken equity in the past have a spinoff rate 1.89 times that of universities that have not taken equity in the past. Similarly, in a survey of universities engaged in technology transfer in the United Kingdom, Lockett *et al.* (2002) found that those universities that generated more spinoffs were more likely than other universities to have taken equity in their spinoffs, and were less likely than other universities to have created spinoff companies in which the university had no equity involvement.

More qualitative studies confirm these quantitative findings. Roberts (1991a) observed that, when MIT adopted its current policy of taking equity in spinoffs, its rate of spinoff activity accelerated dramatically. Hsu and Bernstein's (1997) interviews with licensees of MIT and Harvard University technology reveal that the spinoffs from these universities would not have been formed, particularly in the physical sciences, if the universities had been unwilling to capitalize the upfront royalty payments and patent costs in the form of equity. For example, Hsu and Bernstein (1997) explain that Jim Dwyer, a founder of MIT spinoff Lab Connections, considered licensing a Harvard University technology before starting a company based on MIT technology. However, he decided to license the MIT technology because Harvard University was unwilling to accept equity in his company in lieu of patent costs. Dwyer explained that licensing from Harvard University would have forced him to expend too much cash and so would have hindered his new venture.

Similarly, Mowery and Ziedonis (2001) interviewed the founders of spinoffs from Lawrence Livermore Laboratory and found that spinoff activity from that laboratory was very low because the government would not allow the laboratory to take equity in spinoffs and, instead, demanded large upfront payments for licenses, an arrangement that was not viable for cash-constrained start-ups.

Leaves of absence

A third university policy that leads some universities to have more spinoff activity than other universities is the institution's policy toward leaves of absence and outside work. Universities typically allow faculty to spend only one day a week consulting and many institutions do not permit them to serve as corporate officers. As a result, faculty must often take leaves of absence to start companies.

Permitting part-time employment and leaves of absence are important to encouraging spinoff company formation because many academics do not want to leave their positions permanently and give up tenure and secure salaries to spin off companies. Used to the common arrangement of having one day per week available for consulting, faculty at most US academic institutions think in terms of undertaking part-time entrepreneurial activity. Forcing academics to undertake their entrepreneurial activity on a full-time basis, without the security of their primary academic position, increases the risk of being an entrepreneur and so discourages spinoff activity.

Moreover, university policies that discourage university inventors from serving as principals in companies based on their inventions also discourage spinoff activity. For example, some universities bar faculty from serving in an operating position at a company while employed in a full-time capacity, limiting involvement to serving on the board of directors and consulting. In contrast, other universities do not impose such restrictions on their faculty, allowing them to serve in an operating capacity in spinoff companies.

By restricting the inventors' involvement to a consulting or contract research role, universities make it difficult for inventors to start companies based on their own research (Tornatzky *et al.*, 1999). Because most university technology is at a very early stage at the time that it is first licensed, university spinoffs must conduct a significant amount of additional development on that technology to commercialize it. If the knowledge of how that technology needs to be developed is tacit, inventor involvement is crucial to its further advancement (Jensen and Thursby, 2001). By limiting the way in which inventors can get involved in spinoff companies based on their early-stage inventions, universities greatly inhibit the transfer of knowledge from the inventor to the spinoff and hinder the development of the technology. However, it is more important to note that some universities with restrictive formal policies have informal arrangements that encourage spinoff activities. For example, the University of California schools often provide unofficial leaves of absence approved by department chairs for the purpose of creating spinoffs.

Several studies provide empirical evidence that those universities that allow faculty members to work as principals in spinoffs created to exploit their research, and that permit faculty to take temporary leaves of absences to found firms, have more spinoffs than other universities. For example, Tornatzky *et al.* (1995) report the results of a survey of southern universities which shows that those institutions which have more spinoffs also have more flexible personnel policies, particularly toward faculty consulting, part-time appointments and leaves of absence.

In addition, in a study of spinoff activity from federal laboratories, the founders of several spinoffs from Lawrence Livermore Laboratory told Mowery and Ziedonis (2001) that the laboratory's policies restricted them from doing part-time work, so that they had to resign if they wanted to pursue a spinoff. The respondents also suggested to the authors that a leave of absence policy would help to enhance spinoff activity from Lawrence Livermore Laboratory.

Furthermore, Kenney and Goe (forthcoming) compared the leave of absence policies at the University of California at Berkeley and Stanford University to explain why there are more computer science spinoffs out of Stanford than out of Berkeley. The authors found that, if a Berkeley professor wants to serve as an officer of a spinoff, he or she needs to take a leave of absence from the university, whereas a Stanford professor does not have to leave the university to be a corporate officer. Moreover, an untenured professor at Berkeley cannot take a leave of absence of more than one year, which effectively deters junior faculty from starting companies. Lastly, the Berkeley policy requires the department chair to decide whether to offer a faculty member a leave of absence, and thus leads many faculty members to conclude that it is not worthwhile to try to obtain a leave of absence to start a company (Kenney and Goe, forthcoming).

Use of university resources
A fourth policy difference that makes some universities more likely to generate spinoffs than others is that concerning the use of the university's resources for the development of companies. In general, universities that have more lenient rules about the use of university resources to enhance spinoff company development have more spinoff activity. Tornatzky *et al.* (1995) report that universities that offer flexible leasing arrangements for equipment and lab space or that allow their facilities to be used for free or at marginal cost tend to have more spinoffs than other universities.[4]

For instance, Carnegie Mellon may have a large number of spinoffs because of policies that it instituted to help develop the software spinoff, Lycos, and then were institutionalized for future spinoffs. In its early days, before it obtained venture capital financing, Lycos was incubated in the bowels of the university's computer science building. Moreover, it received a $100 000 investment of university operating funds, which was used to purchase servers and pay for the company's marketing expenditures.

In contrast to the liberal policies toward the use of institutional resources at

Carnegie Mellon University, many universities prohibit faculty entrepreneurs from using their facilities for the development of their companies, thereby inhibiting spinoff company formation. This prohibition is particularly true for state universities, which have conflict-of-interest policies that seek to limit access of outsiders to university resources as a way to limit the potential for corruption (Bagby *et al.*, 1995). For instance, UCLA precludes faculty from using university resources for their own companies, and even fired one professor, Isaac Kaplan, for using university labs and equipment for his start-up (Matkin, 1990).

Universities that have strict disclosure rules about the use of university resources also have less spinoff activity, perhaps because these disclosure rules reflect a general concern about conflict of interest rather than a concern about firm formation. Matkin (1990) observed that the University of California at Berkeley has much more restrictive requirements about the use of resources than Stanford or MIT, requiring disclosure of even the smallest amounts of financial support (less than $1000), and also has many fewer spinoffs than these other institutions. Similarly, spinoff activity is very low at schools in Louisiana, perhaps because faculty at institutions in that state are required to get a university-level exemption to be involved in consulting activity with any type of company, including spinoffs (Tornatzky *et al.*, 1995).

Some research has demonstrated that spinoff activity at universities increases when those institutions remove restrictive policies towards the use of institutional resources. For instance, New York University increased its spinoff activities after it eliminated a policy of requiring licensees to enter into sponsored research agreements as a condition of licensing because sponsored research agreements at New York University cannot have a pre-defined product, cannot assign property rights of inventions to the sponsor and cannot involve faculty consulting at university labs (Golub, 2003).

Division of royalties

A fifth policy that influences a university's spinoff rate is the division of royalties between the inventor, his or her department and the overall university. In general, universities earn licensing income in the form of royalties on the gross sales of products or services that use licensed technologies, and split those revenues with inventors and their departments. The division of royalties between the three parties has a counter-intuitive relationship with the rate of spinoff activity. The greater is the inventor's share of the licensing royalties, the lower is the rate of spinoff activity. The logic of this relationship is as follows. When an inventor founds a firm to exploit his or her invention, he or she must pay royalties on the technology back to the university. Because the royalties are shared between the inventor, his or her department and the university, the inventor–founder always pays more royalties to the university than he or she receives back from his or her share of the royalties from licensing. At the same time, the inventor's earnings from licensing to a third party increase with his or her share of the royalties from licensing. As a result, the greater is the inventor's share of royalties from licensing a technology, the more incentive the inventor has to license his or her technology to a third party because the opportunity cost of starting a firm to exploit the invention goes up with the inventor's share of licensing income (DiGregorio and Shane, 2003).[5]

One piece of empirical evidence supports this argument. DiGregorio and Shane (2003) examined the spinoff rate out of 101 universities from 1993 to 1998 and found evidence of this inverse relationship between the inventor's share of royalties and the spinoff rate. The authors observed that increasing the inventor's share of royalties by 10 percent reduces the spinoff rate by 0.40 spinoffs, or 20 percent.

Pre-seed stage capital

A final policy on which universities vary and that influences spinoff rates is provision of pre-seed stage capital to spinoff companies. Pre-seed stage capital is money that is used for further technological development to bring the technology to a stage where it can be financed in the private sector. As Chapter 11 will describe in greater detail, access to pre-seed stage capital is important because entrepreneurs seeking to found companies to exploit university technologies must often develop their technologies further, identify market needs that can be filled by these technologies and establish intellectual property protection, all before they can approach venture capitalists and business angels to fund their new ventures (Wright *et al.*, 2002).

Several studies provide evidence for the positive effect of the provision of pre-seed stage capital on the rate of spinoff formation across universities. For example, Wright *et al.* (2002) found that those universities in the United Kingdom that generated a large number of spinoffs tended to provide their spinoffs with better access to sources of pre-seed stage capital than universities that did not generate a large number of spinoffs.

Similarly, Tornatzky *et al.* (1995) report that universities with more spinoffs have more university-specific programs to fund pre-seed stage proof of concept and prototype development. For instance, Georgia Institute of Technology, and the University of Virginia have a larger number of spinoffs than many other institutions, at least in part because they offer research commercialization awards that allow inventors to further develop the technologies for their new companies and achieve proof of concept (Tornatsky *et al.*, 1995). Carnegie Mellon and Case Western Reserve University have disproportionately large numbers of spinoff companies relative to their level of technology creation because they have developed pre-seed stage funds that make investments of $100 000 to $250 000 in their spinoff companies to help them to develop to a stage that makes them attractive to venture capitalists and business angels.

Moreover, the impact of these pre-seed stage funds may be best measured, not by the number of spinoff companies created, but by the impact of the investment on the creation of valuable companies. For instance, Carnegie Mellon invested $100 000 in pre-seed stage capital to help Lycos develop to the point that professional venture capitalists would invest in the company. That investment was instrumental in the creation of an Internet company that reached a market valuation of over $500 million.

University Licensing Office Characteristics

The nature of the university's technology licensing office also influences the institution's rate of spinoff formation. In particular, three characteristics of licensing offices are important. The first is the level of investment that the university makes in its licensing office. The second is in the expertise of licensing officers. The third is the licensing officers' network of stakeholders. In the subsections below, each of these factors is discussed.

Licensing office resources

Some universities generate more spinoffs than others because they devote more resources to licensing activity in general. Firm formation is more expensive and time-consuming than licensing to established firms. Individual entrepreneurs do not have the corporate staffs of large companies, and so rely more heavily on licensing officers when they work with patent attorneys, negotiate with suppliers or investigate market needs. Moreover, spinoff companies often negotiate exclusive license agreements, which are more difficult and time-consuming to implement than are non-exclusive licenses (DiGregorio and Shane, 2003). Given budget constraints, many universities lack sufficient staff to undertake these extra activities adequately and so have lower rates of spinoff company formation than other universities (Wright *et al.*, 2002).

Company formation expertise

Some universities generate more spinoffs than others because their licensing officers have greater expertise in the process of technology company formation (Wright *et al.*, 2002). Starting high technology companies requires a different set of skills from those needed to license to established companies. For instance, to generate spinoffs, licensing offices need to employ people with expertise in evaluating markets, writing business plans, raising venture capital, assembling venture teams, obtaining space and equipment, and beta testing products (Golub, 2003). Some universities have more licensing officers familiar with these things than other universities.

For instance, a large sample survey of university technology licensing offices in the United Kingdom by Lockett *et al.* (2002) showed that those universities that were most successful in spinning off companies had licensing officers with more experience in spinoff activity than other universities. Moreover, Lockett *et al.*'s (2002) survey showed that UK institutions that were effective at generating spinoffs tended to have specific licensing officers specialize in spinoff creation as a way to create necessary expertise among licensing office personnel.

Some researchers have even documented an upward shift in the rate of spinoff activity at universities as a result of an increase in licensing office expertise working with start-ups. For example, Golub (2003) reports that New York University increased its rate of spinoff formation after its technology licensing office began to offer start-up assistance, such as help with business plan development, to its licensees.

The data on the MIT spinoffs that I collected also point to the effect of licensing office expertise on the level of spinoff activity across universities. Several respondents identified the expertise that MIT's licensing officers had in identifying investors in spinoff companies as important to facilitating that university's high rate of spinoff activity. For instance, a venture capitalist that has invested in spinoffs at several universities explains,

> Spinoffs from MIT are helped by the professionalism of the TLO. I'm dealing with [two institutions] right now and they make it really hard to work with them as a venture capitalist or entrepreneur. They raise the level of difficulty. Lita [Nelsen, the Technology Licensing Office director] and her crew absolutely know the drill. They'll help find people. They'll help find investors. They're there to make you a success.

Other respondents saw the licensing office understanding of how to structure licensing deals that are appropriate to spinoff companies as being something that facilitated the rate of spinoff company formation out of MIT. For instance, one of the founders of an MIT biotechnology spinoff, explains,

> The MIT TLO fostered the entrepreneurial efforts of people to set up their own companies. They served a great role as facilitator. They did not hang the company's head in a noose in order to license this technology. In fact, the initial royalty payments were extremely favorable to the point of a declining revenue scale based upon increasing future sales.

Similarly, an executive at one MIT spinoff, who later advised other spinoffs in their negotiations with universities on technology transfer, explains the benefits of MIT's approach to structuring licensing deals in comparison to the approach employed by other institutions. She states,

When we acquired [one spinoff], we had to go back to [the institution that licensed the technology] and renegotiate the royalty agreement. That little company had been saddled the whole time with a ten percent royalty. You know it's one thing if you've got some up front payment that gets amortized or if the royalty kicks in after a certain volume. But it's another to saddle the company with high royalties. I've dealt with the same thing with [another institution]. If you're an entrepreneur and you're thinking of licensing, then the royalties have to be absolutely minimal. Otherwise, the start-up won't get its feet on the ground.

Licensing office expertise in spinoff company formation also draws external entrepreneurs to the university. For example, Lockett *et al*. (2002) explain that UK institutions that generate more spinoffs tend to involve more professional managers and entrepreneurs in the spinoffs than UK universities that generate fewer spinoffs. Similarly, Wright *et al*. (2002) found that those institutions that provide an incentive for experienced entrepreneurs to become involved with spinoff companies are more likely than other institutions to generate spinoff companies.

Linkage to start-up networks
Another characteristic of university licensing offices that allows some universities to generate more spinoffs than others is the linkage of the technology licensing officers to a network of investors, managers and advisors that provide the human and financial resources that are necessary to start new companies (Dueker, 1997). Better licensing office access to this network makes potential founders more confident in starting companies and makes them better able to execute the spinoff process.

My interviews with the founders of MIT spinoffs revealed the importance of licensing officer networks to the formation of many of the spinoff companies. For example, MIT's technology licensing office facilitated the development of one scientific instruments company by allowing the company's founders to use the university's patent attorneys for legal questions and to gain access to venture capitalists. Similarly, MIT's technology licensing office facilitated the formation of a materials spinoff by introducing the inventor of the technology to a venture capitalist who became the company's CEO.

At MIT, the importance of the licensing officer's network is so important to the spinoff creation process that technology licensing officers consider developing and exploiting a social network to help spinoffs to be part of the office's mission. For example, Lita Nelsen, director of MIT's Technology Licensing Office, explains, 'I sit on the Mass Technology Development Corporation and the board of directors of the Mass Biotech Council. I know people. I do things for people if they're connected to MIT. If they're a professor or whatever, that's my job.'

To embed the licensing officers in networks of investors, MIT maintains an open door relationship with venture capitalists. Venture capitalists often visit the MIT licensing officers to exchange information and search for deals. As one licensing officer explained, 'During a typical week, three or four venture capitalists would walk in our office to chat with us and express what their interests are, what they're looking for, what their recent deal flow has been, where their network of contacts is strong.'

My interviews with the founders of MIT spinoffs indicated that the key role that licensing officers play in facilitating the formation of spinoffs lies in their efforts to link inventors, investors, entrepreneurs and senior management talent. For example, one MIT inventor whose technology led to the founding of a software spinoff explains, 'The TLO played a big role, an essential role, in finding an investor and a CEO for the company.' One of the founders of that spinoff elaborates,

> [The inventor], being a professor at MIT, didn't have time to run a business. I was in engineering and didn't really want to run a business either. So we decided the only way this was going to happen was if we got a business manager involved. Through the Technology Licensing Office, we got both a CEO and a venture capital group to give us $1 million. The licensing officer knew the venture capitalist and he also knew the CEO.

The use of direct ties between licensing officers and investors was one important mechanism through which MIT's technology licensing exploited their networks to facilitate spinoff company formation. For example, MIT's technology licensing officers used a direct tie to convince several Boston area entrepreneurs to come to MIT to license technology and found spinoffs. One of these external entrepreneurs describes that process:

> I know [the licensing officer] very well. [He] and I have done things together for the better part of ten years. He was processing this patent application that had to do with the use of virtual environments to enhance motor skills and he said, 'I want you to take a look at this and tell me what you think.'

A second mechanism that the MIT licensing officers used to facilitate spinoff activity was to refer the founders of promising spinoffs to investors in their networks. The inventors of several MIT spinoffs explained that the Institute's technology licensing officers referred them to several venture capitalists. For example, the inventor–founder of one medical device spinoff, explains,

> The TLO identified potential money sources and set us up together to talk. Basically, [the licensing officer] went through her Rolodex and identified sources. Then she called them and said, 'you ought to talk to this guy.' The next time [he] came down to Boston, he gave me a call and said, 'let's get together.'

Moreover, Shane and Cable's (2002:370) study of seed stage venture capitalists decisions to invest in new technology companies shows the importance of referrals from the technology-licensing officers in facilitating spinoff activity out of MIT. They quoted one venture capitalist that invested in an MIT spinoff as saying,

> We were heavily influenced by [TLO Director Lita Nelsen's] high opinion of [the entrepreneur] because we have a lot of confidence in her judgment based on our prior relationship with the licensing office and with her in particular. We had done several deals with her before. She is an extremely well known person and her competency in these matters is widely recognized.

A third mechanism by which MIT facilitated the formation of spinoffs was by associating the spinoff with the reputation of MIT. Because MIT's reputation as a source of technology creation was powerful, association with MIT could be used to attract investors and management talent. The founder of one medical device spinoff explains,

> My association with MIT and the TLO made starting a company considerably easier. One of my main reasons for coming back and reactivating the case here and working with the TLO was precisely that you need support if you're not a well known faculty member or if you're a post doc or a staff member or a student. You need to have the full force and reputation of MIT behind you to make this work well.

Several other studies also support the proposition that universities whose technology-licensing officers are more deeply embedded in the social networks of stakeholders in new technology ventures generate more spinoffs than others.[6] For instance, a large sample survey of technology licensing offices at UK universities by Lockett *et al.* (2002) found that the universities in the United Kingdom that were most successful in spinning off companies had greater social networks with potential investors and other key stakeholders in new technology ventures than other universities.

Moreover, Hsu and Bernstein's (1997) case studies of spinoffs from MIT and Harvard University demonstrated that the technology licensing officers' contacts in the seed stage investment community made MIT better than Harvard at generating spinoffs. Hsu and Bernstein (1997) explain that Jim Dwyer, a founder of MIT spinoff Lab Connections, first considered licensing a Harvard University technology before starting a company based on MIT technology. Dwyer decided not to proceed with the Harvard technology and start a company based on an MIT technology instead because the MIT Technology Licensing Office had better ties to the venture capital community and so could offer better support than Harvard University in obtaining capital.

Some research even suggests that universities that increase the marketing and networking activity of their technology-licensing officers in the investor community can increase the universities' rate of spinoff activity. For example, Golub (2003) found that New York University increased its rate of spinoff formation after its technology licensing officers began to network with and market to venture capitalists.

Other University Characteristics

Researchers have also identified several other characteristics of universities that influence the rate of spinoffs formation across universities. These characteristics include the university culture, the presence of entrepreneurial role models, the intellectual eminence of the institution, and the source and nature of research funding. In the subsections below, the effect that these characteristics have on the rate of spinoff formation out of universities is discussed.

University culture

University culture influences spinoff activity in several ways. First, as Bauer (2001) explains, some university cultures reinforce entrepreneurial activity, which encourages spinoff formation. In contrast, other universities provide subtle cultural signals that discourage spinoff activity. For instance, interviewing people involved with technology transfer at UK universities, Blair and Hitchens (1998) found that one university had trouble establishing spinoffs because the central administration was uncomfortable entering into relationships in which it would have a minority ownership stake, a common arrangement with spinoffs. Similar cultural obstacles were seen at another university where spinoff companies were seen as diluting academic work and potentially risking the university's reputation (Blair and Hitchens, 1998).

Second, university culture influences the way university inventors and other important stakeholders in the spinoff process perceive technology-licensing offices. At some institutions, technology-licensing officers are viewed as regulators. At these institutions, inventors are wary of licensing offices, which they believe exist to enforce disclosure rules, but do little to help to license technology or create spinoffs. In contrast, at other institutions, the technology licensing office is viewed as a consulting office. At these institutions, inventors are very supportive of technology licensing offices, which they believe provide them with useful services.

Many observers have pointed to MIT as having a culture supportive of spinoffs, which encourages the formation of spinoffs at that institution (Matkin, 1990). My interviews with the founders of MIT spinoffs provide evidence of the effect of a supportive culture that exerts subtle signals in favor of creating spinoffs. For example, one of the MIT inventors whose technology led to a software spinoff explains, 'There was an entrepreneurial attitude among my graduate students and they were all trying to figure out how to start companies.' Similarly, the inventor–founder of another software spinoff explains,

> Ever since I first came to MIT, I was interest in entrepreneurship and the fact that there were a lot of companies that were started at MIT. It's just a great environment. We had lots of seminars on starting new companies and there was the Enterprise Forum and various activities like that which piqued my interest.

Other founders of MIT spinoffs pointed to the consultant culture of the technology licensing office as something that accounted for the high level of spinoff activity at MIT. For example, the inventor–founder of one robotics spinoff says,

> The basic message from the MIT TLO was that we're not the enemy. This was important to a guy who spent his life in the lab who saw these licensing guys as people who wanted to rip stuff out of our lab and give it to other people, people who would make it hard if we wanted to get our hands on it. The licensing office folks said, 'We want this to be successful. If you want to take this and do something with it, we'll make it easy.' I think the key thing is that they meant it. People at MIT and Stanford have this attitude that this is the way to get value out of the technology, rather than put it in a safety deposit box and protect it, which is what I think most universities do.

Several of the investors in MIT spinoffs also point to the technology licensing office's consulting culture as a factor that encouraged spinoff formation from the Institute and makes MIT different from many other academic institutions in this regard. For example, one venture capitalist that invested in spinoffs from several universities describes his experience working with MIT and Penn State on a spinoff. He recounts,

> The venture didn't work out. While MIT was supportive of the process both from an institutional as well as administrative and faculty standpoint, at Penn State this was viewed as in conflict with the objectives and interests of both the institution and the faculty. They didn't understand the importance of starting companies to commercialize technology and how that would be beneficial from the point of view of the government's perception of what the university was doing, and how the alumni perceived what the university was doing, as well as from the standpoint of retaining key faculty who are interested in making a dollar.

Similarly, a Boston area business angel that invested in an MIT mechanical device spinoff explained how the culture of MIT encouraged the support of external stakeholders, particularly investors like him, in the formation of spinoffs. He explains,

We only participate in one organization that allows us to see business plans – the MIT 50K competition [a student business plan competition]. We do that one in part because it's local and in part because I've seen a lot of deal flow from MIT. The 50K is well recognized as something that the MIT community tries to support. Also, they have some pretty good quality coming out of there. I think part of it is because it has been built up over the years and part of it is just the environment of so many companies having been founded at MIT.

Studies of spinoff activity from other universities also support the proposition that certain universities have cultures that encourage more spinoff activity than others. In a comparison of the electrical engineering and computer science departments at the University of California at Berkeley and Stanford University, Kenney and Goe (forthcoming) found that fewer spinoffs emerged from the Berkeley departments than from the Stanford departments because Berkeley had a much less supportive culture for spin-offs. Similarly, Louis *et al.* (1989) surveyed life science faculty at American universities and found that differences in organizational attitudes and culture predicted whether faculty held equity in new companies based on their own research, as well as whether they engaged in other entrepreneurial activities.

Entrepreneurial role models

Another difference across universities that influences the level of spinoff activity is the presence of entrepreneurial role models. The presence of entrepreneurs either among faculty or in the surrounding business community is crucial to the formation of spinoff companies (Hsu and Bernstein, 1997). Bauer (2001) explains that faculty entrepreneurs provide other faculty and graduate students with an 'informal curriculum' in such things as how to find venture capital and how to start firms. This informal curriculum helps to facilitate the formation of spinoff companies at the margin.

Moreover, Kenney and Goe (forthcoming) argue that the existence of role models motivates people to try entrepreneurial activity by providing them with successful examples to emulate. Because many people learn to do new things by observation of successful others, this argument suggests that the presence of role models is important to facilitating the creation of university spinoffs.

Some empirical evidence supports this proposition. For example, Golub (2003) attributes the growth in spinoff activity at Columbia University, at least in part, to the example provided by pioneers in health sciences who had established companies in the early 1990s. She quotes Paul Maddon, the founder of Progenics Pharmaceuticals, the first spinoff from Columbia University, to explain how growth in the number of role models increased spinoff activity at that institution. He says,

> I was interested in business and becoming an entrepreneur. The mid-1980s were the heyday of biotech and many companies were starting. . . . Prior to this time, scientists who had dealings with companies were labeled as greedy or not good scientists. The best researchers did not go into industry – it was a default job for those who couldn't get an academic position. Then things began to change and it became widely accepted that great scientists could be found in companies. (Golub, 2003: 91)

My interviews with founders of MIT spinoffs provide similar evidence of the role model effect on the rate of spinoff activity. For example, the founder of one MIT software spinoff established in 1982 points to the long tradition of role models at MIT as something that motivated him to create a spinoff company. Describing companies that had been formed out of his department in the 1950s and 1960s, he explains,

> I was in the chemical engineering department. There had been companies formed. Ionics was one of the early companies that had been formed. Ed Gill was the department head at the time and was actually working with American Research and Development and was a consultant until now. It was just a good climate for entrepreneurship and for the idea of starting a company.

One large sample scholarly study also supports the proposition that universities with more entrepreneurial role models have more spinoff companies. Kenney and Goe's (forthcoming) comparison of the spinoff activity out of Stanford University and University of California at Berkeley electrical engineering and computer science departments showed that the Stanford University faculty were more motivated than the Berkeley faculty to become entrepreneurs because of the inspiration they took from the observation of prior faculty spinoffs.

University quality

Another factor that influences the rate of spinoffs out of universities is academic quality. Researchers have shown that spinoffs are more likely to be founded to exploit the technology of more prestigious universities than to exploit the technology of less prestigious ones. Zucker *et al.* (1998b) provide one explanation. They argue that faculty members found spinoff firms to capture the rents generated by their intellectual capital, which is tacit and cannot be easily transferred to others. Because the researchers at higher quality schools have better intellectual capital, on average, than the researchers at lower quality schools, higher quality schools generate more spinoffs than lower quality schools.

A second explanation for the higher spinoff rate out of more prestigious academic institutions is that university prestige makes it easier for entrepreneurs to persuade investors to provide the resources needed to found new ventures. Because information asymmetry and uncertainty make it impossible for investors to evaluate the quality of new technology completely, financiers often make decisions about which university spinoffs to fund on the basis of their perceptions of the quality of the inventors whose technology is being exploited by the new company (Podolny and Stuart, 1995). Investors often believe that the inventions coming from higher quality universities are better than inventions coming from lower quality institutions. Therefore they are more likely to finance those inventions coming from higher quality institutions, enhancing the rate of spinoff formation from prestigious institutions (DiGregorio and Shane, 2003).

Several large sample statistical studies provide empirical support for the proposition that higher quality academic institutions produce more spinoffs than lower quality academic institutions. For instance, Louis *et al.* (1989) surveyed life science faculty members about their entrepreneurial activities and found that equity holding in a company based on the faculty member's research was concentrated at the top universities. Moreover, DiGregorio and Shane (2003) examined the spinoff rate out of 101 universities from 1993 to 1998 and found that a one-point increase in the Gourman Report ranking of a university led to a 68 percent increase in its spinoff rate.

My interviews with people involved in the formation of MIT spinoffs also provide support for the proposition that institutional quality enhances the rate of spinoff activity out of universities. Several interviewees pointed out that MIT's prestige facilitated the acquisition of financial resources from investors, enhancing the spinoff rate from that institution. For example, a venture capitalist that backed one of the MIT software spinoffs explained the value of MIT's prestige in the venture financing process. He says, 'Having come from MIT was a significant factor in our decision to accept the referral. If it comes from MIT, the technology is apt to be significant. It's as simple as that.'

Similarly, one of the founders of an MIT biotechnology spinoff explains how MIT's reputation helped the founders of that company to obtain resources when they were starting their company. He says, 'I think MIT is probably the premier institution for licensing its technology. If this technology were based at a much less prominent university, it never would have gotten out the door.' The founder of another MIT biotechnology spinoff explains, 'Having a technology from MIT helps to raise money', while the founder of an MIT semiconductor spinoff says, 'The venture capitalists are really starved of good ideas. They jump at the opportunity to work with good people, especially from a place like MIT.'

Other interviewees pointed out that MIT's prestige enhanced the spinoff rate by facilitating access to customers. For example, a founder of an MIT optics spinoff explains, 'We had wonderful credentials. Because we were MIT people, we could go in and talk to the highest engineers in the companies that were developing things, and that was really our market. So we had access to market information to a large extent because we came from MIT.' Similarly, the founder of an MIT mechanical device spinoff states, 'The MIT name opens doors to conferences. I was able to present and talk to customers and they gave me feedback.'

Industry-funded research

A final characteristic that makes some universities more likely to generate spinoffs than other universities is the tendency of the university to conduct research funded by industry rather than by government agencies or foundations. Industry funding enhances spinoff activity for at least three reasons. First, private firms are more likely than government agencies to fund research that has commercial applications, and this commercial bias increases the likelihood that the technological inventions resulting from the research effort can be transformed into products or services that satisfy market needs. Second, government-funded research tends to be more basic than industry-funded research (Arrow, 1962), leading to information asymmetry problems that make it more difficult for entrepreneurs to finance new companies based on government-funded research than to finance companies based on industry-funded research (DiGregorio and Shane, 2003). Third, industry funding provides inventors with skills that help them to work with the private sector effectively. For example, one of the MIT technology-licensing officers explained, 'Consulting agreements probably were the number one indicator of whether the inventors knew what industry wanted and could start companies. The ones who consult a lot were good. The ones who didn't consult a lot were naïve.' The founders of one of the MIT biotechnology spinoffs concurs, stating, 'Not being a naïve academic is important to starting a company based on university technology' and the ties to industry that come from industry funding reduce academic naïveté.

Several researchers have documented the relationship between the level of industry funding and spinoff activity. At a micro level, Blumenthal *et al.* (1996) surveyed university faculty in the life sciences and found that those faculty members who received industrial support were more than twice as likely to found a company as a way to commercialize their research than those who did not receive industrial support (14.3 percent to 6 percent). Similarly, Campbell *et al.* (1998) surveyed 2167 life sciences researchers at 50 universities and found that the probability that the researchers would start a company to exploit their research was more than twice as high if they received a corporate gift than if they did not (13 percent to 6 percent).[7] Furthermore, Allen and Norling (1991) surveyed 912 faculty members in science, engineering, business and medicine at 40 educational institutions and found that faculty members were more likely to engage in start-up activity if they had been asked by private sector firms to cooperate on commercial projects.

Research at a more macro level of analysis also shows that universities that receive more industry funding generate more spinoff activity than other universities. Both quantitative and qualitative research results support this proposition. On the quantitative side, DiGregorio and Shane (2003) examined the spinoff rate out of 101 universities from 1993 to 1998 and found that a $10 million increase in industry funding increased spinoff activity at the average university by 0.13 firms, or 6.7 percent.

On the qualitative side, Feldman (1994) explains that the heavy reliance of Johns Hopkins University on the Department of Defense for research funding inhibits spinoff activity from that institution. In particular, she explains that the conditions attached to Department of Defense funding for the Applied Physics Laboratory, Johns Hopkins' biggest research unit, preclude it from making technology available for commercialization by private companies, which, in turn, inhibits spinoff activity.

My interviews with the founders and investors in MIT spinoffs also provide qualitative evidence of the importance of industry funding to generating spinoff companies. The interviews showed that industry funding enhanced the credibility of inventors' claims with investors who were being asked to finance the spinoffs. For example, one venture capitalist that invested in a semiconductor spinoff explains his willingness to investigate that spinoff. He says,

> [The founder] described something that quite frankly I didn't understand. You know there were two lasers. You bounce them off a point on the wafer. You measure the acoustical wave disturbance. You run it through some device, and presto you have a measurement. So being polite, I said something along the lines of, 'Well that's really great but does it have any commercial significance?' And this is one of the key parts about MIT being different than other places. He said, 'Well the work is funded by Intel and IBM.'

Industry funding also increased the likelihood that there was a market for the spinoff's technology. The founder of another MIT semiconductor spinoff explains that industry funding provided evidence of demonstrated market interest. He says, 'We knew that the semiconductor industry was interested. Almost all of [our] funding was from industry.' Similarly, Davies (1981:2) explains that, because MIT spinoff Aspen Technologies' software was based on work with 50 major petroleum and chemicals companies, there were 50 companies that were ready buyers of a maintenance service, facilitating company formation as a way to exploit the technology.

Industry funding of research also increases the knowledge that spinoff founders have of the needs and interests of specific companies. This knowledge is valuable in motivating the founders of spinoff companies to believe that they have a technology that is appropriate for the commercial market. For example, the founder of one MIT semiconductor spinoff explains that he was able to convince a major firm to sign a two-year contract from them to develop a product when he first started his company because they had funded his research. He explains, 'I was engaged with [the company]. I had been interacting with their staff, their VPs, their divisions. So I had some visibility of what difficulties they face and I had some idea of the business even though this was more by observation as opposed to doing business.'

SUMMARY

This chapter has examined the variation in spinoff activity across academic institutions. Research has shown that the rate of spinoff company formation varies significantly across universities and is not explained simply by the level of technology production. Rather, differences in university policies, licensing office strategies and other university characteristics account for this variation.

Among the university policies that enhance the rate of spinoff formation from universities are the following: allowing exclusive licensing; permitting equity investments in spinoffs, offering leaves of absence for inventors who wish to found companies, permitting spinoffs to use university resources to develop technology, allocating a lower share of royalties to inventors, and providing spinoffs with access to pre-seed stage capital. Allowing exclusive licensing enhances spinoff activity by encouraging entrepreneurs to bear the risks of developing new technology and facilitating the financing of new ventures. Permitting equity investments enhances spinoff activity because these investments minimize founders' cash outlays and provide spinoffs with institutional legitimacy. Allowing leave of absence for inventor–entrepreneurs enhances spinoff activity because many academics do not want to leave university positions to found companies. Permitting spinoffs to use university resources for technical development enhances spinoff activity because this arrangement allows the new companies to use expensive equipment at a lower cost. Giving inventors a larger share of royalties hinders spinoff activity because the inventor's royalty share increases the opportunity cost of firm formation. Finally, providing spinoffs with access to pre-seed stage capital increases spinoff activity because these resources allow founders to prove concepts and develop prototypes, both of which are necessary activities to interest private sector investors in financing spinoffs.

The characteristics of the university's technology licensing office also influence its rate of spinoff company creation. Universities that provide their licensing offices with more resources generate more spinoffs than other institutions because firm formation is more expensive and time-consuming than licensing to established companies. Universities whose licensing officers have more expertise in firm formation generate more spinoffs because creating companies requires a set of skills that are different from licensing to established firms. Universities that embed their licensing officers in a network of start-up company stakeholders generate more spinoffs because the linkage to a network of investors, managers and advisors provides these companies with access to the resources and information needed for firm formation.

Several other university characteristics also influence the rate of spinoff activity. Spinoffs are more common in universities with cultures that reinforce entrepreneurial activities rather than in universities with cultures that discourage entrepreneurial behavior. Spinoffs are more common in universities with more entrepreneurial role models than in universities with fewer entrepreneurial role models because existing entrepreneurs educate potential entrepreneurs about the firm formation process and serve as examples that motivate others to start new firms. Spinoffs are more common in more prestigious universities than in less prestigious institutions because faculty members found firms to capture the rents generated by their intellectual capital and because university prestige facilitates resource acquisition under uncertainty and information asymmetry. Finally, universities with more industry funding generate more spinoffs than other institutions because private firms are more likely than government agencies to fund research that has commercial applications, because government-funded research tends to be more basic than industry-funded research and because industry funding provides inventors with skills that help them to work with the private sector effectively.

Having described the variation in spinoff activity across universities, I now turn to environmental influences on spinoff activity, the subject of Chapter 5.

NOTES

1. Measures of entrepreneurial activity related to university spinoff activity show similar patterns. For example, Louis *et al.* (1989) reported that faculty equity holding in start-up companies is found in only a few universities. Similarly, Cohen *et al.* (1994) observed that only 22.5 percent of university–industry research centers reported the formation of new companies, with a mean of 2.38 new companies per center, but three centers reported 10 to 20 new companies.
2. Many more universities take equity in lieu of royalties and fees for their intellectual property than make equity investments in those companies. Therefore this section discusses equity holdings rather than equity investments. However, some universities, like Carnegie Mellon University, Boston University and Case Western Reserve University make equity investments in their spinoff companies. Some of these equity investments can generate very large returns. For example, Carnegie Mellon invested $100 000 of its operating funds in its spinoff, Lycos. That investment resulted in the university receiving divested equity of $20 million.
3. Many universities are reluctant to take equity in spinoffs because their risk aversion leads them to focus on royalties (Siegel *et al.*, 2002).
4. These policies may be particularly important in the early days of spinoff company creation at a university. Several of the founders of MIT spinoff companies that were established before the mid-1980s attributed significant importance to MIT's willingness to allow them to make use of the Institute's resources in the formation of their spinoffs. For example, the founder of

one MIT software spinoff that was established in 1982 explains, 'We got a lot of help from MIT. We bought the furniture from MIT, which MIT didn't need once our project wound down. We leased computer time from MIT. We leased space from MIT.' However, MIT no longer allows licensees to use its facilities for the development of new companies or technologies. None of the founders of the MIT spinoffs established after the mid-1980s considered the use of Institute facilities to be an important factor in enhancing the rate of spinoff companies from MIT.

5. At the time that this book was being written, Cambridge University in the United Kingdom was proposing a policy in which the share of income from university licenses would be allocated 90 percent to the inventor for the first £20 000 and then be reduced to 70 percent for the next £40 000, to 50 percent for the next £40 000 and to 33.3 percent for all net income above £100 000. Given the findings of DiGregorio and Shane (2003), if Cambridge University adopts this policy, it should see an increasing interest in spinoff activity among its faculty as the expected value of their inventions increases.

6. In a series of four in-depth case studies of university spinoffs in the United Kingdom, Vohora *et al*. (2002b) found that, in two of the cases (3G Wireless and Optical Company), the social networks of technology licensing officers actually filled a gap in the linkage of entrepreneurs to investors, enabling them to obtain needed capital.

7. In addition, faculty members who received discretionary funds were twice as likely to start a company to exploit their research than those who did not (18 percent to 9 percent).

5. Environmental influences on spinoff activity

Does the geographic location of a university influence its tendency to found spinoffs? Some researchers suggest that the answer to this question is 'yes'. For example, DiGregorio and Shane (2003) argue that the geographic location of academic institutions influences spinoff activity because some economic, legal and cultural environments are more supportive of spinoffs than others.

This chapter explores the theoretical arguments for, and empirical evidence of, the effects of environmental influences on spinoff activity. The chapter is divided into two sections. The first section provides evidence that spinoff activity does, indeed, vary significantly across geographic locations. The second section discusses the possible explanations for this variation, focusing on access to capital, locus of property rights, rigidity of the academic labor market and the industrial composition of the area.

VARIATION IN SPINOFF ACTIVITY ACROSS GEOGRAPHIC LOCATIONS

University spinoff activity varies significantly across countries. Although a variety of anecdotal evidence supports this proposition, the best evidence for it lies in comparisons of the results of surveys of university technology transfer operations in the United States, Canada and the United Kingdom. Using data from the Association of University Technology Managers, Pressman (2002) found that Canadian educational institutions were much more likely than US educational institutions to generate spinoff companies; in 2000, 15.2 percent of licenses from US institutions were executed with spinoffs, while 22 percent of licenses from Canadian institutions were executed with spinoffs.

Other researchers have compared the rate of spinoff activity, not per license, but per dollar of research and development expenditure, and also have found significant national differences in university spinoff activity. Comparing the results of a survey of UK licensing offices with the data published by the Association of University Technology Managers, Wright et al. (2002) found that the United Kingdom was significantly more productive than the United States and Canada at spinoff company creation. Their results showed that more university spinoffs were created per dollar of research funding in the United Kingdom than in Canada or the United States. Similarly, Charles and Conway (2001) report that, in 2000, each spinoff in the United Kingdom cost $13.67 million in research and development expenditure to create while, in Canada, the cost was $22.1 million and, in the United States, the cost was $84.43 million. For 2001, the data are even more skewed. In that year, spinoffs are almost ten times as costly to create, in terms of R&D dollars, in the United States as in the United Kingdom (Wright *et al.*, 2002).

In contrast to the data on spinoffs, the data on licensing to non-spinoff companies show that the United Kingdom is clearly less productive than the United States or Canada. As Table 5.1 shows, in the United Kingdom, universities earn significantly less in royalties from licensing their inventions than do universities in Canada and the United States. Moreover, they spend more in research and development expenditure to create each dollar of royalty income (Wright *et al.*, 2002). As a result, the return on each research and development dollar devoted to licensing in the United Kingdom is significantly lower than the return on research and development in the United States and Canada. Given that the cost of each spinoff is lower in the United Kingdom than in the other two countries, it appears that universities in the United Kingdom are better at developing spinoffs than universities in the United States and Canada, but the latter are better than the former at licensing to established companies.

But why are UK universities better at generating spinoffs and American and Canadian universities better at licensing to established companies? The next section seeks to answer this question by exploring the reasons why spinoff activity varies across geographic locations.

Table 5.1   The cost of creating spinoff companies and income-generating licenses

Dimension	United States	United Kingdom	Canada
Cost per income-generating license	US$3 780 953	US$4 537 968	US$2 985 546
Financial return on R&D dollar	US$0.06	US$0.02	$0.03
Cost per spinoff created	US$141 212 400	US$14 137 771	US$39 238 884

Note: At the British pound to US dollar exchange rate of 1:1.59.

Source: Adapted from M. Wright, A. Vohora and A. Lockett, 2002, *Annual UNICO-NUBS Survey on University Commercialisation Activities: Financial Year 2001*, Nottingham, UK: Nottingham University Business School.

WHY SPINOFF ACTIVITY VARIES ACROSS GEOGRAPHIC LOCATIONS

Four factors appear to influence the variation in the level of spinoff activity across locations: access to capital, locus of property rights, rigidity of the academic labor market, and the industrial composition of the area. Each of these factors is discussed in turn.

Access to Capital

Differences in access to capital across geographic locations influence the rate of spinoff activity from universities. Spinoffs generally need external capital to finance the development of their technologies. Given the early stage of development of most university technologies at the time that spinoff companies are formed, they need to conduct additional technical and market development, which is costly. The importance of external capital to spinoff company development means that potential entrepreneurs find the formation of companies easier in places where capital is more readily available than in places where capital is difficult to find. Capital availability generates competition among investors to finance entrepreneurs, thereby reducing the price at which investors will provide capital to entrepreneurs (Amit *et al.*, 1998). Therefore, in places where capital is more readily available, more potential entrepreneurs can obtain external financing for their ventures, leading more of them to found spinoff companies.

In particular, the availability of two types of capital encourage the formation of university spinoffs: pre-seed stage capital and seed stage capital. As discussed in Chapter 3, university inventions often require a significant amount of additional technical development before they become of interest to private capital markets. One of the reasons offered in Chapter 3 for the rise in spinoff activity in the United States in the 1980s was the increase in government financing mechanisms to address the financing gap between the stage of technology development at which university research leads to the creation of spinoff companies and the stage of technology development at which the private sector will provide financing to spinoffs. If pre-seed stage funding led to an increase in spinoff activity in the United States over time, then it stands to reason that geographic locations with more pre-seed stage funding programs will have more spinoff activity than other geographic locations. Universities in locations with more pre-seed stage funding can fill the funding gap between spinoff company formation and private sector financing more easily than can universities in other locations.

Several researchers have argued that access to the pre-seed stage capital that the founders of university spinoffs use to demonstrate market need for new technology explains the high level of spinoff activity in the United Kingdom (Wright *et al.*, 2002). The Bank of England (2002) explains that, in the UK context, arrangements such as the University Challenge Funds, Science Enterprise Challenge and the Scottish Proof of Concept Funds facilitate the formation of spinoff companies by allowing founders to develop prototypes from their university inventions. By advancing the development of technologies beyond the proof of concept stage, and by providing a signal that the venture has been screened by external evaluators, these pre-seed stage investments help advance university technologies to the stage at which they might interest private investors (Wright *et al.*, 2002). As a result, in other countries, such as the United States, which has fewer sources of pre-seed stage funding than the United Kingdom, spinoff companies are less prevalent.

Moreover, even within the United States, there is evidence that pre-seed stage funding encourages the formation of spinoff companies. For instance, Tornatzky *et al.* (1995) examined variation across US states in the level of spinoff activity from universities and came to similar conclusions about internal pre-seed stage financing programs. They found that those states that have pre-seed stage financing programs have more university spinoffs than other states.

Another factor that researchers have hypothesized is important in influencing the level of spinoff activity across geographic locations is the level of angel and venture capital financing in the area around the university. Venture capital encourages the formation of new technology companies, including university spinoffs, by providing risk capital and operating assistance to new firms (Florida and Kenney, 1988). In particular, venture capital plays a central role in the formation of biotechnology spinoffs because it provides a major source of funding for the formation of these companies. This is important because biotechnology companies are both capital-intensive and tend to be based on technology that is created in universities (Zucker *et al.*, 1998b).

The amount of local venture capital in a geographical area is important to generating university spinoffs because venture capital is a local business. The uncertainty and information asymmetry present with early stage technology companies make investor monitoring and involvement crucial to the development of new firms. Consequently, venture capital investments tend to be made locally (Sahlman, 1990). Geographic proximity facilitates the creation of social ties that allow investors to gain access to private information (Sorenson and Stuart, 2001), as well as reducing the cost of monitoring new ventures (Gompers and Lerner, 1999; Gupta and Sapienza, 1992; Lerner, 1995; Sorenson and Stuart, 2001). Moreover, investors often link new ventures to networks of managers, suppliers and customers, an activity that is facilitated by active involvement of the venture capitalists in a local entrepreneurial network (Sorenson and Stuart, 2001). Furthermore, the ability to offer operating assistance to investee companies depends heavily on proximity to those companies (Gupta and Sapienza, 1992).

To date, no large sample statistical studies have found support for the capital availability argument for geographical variation in spinoff activity. DiGregorio and Shane (2003) examined the effect of local venture capital in the areas around US universities on the spinoff rate out of 101 universities from 1993 to 1998. However, they found no evidence that the number of venture capital investments, the amount of venture capital invested, the number of venture capitalists, the amount of their capitalization or the presence of university venture capital funds had a statistically significant effect on the level of university spinoff activity in a geographic area. In fact, the authors explain that venture capital funding appears to be proportional to the amount of spinoff activity in a locale. Nevertheless, the authors point out that the availability of angel capital, which they could not measure, might matter more than formal venture capital in encouraging spinoff activity.

Moreover, these authors do not address the cross-national variation in venture capital funding of spinoffs, which might explain variation in spinoff activity at the national level, even if it has no significant effect across locations within the United States. Cross-national variation in capital availability may be important in explaining the limited growth in university spinoffs in the European Union. In Europe, governments are not permitted to provide regional development funding assistance to university spinoffs that are more than 25 percent owned by universities because such funds are not permitted to make investments in small and medium-sized entities owned by larger organizations, keeping many university spinoffs from obtaining the capital that they need to grow (Davis, 2003:1).

Furthermore, some qualitative evidence supports the proposition that the availability of capital encourages spinoff activity in a particular geographic location. Lerner (1998) explains that, when university technology transfer officials identify a technology that provides the basis for the formation of a new company, they tend to contact local venture capitalists. As a result, geographic locations with more venture capitalists should support more spinoff companies.

My interviews with investors and founders involved in the formation of MIT spinoffs also provide support for this argument. For example, the venture capitalists that invested in several MIT spinoffs explain that MIT's location facilitates the financing of those spinoffs because its inventors were part of the investors' social network.

Locus of Property Rights

A second environmental factor that affects spinoff activity across geographic locations is the locus of property rights to university inventions. Because intellectual property laws tend to be made by federal governments, rather than by state or local governments, the differences in the effect of intellectual property laws on university inventions tend to be found at the country level of analysis. Across countries, two major alternative approaches to university property rights exist: in some countries, like Sweden, property rights belong to the inventors of the technology, whereas in other countries, like the United States and the United Kingdom, property rights belong to the university in which the invention was created.

Perhaps counter-intuitively, spinoff activity is more common in those areas where property rights rest with universities rather than where they rest with inventors. Several explanations for this have been proposed. First, some researchers have argued that, when the property rights to inventions rest solely with inventors, the rest of the inventor's department and university do not gain from the inventor's entrepreneurial activity, leading an anti-entrepreneurial attitude to develop among faculty and university administrators (Goldfarb and Henrekson, 2003). As the previous chapter explained, the culture and attitudes at an institution influence the willingness of people at that institution to found companies. Thus, in places where other members of the university do not gain from an inventor's entrepreneurial activity, the anti-entrepreneurial culture makes inventors less willing to start companies. Moreover, those inventors who do start companies in anti-entrepreneurial cultures feel the need to hide their efforts, limiting availability of the role models that Chapter 4 showed were important to facilitating the development of spinoff companies (Henrekson and Rosenberg, 2001).

Second, Goldfarb and Henrekson (2003) argue that spinoff company generation is enhanced when the rights to university inventions reside with universities rather than with individual inventors because this arrangement leads to the creation of technology-licensing offices with expertise in developing new companies that the last chapter explained is important to encouraging spinoff activity. In the absence of the assignment of the rights to inventions to universities, there is no reason for universities to create technology-licensing offices, nor is there reason for the members of the university administration to develop expertise in developing spinoffs (Henrekson and Rosenberg, 2001). As a result, specialized knowledge of how to create spinoffs is not established and stored within universities.

Moreover, the assignment of inventions to universities allows the institution to share the risks and expense of protecting and marketing inventions over a larger pool of technologies (Goldfarb and Henrekson, 2003). Universities can also amortize the cost of finding external entrepreneurs and managers for spinoffs across a wider range of inventions than individual inventors can, thereby enhancing the quantity of spinoffs that they produce. As a result, universities, which are diversified across a portfolio of inventions, are more willing to support the creation of spinoffs to exploit riskier technologies than undiversified individual entrepreneurs. At the margin, this diversification leads universities that receive the property rights to inventions made by faculty, staff and students to create more spinoff companies.

The assignment of inventions to individuals rather than institutions creates a third problem for generating spinoffs. Inventors are unlikely to see many commercial applications for their technologies, making them less likely to patent those inventions and start new companies. Wallmark (1997) explains that, because Swedish inventors have to bear patenting costs themselves, they are much more critical in their screening of inventions than is the case for technology-licensing officers at American universities. These more critical screening criteria hinder the formation of spinoffs when the commercial application of the technology is not obvious to inventors. As will be explained in more detail in the next chapter, the university technologies that lead to spinoffs are often general-purpose technologies at very early stages of development. Consequently, commercial applications for these technologies are difficult to identify initially, and rigid screening criteria are often inappropriate. As a result, leaving the decision making about the disposition of technologies to inventors alone inhibits spinoff company formation.

Rigidity of the Academic Labor Market

A third environmental factor that affects the level of spinoff activity across geographic locations is the rigidity of the academic labor market, or the ability of academics to change institutions or move between industry and academia. Researchers have observed the effect of geographic variation in labor market fluidity on spinoff activity mostly at the country level of analysis because academic labor markets tend to be national markets, leading their differences to be apparent only across nations. Nevertheless, the existing evidence indicates that labor market rigidity hinders spinoff activity in three ways. First, when academic researchers cannot move easily from one academic institution to another, they cannot use labor market mobility as a way to leverage the resources that are necessary to create new technologies. As a result, they generate fewer technologies that are appropriate for the formation of spinoff companies.

Second, when labor markets are rigid, it is difficult for academics to take leave of absence to start companies. Particularly in those countries where faculty and research staffs are national civil servants, it is difficult for academics to take time off to exploit technologies through firm formation. As explained in the previous chapter, when inventors cannot take leave of absence to start companies, the risk of company formation is increased, thereby reducing the willingness of academics to engage in that activity (Stankiewicz,

1986). Thus rigid academic labor markets discourage entrepreneurial activity by increasing the downside loss to academics if the effort is not successful (Goldfarb and Henrekson, 2003).

Third, when labor markets are rigid, academics cannot easily move back and forth between the academic sector and the private sector. Under these circumstances, spinoff activity is discouraged because academics are reluctant to become commercially oriented. Lacking information about what the private sector wants or needs, these university inventors are less able to create technology that would support the creation of spinoff companies. While very little research has been conducted to investigate this proposition, at least one case study of academic labor markets supports this observation. Keck (1993) found that the lack of commercial activity on the part of German academics makes them intellectually anti-commercial and hinders the formation of spinoff companies in Germany.

Moreover, researchers have found that, even in biotechnology, an industry that is driven largely by university spinoffs in the United States, rigid academic labor markets discourage entrepreneurial activity in other countries (Kenney, 1986). For instance, Darby and Zucker (1997) found that, unlike the situation in the United States, where academic researchers found spinoffs as a way to commercialize university research in biotechnology, in Japan companies place scientists in university research laboratories as a way to develop and commercialize university research.[1] These authors attribute the reliance on this arrangement in Japan to the rigidity of that country's academic labor market.

Industrial Composition of the Area

A fourth environmental factor that influences the level of spinoff activity across geographic locations is the industrial composition of the area in which the university is located. Spinoffs are more common in places where high technology start-ups, in general, are more prevalent because the components necessary to create spinoff companies – experienced managers, customers and suppliers, and so on – tend to be present.

Several observers have attributed the high level of spinoff formation out of universities in Boston and San Francisco to the entrepreneurial infrastructure in these areas, including the presence of experienced managers, suppliers and customers. In contrast, the lack of an entrepreneurial infrastructure in other locations reduces the rate of spinoff formation in those locales. For example, Reid (1997:21) describes Marc Andreessen's decision to found Netscape in California rather than in Illinois, where he invented the web browser:

> He had in fact first considered the possibility of building a business around Mosaic back in Illinois. But he hadn't known the first thing about starting businesses. And

'there's no infrastructure at all in Illinois for a start up company,' Marc explains. 'It's not there. No one does it. They just don't know how to react to it. No one really knows if it's a good or bad thing.'

Some more scholarly research also supports the proposition that the industrial composition of the area influences the rate of spinoff activity out of universities. For instance, Golub (2003) found that the rate of spinoff formation out of Columbia University and New York University is inhibited by the fact that New York is not a good geographic location for the creation of new companies, leading spinoffs from those institutions to have an uncharacteristically high tendency (for spinoffs in general) to relocate to other places. Moreover, in a large sample study, Audretsch and Stephan (1998) found that university scientists tend to start biotechnology firms at a younger age when they are located near clusters where a large number of biotechnology companies are started, suggesting that these clusters transmit information about the firm formation process that facilitates the formation of spinoffs.

Other researchers have sought to identify the specific mechanisms through which the industrial landscape surrounding a university encourages or discourages the formation of spinoffs. One mechanism is through the embedding of spinoffs in a network of suppliers and customers. For instance, in their case studies of spinoffs from MIT and Harvard University, Hsu and Bernstein (1997) found that, in some industries, the presence of upstream and downstream technology firms facilitated spinoffs from these institutions by making it possible for the founders of spinoffs to interact with their customers and suppliers more easily and at a lower cost than spinoffs from universities located in places with fewer high technology companies. In places where investors, managers, customers and suppliers of high technology companies are all co-located, it is also easier for spinoff companies to form because these different participants can be brought together through social networks.[2]

Several of the investors in the MIT spinoffs that I interviewed said that they learned of the spinoffs that they funded by networking with local attorneys and accountants or by participating in the MIT 50K Business Plan Competition. Similar patterns are true for external entrepreneurs who started companies by licensing MIT inventions. For example, the founder of one MIT software spinoff explains,

I found out about the MIT invention through a lawyer who taught a class at [the] Sloan [School of Management] called the Nuts and Bolts of Business Plans. I had met him when he was representing a company that had licensed some MIT technology that we were trying to license from them. We struck up a quasi-relationship. After I sold my company, [he] invited me to come up and present to his class in a session on war stories.

Another mechanism through which the industrial landscape encourages spinoff company formation is through support organizations that offer assistance to prospective entrepreneurs. Tornatzky *et al.* (1995) report that universities with more spinoffs tend to be located in places with more support mechanisms, such as business incubators, because these organizations provide information to potential founders, which helps them to form new companies.

A third mechanism through which the industrial landscape encourages spinoff company formation is by making more skilled labor available to new companies. Blair and Hitchens (1998) explain that universities in places with more high technology employees find it easier to create spinoff companies than those in more isolated or less technologically focused locales because more high technology employees are available in the former than in the latter.

My interviews with the founders of MIT spinoffs illustrate this point. For example, the founder of an MIT biotechnology MIT spinoff explains,

> We're right next door to the largest medical center in the world. I was able to teach and meet with the professors in the bioengineering group. They referred the good students to me. I was able to offer these students three months of work in a biotech firm, and the ones that really liked it and that we liked, we kept as full-time employees. So that's worked out pretty well. It's been a nice kind of coop program.

The effect of the geographic location of an academic institution on the ability to find employees, and thereby facilitate the formation of spinoffs, extends to hiring high-level employees as well as the low level ones just described. For instance, the founder of an MIT mechanical device spinoff explains how he found a CEO for his company. He says, 'I started through all of the reasonable channels that you would expect and went through the TLO. I found [our CEO] because he was in the same office space as us, sharing a conference room with the company that I was starting. It's one of those intangibles of being within 300 yards of the MIT campus.'

SUMMARY

This chapter has examined the effects of environmental forces on the rate of spinoff company formation across geographic locations. The first section of the chapter provided evidence that spinoff activity varies significantly across countries. For instance, Canadian educational institutions are much more likely than US educational institutions to generate spinoff companies; and UK universities produce more spinoffs per dollar of research funding than American and Canadian universities.

The second section showed that four factors influence the level of spinoff activity in a particular location: access to capital, locus of property rights, rigidity of the academic labor market and the industrial composition of the geographic area. Access to pre-seed stage capital enhances the rate of spinoff activity in a particular locale because it facilitates the ability to establish the proof of concept and develop the prototypes that are necessary for new companies to attract the attention of private sector investors. Moreover, the availability of local venture capital is thought to enhance the rate of spinoff company formation in an area because university spinoffs often need external capital to undertake further technological development, and venture capitalists tend to make geographically localized investments.

Spinoff activity is more common in areas where the property rights to inventions made by university inventors reside with the institution rather than with the inventors themselves, because such an arrangement minimizes the development of the anti-entrepreneurial culture, facilitates the creation of an institutional expertise in firm formation, makes people more willing to incur the risks associated with firm formation than if those risks could not be amortized across a large number of spinoffs and allows the risks of spinoff company formation to be diversified across a larger number of technologies.

Spinoff activity is more common in geographic locations with less rigid labor markets because labor market immobility inhibits the ability of inventors to generate the resources that they need to create the technologies that underlie their companies. Moreover, the inability to take a leave of absence to start a company increases the university researcher's risk from becoming an entrepreneur, thereby reducing inventors' motivation to found companies. Finally, labor market rigidity reduces the mobility between academia and industry, reducing the amount of commercial knowledge available to academic researchers.

Spinoffs are more common in places where high technology start-ups are more common because the components necessary to create spinoff companies (experienced managers, customers and suppliers, and so on) tend to be present in those areas. Specifically, a high technology infrastructure facilitates access to suppliers and customers, provides support organizations that offer information useful to firm formation and facilitates access to skilled employees and managers.

Having described the effect of environmental forces on spinoff activity, I now turn to a discussion of the types of technologies that lead to the founding of spinoffs, the subject of Chapter 6.

NOTES

1. Rigid labor markets are not the only reason why university research in biotechnology tends to be exploited through the founding of spinoff companies in the United States and through other mechanisms in other countries. Gittelman (2001) found that biotechnology spinoffs are

more common in the United States than in France because French academics are not allowed to own shares in a company they are affiliated with, as is permitted in the United States.

2. However, the presence of a network of suppliers and customers does not appear to matter for the creation of biotechnology spinoffs. In that industry, clusters of spinoffs appear to form even where pharmaceutical firms are not present. Many of the previous studies that have shown the effect of networks of suppliers and customers on the formation of spinoffs did not look at biotechnology, but instead drew their conclusions from the investigation of other industries.

6. The types of technology that lead to university spinoffs

Established firms have a variety of advantages in commercializing university technologies. For instance, they have market knowledge, relationships with customers, distribution systems and related products, all of which facilitate the creation and sale of new technology products and services (Lowe, 2002). As a result, established companies can often make money by commercializing technologies that do not justify the expense of creating a new firm. Therefore most university technologies are licensed to existing companies, and very few university inventions are appropriate technologies for creating spinoffs. In fact, some observers have argued that only about 3 percent of all university inventions are right for founding spinoffs (Nelsen, 1991), although the proportion of spinoff-appropriate inventions being developed in universities has probably risen in the last decade.

The fact that most university technologies are licensed to established companies, but that certain technologies make spinoffs possible, begs the question: what kind of university technology enhances the likelihood that spinoffs will be founded? As Table 6.1 summarizes, university spinoffs tend to be founded to exploit technologies that are radical, tacit, early stage and general-purpose, which provide significant value to customers, represent major technical advances and have strong intellectual property protection.

Table 6.1   The types of technology that lead to spinoffs and established firm licenses

Spinoff firm	Established firm
Radical	Incremental
Tacit	Codified
Early stage	Late stage
General-purpose	Specific-purpose
Significant customer value	Moderate customer value
Major technical advance	Minor technical advance
Strong IP protection	Weak IP protection

This chapter explores these seven aspects of technology, explaining why they make a university invention a good basis for a spinoff.

RADICAL TECHNOLOGY

Most university inventions are not appropriate for founding a spinoff because they are single product extensions that are too incremental to justify the creation of a company. Consequently, they would better complement a business unit within an existing company (Tornatzky *et al.*, 1995) because existing companies already know how to exploit inventions in a particular market or technical field and so would have an advantage over a new firm in the exploitation of an existing technology. Thus, as Lita Nelsen, director of the MIT Technology Licensing Office explains, 'A process invention that improves an existing way of doing things doesn't work well for starting a company. You need more than a tweak on an existing process. You'd need a fundamentally new process.'

In my interviews with the founders of MIT spinoffs, many of them explained the importance of having a radically new technology to create a spinoff. In particular, they talked about having technologies that represent transitions in the market place or that generate revolutions in the way that products or services are created. For example, the founder of one semiconductor spinoff explains that you 'have to ride transitions. As a startup you don't have the same resources as an established company so you have to take advantage of transitions in the market'.

Similarly, the founder of an MIT mechanical device spinoff explains that his decision to start a company was very much influenced by the radicalness of the technology that he was exploiting:

> When I was looking at the different manufacturing industries, it became apparent to me that metal casting is probably one of the basic industries that nobody ever tried to change. All the developments in metal casting were in metallurgy or in putting in robots to replace work that people did, but nothing beyond that. The problem of casting is the paradigm of making a tool first before you make a part. It's a discombobulated way of doing things. I said to myself, 'If you can make a machine that can give you even a small quantity of functional metal parts and you can delay the making of expensive artwork until after you know that there are no changes so you will get the production tooling right the first time, that is a big, big thing.'

Several academic studies also show that radical technologies tend to provide the basis for the creation of university spinoffs, while incremental technologies are more likely to be licensed by established companies. In a study consisting of four in-depth case analyses of university spinoff companies in the United

Kingdom, Vohora *et al.* (2002a) found that all four technologies were competence-destroying innovations that could disrupt existing markets or create new ones. In a larger sample statistical study, Shane (2001a) examined the hazard of firm formation for the 1397 MIT-assigned patents between 1980 and 1996, and found that more radical inventions were more likely to be exploited by spinoffs than more incremental inventions.

Researchers have offered three explanations for the tendency of university spinoffs to exploit radical technologies: first, radical technologies cannibalize existing assets; second, radical technologies undermine existing organizational competencies; third, established firms tend to react to radical technologies with disbelief. Each of these three explanations is developed further in the subsections below.

Cannibalizing Existing Assets

Utterback (1994) explained that established firms with a dominant market position in an industry rarely adopt radical innovations because those innovations would cannibalize the sales of their existing products or services. In fact, whenever new technologies undermine the value of existing assets, established firms are reluctant to invest in them (Arrow, 1962) and cede the opportunity to develop these assets to spinoffs, which do not have existing assets and so are more likely to exploit new technologies that rely on the creation of new assets.

Some qualitative evidence that I collected from interviews with the founders of MIT spinoffs supports the argument that established companies will not exploit radical technologies because these technologies would cannibalize their existing assets. The inventor–founders of the MIT spinoffs clearly saw that the managers of large established organizations were unwilling to invest in radical technologies coming out of the Institute because they had no economic incentive to do so. As a result, they needed to establish new companies to commercialize those radical technologies. For example, the inventor–founder of one MIT medical device spinoff explains,

> The guys in large companies are not willing to take a chance on these kinds of market opportunities because it's not in their interest to. They're making money with the old technologies. But the new technologies take people who don't have a vested interest in the old technology and that's where I was.

Competence-destroying Technology

Researchers have also shown that radical technologies are more likely than incremental technologies to be exploited through the creation of university spinoffs because they replace existing production processes or change product composition, undermining the competencies and skill base of existing firms. Because organizational competencies and skills are expensive and difficult to create (Nelson and Winter, 1982; Hannan and Freeman, 1984), established firms do not want to change them. Hence they do not like to exploit technologies that are based on new technical competencies and skills, and cede radical technologies to independent entrepreneurs (Shane, 2001a).

The qualitative data that I gathered from interviews with the founders of MIT spinoffs indicate that established companies licensed the technologies from the Institute that fit their existing production processes and rejected those technologies that require an investment in new production processes. For example, one manager at an established company that makes advanced porous ceramics for process industries explains why his firm did not license MIT's Three Dimensional Printing Technology to produce ceramic filters for power plants and let an MIT spinoff form to exploit that opportunity:

> We are in a similar business to [the spinoff company]. They saw something different in the technology than we saw because we started from an existing chemical system and chose to stay with it as opposed to go through the gyrations of modification. For us to use Three Dimensional Printing would have required us to change our binder chemistry, which is a major thing. If you know anything about the hot gas filtration system, you know it can take five to seven years to get a new binder tested and accepted in the market place. The stakes are high for users since they're protecting a ten million dollar turbine down stream. They're not interested in radical new technology or any change in technology unless they have a really strong comfort level.

One of the founders of the spinoff company referred to above explains that the answer given by the manager of the established firm explains why the Three Dimensional Printing technology offered an opportunity to found a firm. He says,

> Companies have their own established processes to make filters. That's what they know how to do. If they have a process and I think that [the established company] probably had a handful of processes to make ceramic filters, and somebody comes along and says we have a process you can make filters from, and by the way you are going to pay an up front cost and a royalty, they will probably say no.

Responding directly to the established company manager's point about the need to modify binder chemistry to use the MIT technology to make ceramic filters for power plants, another founder of the MIT spinoff adds that it was not clear that the spinoff's binder or ink technologies were compatible with chemical binder systems used to make ceramic filters. However, the founder's approach to this problem was different from that expressed by executives at established companies because the spinoff had no existing technology. He says,

I bet [the managers at the established company] knew all this stuff too. They just didn't want to put the money and effort into taking a process from MIT's lab bench and making it into a production process. We didn't have a ceramic filter we were trying to improve. We weren't really encumbered by any previous work that had been done. We started with a clean slate.

When technologies are radical, they also impose changes on the composition of products. These changes undermine the competencies of existing firms because they require firms to change the materials used and methods employed to create products. As a result, established firms cede radical technologies that change the composition of products to spinoff firms. The founder of an MIT semiconductor spinoff provides the example of his spinoff and the established semiconductor manufacturers to illustrate this point:

The semiconductor firms didn't license the technology that led to the founding of [our company] because we were at the very bleeding edge of opportunity. It was a new semiconductor material. The traditional semiconductor firms only know devices based on silicon. That's all they know. They research silicon-based devices. If you're a device designer at Siemens or Westinghouse and your job is to make a power semiconductor, what's the first thing that you're going to do? You ask, 'Where's the appropriate silicon materials that I need?' The guy has but one challenge, not to invent a whole new technology base, but to invent and develop a device that is an incremental enhancement over something you're already doing. You turn that into a manufacturable element that you can put out into the market. With diamond thin film, no one in the traditional industry understood how to synthesize the material or how to manage it as a semiconductor.

Similarly, the CEO of another MIT semiconductor spinoff explains how a radical technology invented by an MIT faculty member changed the nature of semiconductor design and therefore required the formation of a new company. He says,

[He] had developed a very interesting design automation technology that was at the forefront of a change in the design paradigm in the semiconductor industry. It was very different and it had a characteristic that allowed system engineers to do complex chip design and allowed a very short design cycle compared to traditional methodologies. This allowed for a new paradigm for a semiconductor company that was based on design automation as opposed to the traditional silicon processing technology. This was a great idea for a new company.

The CEO elaborates on why this radical technology was appropriate for a spinoff. Because established companies develop routines and procedures based on the type of technology that they have, it is easier to start a new company than to get an established company to change its basic technology. Likening a change in core technology to a change in religion, he explains,

You could do more with it as an independent company than trying to bring it into the company because within the company you have to get people to change religions. The design methodologies or actually any methodologies that a person uses, whether it's an accounting or a design methodology or a forecasting system or whatever, become a religious thing in their minds and its very difficult to move people from one to another.

The inventor of the technology that led to a third MIT semiconductor spinoff explains why attempts to convince established companies of the value of radical technologies usually fail, reinforcing the argument that it is easier to start a new company than to change the core technology of an established one. He explains,

We created a company because you come up with an idea and there's a lot of resistance to this way of doing things as opposed to the traditional approach. You can show existing companies that performing this operation in a different way would involve a cheaper, more reliable, and more robust process. You can show them and present it to them and prove it up and down. But to make a company actually change the way they do business, even if it would be cheaper for them, is extremely difficult. To make them actually change the way they do something, it would take another company coming in and competing with them. Companies are very reluctant to change. The only way to get a technology into the industry is to actually start up a company because then the [established companies] are going to lose money and they are going to have to sublicense it.

My interviews at MIT also showed that established companies licensed technologies from the Institute that fit their existing product lines and rejected those technologies that require an investment in new product lines. For example, the founder of an MIT scientific instruments spinoff explains why an established firm did not license his technology, which he ultimately used to found a firm:

The major firms were looking for something that would have a direct fit into their existing product line or that would give them incremental sales with relatively little investment and time. They would not be satisfied with something that would have to grow from a zero base and gradually find its place in the marketplace. A startup is a completely different situation.

Disbelief

A third reason why radical technologies lead to the creation of university spinoffs is that established companies dismiss their value when they learn of their existence. Companies create routines to limit information overload by allowing only that information which appears valuable to their current operations to enter the firm, as a way to avoid diverting organizational attention away from core activities (Henderson, 1993).

Organizational filters have a profound effect on the way established companies deal with new technologies invented elsewhere, whether in a university setting or not. In general, these filters lead established companies to search for those technologies that are closest to the technical processes and market needs that they already have (Podolny and Stuart, 1995). When new, externally created technology is logically different from, rather than an extension of, the organization's existing technical and market knowledge, established organizations have a difficult time understanding, evaluating and incorporating it (Rosenbloom and Christiansen, 1994). As a result, they tend to reject the new technology, claiming that it is 'not valuable' or 'ineffective'. This rejection of radical technology creates an opportunity for people to create new firms to exploit the technology (Shane, 2001a).

My interviews with the founders of several MIT spinoffs point to the importance of the rejection of the value of radical technology by established firms in the formation of spinoff companies. For example, one of the MIT professors that I spoke to describes the rejection by established firms of a technology that he and his student had developed, leading the student to found a spinoff. He explains,

> The alternative of licensing to an existing company was rejected. The technology is unorthodox. The community that does this sort of thing does not believe that it is a viable solution. I can show you some of the reviews we received on our papers when we tried to publish this work initially. They were quite strongly negative, saying things like, 'Don't you guys know that this was disproved in 1960?' and that kind of thing. In general, the community of people who would sell these services had no interest in licensing them because the word on the street was that the technology doesn't work. What [we] did, in fact, was to develop an angle on the technology that nobody had thought of before. But because there is this sense that you can't solve the problem this way, people haven't been inclined to look at it.

Similarly, the founder of an MIT computer hardware spinoff describes the rejection by established companies of a radical technology he invented:

> It was controversial to this day. I had all kinds of proof that nobody understood because we used a different kind of theory than most people in the area used. It also suffered because there had been some premature attempts to do things like this that never amounted to much. It was quite controversial technology-wise.

The skepticism of people in established firms about the value of radical new technologies technology leads the inventors of the radical technologies to found new companies to prove the value of their inventions. For example, an inventor–entrepreneur who founded an MIT semiconductor spinoff explains,

> When you publish papers on this, people don't believe it. There was one dominant competitor in the field and he would come to our presentations and he would

pooh-pooh this stuff. They would say, 'this is academic stuff. It will never work. It's nonsense and they're useless' and so on. But then we did it and they tried to acquire us and now they're doing the same thing themselves.

In general, established companies reject the value of radical technologies because they operate in a particular technical paradigm that other engineers and scientists come to believe is the 'right' way for a particular technology to operate. This paradigm leads researchers to believe that one must focus on certain designs, materials, composition and so on in a particular technical area. Those developing the technology from within this paradigm reject efforts that do not work within the existing paradigm as 'wrong'. The CEO of one of the MIT biotechnology spinoffs provides the example of his company's technology to illustrate this point. He says,

[The inventor's] patents covered inventions that were not common. A lot of the patents had to do with the use of nutrients in a particular way. There were not companies at this time that were exploring the use of nutrients. The pharmaceutical houses were comfortable with drugs and not with nutrients.

Even when inventors can prove the technical superiority of a radical technology to established firms, the latter are often still unwilling to license the technology because the inventors cannot demonstrate the existence of a market for products and services based on the new technology. For example, the founder of another MIT biotechnology spinoff explains,

We went to a number of different companies trying to get them interested in this idea [electronic DNA chips]. At the time, it was totally off the wall and people were a bit skeptical. We realized that we couldn't find a company that was willing to make these chips for us because it was so novel and unusual and none of the big chip companies like the TIs and the HPs and so forth had people in the business area that really understood the market so that they could sell the product. It became clear that if we wanted to drive this we would have to spin out a company.

In short, spinoff companies tend to be founded to exploit radical technologies because established firms tend to reject these technologies for three reasons. First, radical technologies cannibalize existing assets; second, radical technologies undermine existing organizational competencies; third, established firms tend to react to radical technologies with disbelief.

TACIT KNOWLEDGE

When the knowledge necessary to exploit a new university technology is tacit, or held largely in the minds of inventors, spinoff companies are more common than when the knowledge needed to exploit the technology is codified, or documented in written form. Licensing an invention to a non-inventor works best when technology can be codified and made understandable from information stated in contracts or patent documents (Arrow, 1962). However, if knowledge is tacit and potential licensees cannot understand the inventor's technology as well as the inventor, it is important to involve the inventors in the commercialization of the technology (Jensen and Thursby, 2001; Lowe, 2002).

Several pieces of evidence support the proposition that inventor-founded spinoffs are more common when knowledge is tacit than when it is codified. In a study consisting of four in-depth case studies of university spinoff companies in the United Kingdom, Vohora *et al.* (2002a) found that spinoffs were created because existing firms lacked the tacit knowledge necessary to license the technology and exploit the inventions themselves.

My interviews with the founders of MIT spinoffs showed similar results. For example, one MIT software spinoff was founded because the only group with the experience and knowhow to support and modify the software was the group that had created it during the research project. Similarly, the founder of another MIT spinoff explains that he could not license his technology to an established firm because there was too much uncodified knowledge for someone else to take over its development.

The founder of an MIT semiconductor spinoff explains that tacit knowledge inhibited the licensing of his technology by an established firm and led him to establish a spinoff. He says,

> The technology was available to be licensed from the university all along. It wasn't licensed because industry is not able to absorb the technology just by taking a license. In order for the technology to be brought to fruition, you needed not only to license it, but the companies needed the team. So either this had to be done at a more applied level at the university, as opposed to research, almost industrial development at the university or it had to be done in [the company where the research had been conducted] or a start up, which in effect was literally a captive developer for [the company where the research had been conducted]. It was clear that this couldn't be done at the university and I didn't want to let it die. [The company where the research had been conducted] was willing to give a two-year contract to develop the design system that would be needed to effectively utilize the methodology.

When knowledge is tacit, spinoff formation is more likely than licensing to established firms, for two reasons. First, tacit knowledge makes it difficult for anyone other than the inventor to see how an invention could be further developed into a commercializable technology. For example, the founder of one of the MIT biotechnology spinoffs explains,

> I was intimately involved with the research and it gave me an advantage in under-
> standing. The patents that had been filed didn't really identify specific commercial
> applications. They were more related to a broad technology. So it would still take a
> leap of faith to go from that stage to understanding where the commercial applica-
> tions would be.

Similarly, the founder of another MIT biotechnology spinoff explains,

> There were not a whole lot of people capable of taking this kernel of a discovery
> and converting it into something practical without having the vision and under-
> standing that I and some of my colleagues had. The only way to do it was starting
> a company. I had knowledge of how to execute this stuff.

As a result, the formation of inventor-led spinoff companies is a common
mode of commercialization of technologies based on tacit knowledge. When
knowledge is tacit, other people cannot develop the technology and the inventor's involvement becomes crucial to the successful commercialization of the
technology. While, in theory, an established firm could solve this problem by
employing the inventor, that solution presupposes that the licensee is willing
to devote resources to the development of the uncertain new technology.

Moreover, even if the licensee would devote resources to developing the
technology, the problem of providing incentives to inventors remains. To motivate the inventor to become involved, the licensee needs to offer equity ownership to the inventor as a way of overcoming moral hazard problems present
with other compensation schemes (Jensen and Thursby, 2001; Lowe, 2002).
Because it is more difficult to offer equity in an established firm than in a start-
up firm, particularly if the established firm is large, tacit knowledge motivates
the formation of spinoffs.[1]

Second, when knowledge is tacit, spinoffs are necessary because the tacitness of the knowledge makes it difficult for people in established companies
to believe that the invention actually works. That is, they misattribute their
inability to do what the inventor's tacit knowledge enables him or her to do to
problems with the technology. For instance, the founder of one MIT medical
device spinoff, explains, 'The technology is so esoteric. You can tell people I
can do this, I can do that, but it's difficult to convince them. I believed that
people would only appreciate it if I built it.'

To summarize, when the knowledge underlying their inventions is tacit,
university inventors often found spinoffs because the tacitness of knowledge
makes it difficult for anyone other than the inventor to see how an invention
could be further developed into a commercializable technology. Moreover, the
inventors found companies as a way to prove that technology that is based on
their tacit knowledge actually works because the managers in established
companies generally do not believe that the new technology has value.

EARLY STAGE INVENTIONS

Many university inventions lead to the formation of spinoffs because they are early stage technologies that are little more than 'proofs of concept' when the researcher discloses the invention to the university technology-licensing office. Research has shown that, when a university technology is at a very early stage of development, and so is 'unproven', it cannot be licensed easily to established firms. As a result, early stage inventions tend to lead to the formation of spinoffs (Doutriaux and Barker, 1995).

My interviews with the founders of MIT spinoffs support this proposition. For example, the founder of an MIT biotechnology spinoff explains why established pharmaceutical companies did not license the inventions that led to the founding of his company. He explains that pharmaceutical firms want to license new drugs and 'we don't really do any true drug development in my laboratory. We're a basic research house. A pharmaceutical company doesn't want to invest in something straight out of basic research in academia.'

To license a university technology successfully, that invention needs to be developed to the point where there is proof that it works, rather than just being an idea that has the potential to improve the way something is done. Otherwise, there is nothing to show potential buyers that would lead them to believe that there is something that they should license. For example, the founder of an MIT mechanical device spinoff explains that he started a company to exploit his technology because 'we started at the idea stage, not at here's the technology, here's the proof it works. We weren't at the here's why you should license stage'.

Several scholarly studies also have found that established companies are unlikely to license early stage university technologies, and that spinoffs tend to exploit these inventions. For instance, Thursby and Thursby (2000) surveyed 300 executives from the Licensing Executive Society and found that one of the two most important reasons why established companies do not license university inventions is the early stage of the technologies. Moreover, Thursby *et al.* (2001) surveyed licensing officers at 62 universities and found that new and small companies tend to license early stage inventions, whereas established firms tend to license later stage technologies.

Observers of the technology licensing and spinoff creation process have offered several reasons for the tendency of early stage technologies not to be licensed to established firms and instead to lead to the formation of spinoffs: the uncertain value of early stage technologies, the focus of established firms on existing operations, the lack of expertise in conducting radical product development in established firms, the difficulty of communicating information about early stage technology, the difficulty of capturing value of early stage technology through licensing, and the short time horizons of large, established firms, particularly publicly traded ones. These reasons are discussed in turn in the subsections below, beginning with uncertain value.

Uncertain Value

Early stage university technologies are difficult to license because managers of established companies, like most people, find it difficult to see the value of early stage technologies. Before a technology has been proven and its efficacy demonstrated, people cannot know for sure if an invention will be valuable. The lack of proof of the effectiveness of a technology undermines the ability to establish its value. Therefore it is difficult to set a price for uncertain technology. As a result, managers of established companies, who are not intimately familiar with a new technology, prefer to wait for further development to take place before they license it. If that development proves that the new technology has significant value, then the established company will license it. However, if additional development shows that the technology does not have much value, then the established company will pass on licensing.

Some qualitative research supports this proposition. For instance, Vohora *et al.* (2002b:11) quote one biotechnology entrepreneur as saying,

> Commercial partners and industry were not interested. It was so early stage they thought it was a bit wacky. They all had the first option to acquire the patents that had been filed from the sponsored research but did not take any of them up, which left the university in an interesting position with a huge patent portfolio to exploit commercially.

My interviews with the founders of MIT spinoffs also demonstrate that established firms will choose not to license early stage technology because they cannot determine its value. For example, one of the founders of an MIT computer hardware spinoff explains, 'The technology was hard to license because it was not finished. No one knew what to do with it.' Similarly, the founder of an MIT mechanical device spinoff explains why none of the established firms that funded the research that led to the development of MIT's Three Dimensional Printing technology licensed it. He says, 'At the time, all [the inventor] had was a little machine made by students, spitting out one filter every two days. It was not clear that the technology could be used for manufacturing.'

In many cases, spinoff firms serve as a mechanism to bridge the development gap between university technology and private sector products and services. By further developing early stage technology, spinoffs prove the commercial benefit of those technologies, making them more valuable for established companies to license. Consequently, spinoffs often sell out to established firms, rather than competing with them, after they have proved the value of the technology.

The founder of one MIT semiconductor spinoff explains the role that spinoffs play in bridging the gap between university technology and private sector products and services:

> We decided to form [our company], in part, to bring this invention to market. Our more general goal is to fill the existing technology transfer gap between university level research and industrial practice in the semiconductor industry, specifically in the area of integrated sensors used to monitor semiconductor manufacturing processes.

The Focus of Established Companies on Existing Operations

The managers of established companies often are not interested in licensing early stage university technologies because they focus their activities on enhancing the returns from their existing operations, and early stage technology that is not yet commercially useful does not do this. Take, for example, the explanation provided by a corporate venture capitalist working for one large medical device company for that firm not licensing MIT's Three Dimensional Printing technology. He explains,

> A lot of people seemed interested, but it seemed so far away. [Our] operating companies are very focused on existing businesses and existing markets. When it comes to actually developing a broad enabling technology that could some day enable them to do something, it is very difficult to get their involvement.

The managers of established companies usually want someone else to develop a technology before they will license it for ongoing operations. That someone else is typically a spinoff company. Once the spinoff creates a product or service from the technology, the established firm then seeks to acquire the spinoff company or forms a strategic alliance with the firm. For example, another corporate venture capitalist at the medical device firm described above uses the example of MIT's Three Dimensional Printing Technology to show how operating companies view licensing MIT inventions. He says, 'The conclusion from all of our operating groups, who are nearer the product stage, was "Gee, this sounds great, but it ain't ready for prime time yet. Why don't you guys invest in it and call us back in a year or two?" '

In particular, the managers of operating companies want to wait until someone, such as a spinoff company, has developed the university technology to the stage of being a product that is ready for testing before they will consider licensing it. One of the venture capitalists at the medical device company explains his firm's perspective on MIT's Three Dimensional Printing Technology:

> I believed that we should explore the technology for making artificial bone. The operating guys looked at the 3DP process and said, 'Yeah, this is a great technology. Once we know which pore size, which combination of absorbable polymers, which degradation rate, etc. . . . and the answer to all sorts of bone biology questions, this would be the perfect way to build those.' The problem is that there were so many variables. We could build 50 variations and put all those into long-term tests. So there was a lack of enthusiasm to jump into what sounded like academic research. They were saying, 'Nice job. Call us when you can test some product concepts.' When it comes to a big company, the most common response is 'Great. Show me construct A, B, and C with features D, E, and F.'

The desire of established firms to wait until the technology has been developed into a product or service before they will consider licensing it also means that they will not purchase raw technology. As a result, entrepreneurs often need to found firms to develop university technology into products and services that can be sold to other firms. The founder of one of the MIT software spinoffs explains his spinoff's experience trying to sell basic technology to established firms. He says,

> No one wants to buy ideas, a technology that's very vague. People want to buy something ready to go out of the box. When we got down to it, there was nothing for them to really buy. We had nothing that we could just say, here it is, other than this piece of paper that says its okay for you to develop this technology that noone wanted to spend the development money to do. No one would say yes to licensing until they could actually see the stuff working. They figured that it was our job to do the development and research on it, not theirs.

Even to research-intensive companies, which could do further development work on university inventions, it is difficult for universities to license early stage technologies successfully. In research-intensive companies, the problem is that managers often reject early stage university technologies because the adoption of those technologies would undermine existing research activities within the established organization. For example, the founders of one of the MIT biotechnology spinoffs explains,

> My experience in biotechnology has been that mature companies usually do not want to license technology that is not yet in development and hasn't shown lead candidates in drug discovery. And the reason is that they've got a large budget of their own devoted to discovery. Licensing is a line item on their budget and they have a research head that has to make a decision to drop his own discovery programs and reallocate his own human resources in order to in-license a discovery effort from academia and transfer his resources to that discovery effort. Usually a Merck or Pfizer or Johnson and Johnson won't do that.

Similarly, an MIT inventor–entrepreneur whose inventions led to the founding of another MIT biotechnology spinoff explains that he started a company because large, established pharmaceutical companies would not license and develop his inventions. In particular, he explains that the obstacle to licensing was that research and development managers in large pharmaceutical companies were resistant to devoting their research budgets to the further development of technologies that came from outside the organization. He says,

> We tried to license the technology and I was getting quite frustrated with the inability to get the patent to where it could be a very useful product. I decided to start a company with a venture capitalist because companies in the pharmaceuticals industry have their own very large research departments. It would not be a happy reflection on the intramural group if a company felt it had to go outside to license something.

The problem of resistance of managers at large companies to the development of university inventions is not simply an MIT problem, or even an American problem. Barnes (2002) explains that Mark Ferguson, a University of Manchester professor whose spinoff, Renovo, was the largest university biotechnology spinoff in the United Kingdom, founded his company because large pharmaceutical companies with which he worked were unwilling to undertake further development of his inventions. Barnes (2002:8) quotes Mark Ferguson as saying,

> It seemed that no internal resources had been assigned to picking up inventions from the academic programmes and no-one seemed to have the time nor responsibility within the companies. When I started to push harder to try to make progress, friends within the company became resentful as if you were trying to push their projects off the agenda. It was perhaps seen as a quality judgment that the external research was better than in-house programmes.

Product Development Expertise

Spinoffs are often used to commercialize early stage technologies because established companies find it more efficient to buy already developed technologies rather than to develop these technologies themselves. Because their comparative advantage does not lie in technology development, established companies do not like to devote resources to that activity.

My interviews with the founders of MIT spinoffs provide empirical support for this proposition. For instance, the founder of one MIT mechanical device spinoff says,

> The licensing office tried hard to market this technology to some large companies, but at the time I saw the technology it was very, very early stage. It was a pretty risky stage in terms of believing in what it could be. It was a proof of principle

prototype. All it did would show that the concept would work. I think that a large company needs something that's much closer to a commercial product. Large companies would much rather buy a technology that's proven and spend $10 million for the technology than to buy it for $50,000 and go through that [product development] cycle. Large companies are not that great at taking a product from the early conceptual stage to finished product.

In general, established firms suffer from two major disadvantages in developing new technology: first, managers in established companies are not rewarded sufficiently for bearing the risks of technology development, undermining the incentives for this activity; second, most new companies lack the capabilities to undertake these activities successfully. As a result, most established companies cede technology development to new companies that develop these technologies and then sell the new products and services that result from them to established firms.

Focusing on the lack of capabilities for technical development in established companies, the founder of one MIT software spinoff explains why his spinoff was needed. He explains that established companies often have difficulty taking an idea stage technology to the point of commercial usefulness because of the complexity of mixing different technical skills together in a new way to create the new product or service:

> I think the reason the technology wasn't licensed to an established company was that it isn't the kind of technology you can just turn over to capable engineers and say 'Here, have that'. It's a very complex technology that needs to be developed with specific applications in mind with a very diverse set of engineering talent that I don't think most companies have. We had to go recruit a bunch of different engineering talents, human interface people, telephony people, DSP engineers. Most of the established companies that MIT licenses to put technologies in a very ethereal R&D department. Our technology just wasn't ready to be licensed to a company. It wasn't a commercial product. It needed another three years of applied development.

In addition, large corporations often find it difficult to assign talented people to the development of new technology. People with cutting edge product development skills often prefer to work for start-up companies where they have the opportunity to make large sums of money through equity ownership. Large corporations also make significant amounts of money from their existing operations, leading them to devote their best people to those operations. As a result, the founder of one MIT mechanical device spinoff explains that established companies simply do not have the right people to assign to transform university technologies into products and services. He says,

> Established companies really cannot pursue these opportunities. They cannot develop equipment full stop. Pratt and Whitney and Johnson and Johnson or General Motors, or whoever was in this consortium, did not have the talent to

develop such complex equipment. Even if they had the talent, they would never have succeeded because there are very few people who are capable of combining so many engineering disciplines and end up with a machine. The people who work in large companies are assigned to the bread and butter of the companies and they will not be assigned to some miniscule activities unrelated to the mainstream of the company. In order to succeed you need the first league. The best people you can find are in startups. You have to have someone who is very good and puts 100 percent of what he has into this program, which you can never get in a large company.

Established companies are also too bureaucratic to develop new products and services from the idea stage in an effective manner. Large companies are handicapped at product development because they must deal with legacy issues, bureaucracy and the constraints of hiring effectively across a large number of people, which hinders their ability to operate at the same pace as spinoff firms. As a result, spinoffs can conduct product development much more efficiently and effectively than established firms. For instance, the founder of one of the MIT mechanical device spinoffs explains how his company solved product development problems that would have stymied large organizations:

> Just being two guys without having to have a meeting to discuss it, we just did it. In larger companies, it's more difficult to do. There're lots of decisions by committee and things get bogged down and nobody wants to stick out their neck and try something even if it looks good. If I'd have tried this at my old company, I'd have had almost no chance of success at all.

Some observers have even noted that established firms operate too slowly even to learn that they should develop a particular university technology, let alone actually develop it. For example, the founder of one of the MIT biotechnology spinoffs explains that, to take advantage of early stage inventions, 'you need a start-up. The big companies respond too slowly. I work with a number of big pharmaceutical companies and just to get some novel idea in front of them takes forever.'

Similarly, one of the inventors of a technology that led to one of the MIT mechanical device spinoffs explains the difficulty he faced in simply getting his early stage technology in front of managers at large established companies. He explains,

> We tried to get HP to answer the telephone. They never answered when we called them. The Xerox technical people came down and looked at it. They were very friendly, but they were very slow to respond. Apparently, if you're trying to get a big company interested, it takes a long time. You have to percolate up to the level where they make decisions and then they have to make the decision.

Communicating Information about the Technology

The early stage of university technologies at the time that they are available for license also leads to the creation of spinoffs because it makes it makes it difficult for inventors to communicate things about the technology to others. One part of this problem is the inability of the inventors to transmit key information about early stage technology that would be necessary for the further development of the technology because the key information is not yet known. Because the value cannot be communicated easily to others, inventors often found firms to develop the technology further until it has reached a point where its value can be communicated to others.

My interviews with the founders of the MIT spinoffs provide support for this proposition. For example, the founder of one of the MIT computer hardware spinoffs explains that he started a company, rather than licensing his technology to an established company, because 'there was a lot of development that had to get done. I didn't think it was at a mature enough level that it would work. I didn't think it was mature enough to transmit to others.' Similarly, the founder of an MIT software spinoff explains,

> The technology involved was a little complex. It wasn't clear that people were going to recognize the benefit until you had something to demonstrate. After that they could actually see it and use it. They would appreciate that it's good technology. From just reading a write up and looking at software most people weren't able to see that. Most people weren't interested in just code, they wanted to see an example.

Other researchers have observed the same patterns that come out of my interviews with the founders of MIT spinoffs. For instance, in his study of the inventor spinoffs from the University of California system, Lowe (2002:57) quotes the founder of Calimetrics who explains that the university could not get Japanese firms manufacturing CDs to license the technology that the firm was founded to exploit because there was no prototype, just some test results: 'We spent 5½ years [at Calimetrics] getting to the point where we could even bring in Japanese companies and they could see the technology.'

Ability to Capture Value

The early stage of university technology also makes it difficult for inventors to reap much value from licensing their inventions. Most of the value from university inventions is created through the process of transforming the technologies into products and services that meet market needs, not in the ideas themselves. Therefore an established company sees no reason to offer a large amount of money to license the early stage technology. As a result, the inventors of these technologies are often unwilling to license early stage technology to established firms, preferring to start firms to capture more of the value of their inventions.

The data on MIT spinoffs that I collected support this proposition. For example, one of the MIT technology-licensing officers says, 'Envision the conversation with the President of Dupont. You say, "one of our scientists at MIT understands that if you nanotexturize materials, you might be able to change energy, would you like to license this and commercialize it?" He says, "Yeah, I'll give you $25 000 for a license." '

Another problem with capturing value from licensing early stage technology to an established firm is that it is very difficult to sell ideas. Because they are intangible, ideas are very hard to specify in a form that makes it possible for a buyer and seller to agree on what they are contracting over. For example, the founder of one of the MIT biotechnology spinoffs explains how the difficulty of selling ideas led to the founding of that company. He says that the knowledge on which it was based

> was more of a concept than anything. It wasn't even clear why you'd want to patent something like that. It was more of a concept of how things worked. It wasn't a composition of matter patent. It was more of a way of proceeding. There was no technology to license. It was just ideas. It was our knowledge and insight. It's not that I had a specific gizmo that we developed as we started our own company. You see, I've started a bunch of companies and none of them were based on specific experiments or specific things being done in my lab. It was more general concepts that I was aware that you could bring to market.

Moreover, even if the buyer and the seller can agree on what idea they are contracting over, establishing a price for that idea is a problem. Because ideas are intangible, it is hard for buyers and sellers to agree on what they can and cannot do. This disagreement, of course, makes it hard to establish a price for ideas. As a result, the buyer and seller cannot consummate a transaction. The founder of one MIT robotics spinoff explains his decision not to license the technology initially and to found a company instead. He says, 'When you've got something that's completely new and an acknowledged market for it doesn't exist, you really can't go out and get the value for that idea that you might be placing on it.'

Time Horizons

Early stage university technologies are hard to license to established firms because those firms do not like to make investments in technologies that have unknown or long time horizons. When technologies need further development before they reach commercialization stage, often established companies have time horizons that are too short to undertake this development. Managers in established firms are judged on their financial performance, particularly in public companies. As a result, they tend to favor activities with shorter time horizons. In contrast, entrepreneurs often pursue opportunities to achieve personal goals, such as independence or making a technology work, and so are more accepting of longer time horizons for the activities in which they engage. As a result, spinoffs are a common vehicle for the commercialization of early stage university technologies that have long or uncertain time horizons for their further development.

The data that I collected on the MIT spinoffs provided empirical support for the proposition that spinoffs are a more common vehicle to exploit early stage technology because entrepreneurs have longer time horizons than the managers of large firms.[2] For instance, one of the MIT technology-licensing officers describes the perspective toward early stage university technologies prevalent at large established public corporations. He says, supposing that you talk to the CEO of a major company:

> The guy's going to say, 'What the hell are you talking about? What application does it have?' You say, 'I don't know yet, but if you spend $10 million to work on it for three years, you're going to come up with something.' He's going to say, 'I'm accountable to my board of directors next quarter on what my profits and losses are. You want me to spend money on something that I can't even see a pathway to in a three-year horizon to see if we've got anything. You've got to be crazy.'

The inventors of new technologies often have the patience and commitment necessary to develop early stage technology to the point of commercialization because patience and commitment are necessary for invention in the first place. As a result, many inventors found companies instead of licensing out their early stage inventions. For example, the founder of one of the MIT materials spinoffs explains,

> We had considered licensing but we never found an appropriate place for licensing. You could license something, but you had to really pay attention to it. Most companies would not have had the patience to do the development work that had to be done. There are competing technologies that are around that are more established and it's a matter that the markets had to be built as the technology was being built.

Similarly, the founder of an MIT biotechnology spinoff explains that he had a commitment to develop his technology that was not present in established companies that might have been appropriate targets to license the technology. He says, 'There was no interest when we started this. None of these companies really had the commitment to this that was required to make this a success.'

Part of the reason for the greater commitment of the founders of spinoffs to long-term technology development is the enthusiasm that inventors have for their own technology. This enthusiasm, coupled with a focus on the development of the technology, facilitates its advancement over long periods of time. As the founder of one MIT biotechnology spinoff explains, 'When you start off in something like this, you have unbridled enthusiasm. You're not restricted by a detailed, hard earned knowledge of those industries. You've got to learn that.'[3]

GENERAL-PURPOSE TECHNOLOGIES

University spinoffs also tend to exploit general-purpose technologies, or basic inventions with broad applications in many fields of use (Nelsen, 1991). A good example of a general-purpose technology that led to an MIT spinoff is a piezoelectric device. The technology combines piezoelectric material with active control systems to remove vibrations. Among the applications to which this technology has been put are electric shocks on airplane wings, bicycles, skis, baseball bats, automobiles and medical devices. In the biomedical area, tissue-engineering technology provides another example of a general-purpose technology because it can be used for the development of a variety of different products.

General-purpose technologies tend to be exploited by spinoff companies for two reasons: first, they offer multiple market applications; second, established companies have trouble identifying what to do with the general-purpose technologies. These two explanations are discussed in greater detail in the subsections below.

Multiple Market Applications

General-purpose technologies, or platform technologies as practitioners often call them, provide a good basis for starting a spinoff company because they allow founders to change market applications if the first application that they pursue turns out to be a dead end (Tornatzky *et al.*, 1995). This flexibility is important to the survival of new companies, which have no existing products to fall back on should an application for a new technology prove to be unviable.

Second, general-purpose technologies allow spinoffs to diversify risks and amortize their costs across different market applications, both of which are important to the establishment of successful new firms. Lita Nelsen, the director of the MIT Technology Licensing Office, explains the value of diversification and amortization provided by general-purpose technologies:

To start a company, I would want a technology that was multi products. Having many products permits you to spread the cost [and risk] of development across a group of products. For example, we had one technology that was a single product idea, a technology for transcribing stuff off a blackboard or whiteboard. Even if it's a wonderful idea, it's a single product and very hard to attract investors because it's too many eggs in one basket.

Third, a general purpose technology provides the new firm with potential market applications that are achievable at different points in time: some in the short term, others in the medium term, and still others in the long term (Nelsen, 1991). This flexibility allows the founders of the spinoffs to match the pursuit of market applications to resource assembly over time and so better manage the firm creation process.

Fourth, general-purpose technologies allow the founders of spinoffs to compare different potential market applications to figure out the best one to pursue. Several of the founders of the MIT spinoffs pointed out that the ability to compare alternative applications for general-purpose technologies influenced their decisions to establish spinoffs. For example, the founder of one of the MIT biotechnology spinoffs indicated that the technology she investigated was worthy of founding a company because 'it was a broad technology, not narrow or incremental, like many inventions. As a big idea with many uses, we could figure out the best thing to do with it.' Similarly, an MIT inventor whose patents led to the founding of one of the MIT software spinoffs explains why a spinoff was founded to exploit his inventions: 'Artificial intelligence was what we started with, as an instrument, a guiding star. Artificial intelligence can be applied to almost anything, which meant that any interesting idea could be explored.'

Fifth, the possession of a general-purpose technology facilitates the financing of university spinoffs because it increases the likelihood that the spinoff will identify a valuable market application for the technology. As a result, investors favor university spinoffs that exploit general-purpose technologies. For example, one of the venture capitalists that invested in an MIT biotechnology spinoff explained that he had evaluated several MIT technologies, but was interested in one company's technology because, 'if you had an immunomodulator in a carbohydrate, you might have a whole line of products'.

Established Firm Difficulty with General-purpose Technologies

Not only are spinoffs more likely to exploit general-purpose technologies than single purpose technologies for the reasons described above, but they are also more likely to exploit these technologies because established companies tend to avoid them. The very advantages of flexibility and diversification that general-purpose technologies provide to spinoffs create problems for established companies. This seeming paradox occurs because new firms look for the best technology for starting a company, regardless of the industry or stage of the value chain at which that technology can be applied. In contrast, established companies look for the best technology to support the further development of the products and services they already make in an industry in which they already operate. Because general-purpose technologies can be applied in a variety of different markets and at a number of different stages of the value chain, they tend to be difficult for established firms to evaluate and exploit.

For example, the founder of one of the MIT mechanical device spinoffs explains why the founders of that company and several other spinoffs were so interested in a particular MIT invention that established companies, including those that funded the research leading to the invention, were not interested in licensing. He explains,

> The difference was simply that we were coming in looking for any technology that we could use to start a company and make money. The other people were coming from companies and they were given a direction to go. They weren't looking to find a technology to start a company, but they were looking at this as the right technology to solve their problems.

The subsections below explore the problems that general-purpose technologies impose on established firms both because they can be exploited in multiple markets and because they can be exploited at multiple stages of the value chain.

The problem of multiple market applications
The fact that a general-purpose technology can be applied in many industries poses a problem for established firms and leads spinoffs to exploit these technologies. University technologies often require significant investment in further development before they can be used commercially. Much of this investment needs to be conducted before a licensee can know if the technology will have value in a particular industry. Most established companies are reluctant to make investments in new technologies under these circumstances because they seek new technologies that enhance their ability to produce products or services in the industry that they are already in. Because the strategies of established firms lead them to focus on their core businesses, they are usually unwilling to bear the risk that a technology has commercial value, but in another industry. As a result, established firms generally are unwilling to license general-purpose university technologies and cede these technologies to spinoff firms.

The data that I collected on the MIT spinoffs support this argument. For example, one MIT software invention focused on planning and execution of complex coordinated movement, as well as mental process and representations used for learning. The founder of an MIT spinoff that exploited this invention explains why an established company did not license the firm's technology: 'In fairness, people don't understand what the hell this thing was. Is it software? Is it hardware? Are you sports? Are you entertainment? Is this Nintendo? Are you healthcare? What is this?'

In many cases, established companies actually evaluate and reject general-purpose technologies because they cannot see the use for those technologies in their industries, giving spinoffs the opportunity to exploit these technologies. Take, for example, MIT's Three Dimensional Printing invention, a general-purpose technology that ultimately proved useful in making dinnerware, filters for power plants, drug capsules, concept models for architects, and ceramic molds for metal parts. Several established companies evaluated the technology, but decided not to license it, allowing a variety of different entrepreneurs to use this technology as the basis for spinoff companies.

In general, the established firms that decided against licensing the Three Dimensional Printing Technology reported that they did so because the technology was not useful in their industries. For example, the founder of one established firm explains,

> We examined MIT's Three Dimensional Printing Technology and concluded that the process had a couple of impediments for our business. One, it wasn't clear that the binders or the ink were compatible with or could be adjusted to deal with the binder systems that we use chemically. Two, it appeared to be a fairly expensive process for the relatively limited number of parts we needed to have made.

Similarly, an executive at another established firm who also decided not to license MIT's Three Dimensional Printing Technology explains, 'I wanted to see if there was an application for Three Dimensional Printing in my own field and whether it made any sense for this company to consider building that type of machinery and offering it as a product line. But it didn't.' A manager at a third established company explains his company's decision not to license MIT's Three Dimensional Printing Technology. He says, 'I showed the information on Three Dimensional Printing to my boss. He wasn't impressed so we didn't really take it any further. It wasn't that easy to attach to our business. There were some merits but it didn't really fit. It wouldn't have helped us.'

Even when established companies fund the research that leads to the creation of the new general-purpose technology, they often opt against licensing it if it is not clear that it will be useful in developing products or services in their industry. For example, the inventor of a software technology that led to the founding of an MIT spinoff explains why the company that funded the research that led to the invention of this technology chose not to license it, even though the company had the right of first refusal to do so: 'The research cost them $5 million. They had the rights to the patent. The company was not the slightest bit interested in becoming an electronics manufacturer. They wanted to print newspapers. That was their goal.'

In contrast to the negative view of the multiple market applications of general-purpose technologies that established firms have, the founders of university spinoffs tend to express a positive view of the multiple market application potential of these inventions. Moreover, the founders of spinoffs see the multiple industry potential of general-purpose technologies as offering them an advantage precisely because established companies tend not to be interested in them. For instance, the founder of one of the MIT biotechnology spinoffs explains,

> Most of the companies were focused in one industry and so even if they did understand the full potential of our inventions, they weren't in a position to take advantage of it. For example, there was a food company that was very interested, but they were in a position only to take advantage of the food applications. There was also a company involved in waste treatment and they could only take advantage of a certain component of the technology. So no one was in all of these different business areas and so couldn't appreciate the full span of the technology.

The problem of different stages of the value chain

Sometimes established companies choose not to license general-purpose technologies because the technologies would be used at a different stage of the value chain from the stage at which the companies currently operate, and the companies do not want to operate at other stages of the value chain. The tendency of established companies to maintain a strategic focus on a particular stage of the value chain creates the opportunity for spinoffs to exploit the new technology because the established companies often support the efforts of the spinoffs, which they view as complementary to their own. For example, the inventor–founder of one MIT software spinoff explains that the companies that funded the research project that led to his invention supported the founding of his spinoff, which was designed to provide project management software for firms in the chemicals industry. Because the chemicals companies were not in the software business, they were not interested in developing the technology themselves. Instead, they wanted to become customers of the spinoff.

Even when the companies fund research, and so have a right of first refusal to technologies that emerge from that research, they often prefer to be customers of the spinoffs that commercialize the technologies than to develop products or services that compete with the spinoff. For example, an inventor of a software technology that led to one MIT spinoff explains how the sponsors of the research that led to her invention wanted the inventors to start a company, even though they had a right to license the technology themselves. She says,

The idea of sponsorship is that a company picks up some good technology and then commercializes it. We were surprised that none of our sponsors were taking up the technology. It turns out that, in many cases, we actually developed a technology that doesn't fit as an additional feature in one of their products and doesn't fit their business plans. So even though they're extremely excited about it, they want to be either users of it or distributors, they don't want to make it.

In some cases, the managers of established companies that could have developed products or services from the technology are so supportive of the development of the new technology that they even go out of their way to help the spinoffs to develop it. For example, a venture capitalist that invested in one of the MIT optics spinoffs explains the relationship between that company and IBM:

IBM had more to do with funding this thing and with convincing investors and management that all we had to do was to develop it than anyone. We had this guy at IBM who was absolutely key in terms of giving the money and answering questions about markets, technology, competitors and products. But they would never have licensed this, nor would Intel, who also funded the research. They're not in the tool business. At the end of the day, they're not in the business of making tools, they're in the business of using them.

Similarly, Kelleher (1995:24) explains that large firms supported the formation of MIT spinoff Metal Matrix Cast Composites by becoming initial customers for that company's products rather than by licensing the technology themselves. He says,

Cornie's idea for spinning off a business began to gel when an apparatus designed and built as part of the research project attracted the interest of some of the private firms that had been supporting the research along with the government. They asked for copies of the machine – which could produce a high quality composite and make evaluation materials – and Cornie and his team sold a number of them.

Thus, in many cases, university spinoffs are founded because established companies support their efforts to exploit technology that the established companies had funded. In these cases, the established firms want to be suppliers to or users of products created by firms at a different stage of the value chain from the one at which they operate.

TECHNOLOGIES THAT PROVIDE VALUE TO CUSTOMERS

Spinoffs are more likely to be formed when a new technology generates significant value for the customer than when it does not. While an established company can exploit a technology that offers only a small improvement in customer value, a new firm cannot afford to pursue the same type of technology. Because a new firm needs to assemble from scratch the assets used to exploit an opportunity, it requires a more valuable opportunity to act than an established firm, which exploits an opportunity with existing assets.

The emulation technology that led to the founding of one MIT software spinoff is a good example of the level of customer value that is necessary to justify the formation of a spinoff. This technology allowed the spinoff to reduce the cost that emulation system vendors charged per semiconductor gate from $1 to $0.20. Because this technology had a five times greater efficiency than competing technologies, it offered enough of an advantage over existing technologies to allow the spinoff to compete with existing firms, which have the advantage of existing, efficient operations, relationships with customers, distribution channels, and so on.

Moreover, the greater the amount of customer value that the new technology creates, the better the justification of a spinoff to potential stakeholders of the new firm. As a result, spinoffs that generate more customer value find it easier to assemble resources than other spinoffs, facilitating their development. For instance, one venture capitalist that invested in several MIT spinoffs argues that university spinoffs need to have a technology with 'at least a 10 times and maybe 100 times economic advantage over competing approaches' to justify founding a firm to exploit the technology. He argues that the general advantages of existing firms over new firms, combined with the difficulty of creating companies to commercialize university technology successfully, require very high magnitudes of improvement over existing firms' alternatives.

Not only do university spinoffs need to exploit technologies with greater customer value than established companies need to exploit, but also demonstrating the value of new technology to customers is much more important for spinoffs than for established firm licensees. Established companies can sometimes make use of technologies that they cannot demonstrate to have significant value because they can use the technologies to improve their own operations. However, spinoffs need to show that their technologies offer significant value to customers because customers will not switch to spinoffs as suppliers unless the new companies provide solutions to customer needs that are better than the solutions that existing suppliers provide (Roberts and Malone, 1996).

Interesting Shoppers

One mechanism through which high levels of customer value enhance the formation of university spinoffs is through the attraction of external entrepreneurs.[4] As will be explained in greater detail in Chapter 10, entrepreneurs who shop for technologies at university technology-licensing offices lead efforts to start a significant number of university spinoffs. When people come to technology-licensing offices to shop for technology, evidence that an invention will generate customer value often leads the entrepreneurs to select that technology from among the pool of alternatives. For example, the founder of one MIT optics spinoff explains, 'I looked at five different opportunities and the technology [that I selected] was by far the most compelling story in terms of competitive advantage to the customer. It provided the most exciting change for customers.'

Similarly, the founder of one MIT biotechnology spinoff explains how the technology that led to the founding of that company differed from other MIT technologies that he looked at but chose not to exploit in the past. He says, 'It seemed to me that there was a more compelling relationship between diseases and the normality with the proteins than the others had identified.'

Motivating Inventors

Another mechanism through which high levels of customer value enhance the formation of university spinoffs is the motivation of inventors to found firms. When a newly invented technology has significant value to potential customers, those potential customers often express interest in obtaining products or services that use the new technology. This potential customer interest, in turn, motivates the inventors to found companies to supply those products or services. For example, the founder of one of the MIT medical device spinoffs explains that he started a company in response to customer interest in his technology: 'We undertook a market survey by talking to the customers. We interviewed people practicing gastroenterology and described the technology to them and got their reaction. The feedback from the physicians involved was that this is an excellent thing. People will want this.'

Value to potential customers can sometimes be so high that the inventors cannot help but see the potential for profit in starting a company to supply products or services based on the new technology. As a result, they are quickly drawn into founding new firms. For example, one MIT software spinoff was founded because the researchers who invented the technology underlying it had to turn down potential customer sponsors seeking their expertise because of limited capacity at the Media Lab. As a result, it was clear to the founders that their idea had value. They had expertise that met customer needs and for which customers were willing to pay.

In some cases, the inventors did not even need to seek information from the market place to learn that the technology had value to customers. Rather, potential customers volunteered that the invention was valuable and that they would be interested in obtaining it. For example, the inventor of the technology that led to one MIT software spinoff knew that there was customer value without even asking potential customers for feedback because the interest of Media Lab sponsors and the press in her invention was so great. She says,

> The Media Lab is a very open kind of place because we are entirely funded by industry. We basically have sponsors coming through here at the rate of two or three groups a day just in my group. We showed all of these industry people the prototype and they got very excited. They realized that there was a lot of value in this prototype and the concept we had made. So we realized that we had something special at hand.

In some cases, the demonstration of a technology was enough to show that there was sufficient customer interest for an inventor to found a company. For example, the inventor of a software technology whose invention led to the founding of a spinoff explains that he knew that there was demand for a product based on his technology just from the feedback from the observers of the demonstrations of the technology. He says, 'So many visitors were really enthusiastic about the technology, among them several people who had companies in the area. They said, "You have a gold mine here. Why don't you start something? I'd be ready to invest." '

In a few cases, the inventors of university technology knew that the customer value of their technologies was very high because customers actually tried to purchase the prototypes. As a result, they decided to found spinoff companies so that they could sell products and services derived from their inventions. For example, the founder of an MIT robotics spinoff explains, 'In the course of demo-ing to a lot of people, I found two or three who said they would actually buy it. I just came up with a price and they were still interested in buying it.'

Similarly, the founder of an MIT software spinoff describes how he knew his technology had value to customers:

> I took my prototype to Singapore for a conference and showed it to some practitioners in the field and they got very excited. That gave me the information that this would be pretty useful to a lot of people. Then I took it to a large trade show and I made a little brochure about it. I got people to come over to my hotel room because I couldn't afford a booth on site. A bunch of professors and stuff came over and they started jumping up and down and said, 'I want one, how much is it?' It was the reaction of all these potential customers who were just floored by the thing and said, 'I will definitely buy one if this could be a product.

In a few cases, inventors started companies because their efforts to purchase the same technology proved impossible, demonstrating to them the presence of a clear market need. Figuring that other potential customers had the same unfulfilled need as they did, the inventors created a new product or service to satisfy that need and started a company to offer that product or service to others. For example, the founder of one MIT software spinoff explains,

> In some sense we were the customer in our own group when I saw a need in our own group for such a device. Had it existed I would have bought the device to verify our own chip. We faced the same issues like industry. They made chips, just like we made chips.

SIGNIFICANT TECHNICAL ADVANCES

For a technology to be appropriate to the founding of a spinoff company, it also needs to be a significant advance in a scientific field (Del Campo *et al.*, 1999). The technology needs to be cutting edge and not duplicative of previous technologies, for two reasons. First, a spinoff needs a technology that will have significant economic value, and technologies which make a greater technical advance have greater economic value (Harhoff *et al.*, 1999). Without a technology that has significant economic value, a potential entrepreneur cannot justify starting a company to exploit the technology because the profit that the entrepreneur expects will not be greater than the sum of the opportunity cost of alternative activities (Amit *et al.*, 1995), a premium for making an illiquid investment in a new firm (Venkataraman, 1997) and an uncertainty premium (Khilstrom and Laffont, 1979). Most inventions make too small a technical advance to justify the investment of financial and human resources that starting a firm demands (Shane, 2001a).

Second, when technology is far advanced technically, relative to what established companies are doing at the time, it is hard to license the technology to them. If the gap between the technology that the established firm is currently using and the technology that the inventor has created is too great for managers in established firms to understand the new technology, the inventor cannot persuade them of the value of changing technologies. As a result, inventors have to found spinoffs as a way to commercialize the technology. Only through the creation of products and services can the inventors convince established firms that an invention that makes a major technical advance should be adopted. For example, the founder of one MIT mechanical device spinoff explains that he started a company when his efforts to license them to established companies failed because the

> patents were too far advanced from what the companies were doing at the time. What happened was that there was a fair amount of interest from the machine tool companies but the inventions were really on the very high end of performance at the

time. They were too far ahead and industry wasn't ready for it. There were a lot of nibbles but no takers.

Moreover, even when the managers in an established company understand the potential of a new technology, the inventors face the difficulty of overcoming the 'not-invented-here' syndrome, which leads the managers in established companies to underestimate the value of the university inventions. As a result, the university often fails to license the invention to established companies, leading inventors to found companies as a way to commercialize significant technical advances. The founder of one MIT software spinoff explains,

> Trying to convince somebody on the outside of the value of this technology which is out in front of the marketplace is much more difficult than starting a company. You'd have to find somebody that had equivalent products in the marketplace or aspirations to do that, which means that you already have in house people who say to their bosses, 'Oh yes, they have an interesting thing there but we can do that inside.' So that becomes very difficult.

One large sample statistical study provides empirical support for the proposition that spinoffs are more likely when university inventions are more significant technical advances. Shane (2001a) examined the hazard of firm formation for the 1397 MIT-assigned patents between 1980 and 1996 and found that more technically important inventions were more likely to be exploited by spinoffs.

TECHNOLOGIES WITH STRONG INTELLECTUAL PROPERTY PROTECTION

A final dimension of university technology that facilitates the creation of spinoffs is strong intellectual property protection (Nelsen, 1991). Strong intellectual property protection is important for spinoff companies because it is the only competitive advantage available to a new firm at the time when the company is first created. When a new firm is founded, it does not have advantages based on superior manufacturing or marketing and distribution, which allow it to out-compete other firms (Teece, 1987). Thus the existence of strong intellectual property protection enables the founder of the spinoff to build the value chain for the new firm before competitors have copied its new technology. In general, spinoffs are more likely to be founded when a large portfolio of broad scope patents[5] protects an invention.

Portfolio of Patents

Spinoffs are more likely to be founded to exploit a technology if the invention yields several interlocking patents that build a wall of protection around it.[6] Interlocking patents are important to spinoffs because they allow the companies to control more of the technology necessary to exploit an invention. This characteristic is important because spinoffs have many disadvantages when competing with established firms in the market place.

My interviews with founders of MIT spinoffs illustrate the importance of large patent portfolios to the founding of university spinoffs. For instance, the CEO of one biotechnology spinoff explains how the establishment of a portfolio of patents was central to the founding of that firm. He says,

> The company originally was set up as an independent entity based on inventions from University of Illinois at Chicago. However, just before they were about to bring the money in, the due diligence showed that there were a couple of patents, including the MIT patent that demonstrated that the original intellectual property from the University of Illinois was probably not going to be sufficient to fully protect the use of the gene for gene therapy, and there was some hesitancy about actually going forward with starting the company. So at the end of the day, we decided that the two key patents were the one from Illinois and the one from MIT and so we started with those.

Because patent portfolios are so important to the establishment of university spinoffs, entrepreneurs interested in creating spinoff companies often shop around at several universities to create the right patent portfolio: that is, a portfolio which is strong enough to justify the establishment of a spinoff. For example, the founder of one of the MIT biotechnology spinoffs explains that he established a strong portfolio of 30 patent families that included 19 patents on cell death from eight universities so that he could found a firm.

The importance of patent portfolios to the founding of university spinoffs is not limited to biotechnology. The founders of university spinoffs exploiting other types of technologies described similar patterns. For example, the founder of one MIT materials spinoff describes the importance of assembling a patent portfolio across several universities his decision to found a firm:

> I got the processes and know how to make diamond thin films from Penn State. MIT Lincoln Laboratories knew how boron doping is done in films and also had the patent portfolio in another area. Another department at Lincoln Laboratory had the knowledge for the p-type of semiconductor and some friends out at UCLA had invented a process for making a certain type of millimeter wave device. From an expert at UCLA, I got the technology on how to make the right substrate on which to grow diamond. So what I did was put together knowledge from MIT, Lincoln Labs, Penn State and UCLA. I went out and systematically put together

license agreements with MIT, Lincoln Labs, Penn State and UCLA and I actually ended up holding the entire intellectual property for this whole package of technologies.

A large sample study by Wallmark (1997) also supports the observation that having a portfolio of patents is important to the creation of university spinoffs. This study found that many of the spinoffs of Chalmers Institute of Technology occurred after inventors spent many years conducting research and developing a family of patents that together formed strong intellectual property protection for a spinoff.

Broad Scope Patents

Spinoffs are also more common when patents are broad in scope because broad scope patents allow a spinoff to block competitors from exploiting the same technology that they exploit, providing a stronger competitive advantage. The broader the scope of the patent, the more likely it will be that competing products and services will infringe the patent and the more effective the intellectual property will be (Merges and Nelson, 1990).

The data that I collected on the MIT spinoffs provides support for the proposition that spinoffs are more likely to exploit broad scope patents than to exploit narrow scope patents. For instance, Lita Nelsen, the Director of the MIT Technology-Licensing Office explains that, for an entrepreneur to establish a spinoff successfully, there should be few competing patents to the technology that the spinoff will exploit:

> If there aren't competing patents that are very similar to our invention or someone else doesn't hold the dominating patent, we are in good shape for startup. It's a good situation if we do a patent search and there aren't patents out there. However, if another patent is already covering so much of the field that we can only get a very narrow claim that someone can design around, it's not very good. The invention needs to be early and the patents strong enough to dominate the field.

Many of the founders of MIT spinoffs that I interviewed pointed out the importance of broad intellectual property protection in their decision to found a company to exploit the invention. For example, in the case of one mechanical device spinoff, the founders explained that they decided to create a spinoff company once patent counsel told them that they would be able to obtain broad scope patents on their inventions. Similarly, the founder of a biotechnology spinoff explains that she considered it worthwhile to found that company once her patent attorney indicated that the patents on the technology would have broad claims and would not infringe other parties' patents.

Of particular importance in defining whether a patent is broad and therefore supportive of a spinoff is the scope of the first claim. Several of the founders of MIT spinoffs indicated that the strength of the first claim on the patent is important in the decision to establish a spinoff. For instance, the founder of one mechanical device spinoff explains, 'It was a broad patent. You read the first claim and it's not covering any specific embodiment. It's just covering the basic concept and so there's not any way to get around the basic concept.'

Similarly, the inventor of a software technology that led to the founding of a successful MIT spinoff emphasizes the importance of the first patent claim on that technology in motivating the formation of the spinoff. He says, 'I have a lot of patent experience. I have a lot of patents myself and I serve as an expert witness on a lot of patent cases. This was an extremely broad and powerful patent. Claim one is breathtaking.'

One large sample statistical study also supports the proposition that broad patents encourage the formation of university spinoffs. Shane (2001a) examined the hazard of firm formation for the 1397 MIT-assigned patents which led to the formation of new companies between 1980 and 1996 and found that that broader scope patents were more likely than narrower scope patents to be exploited by new firms.

SUMMARY

This chapter has examined the types of technologies that lead to the formation of university spinoffs. Because established firms have a variety of advantages in commercializing technology, only a small percentage of university inventions are appropriate for creating spinoffs. Research shows that radical, tacit, early stage and general-purpose technologies, which provide significant value to customers, represent major technical advances and have strong intellectual property protection, are more likely to provide the basis for a spinoff than other technologies.

Radical inventions are more likely than incremental innovations to lead to the formation of university spinoffs because radical inventions cannibalize existing assets, undermine existing organizational competencies and are often rejected by managers in existing companies. Spinoff companies are more common when the knowledge needed to exploit a technology is tacit than when it is codified. Tacit knowledge makes it difficult for anyone other than the inventor to understand how to commercialize the technology; and spinoffs are a better vehicle than established firms for securing inventor involvement in the exploitation process. Moreover, tacitness of knowledge leads managers in established companies to believe that an invention does not work, causing them to reject the technology.

Early stage inventions lead to the formation of spinoffs because 'unproven' technology cannot easily be licensed to established firms. First, managers of established companies, like most people, find it difficult to see the value of unproven technology. Second, the managers of established companies are often not interested in early stage technology because they are focused on enhancing returns from existing operations. Third, the managers of established companies prefer to buy already developed technologies rather than to develop these technologies themselves, because their firms are often not very good at full-scale product development. Fourth, inventors find it difficult to communicate information about early stage technology to others. Fifth, inventors find it difficult to reap any value from licensing early stage inventions. Sixth, established companies have time horizons that are too short to undertake the development of early stage technology.

Spinoffs tend to exploit general-purpose technologies, or basic inventions with broad applications in many fields of use. General-purpose technologies offer multiple market applications, allowing entrepreneurs to change direction if the first application turns out to have limited value. Moreover, established companies have trouble identifying what to do with general-purpose technologies, given the different market applications and stages of the value chain at which they can be applied.

Spinoffs are more likely to be formed when a new technology generates significant value for the customer than when it does not because significant customer value attracts external entrepreneurs to license the technology and because it motivates inventors to turn into entrepreneurs. Demonstrating the value of new technology to customers is much more important for spinoff formation than for licensing to established firms because established companies can use new technology to improve their own operations and because their existing activities allow them to benefit from marginal improvements to products and services.

Inventions that represent major technical advances are more likely to be exploited by spinoffs because spinoffs require technologies that have significant economic value, which major technical advances offer. Moreover, when technology is far advanced technically relative to what established companies are doing at the time, it is hard to license the technology to them.

A final dimension of university technology that facilitates the creation of spinoffs is strong intellectual property protection because the existence of such protection enables the founder of a spinoff to build the value chain for the new firm before competitors have copied its new technology. Therefore spinoffs are most likely to exploit technologies that are patentable, particularly those that can be protected by a portfolio of broad scope patents.

Having described the types of technologies that lead to the founding of spinoffs, I now turn to a discussion of the industries in which spinoffs tend to be founded, the subject of Chapter 7.

NOTES

1. As the founder of one MIT mechanical spinoff explains, 'I realized that there was interest at companies like GE, but I also realized that's not how things work at major corporations. You don't join by bringing in a project like this.'
2. The founder of an MIT biotechnology spinoff explains that he did not license his technology to an established firm but founded a company instead because 'people saw the market, but they said, "It's ten years away." So it wasn't valuable at the time.'
3. Despite the advantage of new firms at the development of early stage technologies, some time horizons are too long for even spinoffs to pursue. As a result, many founders of university spinoff companies explain that they acted to commercialize only those inventions that showed a clear commercialization path, which could be achieved in a reasonable amount of time. For example, an MIT inventor whose technology led to the founding of a software spinoff explains his decision to found a company to exploit certain of his inventions, but not others. He says, 'The reason this software led to a start-up and my previous ones didn't was that the other technology just seemed farther off. In the long run a lot of people might want the other software but it's kind of farther off. It's much less obvious what the path is to making a commercial product out of it. So it's much less compelling of a product possibility. It was less obvious who would buy it, why they would buy it, and what it would be coupled with.' Similarly, an MIT inventor who founded a software spinoff explains his decision to found a firm. He says, 'I've done a fair bit of things along the way but many of the other things were very futuristic. Going into it I did not see a commercial application right away. But this thing was compact enough, crisp enough that I could see an immediate market and an immediate need for it. I could see how to turn this into a company and so I decided to go ahead with putting something together.'
4. Of course, other factors also lead external entrepreneurs to choose one technology over another. For example, the founder of one MIT spinoff explains, 'What really got me interested in this technology was that the technology was almost invisible. You could put together a product where you got all kind of advantages from the technology, but the product looked, acted, felt and tasted like the product we were selling through distribution channels today. So it wasn't like a pipe dream that you didn't know where the market was. You didn't know what the product was. You didn't know who was going to sell it. You didn't know who was going to buy it.'
5. Spinoffs are more likely if the invention can be protected by patents rather than by other forms of intellectual property protection. Several sources of data provide support for this proposition. A large sample statistical study by McQueen and Wallmark (1991) reports a strong relationship between patent production and spinoff activity from Swedish universities; technologies that are patentable are much more likely than other technologies to lead to spinoffs. My interviews with founders of MIT spinoffs also support the proposition that spinoffs are more common when an invention can be patented. For instance, one professor of mechanical engineering at MIT describes the decision by his student to found a spinoff once he learned that a patent could protect their joint invention. He says, 'The TLO said it would be possible to patent these software methods and that was news to everybody. [He] thought he could patent something. When he did, he began to think about how he could turn this into something he could do after he graduated.' Furthermore, my interviews with entrepreneurs who came to MIT to shop for technologies to start companies also provide evidence of the importance of patent protection in the decision to found a spinoff company. Many of the external entrepreneurs that I interviewed reported rejecting technologies because they could not obtain the patent protection that they would need. For instance, the founder of an optics spinoff explains that he decided against one MIT technology because 'there wasn't much upside in the technology MIT had. Actually, the upside was in the package and the solution and someone else had the rights to that.'
6. Lita Nelsen, the Director of the MIT Technology Licensing Office confirms the importance of multiple patents to the formation of spinoffs. She explains, 'Large established companies tend to license one invention at a time, but startups are interested in a portfolio of patents.'

7. The industries where spinoffs occur

One notable characteristic of university spinoffs is that they are more likely to be founded and to commercialize technology in certain industries than in other industries. This chapter discusses the variation across industries in the creation of university spinoffs. The first section of the chapter provides empirical evidence of the uneven distribution of spinoffs across industries. The second section discusses why spinoffs are more common in biomedical industries than in other industries. The third section of the chapter identifies specific industry characteristics that are associated with higher rates of spinoff formation. The last section of the chapter discusses why spinoffs are more likely to commercialize university technologies successfully in some industries than in others.

THE UNEVEN DISTRIBUTION OF SPINOFFS ACROSS INDUSTRIES

University spinoffs are not evenly distributed across all high technology industries. Rather, several studies have shown that these firms are concentrated in only a few industries. The most common industry for university spinoffs is biotechnology, followed by computer software. As Table 7.1 shows, more than half of all of the spinoffs founded at MIT between 1980 and 1996 are biotechnology and software companies. Similarly, Sobocinski (1999) found that over two-thirds (68 percent) of new ventures at the University of Wisconsin over the past decade were life sciences firms. Lowe (2002) found that two-thirds of the inventor-founded spinoffs from the University of California system were biotechnology, pharmaceutical or medical device firms. Golub (2003) reports that half of Columbia University's spinoff companies are biomedical firms, with the remainder found in electronics and software, while most of New York University's spinoffs are in the biomedical area, with the rest in software.[1]

Similar patterns have been observed in other countries. In Sweden, for example, Olofsson and Wahlbin (1992) found that 20 percent of university spinoffs are in biotechnology and medicine, 16 percent are in computers, 13 percent are in electronics, and 12 percent are in industrial equipment and

Table 7.1   The industry distribution of MIT spinoffs from 1980 to 1996

Technology	Percentage of spinoffs
Biotechnology	31
Computer hardware	6
Materials	11
Mechanical devices	7
Medical devices	10
Optics/lasers	3
Robotics	4
Semiconductors	4
Software	23

Source: Author's compilation from records of MIT's Technology-Licensing Office.

machinery. In a more focused study of just one Swedish university, Dahlstrand (1997) found that 23 percent of the spinoffs from Chalmers Institute of Technology from 1960 to 1993 were software firms. In France, Mustar (1997) found that 28 percent of the spinoffs were found in biotechnology, and 27 percent were found in computer science and software engineering.

WHY ARE SPINOFFS SO COMMON IN BIOMEDICAL INDUSTRIES?

As Table 7.2 summarizes, several possible explanations have been offered for biomedical inventions being fertile grounds for the creation of spinoffs. One explanation lies in the nature of the science itself, with the collapsed discovery process in biotechnology allowing basic academic research to yield directly commercializable outcomes, as opposed to requiring the technology first to be put into a form that can be turned into a product or service (Miner *et al.*, 2001). This collapsed discovery process means that university

Table 7.2   Why biomedical inventions are likely to generate spinoffs

Collapsed discovery process
Long product development horizons
Locus of expertise in technology creation in universities
Focus of customers on product efficacy rather than on cost
Discrete nature of biomedical inventions
Strong patent protection

researchers in biotechnology are not as severely handicapped by a lack of market expertise as are researchers in the physical sciences.

A second explanation lies in the commercialization horizon in the physical sciences. Ku (2001) explains that university spinoffs are a better commercialization vehicle in the life sciences than in the physical sciences because the commercialization time horizon is much longer. She argues that product development cycles of 18 months in the physical sciences are too short for university spinoffs. Because university inventions are typically very early stage technologies at the time of invention, they require significant amounts of subsequent development time before they can be brought to market. In industries in which product development times are relatively short, spinoffs are unable to raise capital from private markets, contract with suppliers or customers, or attract other stakeholders, who have expectations of short product development cycles (Ku, 2001).

A third explanation for the disproportionate likelihood that biomedical inventions will lead to spinoffs lies in the expertise of universities in the creation of biomedical inventions. In contrast to technologies like computer software, where the true technical experts are often employed in industry, the concentration of biomedical expertise lies in universities (Kenney, 1986). As a result, university researchers invent a much larger percentage of patented technologies in biomedical fields than in other domains; and this ability to produce more valuable and useful technology facilitates the creation of biomedical spinoffs.

The example of molecular biology is a case in point. Before 1976, molecular biology was not a part of the domain of the pharmaceutical industry, which employed mostly biochemists and microbiologists (Kenney, 1986). The development of rDNA changed the importance of molecular biology to the pharmaceutical industry (Matkin, 1990). Because almost all the experts capable of making use of this new technology for commercial purposes were found in academia, professors and graduate students had strong incentives to form companies to take advantage of their knowledge (Kenney, 1986). In fact, Zucker *et al*. (1998b) have found that the biotechnological expertise of academic researchers is directly related to the formation of biotechnology spinoffs.

Two pieces of empirical evidence support the proposition that spinoffs are more common in fields in which the locus of expertise in technology creation lies in universities rather than in the private sector. First, Hsu and Bernstein (1997) report that the importance of universities to the creation of technology in an industry was an important factor in enhancing the formation of spinoffs from MIT and Harvard, and made spinoffs in biomedical fields prevalent at both those institutions. Second, Shane (2001b) examined the frequency with which the 1397 MIT-assigned patents led to the formation of new companies between 1980 and 1996. He found a significant positive effect of the proportion of university patents in a three-digit patent class on the likelihood that a patent would be a firm formation patent. That is, spinoffs were most common in technology classes in which universities accounted for the largest proportion of patented inventions.

A fourth explanation for the tendency of spinoff companies to be found in the biomedical area lies in the decision-making criteria of potential customers. In the biomedical area, customers tend to prefer the product that is most efficacious, regardless of cost. However, in the physical sciences, customers often trade off cost for efficacy. For example, spinoffs that create the most effective cure for cancer are more likely to find a ready market than spinoffs that generate the fastest supercomputer. Conditional on their approval by insurers, medical professionals typically select drugs and other medical treatments on the basis of efficacy. However, customers of supercomputers are much more likely to incorporate price into their purchasing decisions. Universities tend to be much more successful at generating cutting edge products that can provide solutions which previously were not possible than they are at creating the most efficient new technologies. Because university personnel have significant expertise in research, but lack expertise in product development, manufacturing and marketing, they are biased toward generating the best technical solution rather than the most efficient one. Therefore spinoffs are typically more successful with biomedical inventions than with other types of inventions.

A fifth explanation for the tendency of spinoff companies to be found in the biomedical area lies in the discrete nature of biomedical inventions. Biomedical technologies can often be used independently of other pieces of technology. For instance, a cancer drug can be used independently of other inventions developed by established pharmaceutical companies. In contrast, an automobile ignition system cannot be used in the absence of other inventions established by automobile companies. Because of the discreteness of biomedical technologies, spinoffs that commercialize these technologies can often do so regardless of the technologies used by established firms. In contrast, many physical science inventions require complementary technologies to be effective. Frequently, these complementary technologies are under the control of established firms, making it difficult for new firms to exploit their technologies without first creating a partnership with the established company that controls the existing technology. For example, new firms find it difficult to exploit an automobile engine invention without first having access to complementary technologies in automobile production. In contrast, new firms find it relatively easy to exploit a drug invention because new drugs can be implemented independently of the other technologies employed by pharmaceutical firms.

A sixth explanation for biomedical inventions being more likely to generate spinoffs than other inventions is that biomedical inventions are more easily protected against competitor imitation by patents than other types of inventions. Patents are particularly effective at protecting biotechnology inventions because patents only protect a particular approach to solving a technical problem, not solutions to the problem in general (Levin *et al.*, 1987). Therefore, when multiple solutions to technical problems are possible, patents are relatively weak. Patents on drugs and other pharmaceuticals are relatively strong because a slight change in molecular structure radically alters the efficacy of drugs. In contrast, patents on electrical devices are relatively weak because even a major change in electrical circuitry often has very little effect on the workings of an electrical device.

SPECIFIC INDUSTRY CHARACTERISTICS THAT PROMOTE SPINOFFS

In addition to explaining why spinoffs are more likely in biomedical industries than in other industries, researchers have explored specific industry characteristics that encourage university spinoffs. Among the dimensions that they have identified are the effectiveness of patents in an industry, the importance of complementary assets in marketing, distribution and manufacturing, the age of the industry, the degree of market segmentation in an industry and the average firm size in the industry. The effect of each of these dimensions on the likelihood of spinoff company formation is discussed in the subsections below.

Effectiveness of Patents in an Industry

Spinoffs are more common in industries in which patents are more effective. In industries with strong patents, firm founders can establish the value chain necessary to exploit a new technology before knowledge of how to imitate it is diffused to competitors (Teece, 1987). Moreover, strong patents facilitate the process of raising capital from financial institutions, which is important for new firms that lack cash flow from existing operations (Lerner, 1994). Furthermore, strong patents also allow new firms to adapt technologies to market needs before competitors can imitate them, even if there is technological or market uncertainty that prevents the initial identification of the correct market application (Teece, 1987). Finally, strong patents allow new firms to maintain a differentiation strategy, permitting them to compete effectively with large, established firms that have economies of scale and other production cost advantages over them (Shane, 2001b).

Two pieces of empirical evidence support the proposition that industries in which patents are more effective have more spinoff activity. First, Hsu and

Bernstein (1997) report that the strength of patent protection in a technical field is important in explaining the willingness of entrepreneurs to found spin-off companies from MIT and Harvard. Second, Shane (2001b) examined the frequency with which the 1397 MIT-assigned patents led to the formation of new companies between 1980 and 1996 and found that, the stronger patent protection was in an industry, the more likely it was that an MIT patent in that industry would be exploited by a spinoff.

Complementary Assets in Marketing, Distribution and Manufacturing

Spinoffs are relatively infrequent in industries in which the magnitude of complementary assets in manufacturing, marketing and distribution is very large. In industries in which these complementary assets are important, spin-offs find these assets difficult to obtain (Shane, 2001b). Established firms tend to obtain control over these assets, particularly if they are specialized with the new technology because this specialization creates asset specificity. Asset specificity, in turn, causes bargaining problems when market mechanisms are used to govern the exchange of assets (Williamson, 1985). As a result, established firms obtain control over these assets and the vertical integration of the value chain makes it difficult for new firms to obtain them, except by building them from scratch, which is a costly endeavor (Teece, 1987).

One empirical study provides support for the proposition that industries with a greater reliance on complementary assets in manufacturing, marketing and distribution have fewer university spinoffs than other industries. Shane (2001b) examined the frequency with which the 1397 MIT-assigned patents led to the formation of new companies between 1980 and 1996 and found that, the more important complementary assets in marketing and distribution were in an industry, the less likely it was that a patent in that industry would be exploited by a spinoff.

Age of the Technical Field

Spinoffs are more common in industries with a younger technology base. Researchers have provided three explanations. First, when the technical base of an industry is young, the amount of accumulated knowledge necessary to compete in the industry is relatively small, as the knowledge has been developed for a relatively short period of time (Shane, 2001b). Because established firms develop an advantage by making use of technical knowledge for a longer period of time, the older the technical knowledge in an industry, the greater is the advantage of older firms, and the harder it is for new firms to enter an industry (Nelson, 1995). Second, as the technological base of an industry matures, the basis for competition shifts. Product innovation, which is paramount when the technological base is young, becomes less important as the technological base ages, and process innovation and efforts to lower production costs become more central (Pavitt and Wald, 1971). Because new firms are disadvantaged at process innovation relative to established firms, the competitive advantages of new firms decline as the technological base of an industry ages (Shane, 2001b). Third, established companies tend to acquire the complementary assets necessary to exploit a technology in an industry. Thus, as the technological base of an industry ages, these assets become more and more difficult for new firms to obtain (Teece, 1987).

One empirical study provides support for the proposition that spinoffs are more common in industries with a younger technological base. Shane's (2001b) examination of the frequency with which the 1397 MIT-assigned patents led to the formation of new companies between 1980 and 1996 showed that, the older the class to which a patent was assigned by the US Patent and Trademark Office, the less likely invention in that technical field was to be exploited by a university spinoff.

Market Segmentation

University spinoffs are more common in markets that are segmented. In general, new technologies tend to be exploited first in small market segments by new firms because new technologies begin with limited reliability and relatively high costs, requiring their exploiters to focus on the segments in which the advantages of the technology are greatest (Utterback and Kim, 1984). After the initial advantage of new technologies is demonstrated in the initial segments, the technologies spread to the mainstream of the market (Christiansen and Bower, 1996).

Large, established firms allocate their resources to satisfy the demands of their major customers (Christiansen and Bower, 1996). Because the initial market segments tend to be small, and do not generally include mainstream customers, established firms cede these segments to new firms with low opportunity costs (Shane, 2001b). As a result, in segmented markets, new firms can often enter successfully before facing competition from established firms. In unsegmented markets, however, new firms face immediate competition from established firms who are focused on meeting the needs of their major customers who are present in the markets targeted by new firms (Christiansen and Bower, 1996). Consequently, new technologies are more difficult to exploit through the creation of new firms in markets that do not tend toward segmentation than in markets that do.

One empirical study provides support for the proposition that spinoffs are more common in industries that are more heavily segmented. Shane (2001b) examined the frequency with which the 1397 MIT-assigned patents led to the formation of new companies between 1980 and 1996 and found that, the greater the segmentation of a market, the more likely a university invention in that market was to be exploited by a spinoff.

Average Firm Size

Spinoffs are less common in industries in which firms tend to be of large average size. Researchers have offered two explanations for this pattern. First, large average firm size means that the minimum efficient scale in an industry is relatively high, raising the cost of entry, and inhibiting that activity (Audretsch, 1995). The cost of entry is higher in these industries because new firms typically enter industries at less than minimum efficient scale and so must operate for a time less efficiently than established firms, and have to grow more to reach an efficient size (Shane, 2001a).

Second, large average firm size in an industry means that new firms need to raise a significant amount of external capital to begin operations. Because capital is so expensive for new firms to obtain, this requirement discourages spinoff companies from entering these industries. For example, industries like software and expert systems have a large number of spinoffs because the capital needs of new businesses in these industries are small, but industries like chemicals or steel making are too capital-intensive for spinoffs. Capital-intensive industries require so much investment to exploit new technologies that only established companies can pursue opportunities in those industries (Wilson and Szygenda, 1991).[2]

One empirical study provides support for the proposition that spinoffs are less common in industries of larger average firm size. Shane (2001a) examined the hazard of firm formation for the 1397 MIT-assigned patents between 1980 and 1996 and found that larger average firm size in an industry reduced the likelihood of a spinoff being formed to exploit an MIT patent.

INDUSTRIES WHERE SPINOFFS COMMERCIALIZE TECHNOLOGY

Some research has also examined the industries in which spinoffs are most likely to commercialize university technology. This research has shown that three industry characteristics enhance the ability of spinoffs to commercialize university inventions: number of firms in the industry, the manufacturing intensity of the industry and the effectiveness of patents in the industry.

Number of Firms in the Industry

Spinoffs are better at commercializing university inventions in industries with more firms, for two reasons. First, when there are large numbers of firms in an industry, market uncertainty is greater (Cohen and Klepper, 1992). Because new firms find it easier to change markets than established companies, which have an existing customer base that constrains them (Christensen and Bower, 1996), they are better able to manage this uncertainty. Second, when spinoffs enter markets with a large number of firms, there are few established competitors with the ability to drive them out of business before they have established a beachhead (Romanelli, 1989). As a result, the new firms can invest in the development and commercialization of their technologies relatively unimpeded by the actions of large competitors. However, when an industry is composed of a small number of firms, new firm commercialization efforts immediately threaten the customer base of established firms, which use their resources to respond by competing with the new firm before it has developed and commercialized its new technology.

One empirical study provides support for the proposition that spinoffs are better than established firms at commercializing university inventions in industries composed of more firms than in industries composed of fewer firms. Shane and Katila (2002) examined the likelihood of commercialization of the 964 MIT inventions licensed to private firms between 1980 and 1996 and found that spinoff companies were better than established companies at commercializing the university inventions in industries that were composed of a larger number of firms.

Manufacturing Value-added in the Industry

Spinoffs are worse at commercializing inventions in industries in which more of the value-added created by those firms comes from manufacturing, for two reasons. First, the information developed from current operations in manufacturing facilitates innovation (Gort and Klepper, 1982) because commercialization often involves use of both manufacturing and research expertise, as is the case when manufacturing engineers and research scientists work together to scale up biotechnology processes (Pisano, 1991). As Teece and Pisano (1994: 540) explain, 'Entrepreneurial activity cannot lead to the immediate replication of unique organization skills through simply entering a market and piecing the parts together overnight. Replication takes time, and the replication of best practice may be illusive.' Thus established firms have an advantage over new firms in the commercialization of technology in industries that require manufacturing knowledge.

Second, spinoffs do not possess the specialized complementary assets in manufacturing that facilitate innovation in manufacturing-intensive industries and so have to build or contract for them before they can commercialize new technologies (Teece, 1987). The time, expertise and cost that it takes to create these assets hinder cash-constrained new firms that lack the tacit knowledge of manufacturing developed through existing operations, and gives an advantage to established firms in manufacturing-intensive industries (Teece, 1998). Furthermore, contracting for these assets is a problem for new firms because they lack the reputation to provide non-contractual safeguards against opportunism (Williamson, 1985).

One empirical study provides support for the proposition that spinoffs are worse at commercializing inventions in industries with more manufacturing value-added. Shane and Katila (2002) examined the likelihood of commercialization of the 964 MIT inventions licensed to private firms between 1980 and 1996 and found that spinoff companies were worse than established companies at commercializing the university inventions in industries that had more manufacturing value-added.

Effectiveness of Patents in the Industry

Although research has not shown that the effectiveness of patents in an industry has a direct effect on the commercialization of university technology by spinoff companies, it has shown that patent effectiveness influences the likelihood of technology commercialization by an important subset of these companies – inventor-founded spinoffs. Research has demonstrated that spinoffs founded by inventors are better at commercializing university inventions in industries in which patents are relatively ineffective (Shane, 2002). When patent protection is relatively weak, markets for knowledge do not work well because moral hazard, adverse selection and hold-up problems plague transactions between buyers and sellers (Arrow, 1962). Fearing that buyers will take advantage of them, sellers engage in actions such as providing limited disclosure or establishing complex contracts that make it difficult to consummate deals effectively when patents are weak (Shane, 2002).

However, strong patent protection allows knowledge to be sold effectively to non-inventors (Arrow, 1962). In general, non-inventors are better at commercialization of university inventions than inventors. Because university inventors focus on academic research, they have much less knowledge of marketing, manufacturing and product development, all of which help firms to commercialize new technology, making non-inventor licensees better at commercializing university inventions than inventor licensees, as long as patent protection is strong enough to permit effective sales of technology to non-inventors (Shane, 2002).

One empirical study provides support for the proposition that inventor-founded spinoffs are better than other firms at commercializing university inventions when patent protection in an industry is relatively ineffective. Shane (2002) examined the commercialization of 966 licenses to MIT inventions from 1980 to 1996 and found that inventor–licensees were more likely than non-inventor--licensees to commercialize inventions (achieve first sale) when patents were less effective in a line of business.

SUMMARY

This chapter has discussed the variation across industries in the creation of university spinoffs. A variety of studies have shown that university spinoffs are most common in biomedical industries, for several reasons. First, the collapsed discovery process in biotechnology allows basic academic research to yield directly commercializable outcomes. Second, the commercialization time horizon in the life sciences is much longer than in the physical sciences, allowing time for university inventions to be developed and brought to market by new firms. Third, universities are the locus of expertise in the life sciences, leading university inventors to found biotechnology firms to earn rents on their intellectual capital. Fourth, in the biomedical area, customers prefer products that are most efficacious, regardless of cost, a condition that favors spinoffs, which are relatively inefficient producers of new technology products and services. Fifth, biomedical inventions tend to be discrete, allowing spinoffs to commercialize them, regardless of the technologies under the control of established firms. Sixth, biomedical inventions are typically protected by strong patents, which provide an important source of competitive advantage that facilitates the formation of new companies.

In addition to explaining why biomedical inventions are more likely than other inventions to lead to spinoffs, researchers have explored specific industry characteristics that encourage the formation of university spinoffs. Spinoffs are more common in industries in which patents are more effective because strong patents allow firm founders to establish the value chain to exploit their technology opportunities before knowledge of them is dispersed to competitors. Spinoffs are less common in industries that require a large amount of complementary assets in manufacturing, marketing and distribution because obtaining control over complementary assets is difficult for new firms. Spinoffs are more common in industries with a younger technology base because established firms become relatively more advantaged as the technology base of an industry ages. Spinoffs are more common in markets that are more segmented because new firms can enter these industries and obtain a foothold before established firms respond to their entry. Spinoffs are less common in industries with larger average firm size because minimum efficient scale is high in industries with large average firm size, making new, small firms relatively less efficient in these industries, and because new firms need to raise a significant amount of external capital to begin operations in capital-intensive industries.

Some research has also explored the conditions under which spinoffs are better than established firms at commercializing university inventions. Spinoffs are better at commercializing university inventions in industries with more firms because markets with a large number of firms have fewer established competitors with the ability to drive new firms out of business before they have established a beachhead. Moreover, spinoffs are worse at commercializing inventions in industries in which more of the value-added comes from manufacturing because the information developed from current operations facilitates innovation in these industries. Furthermore, non-inventor founded spinoffs are better at commercializing university inventions in industries in which patents are relatively effective because strong patent protection facilitates the sale of technology to non-inventors, who are better than university inventors at technology commercialization.

Having described the industries in which spinoffs tend to be founded, I now turn to a discussion of the role of people in university spinoffs, the subject of Chapter 8.

NOTES

1. The proportion of biomedical firms may be rising while the proportion of software firms may be falling. Many earlier studies indicated that computer software was the most common industry for university spinoffs. For instance, Smilor *et al.* (1990) found that 43.5 percent of the 23 technology spinoffs from the University of Texas were in computer software.
2. One venture capitalist that funded several MIT spinoffs explains, 'In capital-intensive business there is no way for a company to exploit the technology, develop the market, and create support channels. So they are not appropriate for spinoffs.'

8. The role of people in university spinoffs

University spinoffs do not form spontaneously, but take place in response to the actions of enterprising individuals who decide that university technology is worthy of exploitation through the formation of new companies. This chapter explores the role of people in the university spinoff process. The first section of the chapter discusses the importance of inventors in the decision to create a spinoff, whether or not the inventor is the entrepreneur who leads the effort to found the new firm. The second section of the chapter distinguishes between different types of spinoffs as a function of the different people who lead the efforts to found new firms: those spinoffs whose formation is led by inventors, those spinoffs whose founding is led by external entrepreneurs and those spinoffs whose formation is led by investors.

Although external entrepreneurs and investors are important actors who drive the firm formation process, accounting for the founding of more than half of all university spinoffs, almost all the research on the role of people in university spinoffs has focused on inventor–entrepreneurs. For that reason, the remainder of the chapter focuses on inventors who lead the efforts to found spinoffs. The third section of the chapter discusses the role of the inventor in the decision to create inventor-founded spinoffs. The fourth section of the chapter discusses the effect of different inventor attributes on the likelihood that university spinoffs will be founded. Specifically, it considers the role of the inventors' motivations and career experience in the spinoff formation decision.

THE IMPORTANCE OF INTERESTED INVENTORS

The inventor of a university technology plays an important role in determining whether a spinoff will be founded to exploit an invention. In addition to the obvious point that inventors are important when they decide to found companies to exploit their own inventions, several observers have noted that inventors are also important when other people are the entrepreneurs who lead the efforts to found spinoffs. As explained in Chapter 6, the early stage of technological development at which most university inventions are licensed, and the tacitness of the knowledge that underlies these inventions, mean that inventor involvement is central to spinoff company development. Therefore, for spinoffs to be founded, the inventors of the technology must want a company to be formed (Nelsen, 1991). As Lita Nelsen, the director of the MIT Technology Licensing Office explains, 'We start companies when professors want to start companies. That doesn't mean that the person has to leave MIT, but they have to be enthusiastic about the process, helping to raise the money, that kind of thing. If they're not, then forget it.'

Several pieces of scholarly research support the proposition that inventor interest in spinoffs is central to their formation. Survey evidence of spinoff company activity in the United Kingdom consistently shows that the presence of a committed entrepreneur is crucial to the formation of spinoff firms (Wright *et al.*, 2002). Moreover, Blair and Hitchens (1998) examined the formation of spinoffs from a variety of UK institutions and found that, in almost all cases, spinoffs occurred when an inventor was enthusiastic about starting a new firm.

INVENTOR–ENTREPRENEURS, TECHNOLOGY LICENSING OFFICE SHOPPERS AND INVESTORS

Inventors do not lead the effort to establish all university spinoffs. Rather, the efforts to create these companies are led by three primary groups of people: the inventors of the technologies (inventor-led spinoffs), external entrepreneurs interested in founding companies who license university inventions through technology licensing offices (shopper-led spinoffs) and investors who bring together technology and entrepreneurs (investor-led spinoffs). Take, for instance, three examples of biotechnology spinoffs. The first company, Genetic Systems, was a technology licensing office shopper-led spinoff, created in 1980 when two business people, David and Isaac Blech, approached professor Robert Nowinski to use his inventions as the basis of a new biotechnology company (Kenney, 1986). The second company, Hybritech, was an inventor-led spinoff, established in 1978 when two academics at the University of California, San Diego, Norman Birndorf and Ivor Royston, approached Brook Byers, a venture capitalist with Kleiner Perkins (Kenney, 1986). The third company, Xenometrix was an investor-led spinoff, created when the Castle Group, a venture capital firm, sought out a particular faculty member's research and then found an entrepreneur to lead the formation of a company around it (Lowe, 2002).

These three models of spinoffs all occur with roughly the same frequency, at least at MIT. Research by Roberts and Malone (1996) shows that approximately one-third of the MIT spinoffs fall in each of these categories. Similarly,

Shane and Stuart (2002) confirm these patterns in their study of MIT spinoffs founded between 1980 and 1996.[1]

Although very little research has explored the difference between inventor-led spinoffs, external entrepreneur-led spinoffs and investor-led spinoffs, researchers have identified a few differences between these groups. First, inventor-led spinoffs tend to be more common when intellectual property protection is not very effective, such as when patent protection tends to be weak in an industry (Shane, 2002). As Chapter 6 explained, spinoffs are often used to commercialize university technologies when the knowledge necessary to exploit the invention is tacit and cannot be conveyed easily to others. As a result, the involvement of the inventor is central to the development of the technology, making it difficult to license the invention to other parties. Inventor-led spinoffs are the most common form of spinoff under these circumstances because external entrepreneurs face similar difficulties to established firm licensees in making use of these inventions without the involvement of the inventors.

Moreover, when knowledge is tacit, patents are less effective at protecting knowledge than when knowledge is codified. This means that markets for the sale of technology (to external entrepreneurs) work relatively poorly in situations in which patents are ineffective because of disclosure problems (Shane, 2002). When the seller of a technology cannot be sure that the knowledge that he or she discloses will be protected against appropriation by a prospective buyer, the seller becomes reluctant to disclose how the knowledge works (Arrow, 1962). Given technological uncertainty, the buyer is unwilling to purchase technology without disclosure by the seller of how it works, undermining knowledge markets.

Second, inventor-led spinoffs differ from other types of spinoffs because they are more likely to be established near the university that generated them. This proximity allows the inventor to retain his or her academic employment, a condition that is important to inventor-led spinoffs, but not to spinoffs led by external entrepreneurs or investors (Golub, 2003). Moreover, because they are located near the host university where the inventor is employed, inventor-founded spinoffs are more likely than other types of spinoffs to use university facilities for the further development of their technologies.

Third, investor- and external entrepreneur-led spinoffs are more common in major cities and technology centers, where there is substantial employment of investors and technology managers. Although no research has directly tested this argument, logic suggests that shopping for a new technology at a university technology licensing office will be more frequent in a place where investors and external entrepreneurs are more common than in a place where investors and external entrepreneurs are rare. As a result, technologies that might have remained unlicensed in other locations will be licensed to external entrepreneurs or investor-led spinoffs in these locations.

Fourth, the timing of the founding of inventor-led spinoffs differs from the timing of the founding of other types of spinoffs. Inventor-led spinoffs often occur earlier in the life of university technologies than non-inventor-led spinoffs because they can occur without significant effort on the part of the university to market the technology, an activity that generally does not occur until after patent applications have been filed.

Some empirical evidence supports this proposition about the timing of the formation of inventor-led spinoffs. Roberts (1991b) found that 78 percent of spinoffs that exploited MIT technology as their base had the technology transfer occur immediately upon the founding of the company, and in only one case did the time of technology transfer occur more than 5 to 6 years after company founding. Moreover, data from the MIT Technology Licensing Office that I collected suggest that inventor-founded spinoffs tend to license their inventions prior to patents issuing, largely because the inventors have private information about their inventions. In contrast, external entrepreneur-led spinoffs tend to license their technologies later, often after the patents have been issued, when it is possible for external entrepreneurs to examine the strength of intellectual property protection on the inventions.

Fifth, inventor-led firms are more likely than other types of spinoffs to be founded by part-time entrepreneurs because career goals and university conflict of interest policies often limit the way in which the inventors can interact with their spinoffs after founding them. For instance, Roberts (1991b) compared 32 entrepreneurs who founded spinoff companies based on their MIT technology immediately upon leaving MIT with 93 other entrepreneurs who had once worked at MIT, and found that the founders of the direct spinoff companies were significantly more likely than the other entrepreneurs to start their companies on a part-time basis. Moreover, Roberts (1991a) found that all of the faculty founders of MIT spinoffs that he studied had started their companies on a part-time basis, including such well-known examples as Amar Bose, who started Bose Corporation.

Sixth, external entrepreneur-led firms are more common at universities that generate high numbers of spinoffs as opposed to universities that generate low numbers of spinoffs (Franklin *et al.*, 2001). The explanation for this may lie in the attitudes of licensing officers at the universities that generate the most spinoffs. In a survey of 56 licensing offices in the United Kingdom, Franklin *et al.* (2001) found that licensing officers at the top ten universities for spinoff company formation are significantly more likely than licensing officers at other universities to believe that external entrepreneurs provide the advantages of financial motivation, previous business experience, and social networks, and are significantly less likely to see a problem with the entrepreneur's commitment to the technology or a risk of an outsider using a university asset.

Much more research has been conducted about inventor-led spinoffs (see for example, Roberts, 1991a; Lowe, 2002; Shane and Khurana, 2003; Zucker *et al.*, 1998b) than about other types of university spinoffs. For this reason, the information on the characteristics of entrepreneurs who found university spin-offs is only available for inventor-led spinoffs and therefore the remainder for this chapter focuses on these types of spinoffs.

ENTREPRENEURIAL TYPES

Some evidence suggests that the inventors found university spinoffs because they are 'entrepreneurial types' who have always wanted to start companies, and who use their university inventions as a way to achieve their entrepreneurial goals. For instance, in a large sample statistical study of 1397 MIT inventions patented between 1980 and 1996, Shane and Khurana (2003) showed that 'entrepreneurial type' inventors were more likely to have their inventions exploited by newly founded firms than were other inventors.

In addition, several of the founders of MIT spinoffs that I interviewed explained that they founded spinoff companies because founding companies was something that they had always wanted to do. For example, when asked why he started a biotechnology spinoff to exploit his MIT inventions, one MIT inventor explained, 'I always wanted to start a company. It was always in the back of my mind.' Similarly, another inventor whose technology led to an MIT software spinoff said, 'I've been interested for a very long time in starting companies. I was involved in starting two while still a graduate student. For better or for worse, I think I have an entrepreneurial inclination. I have a long term interest and desire in starting companies.' A third MIT inventor, who founded a materials spinoff, explains,

> I decided in my early teens to start a company. I applied to [MIT's] Sloan [School of Management] and engineering graduate school. I was looking for a research opportunity that would be something to build a business. In fact, I switched to [another] lab because [the professor] had a better understanding of putting science into practical applications.

Finally, the founder of a software spinoff explains,

> I've always been entrepreneurial. I've always run businesses on the side. I own a bunch of condos in Boston that I bought when I was a graduate student and I used to have a little import/export business on the side. I always had in the back of my mind the idea that I might do a company.

THE MOTIVATIONS TO SPIN OFF

The fact that the formation of an important subset of university spinoffs depends, at least in part, on the characteristics of the inventors of the technologies suggests that understanding the motivation of inventors to start companies is important to explaining spinoffs. So why do inventors start companies? Two major categories of explanations have been offered: a psychological explanation in which inventors found companies to put their technology into practice or obtain wealth or independence, and a career-oriented explanation in which inventors found companies because of their career stage at the time of the invention.

Psychological Explanations

A great deal of research by entrepreneurship scholars has shown that entrepreneurs differ from other members of society in their psychological attributes (for a review of this literature, see Shane, 2003). Often researchers have used these differences to infer that these psychological attributes lead entrepreneurs to found companies. Despite the evidence provided by entrepreneurship researchers to show support for psychological explanations of the formation of new companies, the literature on university spinoffs has not explored the effect of psychological characteristics on the formation of inventor-founded spinoffs in any systematic way. Nevertheless, there is a small amount of anecdotal evidence that supports the effect of three psychological attributes that previous researchers have found influence the formation of new companies on the formation of inventor spinoffs: a desire to bring technology into practice, a desire for wealth and a desire for independence.

A Desire to Bring Technology Into Practice
Inventors often start companies because they believe that establishing a spinoff is an effective way to bring their new technologies into practice (Samson and Gurdon, 1993). For example, McQueen and Wallmark (1982) surveyed the founders of spinoffs from the Chalmers Institute of Technology and found that most of them did not found their companies because of a desire to generate wealth, but to fulfill their desire to commercialize their technology.

My interviews with the founders of MIT spinoffs also provide evidence consistent with the observation that many inventors of university technologies found companies because of their desire to bring their technology into practice. For example, the founder of an MIT medical device MIT spinoff explains, 'We wanted involvement and continuing development of the technology. [My co-founder] feels a sort of personal desire to bring to commercialization his efforts in the last dozen years.' Similarly, the founder of an MIT biotechnology spinoff explains that he started a company because

> I, as the inventor, wanted to see this invention get through to a stage of practicality or commercialization. I had a relationship to these discoveries and wanted to be involved in the actual conversion of the early stage intellectual property into something practical.

Several of the MIT inventor–entrepreneurs explained that they did not have confidence that large companies would necessarily develop their technologies once they were licensed. Believing that the established companies might license the technology and fail to commercialize it, the inventors decided to found their own companies instead.[2] For example, the founder of one of the software spinoffs explains,

> We could see that there was more of a market developing for these types of projects and that they would need to be commercialized and distributed so that they could be used effectively by teachers and students. We just didn't want stuff to be researched and then not get used.

Other inventor–entrepreneurs explained that part of their desire to found companies to bring their technologies into practice was a feeling that established company licensees would not involve them very much in the commercialization process. As a result, the inventors felt that it would be difficult for them to fulfill their desire to bring their inventions into practice personally, if the inventions were licensed to established firms. For example, one of the founders of an MIT biotechnology spinoff explains why he and his partner started a company to exploit their inventions. He says, 'As inventors, we wanted to be involved in this development and commercialization. That was very exciting to us. If we licensed it to some other company then we wouldn't necessarily be involved and, if we were, it would just be in a small way.'

Other inventor–entrepreneurs explained that the desire to found spinoffs as a way to bring their technologies into practice is based on a sense that established companies will not move the technology into practice quickly enough because they are not as passionate about the technology as the inventors are. For instance, the founder of one of the MIT biotechnology spinoffs explains,

> One option was to place this technology within a biotechnology company in Maryland. I was too passionate about the science and I did not want to see this science get too remote from me where I could not impact its development, especially at the early stage. I was worried that if I put it in a big pharmaceutical or big biotech company that wasn't as passionate about moving it forward, things were not going to move forward. So I said, 'whatever I can do to have a major impact to move it forward would be better.'

A final part of the inventors' desire to bring the technology into practice through the formation of spinoffs was a desire for quality control. The founder of several MIT biotechnology spinoffs explains why he and his co-inventor did not license one of their inventions to an established company:

> I guess it's a question of how good a job you think they'll do. A lot of this stuff comes down to control. In the end, I had the most faith that we'd do the best job. If you licensed to [a large firm], they might not do a good job at all. In the lab you can control the science.

A Desire for Wealth

Another important psychological attribute that motivates university inventors to found spinoff companies is a desire to get rich. For example, in the case of several MIT spinoffs the inventors explained that they saw their colleagues making money and wanted to do so as well. The founder of one of the MIT semiconductor spinoffs explains, 'I couldn't speak for my partners in all of this, but I think I saw the potential for financial success and I said to myself, "I should start a company." '

Part of the wealth creation motivation for university inventors to establish a spinoff was a realization among the inventors that much more money could be made establishing a successful company than by licensing an invention to an established firm. Several MIT inventor–entrepreneurs described the importance of firm formation for making money from university inventions. For example, the founder of one of the MIT materials spinoffs explains, 'We wanted to do it ourselves because there's a greater potential in terms of financial success rather than simply licensing it.'

Inventors earn significant returns on their inventions only if they found companies because royalties on licenses to university inventions are simply too small to provide a very high return on the invention of university technologies. As a result, inventors need to found companies and take them public if they want to earn large financial returns on their inventions. Several MIT inventor–founders explained that they understood this relationship. For example, the founder of one MIT biotechnology spinoff explains,

> This is the way to make money. If I would license to Pfizer all I would get is the licensing fees plus some consulting fees. The way you make money in this business is to start a company. You take founder's stock not consulting fees. You get the payoff when the company goes public.

A Desire for Independence

A third motivation for an inventor to found a spinoff is a desire for independence. A desire for independence a personality trait which shows that people have a preference for acting alone as opposed to acting in conjunction with others. Much entrepreneurship research has shown that people with a strong desire for independence are more likely to found firms than people with a weak desire for independence (Shane, 2003). While much less research has examined the effect of inventors' desire for independence on the founding of university spinoffs, some evidence does suggest that such a pattern exists. For example, in a survey of 69 entrepreneurs who spun out companies from MIT, Roberts and Wainer (1971) found that the desire for autonomy was the major reason for the entrepreneurs founding their companies.

Moreover, several of the MIT inventors that I interviewed founded companies so that they would not have to work for others. For example, one of the founders of an MIT software spinoff explains,

> We didn't really want to go to work for one of the big companies that were giving us offers after graduation. We wanted to do something different. Something we felt more ownership of. We had offers from Apple and we could have interviewed with General Magic and Oracle and all the big names you could think of and gotten offers from all of them. But the idea of working as one cog in a huge wheel in one of these companies wasn't terribly exciting to any of us. We really wanted to do something of our own.

Career-oriented Explanations

Although research supports the proposition, described above, that some inventors are entrepreneurial types, which provides them with motivations that lead them to found spinoff companies, other research suggests that inventor–entrepreneurs found companies because of career-related factors. Career-oriented explanations for the formation of inventor-founded university spinoffs argue that inventors establish these companies, not because they have motivations that lead them to found new companies at all stages of their careers, but rather because inventors found spinoffs at certain times in their careers and not others. Among the career-related factors that previous researchers have argued influence the creation of university spinoffs are career cycles, academic status, intellectual capital and entrepreneurial experience.

Career cycles

Academic life cycle models argue that in the early part of their careers, academics invest in the development of their human capital both to create an area of expertise and to achieve important academic milestones, such as achieving tenure (Stephan and Levin, 1996). Once these academic career goals have been achieved, researchers try to obtain a financial return on their human capital by, among other activities, starting companies (Feldman *et al.*, 2000). Therefore career cycle models of spinoff company formation suggest that academic researchers establish spinoffs in the later stages of their careers.[3]

Several pieces of empirical evidence support the career life cycle argument for the tendency of inventors to found spinoff companies. First, Audretsch and Stephan (1998) studied the firm formation activity of life scientists and demonstrate that academic scientists tend to start firms at a later stage of their careers than industry scientists, who tend to spin off from their employers at relatively early career stages. Second, Audretsch (2000) found that, in comparison to industrial scientists who start firms, university scientists are older and more experienced at the time that they found their companies, a characteristic that he attributes to the academic reward system. Third, Klofsten and Jones-Evans (2000) studied spinoffs in Ireland and Sweden and found that there were very few young academic founders of spinoff companies in these two countries.[4]

University status

University status models hold that inventors who have achieved a higher university rank should be more likely than other inventors to found spinoff companies. Given the technological and market uncertainty that university inventions face, external stakeholders cannot judge which inventions will be successful and which ones will be unsuccessful (Shane and Khurana, 2003). Under these circumstances, external stakeholders (for example, investors) rely on the inventor's status to decide whether or not to support the opportunity (Merton, 1973; Latour, 1987). External stakeholders will evaluate the inventions of high status inventors more positively, making it easier for high status inventors to obtain the resources that they need to establish new companies (Shane and Khurana, 2003).

My interviews at MIT provide support for the proposition that university status enhances the likelihood that an inventor will found a university spinoff to exploit his or her inventions. For example, Lita Nelsen, the director of the MIT Technology Licensing Office explains that, when at least one of the inventors involved with the spinoff has high status, raising money is easier (Nelsen, 1991). The founder of one of the MIT biotechnology spinoffs describes how the status of the inventors leads external stakeholders to provide resources for university spinoffs. He says that the positions of the scientists 'are important to establishing credibility. Certain people talk and people listen.'

At least one large sample statistical study supports the proposition that academic status increases the likelihood that an inventor will found a company. Shane and Khurana (2003) examined the 1397 MIT-assigned inventions from 1980 to 1996 and found that inventor rank in the university had a positive effect on the probability that an invention would be commercialized by the founding of a company.

Star scientists

A third career-related explanation for inventor-founded spinoffs is the star scientist model. This explanation holds that spinoffs occur because star scientists seek to capitalize financially on the tacit knowledge that they have developed about their inventions (Zucker *et al.*, 1998b). Because only leading scientists have this tacit knowledge, these authors explain that only star scientists can capitalize on this knowledge by starting firms.

Several pieces of evidence support the proposition that spinoffs occur when star scientists seek to earn a financial return on their intellectual capital. Researchers studying the formation and development of the biotechnology industry have discovered that firm founders are often the most successful scientists in their fields (Etzkowitz, 1989). Moreover, Zucker, Darby and Brewer (1998), who examined the formation of biotechnology companies in the United States, have shown empirically that the birth of biotechnology enterprises is directly related to the intellectual capital of their founders. Darby and Zucker (2001) found similar evidence regarding the founding of biotechnology companies in Japan, while Torero *et al.* (2001) show evidence of the star scientists' effect in the semiconductor industry.

Other support for the star scientist hypothesis comes from the qualitative evidence that I collected at MIT. If the star scientist hypothesis is true, then technology-licensing offices should be more likely to encourage inventors to start companies when they have significant intellectual capital in a particular field than when they do not. The MIT technology-licensing officers confirm that they are more likely to encourage inventors to found companies to exploit their inventions when the inventions are made in a technical area where the inventors are truly the world's intellectual leaders. For example, one of the licensing officers that I interviewed explained why she encouraged an MIT inventor to found a spinoff: 'He was a real expert in the area. Frequently, we get people who want to start businesses in areas that they are not expert.' She then added that inventors found the most successful companies when they are experts in a field.

Another licensing officer explains that, when inventors found companies to exploit technologies in areas in which they are not experts the spinoffs run into problems that hinder the performance of their new companies, particularly problems with obtaining strong intellectual property protection for the spinoff. He explains that, when inventors 'invented totally outside their area of expertise, we found that it was always harder for them to start companies because they didn't know what was going on there. We almost always found prior art that hurt us and so on.'

Entrepreneurial experience

A final career-related factor that research indicates increases the likelihood that inventors will found companies is their level of entrepreneurial experience.

Prior experience starting new ventures increases the likelihood that an inventor will found a company as a way to exploit their invention because prior entrepreneurial experience makes inventors better at forming companies (Jovanovic, 1982; Hebert and Link, 1988). For example, creating organizations provides knowledge about firm organizing routines (Bruderl *et al.*, 1992), and making decisions about opportunities teaches entrepreneurs how to make these decisions effectively (Duchesneau and Gartner, 1990). Moreover, experience in founding firms incorporates the inventor in a network of suppliers, investors and customers that help the inventor to found a new company (Campbell, 1992).

Individuals involved with the MIT spinoffs provide anecdotal evidence to support the proposition that university inventors with more firm formation experience are more likely to found spinoffs to exploit their inventions. For instance, the inventors of several MIT spinoffs explained that their experience founding one spinoff made it much easier to establish and raise money for subsequent ones. In particular, the MIT interviewees pointed to the importance of spinoff company experience in providing credibility with stakeholders. One of the licensing officers explains,

> There's no predictor of success that's better than past success. So when [an experienced inventor–entrepreneur] says 'I've just hit gold. This is the best invention I've ever had since I got to MIT', he'd have everyone listening to him with great intensity. It's clear that the people who had success were those that we should take seriously.

The experience of one multiple venture inventor–entrepreneur allows a dynamic look at how entrepreneurial experience facilitates spinoff activity. As one of MIT's most prolific inventor–entrepreneurs, this person has founded many companies to commercialize his discoveries. He explains that he finds the process of establishing spinoff companies to exploit his inventions has become easier as he has created more companies, increasing his probability of founding spinoffs to exploit his inventions as time goes on. He says,

> This is 1997. People certainly wouldn't have had the interest ten or 15 years ago. I'm doing better now because I'm more experienced. Also, I've had a number of products based on my patents that have gone to the FDA and others that are in very advanced clinical trials. In 1987, I couldn't say that. Even in 1992, it was hard to do.

One large sample statistical study also provides support for the inventor experience effect on spinoff activity. Shane and Khurana (2003) examined the 1397 MIT-assigned inventions from 1980 to 1996 and found that each of an inventor's prior spinoff company patents increased the probability of a patent being exploited by a spinoff by 8 percent.

SUMMARY

This chapter has explored the role of people in the university spinoff process. Inventors play an important role in determining whether a spinoff will be founded to exploit a university invention, with spinoffs occurring more often when inventors are interested in the formation of a new company as a way to develop the invention than when they are not.

While university inventors are important influences on the formation of university spinoffs, inventors do not always lead efforts to found these companies. Rather, their formation is led by three primary groups of people – the inventors of the technologies (inventor-led spinoffs), external entrepreneurs interested in founding companies who license university inventions through technology-licensing offices (shopper-led spinoffs), and investors who bring together technology and entrepreneurs (investor-led spinoffs). Research has shown that these three types of spinoffs all occur with roughly the same frequency, at least those out of MIT.

Although very little research has explored the difference between inventor-led spinoffs, external entrepreneur-led spinoffs and investor-led spinoffs, researchers have identified a few differencess. First, inventor-led spinoffs are more common when intellectual property protection is not very effective, such as when patent protection tends to be weak in an industry. Second, inventor-led spinoffs are more likely to be established near the university that generated them. Third, investor- and external entrepreneur-led spinoffs are more common in major cities and technology centers where there is substantial employment of investors and technology managers. Fourth, inventor-led spinoffs are more likely than other types of spinoffs to be founded before patents are issued. Fifth, inventor-led firms are more likely than other types of spinoffs to be founded by part-time entrepreneurs. Sixth, external entrepreneur-led spinoffs are more likely to occur at universities that generate greater numbers of spinoffs than at universities that generate fewer.

Some evidence suggests that the inventors found university spinoffs because they are 'entrepreneurial types' of people who have always wanted to start companies and who use their university inventions as a way to achieve their entrepreneurial goals. Anecdotal evidence suggests the effect of three psychological attributes on the formation of inventor-founded spinoffs: a desire to bring technology into practice, a desire for wealth and a desire for independence.

Although some evidence supports the proposition that some inventors are entrepreneurial types, providing them with motivations that lead them to found spinoff companies at all stages of their careers, other research suggests that inventor–entrepreneurs found companies because of career-related factors. Academic life cycle models suggest that academic researchers establish spinoffs later in their careers, having first invested in the development of their human capital. Status models hold that inventors who have achieved a higher university rank are more likely than other inventors to found spinoff companies because their status facilitates resource acquisition under uncertainty. The star scientist model holds that spinoffs occur because leading researchers capitalize on tacit knowledge of how to exploit their inventions. A final career-related factor that research indicates influences the likelihood of spinoff company formation is the inventor's level of entrepreneurial experience. Research has shown that each prior firm-founding patent that an inventor has increases the likelihood that a spinoff firm will exploit the inventor's subsequent invention by 8 percent.

Having described the role of people in university spinoffs, I now turn to the process of spinoff company creation, the subject of Chapter 9.

NOTES

1. While spinoffs can be categorized according to whether the primary agent that led to the foundation of the company was an inventor, external entrepreneur or investor, these categories can also be further subdivided. For instance, inventor-founded spinoffs can be further divided into those companies in which the inventor leaves the university upon founding the firm and those where the founder remains an employee of the university, sitting on a scientific advisory board or the board of directors, but remaining in his or her original faculty role (Nicolaou and Birley, 2003). The distinction between spinoffs where the inventor leaves the university and spinoffs where the inventor does not is important because the situations where the inventor does not leave the university are more likely to lead to conflict of interest issues. Moreover, the characteristics of the two groups of founders are different. For example, Nicolaou and Birley (2003) found that the inventor founders who left the university had stronger social ties to the business community than those who did not.
2. This quotation does not only indicate that psychological factors influence the decision to spin off. It also suggests that the different economics faced by new and established companies influences the decision to found a spin off.
3. As university spinoffs become more common, the effect of the career cycle on the tendency of inventors to found university spinoffs may be weakening. In addition, the career cycle explanation for inventor-founded spinoffs may have greater predictive validity in the United States than in Europe, which has less stringent tenure systems in its universities.
4. However, Wallmark (1997) finds evidence that contradicts the life cycle model. He shows that two-thirds of all the patents at Chalmers Institute of Technology are assigned to faculty, but that only one-third of the spinoffs are founded by faculty, suggesting that students have a greater willingness than faculty to bear the risk of founding new companies.

9. The process of spinoff company creation

This chapter discusses the process by which a university spinoff is created and developed. The first section of the chapter discusses the research that leads to the creation and disclosure of a university invention. In particular, it explains how university researchers use research funding from companies, foundations and government agencies to invent new technologies. It also discusses the university's evaluation of the invention and its patenting decision, explaining how personnel in the university technology transfer office evaluate these inventions to verify that they are inventions for which property rights reside with the university and inventions worthy of intellectual property protection.

The second section of the chapter examines how universities market their inventions. In particular, it explains that the marketing of university inventions involves a variety of activities by both licensing officers and inventors to find companies interested in licensing the inventions. This section also discusses the decision to license the technology to an entrepreneur who founds a spinoff company.

THE RESEARCH AND INVENTION CREATION PROCESSES

As Figure 9.1 indicates, the creation of the technology used by a university spinoff is a multi-stage process. Funding from the federal government, private firms and foundations is used to support scholarly research in science and engineering. Some of this research results in the creation of new technology, some of which is disclosed to the university. The university technology-licensing office then decides whether or not to seek intellectual property protection for the inventions, after which efforts are made to find licensees for them. In most cases, established companies are the licensees of university inventions, but in some cases newly formed companies are the licensees. Beginning with the initial research phase, the process of university technology development involves significant amounts of winnowing, with only some efforts leading to outcomes that mark progression to the next stage.

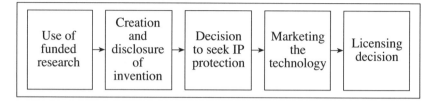

Figure 9.1   The process of university technology development

The first stage of the process by which a university spinoff is created is research. University faculty, staff and students use funding from companies, foundations and government agencies to obtain human and physical resources for the research effort. Unlike research in private sector firms, the main goal of this research effort is generally the production of new academic knowledge, not the creation of new technology that has commercial potential. However, the pursuit of academic knowledge in engineering and science sometimes results in the creation of new technical knowledge that has the potential to lead to new products and services. That is, some of the time, academic research in science and engineering results in the creation of invention disclosures.

Because the goal of university research is not to create invention disclosures, the process of generating these disclosures from university research is not at all efficient. Most financial and human resources that are invested in academic research in science and engineering yield no tangible results in the form of invention disclosures. Moreover, the 'cost' of creating each university invention disclosure is quite high. The Association of University Technology Managers (Pressman, 2000) estimates that universities spend $1.2 million in research funds to produce each of their invention disclosures. Despite the inefficiency of this process, some of the research effort yields potentially valuable inventions that can then become the basis of a license to an established or new company (Roberts and Malone, 1996).

Patents, copyrights or other forms of intellectual property protection are used to secure property rights to only some of the inventions that are disclosed to universities. From the pool of invention disclosures, universities winnow out those disclosures that are not true inventions, those for which the university does not believe that seeking intellectual property protection is worthwhile and those for which the inventions did not make material use[1] of university resources.[2] The result of this process is a smaller pool of inventions for which universities obtain intellectual property protection.

After intellectual property protection is secured on university inventions, the university technology-licensing office seeks to market the technologies. Because these inventions are typically early stage inventions of uncertain value, only some of them prove to be appealing to potential licensees. As a result, the university inventions are further winnowed at the marketing stage, with fewer than half of all university inventions that have been secured by intellectual property protection being licensed to private sector firms.

Approximately 14 percent of the university inventions that are successfully licensed are licensed to spinoff firms (Pressman, 2002). As a result, the winnowing process continues at the licensing stage, with spinoffs forming around those inventions that have the right characteristics for spinoff formation, be those characteristics the attributes of technology discussed in Chapter 6 or the attributes of inventors discussed in Chapter 8. Because of the winnowing process from research funding to spinoff creation just described, the level of research funding that is necessary to generate a university spinoff is very large, with the amount of funded research that it takes to generate each university spinoff exceeding \$141 million in the United States (Pressman, 2002).

In the subsections below, stages of the process from research to spinoff company creation are discussed in greater detail.

University Research

Researchers in science and engineering at academic institutions seek to create new knowledge through scholarly research. Unlike the case of social sciences and the humanities, research in engineering and sciences is often expensive. To conduct their research, academics in engineering and science need laboratories with costly equipment, and significant amounts of talented human resources in the form of graduate and post-doctoral researchers. As a result, science and engineering research at academic institutions is heavily dependent on grants and other sources of funding.

The federal government provides more than two-thirds of the funding for this research, largely through the major agencies of the government, such as the National Institutes of Health, Department of Defense, the National Aeronautics and Space Administration, and other government entities. However, unlike the social sciences and the humanities experience, where very little research funding is provided by industry, private firms underwrite a significant minority of science and engineering research. These firms support research in the hope that it will solve basic scientific and engineering problems that will lead to applied development in the future, and because it provides training for students who provide an employment base for the firms.

Most of the research funding with which the federal government and private firms provide academic researchers in science and engineering is used to pursue typical academic goals. For academics to advance in their careers, they must produce cutting edge research that advances scholarly knowledge.

Therefore most of the research conducted by science and engineering faculty and students is undertaken to produce new knowledge that can be published in academic journals. In the course of conducting this research, however, researchers sometimes produce new technology that is novel, non-obvious to experts in the field, and valuable – that is, they produce technological inventions.

Invention Disclosures

If a university researcher believes that he or she has invented a new technology in the course of their employment or education at an academic institution, that individual is expected to disclose the discovery to the university technology-licensing office. Because most academic institutions assert property rights to those inventions created by their faculty, staff and students, almost all universities have policies that require inventors to make such disclosures (Lowe, 2002).

For an invention disclosure to occur, two conditions must be met. First, the inventors must believe that they have invented a new technology, rather than having just produced a research result. This is a relatively rare event because the researchers must believe that they have come up with something that is novel, non-obvious and valuable, and thus an 'invention'. Second, the inventors must believe that they have to disclose their 'invention' to the university, a decision that is influenced by the university's policies toward disclosure, as well as the nature of the technology and the nature of intellectual property protection for the technology. For example, software can be patented or copyrighted. Although software protected by a patent requires disclosure in many academic institutions, software protected by copyright grants no rights of title in many universities and so does not require invention disclosure. Moreover, universities require disclosure of any invention that makes 'material use' of university resources. Therefore the inventor evaluates whether or not they made such use of university resources in their disclosure decision. For instance, a software invention is less likely than a biotechnology invention to make 'material use' of university resources in its development. As a result, more biological inventions than software inventions are disclosed to university technology-licensing offices.

Evaluation of Invention Disclosures

Once an invention is disclosed, the university technology transfer office evaluates it. The purpose of this evaluation is to determine whether or not the institution should seek patent or copyright protection for the invention (Roberts and Malone, 1996). Typically, the university personnel making these decisions are people with technical training in the relevant field, and who have experience at patenting and licensing with university inventions. Moreover, they often involve expert patent counsel in the evaluation process.

In some institutions, invention disclosure also has a second purpose, to determine whether the inventor made 'material use' of university facilities in creating the invention. If the inventor did, then the title to the invention resides with the university and the university manages the disposition of the invention. However, if the university technology-licensing office determines that the inventor did not make material use of university property in generating the invention, the inventor is free to make use of the invention as he or she sees fit. While the university's evaluation of whether an inventor made 'material use' of university resources in the development of an invention is clearly conditional on the inventor's belief that he or she did (or the inventor would not have disclosed), university technology-licensing offices sometimes determine that the inventor did not do so, even when the inventor believed that he or she did.

Perhaps the most notable example of this situation is the case of Yahoo! The founders of Yahoo! disclosed their invention to Stanford's Technology-Licensing Office because they were students at Stanford at the time that they invented the Yahoo! search engine and had used Stanford computers in the process of developing their technology. Stanford University's licensing office, however, determined that Yahoo!'s founders had not made 'material use' of university resources in developing their search engine because the inventors had only used general computing resources. As a result, Stanford exerted no claim on the inventors' intellectual property and allowed the founders of Yahoo! to exploit their invention without first licensing it back from the university.

For a university technology-licensing office to seek a patent to protect a university invention, several conditions must be met. First, the technology-licensing officers must believe that the inventor has made a novel, non-obvious and valuable technological advance because these are the conditions of receiving a patent. Second, the technology must be embodied in some form that can be patented, rather than just being tacit knowledge residing in the inventor's head.

In some cases, the technology transfer officers determine that the disclosure is not an invention because it does not meet criteria of non-obviousness, novelty and value. In that case, the university does not pursue patent protection, and generally does not try to license the invention.[3] In other cases, the technology-licensing officers determine that the invention meets the criteria for patent protection, but expect that the profits from licensing the invention will be too low to justify the cost of patenting it, and the invention passes into the public domain. Given the above criteria for seeking patent protection for university inventions, technology-licensing offices file patent applications on less than half of all inventions disclosed to them. At Stanford University, for example, the technology-licensing office files patents on roughly 40 percent of the invention disclosures that it receives (Ku, 2001).

THE MARKETING, LICENSING AND SPINOFF CREATION PROCESSES

After a university technology-licensing office decides that it will seek intellectual property protection on an invention, it needs to market that technology to the private sector to find a licensee for the invention (although, in many cases, the inventors will opt to license the inventions and found firms themselves). If a new firm is formed to license the invention, then a university spinoff is born. The subsections below describe the processes of marketing and licensing university inventions, as well as the spinoff creation process.

Marketing Technology

One of the jobs of university technology-licensing officers is to market the university's inventions, looking for private sector entities interested in licensing and commercializing those technologies. In general, the 'products' that technology-licensing officers are trying to market are very early stage inventions in need of further technical development. Nelsen (1991:40) provides an excellent description of the products that technology-licensing officers are typically trying to market to private companies:

> Here's what we have found and here's what we are trying to protect (either as patents, copyrights, or perhaps as 'tangible material'). We are not certain it will work, and we are not terribly sure what it is good for. We aren't even sure that any patents will issue. We do know, however, that this invention is based on very good science in a promising field, and it appears to be a potential solution (or at least a clue toward a solution) to an important problem. Our researcher is a leader in her field, and would like to see someone develop the practical side of the invention. She is continuing research on the pure science aspect of the technology, but would be happy to help on a consulting basis with practical development.

Given the 'rawness' of technologies that university licensing officers are trying to sell, the marketing of university inventions involves a variety of activities. These activities include efforts by licensing officers to contact existing licensees and other prospective companies directly to see if they would be interested in licensing the new invention, the listing of university technologies on websites so that potential licensees may search for available technologies, and bulk mailings to technology companies (Hsu and Bernstein, 1997). Researchers have found that universities have the most success at licensing their technologies through direct contact with firms that already license inventions from universities, and have found that direct mailings and website lists are relatively ineffective mechanisms for marketing university inventions (Hsu and Bernstein, 1997). The modal form of direct contact used to market university inventions is a phone call from a technology-licensing officer to a prospective company to ask if they are interested in the invention (Pressman *et al.*, 1995).

Much of the effort to identify prospective licensees is conducted by inventors of the technology. Jansen and Dillon (1999) have found that, when direct contact is used, the inventors are responsible for the identification of approximately half of the actual licensees of university inventions, with the licensing officers identifying the remaining half.

Despite these efforts by technology-licensing offices to attract interest in university inventions among potential licensees, very few private sector firms are interested in licensing the typical university invention. As a result, marketing of university inventions is a very difficult process. Pressman *et al.* (1995:52) explains why marketing university inventions is so difficult:

> University inventions are 'embryonic.' At the time a university is ready to hand off its inventions to industry, most have not even reached the prototype state, much less demonstrated manufacturability and practicality in the market. These inventions will require substantial investments in product and market development, and many will never succeed. Thus the task of the university is to find industrial licensees willing to make the high-risk investment.

Because attracting private sector interest in university inventions is so difficult, even the most successful universities at technology licensing only license about half of their patented inventions. For example, Stanford University reports that it licenses approximately half of its patents (Ku, 2001). Similarly, 50 percent of the MIT inventions patented between 1980 and 1996 were ultimately licensed (Shane 2002). Overall, data from the Association of University Technology Managers (Pressman, 2002) shows that, in 2000, licenses and options executed were 59 percent of patent applications at academic institutions in the United States and Canada and 29 percent of invention disclosures.

Optioning Technology

Perhaps because of the technical and market uncertainty of university inventions at the time of their creation, potential licensees are often unsure whether they would like to license them. As a result, they often take options to license the inventions, giving them time to evaluate the technologies further before they make a decision to license. Thus the process of optioning allows potential licensees to mitigate the technological and market uncertainty inherent in exploiting university inventions by gathering more information about the technology and market, as well as the commitment of the inventors to the process of commercialization.

My interviews with the founders of MIT spinoffs point to the widespread use of the optioning of university technologies. Most of the non-inventor founders of university spinoffs took options, typically for six months, before licensing university inventions. For instance, the founder of one MIT medical device spinoff describes the typical process used by a non-inventor founder of an MIT spinoff:

> When I signed up for the technology, my first step with the licensing office was to take an option. I took an extension on the option because I wasn't really done with my perusal of the market opportunity for things at the time of the option. Then I finally signed up for the license after an eighteen month period.

In addition, the founders of MIT spinoffs often take an option on several technologies and then decide later which technologies to exploit and in what fields of use to license them, an approach that mitigates market uncertainty. For example, when Sherie Oberg founded MIT spinoff Acusphere, she took a one-year option that gave her exclusive rights to the technology in five different application areas: medical imaging contrast agents, cell encapsulation, drug delivery, tissue regeneration and medical devices, in return for 1.4 percent of equity for each application that she ultimately licensed (Hansen and Anderson, 1996). At the end of that year, she identified the specific fields of use to focus on and took a license in those areas (Hansen and Anderson, 1996).

Licensing Technology

As indicated earlier in this chapter, a relatively small percentage of university inventions are successfully licensed. Moreover, when licensing does occur, there is typically only one company interested in obtaining the rights to the technology.[4] For instance, Jensen and Thursby (2001) surveyed university technology-licensing offices and reported that only 22 percent of technologies ever have more than one party interested in licensing them. As a result, universities cannot drive very hard bargains on the terms of the typical licensing agreement, and most of these agreements involve very little in the way of upfront payments to universities. The typical agreement provides only repayment of patent costs. Most of the compensation paid to universities for licensing their inventions takes the form of gross royalties on sales of successfully commercialized products or services that make use of the university intellectual property.

When patents are licensed successfully, universities typically issue two broad types of licenses: exclusive licenses, in which the licensee is the only firm that can use the technology, and non-exclusive licenses, in which a variety of firms can use the technology. When the patent is licensed exclusively, this exclusivity can extend across all fields of use, or can extend only across a particular field of use. For example, a new material patent might be licensed exclusively to one company for the production of aircraft and be licensed exclusively to another company for the production of medical devices.

The most common type of license is an exclusive license within a particular field of use. For example, at MIT, only 163 of the 966 licensing efforts from 1980 to 1996 were non-exclusive licenses, and very few of the efforts were exclusive in all fields of use (Dechenaux *et al.*, 2003).

One reason for the strong reliance on exclusivity within a field of use is that it allows firms to exploit technology without fear that the technology will also be licensed by their competitors, while affording the university the flexibility to license to multiple companies, thereby increasing the probability of commercialization. However, as Chapter 4 explained, wide variation exists in the use of exclusive licensing across universities, with some universities, such as MIT, relying heavily on the use of exclusivity and other universities, such as Stanford University, avoiding exclusive licensing as much as possible. (This variation in exclusivity is important because, as Chapter 6 explained, exclusive licensing is much more common with spinoff companies than with licenses to established firms.)

The Decision to Spin Off

Most of the time, established companies are the firms that license university intellectual property. In fact, Pressman (2002) reports that approximately 86 percent of all licenses go to companies already in existence. However, this means that, approximately 14 percent of the time, new ventures are created to exploit university intellectual property.

It is important to note that university spinoff companies are atypical examples of start-up companies. In addition to their reliance on cutting edge technology that is often based on very sophisticated science or engineering, these companies are also very early stage ventures when they are formed. Comparing university spinoffs to the typical start-up, which venture capitalists refer to as 'seed stage' companies, Lita Nelsen, the Director of the MIT Technology Licensing Office, refers to university spinoffs as 'minus two stage companies'. She explains that, unlike the typical seed stage start-up company, the typical university spinoff begins with a technology that has not been reduced to practice, has no business plan, no management and a need for capital to create the company that would bring these things together.[5]

My interviews with the founders of the MIT spinoffs support the proposition that university spinoffs are 'minus two stage ventures' at the time that they are founded. For example, the founder of one MIT materials spinoff describes the status of his company at the time it was started. He says, 'We started with a clean sheet of paper. We had a research idea to make devices that had never been produced to serve an application that no one had ever targeted.'

The fact that university spinoffs are typically 'minus two stage companies' at the time they are founded raises several questions about them, two of which are discussed in the remainder of the chapter. (The other questions are the subject of the next chapter.) First, given the very early stage of university technology and lack of confidence in the commercial value of university inventions shown by most observers of these inventions, how do the entrepreneurs that found university spinoffs identify the valuable business opportunities in them? Second, do inventors found university spinoffs when markets for university technology fail because others cannot see the value of university inventions that inventors see?

Discovery of business opportunities in university technology

Shane (2000) has pointed out that the entrepreneurial opportunities inherent in university inventions are not obvious from the technologies themselves and are not presented in prepackaged form to the entrepreneurs pursuing them. As a result, most people who look at university technologies at the time that those technologies have been disclosed to university administrators are unable to identify specific entrepreneurial opportunities to pursue with the technologies.

Given the state of the technology that most university spinoffs are founded to exploit, how do entrepreneurs identify business opportunities inherent in these new technologies? The answer appears to lie in the information already possessed by the entrepreneurs who found the spinoffs. Research in the field of entrepreneurship indicates that some people discover entrepreneurial opportunities that other people do not recognize because they have prior information that other people lack (Hayek, 1945; Kirzner, 1973). This prior information makes it possible for the person to recognize an entrepreneurial opportunity in a new technology when other people are ignorant of that opportunity.

Prior knowledge provides an absorptive capacity that enhances the ability to see entrepreneurial opportunities in information about new technologies and markets for two reasons (Cohen and Levinthal, 1990). First, the knowledge a person already has puts new information that a person receives into a context that enhances the person's ability to make use of it (Yu, 2001; Shane, 2000). Second, prior knowledge facilitates the ability to envision solutions to problems that they see (Yu, 2001).

One study provides evidence that prior information facilitates opportunity discovery among the founders of university spinoffs. Shane (2000) examined eight cases of entrepreneurs who discovered entrepreneurial opportunities to exploit the same invention assigned to the Massachusetts Institute of Technology – Three Dimensional Printing. Examining the relationship between the particular opportunities discovered and the entrepreneurs' backgrounds, Shane (2000) found that prior knowledge of a particular market increased the likelihood of discovering an opportunity in that market.

My interviews with the founders of MIT spinoffs reinforce the evidence of the effect of prior knowledge on the discovery of entrepreneurial opportunities in university technology that Shane's (2000) case studies demonstrated. For example, the founder of one MIT biotechnology spinoff describes the importance of his prior knowledge to the identification of entrepreneurial opportunities in his technological inventions. He states,

> There were some important discoveries that I made in my lab in the area of immunology for which it became clear that application of that type of technological and information advance would have some commercial potential. That was a decision that I was able to easily reach on my own because of my prior experience in the industry in general.

Market failure and the creation of inventor-founded spinoffs

Researchers have suggested that inventors found spinoffs when efforts to license their inventions to established companies fail (Lowe, 2002). They do so because prior knowledge enhances the ability to discover entrepreneurial opportunities in newly invented university technology and because the tacit knowledge of inventors often leads them to understand the value of their inventions which is not apparent to others. As Etzkowitz (1998:830) explains, in many cases

> the researchers also tried and failed to get an existing company to develop and market the [technology]. As one of the researchers described their efforts, 'we initially looked for companies that might license it from us, . . . none were really prompted to maintain or develop the [technology] further.'

Prior research provides empirical support for the proposition that inventors often found spinoff companies after established companies fail to license those inventions because inventors have better knowledge about the value of their university inventions than do other parties. For example, Golub (2003) conducted a study of spinoffs from Columbia University and New York University and found several cases of spinoffs that were founded by inventors after efforts to license inventions to non-inventors had failed.

My interviews with the founders of MIT spinoffs also indicate that many university spinoff companies are formed after efforts to license university inventions to established companies fail. For instance, the founder of one biotechnology spinoff explains his decision to found a company: 'I knocked on a lot of doors of big companies like Johnson and Johnson and Abbott Laboratories and smaller testing firms to tell them what I had, but since I had no proof of concept, I got nowhere.' Similarly, the founder of an MIT semiconductor spinoff explains that he founded his company after he failed to sell his technology to existing semiconductor and computer companies.

This pattern of licensing market failure and subsequent spinoff formation suggests that spinoffs, particularly inventor-founded spinoffs, serve a complementary role to licensing to established firms, by promoting the development of university technologies when established firms are unwilling or unable to do so.

SUMMARY

This chapter has discussed the creation of university spinoffs, beginning with the initial scholarly research that leads to university inventions and ending with the discovery of entrepreneurial opportunities and the founding of spinoff companies. The process starts when university researchers use funding from companies, foundations and government agencies to obtain human and physical resources for the research effort. Although this research effort is not designed to create intellectual property, but instead to generate new academic knowledge, technological inventions sometimes result from this research effort.

When university inventors believe that they have come up with a technological invention, they are generally expected to disclose that discovery to their university. The university technology licensing office evaluates these invention disclosures to determine whether the invention can be protected by a patent or copyright and whether the expected return from licensing the invention exceeds the cost of protecting it. If these conditions are met, the university technology-licensing office seeks to patent the invention. In some universities, technology-licensing officers also evaluate whether the invention made 'material use' of university facilities, opting to manage only that intellectual property that does so.

The technology transfer office then markets the technologies to entities interested in licensing and commercializing them. The process of marketing university technology is difficult because of the early stage of university inventions at the time that universities seek to license them. As a result, only about half of all patented university inventions are licensed and most licensed inventions have only one interested licensee.

Established companies are the entities that license most university intellectual property. However, new ventures are created to exploit approximately 14 percent of all university inventions. When universities license technology to spinoff companies, the founders of those companies often option the technology first, as a way to mitigate technological and market uncertainty. In addition, many of the spinoff companies take exclusive licenses to these inventions, at least in a particular field of use, as a way to mitigate competitive uncertainty.

Given the uncertainty and early stage of most university inventions at the time that spinoffs are founded, the entrepreneurs that found these companies typically have prior knowledge of markets that allow them to see entrepreneurial opportunities inherent in the technologies. Moreover, inventors often found spinoff companies after efforts to license these technologies fail because their tacit knowledge allows them to see commercial opportunities that others do not recognize.

Having described the process of spinoff company creation, I now turn to the process of spinoff company development, the subject of Chapter 10.

NOTES

1. Material use generally excludes the routine use of personal computers, offices and libraries.
2. Significant variation exists across academic institutions in the tendency to winnow out those disclosures that do not make material use of university resources. For example, as the Yahoo! example indicates, Stanford University's technology-licensing office does not assume responsibility for the management of intellectual property created by its faculty staff or students if that intellectual property does not make material use of university resources. In contrast, MIT's technology-licensing office will assume responsibility for the management of any intellectual property assigned to it.
3. The major exception occurs when copyrights can be obtained to protect software inventions that do not meet the criteria for patentability.
4. In only a small number of cases do multiple firms investigate and license a particular university invention. However, some of the inventions that are licensed by multiple firms, such as the Cohen–Boyer genetic engineering patent, are very lucrative inventions for universities.
5. Given the stage at which spinoffs start, many university technology-licensing offices help entrepreneurs shape their businesses and provide introductions to investors and managers. Assistance in the funding process will be described in greater detail in Chapter 11.

10. The process of spinoff development

Once spinoff firms have been established and have licensed university inventions, they often undertake efforts to further develop the inventions and identify markets for them. This chapter discusses these two activities.

The first section of the chapter discusses the additional technical development that spinoffs typically undertake. Because spinoff companies are often established at 'minus two stage', the founders of these companies often need to establish proof of principle and then prototypes for their technologies. Even if the spinoffs are established to exploit relatively more mature technologies, the founders of the spinoffs still have to undertake additional development to make the technologies appropriate for the commercial environment. As a result, the founders must often make major changes to the performance, robustness, supporting infrastructure, scale, ease of use, mechanisms and architecture of their technologies to make them appropriate for commercial customers.

The second section of the chapter discusses the process by which spinoffs develop a market for products and services that exploit their technologies. University spinoffs must overcome significant market uncertainty because the technologies that they are founded to exploit are invented as a byproduct of academic research and often are not the result of efforts to meet specific customer needs. The founders of the spinoffs need to gather information about customer needs and how they might satisfy them, as well as to obtain and incorporate customer feedback about the products and services that make use of their technologies. Because the technologies that spinoffs exploit are often early stage, general-purpose technologies, the founders of spinoffs must also choose a market application for their inventions. Finally, the founders must sell their new products and services to customers.

ADDITIONAL TECHNICAL DEVELOPMENT

The 'minus two stage' of most university spinoffs at the time of founding means that almost all of them need to conduct further development of their technologies after they have founded their firms (Nelsen, 1991). As a result, the staff of a university spinoff spends a great deal of time and effort on additional technical development in the early days of the new company (Roberts and Malone, 1996).

The need for the spinoff to further develop the university technology subsequent to founding a firm creates a technical development process through which university spinoffs must travel. For many spinoffs, the first step in this process is establishing proof of principle, followed by prototype development. Then, after prototypes have been created, the founders of the spinoff often need to make their technologies into products and services that are appropriate for the commercial environment. The subsections below describe the process of development that occurs subsequent to the founding of a university spinoff.

Proof of Principle

Many university spinoffs are based on such early stage technology that the founders of the company need to establish proof of principle after the spinoff has been founded. Without proof of principle, it is impossible to create a prototype, let alone create a product or service that would solve a customer problem or meet a customer need.

My interviews with the founders of the MIT spinoffs illustrate this point. For instance, the founder of one of the MIT materials spinoffs explains the need to establish proof of principle as a first step in the development process of a spinoff company and its technology:

> When we were coming out of MIT, we weren't even looking at the fuel business. We were initially looking at energy localization in the context of whether it has applications for nuclear reactions. We were just trying to understand the implications of the technology. We did a whole lot of modeling and thinking and narrowing in on things that we thought might make sense. We didn't have proof of principle until six months after we started the company.

The very need to establish proof of principle to have the potential to solve a customer problem or meet a customer need means that some of the spinoffs fail very early in the development process. Unable to prove the technical principle on which the new company is based, several of the MIT spinoffs I examined failed to develop. For example, the CEO of one of the MIT biotechnology spinoffs explains how this situation affected his company:

> I think it's too grandiose to call what we started from MIT with a technology. It was a science license from MIT in the form of biology patents and some chemistry patents. For the first couple of years we tried to prove the principle of the technology rather than going after a specific marketplace. The technology was unproven in terms of the specific applications. This was a big surprise because the founders gave the expectation that it would immediately work. They said the technology applied to commercial opportunities. But it didn't and it still hasn't.

Even when the founders of spinoffs are able prove the principle behind the technologies that their companies are developing, the spinoff often progresses slowly because the technology is able to do only some of the things that inventors had previously thought it could do. As a result, the potential prototypes that can be developed, the market applications that can be pursued and the customer problems that can be solved are all much more limited than originally anticipated, limiting the direction and pace of the new company's development. For example, the CEO of one of the MIT materials spinoffs explains,

> When academics discover technology they consider it complete before it is even started. If you read some of the earlier papers on this technology you would get the impression that you could take half the material out of a board and have a board that was equally stiff with no degradation in any physical properties at all. But, actually, the material doesn't give you all the properties that people said it would. It isn't applicable to every polymer in the same way. The technology was overstated. We had to reduce it back to human proportions along the way and figure out what to do with it.

Despite the difficulties in proving the principle of university technologies, for a significant proportion of the university spinoffs, the founders are able to prove the scientific principle on which the new technology is based and the spinoffs progress to the next stage of development, the creation of prototypes.

Prototype Development

Roberts (1991a) found that most university spinoffs lack prototypes of their products at the time of spinoff even if they have achieved proof of principle in the laboratory. As a result, after proof of principle has been achieved, the typical university spinoff has to develop prototypes.

My interviews with the founders of the MIT spinoffs support Roberts' (1991a) observation. For example, the founders of one MIT spinoff created to make cars that pollute less than existing vehicles explain that they had no prototype, no model and no tests at the time of founding. Similarly, a venture capitalist that invested in one of the MIT mechanical device spinoffs describes that company at the time of his investment. He says, 'The major risk at the time of financing was whether or not it was going to work. Could we develop a prototype to prove the concept?'[1]

Moreover, the founders of MIT spinoffs that have prototypes at the time that the companies are founded often need to conduct additional prototype development for a variety of reasons. For instance, the founders of some university spinoffs need to engage in prototype development because a change in the market application for the technology necessitates redoing the prototype.

Because of the difficulties of creating prototypes in a university laboratory, the inventors of university technology typically create a prototype for the most likely application or the one for which the technical development can be most easily undertaken. As a result, if the founders of the spinoff identify a different application for the technology after receiving information from potential customers, post-founding prototype development needs to be undertaken.

My interviews with the founders of the MIT spinoffs illustrate this point. For example, the founder of one of the MIT medical device spinoffs explains that his company made use of an MIT technology for which a prototype had been developed, but not one that was also applicable to medical uses. This led to the creation of a new prototype that was appropriate for the new application. He says, 'We had proof of principle. [But] we needed some information for medical use. We had to see if it could work with polymers and other materials. We had to change the bubble jet printing to get FDA approval.'

Prototype development by the spinoff is also necessary when the initial prototype does not work properly. Given the uncertainty of technical development, problems with the technical functioning of prototypes are not rare, and the founders of several of the MIT spinoffs explain that they needed to conduct additional prototype development after the founding of their companies to make sure that their prototypes worked properly. For instance, the founder of one of the MIT medical device spinoffs explains,

> At the time of licensing, the prototype didn't work. So there was no proof of concept. I had to first fix the machine. I had to reduce the invention to a simpler concept that would allow it to succeed. [The] machine is very complex and very expensive to make. While the core concept is excellent, it had to be redesigned in a simpler way.

In some cases, the prototype functions, but not as effectively as the founders need it to work to meet customer needs. Because multiple approaches to solving problems can often be applied to a new technology, the founders of the spinoffs sometimes redesign their prototypes, stripping them back to the proof of principle and developing them along a different technical path. The founder of one MIT mechanical device spinoff provides an example of this type of prototype development:

> What we really licensed from MIT was a concept. We had to change everything beyond that. At the stage that we licensed from MIT, they had a single-jet printing machine. The printer was made as a kluge from a syringe and it worked well on the single jet. But there was no way to make a commercial machine with a single jet. So we had to select a different printing technology from the one that they had. So we ended up developing all the hardware and software. The only thing that we used was the concept of printing glue onto powder and that is basically the MIT patent.

Because university spinoffs often have to engage in prototype development subsequent to founding, many of them spent significant amounts of time and resources on this process. The length of time spent on prototype development for the MIT spinoffs ranged from just under a year to several years. Even in the case of computer-related spinoffs, which had relatively short prototype development times by the standards of all MIT spinoffs, the amount of time spent on the prototype often exceeded a year.

We now examine the next stage in the technical development process after prototypes have been development – making the technology appropriate for the commercial environment.

The Product Development Process

Spinoffs often must undertake additional technical development after founding to make university inventions into products and services that are appropriate for the commercial environment. This product development process involves two separate activities. First, it involves turning the university invention into a product or service. Second, it involves making sure that those products or services meet the standards of the commercial environment. Each of these types of activity is discussed in the subsections below, beginning with the process of turning the university technology into a product or service.

Productizing the invention

The founders of university spinoffs often need to undertake additional technical development of their inventions after they have created their prototypes because they need to turn the technologies into products or services. To have a product or service, the founders of a university spinoff must transform the technology into something that solves a customer need or problem. For example, the founders of MIT spinoff Open Market had to change their technology from an on line payment algorithm into software to manage on line transactions for it to be something that met a customer need (Gogan and Applegate, 1996).

Why product development is necessary   The founders of university spinoffs must transform their university technologies into products or services for several reasons. First, most customers generally do not buy raw technology, but, instead, buy products or services. Therefore the spinoffs need to create something that customers will buy. The founder of one MIT software spinoff explains the importance of transforming university technology into products or services to have something to sell to customers:

> We tried to license to other companies to merge our technology into their products, but it didn't work. It's an interesting psychological thing we found. If we put our

stuff in hardware, then they'll buy it. All we did was put a processor and some software in a little metal box. It could have been done inside of their own computer, yet people who wouldn't buy it in software will pay money for this box.

Second, many customers of new technology products and services do not purchase the technology alone, but instead purchase solutions to their problems. As a result, they are interested in products and services that combine the new technology with standard features that competitor products and services have, such as appropriate documentation, packaging, support services, and so on. To attract customers, the spinoff needs to minimize any differences between its products and services on standard dimensions that all products and services have, and provide features that are not possible in competitor products or services. Therefore the founders of spinoffs often need to create the standard attributes of products and services before their technologies can be considered products or services.

The founders of the MIT spinoffs that I interviewed provided empirical support for this proposition. For example, in describing the development of his spinoff's product, Cornie (1997:2) explains,

> We went far beyond the original ideas in putting the concepts into practice. We had to create a whole new technology (and patents) associated with low cost tooling, casting core, and performance manufacture which helped to convince investors, government project managers, and potential commercial customers that our APIC process was a viable and practical technology. The perfection of our foundry technology is what the first four years of MMCC's existence has been all about.

Third, the university technology must be changed into a form that meets actual customer needs. Because university technology is often created without the goal of satisfying customer needs, potential customers often do not find that university technology in raw form satisfies their needs or solves their problems.

The data from the MIT spinoffs support this proposition. For example, the founder of one MIT software spinoff describes how he needed to transform his technology to meet an actual customer need when he created his new company: 'Things evolved quite differently from the things I invented at MIT. What industry said, was "That's nice but we need to have a decision tool coupled with that." ' This feedback led the founder to develop a decision tool as the central component of his spinoff's product.

Fourth, the creation of a product or service allows the spinoff to obtain additional intellectual property protection on its technology. While university spinoffs often begin with licenses to patented inventions, they can acquire additional protection on their technologies by obtaining patents on the designs of their products or on special features of products or services that they develop. These additional patents provide added intellectual property protection for the spinoff. As Chapters 11 and 12 will explain, strong intellectual property protection enhances the likelihood that the spinoff will obtain external financing and will perform well. Therefore many spinoffs develop explicit strategies for obtaining intellectual property protection on their products and services as they develop them.

Several of the founders of the MIT spinoffs articulated the importance of creating products and services from their basic university technologies as a way to obtain additional intellectual property protection for their technologies. For instance, the founder of one biotechnology spinoff explains, 'Since the MIT days, the company has primarily been engaged in extending the intellectual property position and cementing what we have. The real challenge of the company is to cover the intellectual property front on its technology as broadly as possible.'

Understanding the product development process   Many of the inventor–founders of university spinoffs underestimate the importance of product development, often because they do not know what product development is, or how the process works. This is not surprising given that many of the inventor–founders of university spinoffs have spent their entire careers focused on basic research and have not spent much time in product development or marketing functions.

Academia has large numbers of people with excellent research skills who have a comparative advantage in the invention of new technology. However, academia lacks people with product development skills. The founder of one MIT software spinoff describes how this relative balance of skills influenced the development of products at that company:

> Research is one thing. It's theoretical. You collect data, do tasks and so on. When you're getting into what you might call media technology where you really need to make something that students can use, you need skills that don't exist inside of MIT. Those kinds of skills generally don't live in a university in the way that they can live outside of the university because of the needs of production. [In our case this transformation] was a massive project. Lots of videos had to be compressed, all kinds of information had to be cross-referenced. It had to be put together and breaking free of the bureaucracy of working within the university helped us to finish the project.

Because product development skills are different from the research skills that most university inventors have, inventor–founders often find the process of product development difficult. Moreover, the process requires them to learn new knowledge to be successful. The founder of one MIT software spinoff explains that university inventors need to learn to approach problems differently when they become company founders and engage in product development:

The neat thing about products versus engineering research is that you can cheat on the product. You're supposed to cheat. If you can find some clever way so that from the user's point of view it's the same, but functionally it's much cheaper or it works faster or something, that's great. That's the way to do innovation, but it's not the way to work in the university.

While my interviews with the founders of the MIT spinoffs revealed that some of them understood the different skills that were needed to undertake product development before they started their companies, they also revealed widespread ignorance of the product development process, particularly among many inventor–founders. The founder of one MIT software spinoff provides an example of this ignorance of product development. He says,

When we started I didn't know much about product development. It was a surprise to me how much longer and harder it was to get the product out. When people asked us 'what are your plans for productization?' I didn't quite understand what they meant.

My interviews with the founders of the MIT spinoffs also revealed the specific types of activities that spinoffs need to undertake to turn their inventions into products and services. In particular, turning an invention into a product requires much more iteration and fine-tuning and less elegant theorizing than is the case with inventing itself. As the CEO of one biotechnology spinoff explains, when researchers invent something, they 'find a technological approach and strategy that is elegant as is and the science is correct in its theory'. However, when they create products, they need to undertake 'a lot more work and fine tuning and time and multiple iterations'.

The differences between product development and research mean that the founders of university spinoffs need to change the emphasis of their efforts from the creative part of invention to the nitty gritty process of making things commercially useful when they begin to develop new products and services from university research. Several founders of MIT spinoffs that I interviewed explained that they needed to make these changes when they began the product development process. For example, Jim Cornie (1997:2) founder of MIT spinoff Metal Matrix Cast Composites explains:

Good ideas are necessary but not sufficient. At MIT, I came to appreciate the original creative act. The transition of good ideas into commercial reality requires a whole different discipline and activity. Quite simply it takes a great deal more time and effort to be commercially successful than it does to create the original concept.

Other founders of the MIT spinoffs described the types of changes that they needed to make once product development began. For instance, the founder of one MIT software spinoff describes how the focus of her activities changed as product development got underway:

There's a distinction between research and production. At MIT, the focus is on doing research with a new technology and not on producing a finished product necessarily. What we felt we needed to do was, yes we had laid the groundwork, done the research, and knew what we wanted to do. To actually make the product, it needed a lot of writing. It needed a lot of programming. It needed a lot of sheer production graphics and video. All that goes into making a product is not something that MIT is set up to do. So at that point we needed a finished product. In the early days, in the research phase, well, it's all research. However, there's more production and completion and making it real that happens later on.

The founders of university spinoffs often find the product development process quite challenging because it is not always a direct extension of the research that led to the invention on which the spinoff is founded. In many cases, the technology itself does not indicate what type of product should be created, and the founders of the spinoff have to figure out what product or service to make from the invention.

The founders of several MIT spinoffs explained that this was one of the most difficult parts of the product development process for them. For instance, the founder of one MIT software spinoff explains,

I spent some time over at MIT. I read through all of [the inventor's] research. I talked to him for hours and hours. His demo gave you some idea of what a system could look like, some of the merits of the research, the user benefit. But there wasn't a product there. There wasn't any real idea of a product, just some concepts. So I began to think about how I could use that technology and actually build a product that could serve a very large market. We spent days brainstorming what products could look like. We innovated way beyond the MIT research. After that we boiled all of it down to a first product. We did a real spec, hired a team, began architecting and writing codes. It was really difficult to understand what the customer opportunity was for our idea without going pretty far down a path. So in the early stage, we were trying to figure out what our product plans were and what market we were going after.

The product development time horizon   The amount of activity that needs to be undertaken by the spinoff in product development is often quite large. In general, to develop a commercial product for a university technology takes an average of four years and $4 million after the spinoff is founded, with revenues from the successful commercialization effort not coming until the eighth or ninth year after licensing (Bee, 2002).[2]

My interviews with people involved with MIT spinoffs support this proposition. For example, the founder of one computer hardware spinoff explains that the founders of that company left MIT in 1985 and had their first product in 1995, a decade later. He explains, 'There were a tremendous number of details that had to be taken care of after we left Lincoln Lab. It took us six years before this thing got to a commercial state.'

Moreover, commercialization is slow even if significant development occurred before the spinoff was established. For example, the founder of one semiconductor spinoff invented his technology in 1974, conducted applied research until 1977, and did not found a company until 1981. Nevertheless, the company did not come out with a system to custom design integrated circuits until it had conducted an additional two and a half years of development work, and did not come out with an actual product until 1987, thirteen years after the initial invention was made.

The main reason why product development times for university spinoffs are so long is that university technologies are at such an early stage at the time that the spinoffs are founded. As a result, the founders need to undertake steps – proving the principle, developing a prototype and then conducting product development – to transform their technology into products and services. For example, one of the investors in one of the MIT biotechnology spinoff explains,

What [we] started with was an observation. That's a long way from being able to put an assay on an amino assay machine and get results. Before you got results, you had to build systems to make antibodies, do a sandwich assay, put it on an amino assay machine and develop a system for detection. You had to get the levels necessary to show recurrence of the disease and you had to do FDA trials.

Even with products or services that are close to commercial products at the time that the spinoff is founded, as is the case with many software spinoffs, significant amounts of product development work still have to be done to transform university technology into commercial products.

My interviews with the founders of the MIT spinoffs demonstrated this pattern. For example, the founder of one MIT software spinoff explains,

I think you'd have to say that our software would not have been considered of commercial quality. About three years after [the company] was formed, the software had finally become robust. It took that long to work the bugs out, get decent documentation, fill in the holes of things that needed to be developed and that hadn't been included. Then we had a commercial product. The final software product was different from the software of the project. It had more models. It was more complete. It was debugged. It had more capability. In developing a software product, it's like writing a book or an encyclopedia. You think you're getting there, but the real value comes in getting up to that 99 percent and we were a long way from that.

The long product development times for university spinoffs create several difficulties for the management of the process. The first problem is that markets do not stand still while product development is being undertaken. Customer needs shift and competitors launch products, changing the necessary features and characteristics of the spinoff's product or service. As a result, many university spinoffs miss their market opportunities.

Several of the founders of MIT spinoffs recounted experiencing this problem. For example, the founder of one mechanical device spinoff explains, 'The company started in 1988. By the time we actually had a product that was ready for testing at customer sites, it was 1992. By then the MRI market had matured significantly.'

A second problem that long product development times create is that they lead founders of university spinoffs to underestimate the time and money that it will take to develop a successful spinoff. For instance, the founder of one MIT mechanical device spinoff explains, 'We were also naïve about how long it takes to develop, verify, and apply any measurement made on a living system and then having to do clinical studies. Just having the technology and believing its clinical value is very different than proving it.' Similarly, the founder of an MIT computer hardware spinoff explains,

> In retrospect, I realize that the idea was too far in advance if its time. I was the classic academic with the idea of a great technology facing a big market but not understanding the steps you have to go through. You have too big a job, too much. I mean hardware, physics, algorithms, software, and then all the business. To get the MIT invention into the state in which it would be a salable product in the market place, the basic invention had to be extended in all kinds of ways. All were driven by the need to reduce the hardware requirement. The software had to get a whole lot cleverer. The algorithms had to get a whole lot cleverer. The original invention was pretty raw.

This underestimation of the time and effort that it takes to create products and services from university technology means that the efforts of many university spinoffs are unsuccessful because the founders do not obtain sufficient human or financial resources to complete the process.

The uncertainty of product development   Developing a product or service from a university invention is also highly uncertain. Because the founders of spinoffs must often change university technologies to create products or services, many university spinoffs face considerable technical uncertainty even after they have developed prototypes. Among the aspects of technical uncertainty that founders face are whether the technology will adapt to the commercial environment, whether the founders have the competence to turn a university invention into a product and whether complementary technologies necessary to support a product or service will be developed in time.

My interviews with the founders of MIT spinoffs provide empirical support for the presence of these different aspects of uncertainty in the product development process. Several of the interviewees pointed out that there is considerable uncertainty about whether the technology can be adapted to the commercial environment. For instance, the founder of one optics spinoff explains, 'At the beginning there was the question of would the system work when we adapted it for the commercial arena. We had a scheme for miniaturization and we didn't know if we could shrink the system and still make it work.'

Other MIT founders described a similar type of technical uncertainty in biotechnology. For instance, the founder of one biotechnology spinoff explains,

There's always technological uncertainty. I think people didn't anticipate how much more difficult it was going to be to work with human stem cells than with mouse stem cells. Some of this is endemic to people who come out of basic laboratory settings and are getting into development programs on an industrial scale for the first time and don't have an appreciation for how difficult it is to translate what you do at the lab bench to what you do in a clinical setting or a factory setting.

The founders of the MIT spinoffs and their investors also recounted that the companies faced considerable uncertainty about the ability of founders to transform their technologies into commercially viable products and services. This uncertainty involves both questions about technical possibilities and questions about founder competence. First, there is uncertainty because no one knows if the changes that would be required to make something commercially viable are physically possible. Second, there is uncertainty because no one knows if the founders of the spinoffs are capable of making these changes even if they are physically possible.

A business angel that invested in one MIT software spinoff explains how these two dimensions of uncertainty affected that company at the time he invested:

There were two major risks [with that company]. The first was that the product was not complete. Although it appeared in breadboard, it needed to be put into manu-facturable form and be much more robust than it was, and it wasn't clear that the founders had the experience to know what it would take to get to that stage. That is, it could make a good demonstration on a one off unit, but whether or not it could be robust enough to be sold to the likes of Boeing was questionable.

A venture capitalist that invested in an MIT optics spinoff provides another example of how technical uncertainty affects university spinoffs. He explains,

The biggest uncertainty at the start of this company was whether this technology would work in a way that you could make measurements on real world semicon-ductor wafers with different combinations of metal layers being used and could you make the measurements with reproducibility that would work in that environment?

The founders of the MIT spinoffs also explained that they faced uncertainty in product development because the transformation of the university inven-tions into commercial form requires the development of important component technologies that are beyond the control of the founders of the spinoffs. As a result, there was considerable uncertainty about whether the components would be developed quickly enough for the spinoff to succeed in commercializing its invention. For example, the founder of one of the MIT computer hardware spinoffs describes the situation with his company: 'The major risk was would the product work. It was really a white board thing when we started. It was based on a component that Lincoln Lab was developing and we didn't know when that would be completed.'

The uncertainty of the product development process means that relatively few spinoffs succeed in creating a product that reaches the market. Table 10.1 shows the MIT spinoffs founded between 1980 and 1996 with products on the market. This table reveals that, of the MIT spinoffs founded between 1980 and 1996, by 1996, only 27 percent had a product on the market, and 7 percent had products in clinical trials. While the 1997 cut off for evaluation is probably too soon to determine whether or not many of the later-founded spinoffs would commercialize their technologies, these data do show that the product development process involves considerable uncertainty as to whether or not a product will ever be formed to exploit university inventions.

Changes to make technologies appropriate for the commercial environment

The second part of the product development process involves making sure that the products or services that emerge from university inventions meet the standards of the commercial environment. To meet the standards of the commercial world, the founders of university spinoffs make several changes to their technologies during the product development process. These include improving performance, enhancing robustness, adding supporting technology, scaling up, increasing ease of use and changing mechanisms and architecture.

Improving performance   One way that university spinoffs make their technology more appropriate for the commercial environment during the product development process is by improving performance. When university inventions are first created, they often have limited performance relative to existing technologies. This is not surprising since almost all new technologies begin with levels of performance that are inferior to existing technologies that they aim to replace (Foster, 1986). However, the inferior initial performance of university technologies means that spinoff company founders must expend considerable development effort improving the performance of their technologies after they have founded their new companies. For instance, the founder of one MIT materials spinoff explains why he conducted additional technical development subsequent to founding his firm: 'We had a technology that

Table 10.1   The MIT spinoffs founded between 1980 and 1996 with products on the market by 1997

Company	Product
Active Control Experts	Piezoelectric devices
Active Impulse Systems	Semiconductor testing device
Adreneline Inc.	Vehicle ignition system
Aesop	Machine components
American Superconductor	Superconductors for electric power
Applied Language Technologies	Voice recognition software
Aspen Technologies	Manufacturing software
Aware, Inc.	Data compression software
Barrett Technologies	Robotics for factory automation
Beyond Inc.	Email software
Boston Dynamics	Software to visualize robotics in motion
Cambridge Heart	Cardiac stress test
Cirrus Logic	Computer integrated circuits
Convolve	Software to improve robotics
Digital Optics Corporation	Lens arrays
Diva	Multimedia authoring software
Electronics for Imaging	Software and hardware for color printing
Exa Corporation	Hardware and software for fluid CAD
Facia Reco Associates	Facial recognition software
Firefly	Intelligent agent software
Gel Sciences	Application specific chemicals
Integra Life Sciences	Artificial skin
Integrated Computing Engines	Computer workstation
Inteletech	Software for speech processing
Interneuron Pharmaceuticals	Drugs for CNS disorders
Intersense	Inertial motion tracker
Jentek Sensors	System for materials characterization
Kopin Corporation	Flat panel display
Lab Connections	Analytic lab devices for spectroscopy
Lasertron	Diode lasers
Low Entropy Systems	Wafer imaging interferometer
Manufacturing Software	Scheduling software
Matritech	Bladder cancer test
Metal Matrix Cast Composites	Components of cast metal
Micrion Corporation	Semiconductor equipment
Micromet Instruments	Microdielectrometer
NBX Corporation	Ethernet phone adapter
nFX	Chat software
Open Market	Internet business software
Queues Enforth	Queing software
RSA Data Security	Encryption software
Sensable Technologies	Computer robotic haptic interface
Silicon Process Corporation	3D MEMS structure
Soligen Corporation	Production casting for metal parts
Specific Surface	Ceramic gas filters
Sutek Corporation	Strengthened copper
Thinking Machines Corporation	Supercomputer
USAnimation	Software for animation
Virtual Machine Works	Computer logic emulation systems
Z Corporation	Prototyping machines

Source: Records of the MIT Technology-Licensing Office.

wasn't particularly fast. We have developed now what we consider to be a more efficient technology and our production costs are less.'

The improvement of performance also involves the incorporation of a new set of performance factors that generally are not present in the research environment because the range of performance factors that are important to researchers is quite limited. In particular, most of the performance factors that matter in research have little to do with the demands of customers and rarely incorporate cost considerations. However, making technologies commercially applicable does require consideration of these performance factors. Therefore the founders of university spinoffs often spend considerable time in the product development process trying to improve the performance of the university technologies on dimensions that the commercial world cares about.

My interviews with the founders of MIT spinoffs support this proposition. For example, the founder of one MIT mechanical device spinoff explains that the product development process for that spinoff focused on improving a variety of dimensions of performance not considered during the research process:

> There are many dimensions of performance you can achieve. Can it be produced at low cost? Is it light enough weight? Does it offer efficiency improvements? Is it durable? Can it be maintained? What is the packaging like? Meeting all of these more practical criteria is important to have the product sold.

Enhanced robustness   A second way in which university spinoffs make their technology more appropriate for the commercial environment during the product development process is by making the technology more robust to the stresses of the real world environment. For instance, the founder of one semiconductor spinoff explains why making his university technology more robust was important to making it commercially viable:

> The goal of producing in the university environment is a different goal from producing in the commercial environment. So what comes out of the university environment may be a very long way from ever being a product because it hasn't had to stand some of the tests that the real world might place on it. The environment that the experiment is being done in is less stressful that if it was done at the finest geometries and the most stringent requirements. Therefore, the idea is never tested as much as it may need to be to prove that it's really the basis for a product.

The founders of university spinoffs make technology more robust in a variety of ways. One of the methods involves replacing researcher-created solutions with more commercial versions of the same thing. For example, the CEO of one MIT semiconductor spinoff describes this change to that company's original MIT invention:

[The inventor] had his inventions at MIT, got some DARPA grants, and developed what I refer to as band-aid and bailing wire software. He had the ability to develop a chip, but not anything that was marketable to third parties in the sense that it was easy to use, robust software. It was basically proof of concept. So I had a lot of questions about scaling this up, the complex chips, and doing this in CMOS because no one had done anything in CMOS yet. We had to first demonstrate that we could do this in CMOS versus NMOS.

The inventor of one of the MIT materials spinoffs describes a similar change to his invention during the product development process that made the technology more robust:

At the time of license, it was simply a university invention. We had cobbled together the implementation using a hobbyist's computer. Everything was hand wired. The boards were wire wrapped. The sensor chips were manufactured at MIT and were very fragile. The chips were wire bonded on to headers. We went about hardening the system. So we converted the boards from wire-wrapped boards to printed circuit boards.

The hardening process that the founders of university spinoffs undertake during the product development process does not just occur with computer hardware and mechanical devices, it also occurs with software. In many cases, this transformation means that graduate student-written software has to be replaced by commercial software.

My interviews with the founders of MIT software spinoffs provide support for this proposition. For example, the founder of one MIT software spinoff explains that when we licensed the technology, they had proved 'that it worked at MIT, but that was all. They had done software that made it work, but it wasn't salable. The graduate student written software was terrible. It had six different programs and you had to know what order to do things. It wasn't a usable product.'

In particular, the founders of software spinoffs need to replace research code with code that is less likely to fail and that is easier for non-researchers to understand. As a result, one of the product development activities that the founders of the software spinoffs undertake to make their software more robust is to rewrite the software. For instance, the founder of another MIT software spinoff explains that the founders of that company took

the existing researchy code and rearchitected it and rewrote it so it would be more usable for commercial things, so that it wouldn't crash all the time and so it would be easier to understand. Our first goal was to rewrite all the code I had done at MIT and make sure we could get it to run on Windows. The MIT code was research code and so it was very inefficient. It was pretty much hacked together to make it work, which is unacceptable for the commercial world. We had to go in and re-engineer it from scratch with built in error detection and rewriting all of the libraries so they could be ported easily. All sorts of things like that.

Improving robustness of university technology during the product development process also involves increasing its reliability. The founders of several MIT spinoffs pointed out the importance of increasing reliability as a key aspect of making their technologies more robust during the product development process. For example, the founder of one MIT software spinoff explains,

> The question was: could we deliver something that was reliable? Could we clock it a speed that the customer would like? What we had was a toy. So we had to build something that was useful to somebody else and that was reliable and bug free and could run by itself 2,000 miles away without handholding. We had to build something that could support three different operating systems. We needed something with the right features. We had to meet the customer's need for support and documentation.

Similarly, the founder of another MIT software spinoff explains,

> One difference we have noticed is that in the commercial environment we have a vigorous task master. When it's not research, when it's the product, it has to work. It can't crash everybody's computer. It can't require incredibly specialized things that only one person in a research lab can do.

Moreover, for a technology to be reliable, it has to work after it has been delivered to the customer and the researchers are not available to tweak the devices the way that they can in the research laboratory. Several of the founders of the MIT spinoffs explained that the effort to make sure that their technology would work on the customer premises was an important change from the research stage to the product development stage. The founder of one MIT software spinoff describes this change at his venture. He says,

> It was certainly the first time my robots got out of the lab that we learned the difference between a product and a laboratory creation. A product has to get shipped in a cardboard box all around the world. Someone has to take it out to try it and it works. It always works.

The founder of one MIT optics spinoff explains why reliability has to be built into the product during the product development process. Unlike the situation in the research environment, where there is always someone available to fix the technology, in the commercial environment, this assistance is difficult, costly and problematic to have to rely on. He says,

> When you bring this technology to market, you don't have five graduate students around tweaking the instrument. When you sell them, they have to live on their own and operate on their own in a nasty environment that requires it to operate 24 hours a day, 7 days a week. In the lab, you can have a graduate student stay up till four in the morning tweaking things until they work, but in a real application, you don't have that kind of time. You don't have the kind of liberties that a graduate student

can take. Therefore, it turns out that there's a huge amount of work just getting to know how the process works in the real world. Everybody learns that when you scale up, either in terms of complexity, size or, for us, application specificity, there's a huge amount of work that needs to be done.

The founders of the biotechnology spinoffs from MIT also describe the importance of establishing the reliability of technology during the product development process. For instance, the founder of one MIT biotechnology spinoff explains,

> It's like with any technique that's developed in a research lab. You need to get some folks who can take it and get the technique to work reproducibly. So we had to redesign the whole assay. We didn't have an instrument that was usable to make the microdrop so we had to go out and get an instrument made. We had to sort through alternative reagents and what their plusses and minuses were.

Adding supporting technology   A third way that university spinoffs make their technology more appropriate for the commercial environment during the product development process is by creating tools and technologies that support the original university invention. The development of these supporting tools and technologies is necessary because commercial customers do not purchase technology, they purchase solutions to their problems. As a result, a spinoff must develop all of the things that are needed for a product or service to solve customer problems, even if these things are not part of the original university invention.

Several of the founders of the MIT spinoffs that I interviewed explained the importance of creating supporting tools and technologies as part of the process of making university technologies more appropriate for the commercial environment. For instance, the founder of one MIT software spinoff explains how this process affected the development of his company's product:

> After I licensed the technology, there was much more work to be done. I knew the technology worked. It was fairly simple. But in order for it to be really commercial, a lot more work had to be done. It was easy to underestimate the amount of tools and support software and documentation and refinements to the technique that were needed in order to make something that somebody would consider buying. There are some software tools that are needed that were not there when I did the original work. For instance, the software for generating the numbers that get burned into the code that runs and implements for different kinds of machines was not there.

Sometimes the spinoff cannot make the supporting tools and technologies that it needs to be successful and fails as a result. The founder of one MIT software spinoff explains how his company ran into a dead end because of a failure to create supporting technology:

[The company] was never successful in actually translating into any sort of commercial application because it was relatively unstable and required a lot of computer horsepower to actually be usable for an end user. Only today computers are getting powerful enough to realistically make some product based on that.

Scale-up   A fourth way in which the founders of university spinoffs make their technology more appropriate for the commercial environment during the product development process is by scaling up so that the technology can be produced at commercial levels of production. In the very early period in the lives of university spinoffs, output can be produced only on a very small scale, typically limited to batch mode. Consequently, the founders of the spinoffs must figure out how to produce at higher scale. Because scaling up often requires more than just producing at a higher volume, but rather involves a new way of producing the technology, scaling up often requires significant changes in the technology during the product development process.

The founders of the MIT spinoffs that I interviewed described how they needed to change their technologies to scale them up to commercial levels of production. For instance, the founder of one MIT software spinoff explains,

> We were proposing scaling this to hundreds of thousands of users with real time multiple requests. We had built a system that wasn't designed to scale. So we had to rearchitect the system from ground up. It had to be robust. It couldn't be this dinky little research backend that we did for our research and for our prototype. It had to be an industry database at the backend. We found all sorts of issues when we actually tried to deploy this because these systems weren't designed to scale. They weren't designed for that kind of behavior.

The changes that the founders make to scale their technologies to commercial levels of production are also made so that they can communicate their product concepts to potential customers. Without the changes that allow the technology to be produced on a commercial scale, and hence in a commercial form, customer feedback is often difficult to obtain because customers cannot see a product or service in the form that they would use. For instance, the founder of one medical device spinoff explains,

> There is no question that we changed from an idea to something that people could grasp around the summer of last year. That's when we came up with a really efficient manufacturing process. People could then actually see that we could make a chip that had one hundred to four hundred probes per square centimeter. We could also print the arrays with standard procedures. Now people could realize how they could take the arrays technology and put it easily in their laboratories and use a lot of their existing equipment. So the capability we developed to print efficiently so we could get the arrays down in the order of tens of dollars instead of ten thousand dollars was an incredible advantage. That was probably the pivotal point that really set us apart and brought us from R&D into manufacturing.

Increased ease of use　A fifth way in which the founders of university spin-offs make their technology more appropriate for the commercial environment during the product development process is by making it easier for potential customers to use. Most university technology is very difficult to use because highly trained researchers, who employ shortcuts that the average user cannot understand or replicate, create it. As a result, the technologies often must be changed so that the average user can employ them.

Several of the founders of MIT spinoffs that were interviewed described the importance of making their technology easier to use as a way to make it more appropriate for the commercial environment. For example, the founder of one MIT materials spinoff explains, 'In the beginning I had to perfect the technology. The technology that was sold could be used on a very limited basis. We needed to develop methods to make the technology easier to use.' Similarly, the founder of one of the MIT optics spinoffs explains why ease of use is important to making a university technology commercially useful:

> The science that comes out of MIT is usually fantastic, neat, kind of 'oh, wow' stuff, but it's never ready for a real commercial application. It needs to be simplified so that the labor force can take advantage of it. You need to simplify the data interpretation stage because most of the world is not a PhD and you won't have PhD's operating it.

Increasing ease of use involves undertaking a variety of changes to university technology. First, the technology often needs to be redesigned so that users who are not deeply versed in research can use it. For example, the founders of one MIT medical device spinoff describe the need for a redesign of their device from the MIT version to a commercial version:

> In the MIT unit, a computer keyboard was used for the operator interface. The diagnostic readings are superimposed with the white light image video display on the endoscope monitor. This is complex and must be operated by a researcher. The commercial system must be easy to use by the clinician. Therefore this subsystem will be redesigned.

Second, the form in which the technology is presented to the customer has to be improved so that it looks like a commercial device. For example, the founder of one MIT materials spinoff describes some of the changes that his company had to make so that its university technology conformed to commercial standards:

> We redesigned the chip so that it could go into a circuit package that would be much more useful to customers. We also had to redesign the data acquisition software so it would be more user-friendly and also perform functions of data analysis that the customer would need. Little details like being able to process the data into a

presentable format were important as well as trying to anticipate certain customer needs in the user interface.

In some cases, changing the technology into a form that meets commercial standards means redesigning the device to look like a commercial machine even if it does not involve changing the actual functioning of the device. This is because potential customers have expectations about what products look like, and they do not look like the machines that university inventors create. An executive at one of the MIT spinoffs explains how his company redesigned its machine from the form that the MIT prototype took so that it was appealing to customers. He says, 'The MIT prototype machine is a very crude rendition of what we have since accomplished. It looks like a Rube Goldberg apparatus compared to ours, which is all shiny and runs very smoothly and the products are protected from the outside environment.'

Third, increasing the ease of use means providing customers with proper documentation. Because the commercial users of university technology will not be the research scientists and engineers who developed the technology in the first place, they need documentation on how to use the product or service that the spinoff is producing. Without such documentation, the users will find it difficult to understand how to make productive use of the university inventions.

In many cases, the founders of the MIT spinoffs that I interviewed pointed out that the documentation actually drove the purchase decisions of the customers. For example, one interviewee explained how documentation affected a software spinoff with which he was involved. He said, 'People buy software all of the time and they're really buying the book and the instructions and all that. They didn't know if they were getting two lines of code or twenty lines or a thousand lines.'

Fourth, making the technology easier to use means adapting it to fit the technical standards prevailing in the industry. Because most technical personnel in the private sector are used to using technology that fits prevailing standards, they are most comfortable with technologies that conform to these standards. Moreover, if technology conforms to an industry standard, it can be more easily linked to existing technologies employed by the engineers and scientists at target companies.

The founders of the MIT spinoffs described the importance of changing their technologies to meet industry standards. For example, the founders of one MIT medical device spinoff explain this change in their technology. As they wrote in their business plan, 'This system, being a research tool is not designed or built to commercial instrument standards. . . . A simpler and less expensive, commercially suitable ISF will be developed. . . . The production unit will be smaller, lighter, and consume less power, and will be engineered for routine use during colonoscopy.'

Changes in mechanisms and architecture　A sixth way in which the founders of university spinoffs make their technology more appropriate for the commercial environment during the product development process is by changing the mechanisms and the architecture of the technology itself. The founders of spinoffs do this for a variety of reasons.

First, changes in the mechanisms and architecture are often important because customers prefer a different approach to that which the inventors originally created. To adhere to these customer preferences, the mechanisms or architecture of the technology sometimes need to be changed. One MIT medical device spinoff provides a good example of this need to change mechanisms and architecture. One of the inventors of the technology explains,

> To make a product, we actually had to change the mechanism. It was actually a profound change. We had an invasive procedure. We put catheters in people. We had to figure out a way around that and so we developed a way of doing that with exercise. So, based on market needs, we changed the entire paradigm for how the measurement is made.

Second, the founders of spinoffs often make these changes to reduce the cost of the technology. While the cost of developing a technology is often not important in the initial research process, it is important in product development because cost influences customer interest in adopting the product or service. As a result, design changes that make it possible to use less expensive materials or to use less expensive inputs are an important type of change to make technologies more commercially useful during the product development process. The founder of one MIT medical device spinoff provides an example of this phenomenon at his company. He says that he and his co-founders redesigned their technology during the product development process because

> it had to be a lot less expensive. The MIT invention used a rather expensive laser for a light source in a design set up for research so that you could gather the largest rep of data. But once the research has shown you what you need then you can design a simpler, less expensive system.

Third, spinoff company founders often have to change the mechanisms and architecture of their products so that they can manufacture them. In many cases, the designs of university technologies are effective for producing prototypes or small batches of a product, but are not scalable. As a result, the founders of the spinoffs have to redesign their products during the product development process to make them more appropriate for large-scale manufacture.

My interviews with the founders of the MIT spinoffs provided several examples of this type of change in the mechanisms and architecture of the university technology during the product development process. For instance, the founder of one MIT robotics spinoff explains,

> What I invented is what I call design for graduation. In some ways it was over designed. But in other ways it was using materials and processes that aren't feasible for large-scale distribution. What we had to do was go back and change that design for manufacture and usability.

In some cases, the key change to mechanisms or architecture necessary for manufacturing is not undertaken to improve scalability, but to improve manufacturing speed. By improving speed, the founders of the spinoffs can make manufacturing more effective because speed influences the cost of manufacturing. For example, the founder of one MIT mechanical device spinoff explains the need for his company to change its product design so as to improve manufacturing speed:

> The design we make is very different from MIT's. We make a thin large structure as opposed to a small solid structure. We needed to get the designs to print correctly and we needed to improve the speed. Our machine doesn't really bear much resemblance to the MIT machine except that it operates on the same principle.

Fourth, spinoff company founders often have to change the mechanisms and architecture of their products so that they can use commercial components that are more readily available or more effective. By shifting to such components, the founders of the spinoffs can increase the appeal of their technologies to engineers and scientists employed by potential customers.

Several of the founders of the MIT spinoffs explained the importance of this change during product development. For example, the founder of one MIT medical device spinoff says,

> MIT had a functioning prototype. But I went straight to the design of a breadboard that was more reasonable rather than spending a lot of time trying to make the MIT piece function. It was a big, awkward, heavy case. As I took it apart, there were a lot of things that were not the way products are so I skipped over square one and started to design an engineering model of a product.

Replacing one set of components with another set of components often necessitates changes to the way in which the component parts are linked together or to the materials that are used in the product. As a result, when spinoff company founders change the designs of their products so that they can use different components, they often have to change the product's architecture. For instance, the founder of one semiconductor spinoff explains that, when he redesigned his product to make it commercially viable, he had to create a new device and then rearchitect the relationship between the device and the component parts. He says,

'The camera that we used has serious limitations and we've since built our own camera for that reason. So we had to buy the hardware, make software that communicated to it and make software that was usable to the outside world.'

DEVELOPING A MARKET FOR THE TECHNOLOGY

Even after the founders of spinoffs have undertaken additional technical development to make university technologies appropriate for the commercial environment, they still face considerable market uncertainty. As a result, the founders of the spinoffs need to sell their new technologies, which involves evaluating the market, identifying a customer need, gathering feedback from customers, choosing an application and ensuring that the approach to satisfying customer needs is better than that offered by competitors. In the subsections below, each of these activities is discussed, but first the market uncertainty facing the founders of university spinoffs is described.

Market Uncertainty

When university spinoffs are established, they often face significant market uncertainty because no one knows whether the spinoff can provide a product or service that customers want or need, or that is better than the alternatives offered by competitors. The founders of the MIT spinoffs that I interviewed described several dimensions of market uncertainty that university spinoffs face. First, several of the founders indicated that spinoffs face the uncertainty of whether or not there is customer demand for the product or service provided by the spinoff. For example, the founder of one medical device spinoff explains that, at the time of founding, his venture faced a question:

> Is there a market for what we've got? That's a major risk. You have to be able to look at your products from not only the view of what you know about how it runs, but you have to get out there with the potential customer base and say, 'These are a bunch of people who can use this thing.' They're going to say, 'Gee, that's all academically interesting but we don't know how well it's going to work or anything like that.' So you have to do a lot of application development work and you have to do customer samples. You have to reduce the risk to the customer.

In addition to determining whether there is demand at all, the founders of university spinoffs need to determine the volume of that demand. For the spinoff to be successful, the volume of demand has to be large enough to support the development of a new company. An angel investor in one MIT optics spinoff describes the uncertainty in that company at the time it was founded. He says that the founders faced the question: 'Did you have a tool that you would sell one of to each manufacturer that would go in their QC [Quality Control] lab or did you really have something that could go in line where you could sell dozens of these to people?'

Sometimes demand proves to be insufficient to support the spinoff company. As a result, the spinoff fails to develop. A venture capitalist that has invested in several MIT spinoffs explains that the problem of insufficient demand led to the demise of one MIT materials spinoff that he backed: 'The big risk was whether or not you could find a big enough application. In fact that application was never found.'

Overcoming market uncertainty also means coming up with a product or service that customers are willing to pay for, rather than viewing it as something that they should receive for nothing. For instance, the founder of one MIT software spinoff explains, 'In 1981, when we started, we didn't know if companies would be willing to pay for software. The software industry didn't exist yet. The big risk was if there would be a market.'

Even if the spinoff creates a product or service that customers want and will pay for, the founders face the uncertainty of whether or not the spinoff can produce the product or service economically. Producing a product or service economically means that it can be created at a cost less than the price that customers are willing to pay. For instance, a founder of one of the MIT materials spinoffs describes the uncertainty at the time that his firm was founded: 'The biggest risk was that there were no commercial opportunities for this new understanding of quantum physics or that the cost of implementing the core idea would have exceeded the economic benefits.'

A fourth dimension of market uncertainty is whether the spinoff's product or service provides a better solution to customer needs than the alternative provided by competitors. While a spinoff's product or service may meet a customer need in a cost-effective manner, it will not generate significant sales if its competitors satisfy customer needs more effectively than it does. A business angel that invested in an MIT software spinoff explains how this uncertainty affected that company:

> One big uncertainty was: would [the] approach really prove to be that superior to the existing magnetic tracking approach? We specifically identified targets of opportunity, potential customers in these market segments so that not only would we attempt to sell products to them, but we would attempt to determine what the implications would be from a market potential point of view.

The founder of one MIT biotechnology spinoff explains that the uncertainty of whether the university technology is actually better than the alternative provided by competitors is a problem that affects many university spinoffs. He says,

It's the same when you transfer technology out of MIT. It looks great inside MIT and everybody is very excited. But you transfer it out and suddenly you're out there with thousands of other groups who've transferred their technology and your technology starts to look less and less important and less and less significant.

As a result of this market uncertainty, the founders of university spinoffs need to sell their technology, which involves evaluating the market, identifying a customer need, gathering feedback from customers, choosing an application, and ensuring that the approach to satisfying customer needs is better than that offered by competitors. Each of these activities is discussed below.

Gathering Market Information

To overcome market uncertainty, the founders of university spinoffs need to evaluate the markets for their technologies. Because university inventions are not created with the explicit goal of filling a market need, the founders of spinoffs must determine whether a market really does exist for the technology that their spinoff is exploiting. The need to evaluate the market, however, does not mean that the founders of university spinoffs undertake full-fledged market studies. In fact, most founders of university spinoffs engage in very rudimentary market evaluation. For instance, the founder of one MIT medical device spinoff describes the market studies done by the founders of that company at the time it was started. He says, 'Nobody thought can this technology really be used? Do you have a market if you have to pace invasively? How big is the market?'

Rather than conduct full-fledged market studies, the founders of most university spinoffs conduct relatively simple tests to determine if a market for the spinoff's product or service exists. For example, Sherie Oberg, founder of Acusphere, an MIT biotechnology spinoff, focused just on determining market needs and competitor offerings when she launched that company (Hansen and Anderson, 1996). Despite the very rudimentary approaches used by the founders of university spinoffs, most of the successful university spinoffs engaged in three types of information-gathering activities: identifying if there was a need, determining whether the spinoff could satisfy the need and obtaining customer feedback on the product or service used to satisfy that need.

Identifying a need
One key part of gathering information about the market that the founders of successful university spinoffs undertake is the process of identifying a customer need. Because most university technologies are a byproduct of scholarly research, they do not offer solutions to previously known customer problems. As the founder of one MIT mechanical device spinoff explains, many of the MIT technologies are technologies in search of customer problems. He says,

> We looked at a lot of the MIT technologies and most of the others didn't make
> sense. They were more of a solution looking for a problem. Somebody had a solu-
> tion, but it wasn't clear there was a real need for that. It was just an interesting
> observation and you find that there really wasn't any need for it.

Other founders of MIT spinoffs echoed these sentiments. For instance, the
inventor of the MIT technology that led to the founding of one MIT biotechnology spinoff explains,

> We had a technology in search of a market. We thought we had some neat technol-
> ogy. We had some patents to cover that technology. And we had only a vague idea
> about what specific needs were out there in the marketplace that this technology
> could fulfill.

As a result, the founders of university spinoffs often need to find customer
problems that their technologies can solve. As the founder of an MIT optics
spinoff explains,

> With university technologies you pull the technology out and you run around saying
> 'Where can I stick it?' It's probably much better to say I've heard about these prob-
> lems and I think I can solve it. But with companies coming out of MIT, it's always
> this great thing, what do I do with it to shoehorn it back into industry?

The technology push nature of the creation of products and services by
university spinoffs seems backwards given the standard model that new products and services should be created in response to specific customer problems.
Many of the founders of the MIT spinoffs that I interviewed indicated that they
recognized this sense of backwardness. For instance, the founder of one MIT
software spinoff explains, 'We're backwards. We're technologists who are
doing things and trying to find ways to sell those things. Rather than going and
taking a blank sheet and going out there and saying what needs to be done?'

The technology push nature of university spinoffs also means that the
founders of university spinoffs have to spend a great deal of time and effort
trying to find a use for their inventions. The process of finding a customer need
for the technology is often very slow because the founders of the spinoffs
rarely have a clear vision of how their technology will solve real customer
problems. Because a commercial purpose for the technology was rarely a
guiding force in the research that led to its creation, it is very difficult for the
founders of spinoff firms to identify a customer need that the technology fills.
As the founder of one MIT software spinoff explains, 'We were going to make
a tool so people could create animated models. But we didn't really know who
was going to buy those tools or what we were going to do with those tools
once they were developed.'

Moreover, the founders of university spinoffs are often quite naïve about the importance of identifying a customer need for their technologies. As a result, they do not directly focus on this process, making it take longer than it otherwise would. Several founders of the MIT spinoffs that I interviewed identified this naïveté as an obstacle to their identification of customer needs. For example, the founder of one MIT software spinoff explains,

> We had a school of thought in our company initially which was if the technology is sexy, everyone will buy it. It doesn't matter whether there's an application for it. That's a very naïve view of the world of business. But it comes out of a lot of engineering backgrounds and it took a long time for us to get over that. It was a hard lesson for us to realize that you've really got to build your product based on what customers can really use, even if it doesn't have the coolest technology. We built this really cool product. It was really hard to use. Only those techie geeks could use it and there are only so many of them around. When you got around to deploying it, it took six to nine months and we had to hand hold them all of the way. This was not the way to scale the company. It took three revisions before we got it right.

Eventually those university spinoffs that survive learn the importance of identifying a market need for their technologies. My interviews with the founders of the MIT spinoffs revealed that successful spinoff companies generally figure out, through trial and error, that technology push is a very difficult way to introduce new products and services. As a result, most of the successful spinoffs ultimately identify customer needs and evolve to a market pull orientation. For example, the founder of one computer hardware spinoff explains,

> In the beginning we looked at the technology as a technology push out into the market to try to do a couple of products which we think the market needs. What is successful is more market pull. We sit down with people and find out what the market needs and use our technology to solve their problem. When the product comes out, of course, the people are waiting for it.

Satisfying a need

It is one thing to identify a market need and it is another to come up with a solution that meets that need. For university spinoffs, like all companies, satisfying a market need with a new technology means using the technology to create a solution that customers are willing to pay for.

My interviews with the founders of the MIT spinoffs revealed that many of them began their efforts with the mistaken notion that the key to satisfying a customer need is coming up with the best technology. For instance, the founder of one MIT computer hardware spinoff explains, 'I started with a pretty idealistic idea of blowing the problem away with computational horsepower and that ended up not being feasible on any level. I mean nobody would pay for it.' This mistaken notion is not surprising because, in the academic setting, having the best solution does matter a great deal; rewards in that setting accrue to those people who come up with the most creative and novel solutions.

Because the rules of academia and the product market are different, founders of university spinoffs have to adopt the commercial sector's perspective on how to satisfy customer needs if they are to be successful. My interviews with the founders of the MIT spinoffs revealed that the most successful founders figure out that the key to satisfying a customer need is not coming up with the best technology, but rather coming up with a solution that people will pay for. For example, the founder of one MIT software spinoff explains,

> In general, the founders of the startups coming out of MIT are always in love with all the technology that we come up with and not thinking enough about whether someone would be willing to pay for that. We often make the mistake, as MIT entrepreneurs, that we're in love with the technology, and the science and the cool ideas. But business out there has to have some application for it where it ultimately makes a big difference so they're willing to pay the price that it takes. Even if you have the most exciting technology you can imagine, if there isn't a market for it, it isn't worth the money. It's just not going to take off if it's not changing the bottom line for some client out there.

Coming up with an understanding of how to satisfy customer needs is not an easy process for the founders of university spinoffs even after they learn that the business world rewards the identification of solutions to customer needs rather than the identification of the best technology.[3] To come up with solutions that satisfy customers, the founders of spinoffs sometimes need to recognize that these solutions may not actually require the cutting edge technology that the university inventors created and that the spinoff's best strategy is to abandon its cutting edge university invention. For example, the founder of one of the MIT software spinoffs explains,

> In our case, the customers' first priority was getting a computer to run a web site in the first place and then dealing with a firewall and all these other things that were really must haves and ours was sort of cool to have technology, but not a must have. It was not a problem they needed to resolve tomorrow.

In fact, it is actually very unlikely that the product or service that satisfies a customer need will be as technologically sophisticated as the original university invention that leads to the founding of the spinoff. The reason is that, to satisfy customer needs in a way that allows for sufficient sales, the spinoff has to appeal to a wide variety of customers, and the mainstream of the market does not want technology as cutting edge as university researchers typically develop. As the founder of one of the MIT software spinoffs explains, 'It's got to work for a broad base of people. It can't just be something that one person thinks is a really great idea.' Otherwise, too few people will buy the product or service for the spinoff to make money.

To come up with solutions that satisfy customers, the founders of spinoffs often need to change their technologies. Specifically, they need to develop products and services with the specific features that customers want, even if these features have little, if anything, to do with the core technology developed in the university. For instance, the founder of one MIT software spinoff explains, 'For our product all the cool technology in the world doesn't make any difference. All that really matters is how good your artists are. Without a tool that an artist could understand, we weren't going to get any type of good demos back out.'

Moreover, the spinoffs have to develop these products in a timely manner, which is not the norm in academia. As a result, satisfying a customer need means that the founders of the spinoffs have to figure out how to operate on a commercial schedule. For example, the founder of one MIT software spinoff explains,

> When we have somebody doing graphics, for example, they know they have to get it done. It's not that they're on a funded position for years to come and maybe they'll finish it this month or maybe they'll finish it next month. There's a different mentality. They have to get it done and they have to get it done fast.

Obtaining customer feedback

Because university technology is generally invented without customer involvement, the founders of university spinoffs are usually not able to identify customer needs or come up with solutions to them unless they interact with potential customers to obtain feedback on their technologies. It is the feedback from potential customers that allows the founders of university spinoffs to fashion new products and services from their technologies that actually satisfy customer needs. As the founder of one MIT semiconductor spinoff explains,

> You have to work with your customers. No matter how good your idea is, you have to get to a point where you can actually engage the customer. The engagement allows you to stay on course or for the customer to redefine your product, which will then be guaranteed to meet their needs.

Obtaining customer feedback helps the founders of university spinoffs to fashion new products and services that satisfy customer needs in five ways. First, obtaining customer feedback provides necessary information about market needs that is not available in the university environment. As a venture capitalist that backed one of the MIT software spinoffs explains,

> The real issues that have to be answered are what problems do you solve economically for the customer? The answers to these questions are not technical and they cannot be answered from within the university environment because the university

environment doesn't provide any information about what's going on in the market-place.

Second, obtaining feedback from customers provides fine-grained informa-tion about customer needs that is necessary for the founders of university spinoffs to figure out how to satisfy customers. Several founders of the MIT spinoffs explained that no other source is able to provide this fine-grained information about customer needs. As a result, obtaining feedback from customers is necessary to develop appropriate products and services. The founder of one MIT software spinoff explains,

> The true feeling and understanding of the market comes from being there at trade shows or working with customers. So our understanding of the depth of the markets is growing as we're actually there selling product and figuring out who's buying and who's not buying.

Moreover, in the absence of this fine-grained information, university engi-neers and scientists will exploit their natural academic tendencies to develop elegant technical solutions because this is what they are trained to do. Unfortunately, as was explained earlier in the chapter, customers do not value elegant technical solutions, but instead value solutions that best meet their needs. Several of the founders of MIT spinoffs confirm that it is important to seek customer feedback to ensure that scientists and engineers focus on ways to meet customer needs. For instance, the founder of one MIT software spinoff explains,

> It's very easy to get engineers in the ivory tower to come up with elegant solutions. But they're elegant solutions to problems that nobody particularly cares about. You really have to find out what the buyer wants and say, 'If I do this and this in such a way, would you be a customer?' That's how I did it. We didn't do it in a vacuum. I did it by having vital contact through discussions with various segments of the marketplace.

Third, obtaining feedback from customers helps the founders of university spinoffs to decide what market applications to pursue. As Chapter 6 explained, many university technologies at such an early stage that they can be applied in multiple markets. While the founders of spinoffs can choose which application to pursue on purely technical grounds, they are often better off making the decision on the basis of market-based factors. For this reason, the founders of many university spinoffs seek feedback from potential customers to determine which applications to pursue. For example, the CEO of one of the MIT mate-rials spinoffs explains,

> We went to customers and said, 'We're not looking for some big development commitment here at the moment. We're just thinking if we could make good micro

cellular foam, it would have real applicability to your product line. Could we talk to you about it?' We used that as a vehicle for doing very quick and dirty feasibility assessment on the foaming of different materials and that helped us to decide what directions to take.

Fourth, obtaining feedback from customers provides the founders of the spinoff with information about how to integrate the new technology with existing technologies that are already being employed by potential customers. Because much technology is systemic and needs to be employed with complementary technologies already in place, this feedback is very important to obtaining customer acceptance of the new products and services offered by university spinoffs.

Several of the founders of the MIT spinoffs that I interviewed indicated the importance of obtaining customer feedback as a way for the founders of the spinoff to integrate their new technology with existing technologies employed by customers. For instance, the founder of one of the MIT software spinoffs explains, 'We started talking to customers and it was customer input that really led us to where we had to do a lot more in terms of integrating our technology within their existing messaging infrastructure.'

Fifth, obtaining feedback from customers provides the founders of the spinoff with information about the future technology plans of customers. This is important because most university technology is far from the commercialization stage at the time when spinoffs are founded. By understanding the direction in which customers are moving, the founders of university spinoffs can determine whether or not they are investing in the right areas to support the future development of the technology. For example, the founder of one of the MIT optics spinoffs explains, 'We talked to a lot of folks in the auto industry, which has embraced MEMS more than any other industry at this point in time, and got a sense from them what their plans were and what kind of devices they would like to see in vehicles.'

The difficulty of obtaining feedback from customers

The importance of obtaining feedback from potential customers does not mean that it is easy. In fact, the process of obtaining feedback is very difficult because potential customers often cannot give accurate feedback until the spinoff has invested in the development of the technology. As a result, the founders of the spinoff must make the initial investments in the development of their products and services without the benefit of customer input.

Several of the founders of the MIT spinoffs that I interviewed described the difficulty of obtaining feedback from customers without first developing the technology. The founder of one of the MIT mechanical device spinoffs explains,

> At first we went to the filtering companies and said, 'Anything you want, we'll make it. Tell us what you want.' But as it turns out, they don't really know what they want. It's like selling tires. You go into a tire shop and there are a lot of tires there and you might buy some. It's the same thing with the filters. The filter guys don't really know what they want. They've got some performance criteria that they need, and if you meet that, then that's what they're looking for.

It is difficult for the founders of university spinoffs to obtain feedback from customers not only because customers do not know what they want, but also because some technologies are difficult to understand without seeing them. The founder of one of the MIT software spinoffs describes this situation, saying

> It would be absolutely futile to talk to customers without a demo. How's anyone going to believe that the technology can even be made to work unless you show them that it works? In this particular case, you're trying to sell a concept that the existing technology is bad and what I propose is better. But it's a little bit of a subtle thing because unless they can see the R system running with the magnetic tracker and can see it jittering and they feel sick, they won't have a sense of what you're talking about. I can go out there and say in words that the existing R systems jitter and there's latency and there's range restrictions and these things are very frustrating if you try to use the existing technology. I can say that there's a better way. But how can anyone understand what you mean if you don't show them?

Given the difficulty of obtaining feedback from potential customers without first offering a prototype or demo for them to look at, many founders of the MIT spinoffs had to invest in the development of their initial prototype without the benefit of customer input. The founder of one of the MIT mechanical device spinoffs explains this process in the context of his company:

> We finally had a prototype that was far enough along to ship to customers and get some feedback. It's important to realize that because we were building this new technology and it was so fundamentally different from what the markets had ever had before, nobody was able to give us a real specification. It's not that they wouldn't put the time in, it's just very difficult to know what the specifications would be until they used it. So we spent a hell of a lot of money doing development work. What we had to do was build a cooler to prove that this could be made into a reliable, affordable, low temperature refrigerator.

Because customer feedback is important to the identification of products or services that meet their needs, the founders of university spinoffs cannot develop useful products or services until they receive this customer feedback. As a result, the founders of the MIT spinoffs typically establish their initial prototype in the absence of customer input, test that prototype with customers, and gather information on everything that is wrong with the prototype that the spinoff had created. This list of 'mistakes' can then be brought back to the spinoff, and its technical staff can create a new version of the product that does not have these flaws in it. The founder of one of the MIT mechanical device spinoffs describes this process. He says,

> It's very difficult to address everything up front. We took our best shot to address all aspects. Not just the performance aspect, but all aspects of cost, durability and packaging. We then tried to get the prototype tested as soon as possible so that we could further refine it.

As a result, the process of creating a product or service that meets customer needs is an iterative one. The founders of the MIT spinoffs describe a process of developing a product, obtaining feedback from customers, making changes to the product and obtaining more feedback. For example, the CEO of one MIT semiconductor spinoff explains, 'Basically you get out in front of the customer and tell what you've got. He's going to say, "Yeah, yeah, yeah, that's all great, but . . ." You listen to the buts and go back and fix them real quick and then get back in front of him.'

The need for customer feedback combined with the difficulty of obtaining it means that many university spinoffs seek to get to market quickly with a product and then revise the product in subsequent versions on the basis of customer feedback. While the lack of customer feedback in the initial invention phase precludes spinoffs from creating products or services that meet customer needs completely the first time around, such an iterative process allows the spinoff to obtain more realistic customer feedback than would be the case if the feedback were not provided in a market context.

The founders and investors in the MIT spinoffs that I interviewed described the usefulness of this strategy. For example, a venture capitalist that funded one MIT software spinoff explains,

> The only thing you can really do is get the product to market as quickly as possible and validate it as much as possible along the way. Then you go out and talk to customer prospects and get their feedback and refine positioning in the direction of the products so it's a fit for a problem that they have.

This quick-to-market iteration strategy works best if the spinoff launches a simple, inexpensive product first, and uses this product to gain access to customers. By entering with a product that customers would accept more easily, the spinoff can obtain information useful for the development of products that require much more accuracy in meeting customer needs to be successful. The founder of one MIT semiconductor spinoff explains this strategy:

> We took the technology and made the simplest product we could. It wasn't the best product. The only thing it had going for it was that it was something we could make and it could be applied. We used that product to get entrée into these large companies

to find out what they wanted. If you were their supplier you could learn what they really wanted for the next generation. But if you weren't supplying to them, you had no way to get in the door. So product evolution happened by listening very carefully to some big companies and not from sitting and saying, 'Well this industry is going to need these kinds of products.' You just didn't have the opportunity to learn that as an outsider. You had to be an insider and the way to get to be an insider was to do anything that was useful to get through the door. Once you get close to your customers and have access to what they needed, it is very clear. You just pay attention and you know what to do.

Some of the founders of the MIT spinoffs identified mechanisms to shorten the iterative process of developing a product, obtaining feedback on it and revising the product to meet customer needs. As a result, these spinoffs were able to reduce the market risk that they faced in the product development process. For instance, the founder of one semiconductor spinoff explains how his company developed a process to manage the iterative process of obtaining customer feedback:

> We were going to build a product and the market risk is that you design a product and nobody wants it. So we evolved this technique of writing up the spec before doing the product and taking this spec to the potential customer. We would ask, 'If we offer this would you find it interesting?' At least then we had something to engage with and could get feedback. In fact, interesting feedback that we came up with was that we had designed a product that was too advanced. We went to Seagate and the guys there said, 'You know, we'll need this in five years, but we have this problem today. We need things in CMOS and if you do this and this, we would need it sooner.' So we took the concept back and put it on the shelf for later use and just said, 'Okay Seagate, you're our customer. What do you need? What do you want?' And then we created a new spec that actually solved their problem. So the technique was that of doing this thing of feedback with the customers, just fulfilling their need. We would have mid-course correction to whatever we were trying to do.

Choosing an Application

Another part of the process of overcoming market uncertainty for university technologies involves the selection of a market application in which the founders of university spinoffs would employ their technologies. The process of choosing a market application is difficult for the founders of university spinoffs because the technologies that the spinoffs exploit are often very early stage inventions that are introduced via technology push, making it hard for founders to identify the 'right' market applications for their technologies.

Several of the founders of the MIT spinoffs that I interviewed described the difficulty of selecting a market application for the technology that their company was exploiting. For instance, the founder of one MIT software spinoff explains, 'It wasn't clear what market you should target because technically you want to be in all markets that use audio.' Similarly, the founder of one of the MIT optics spinoffs explains, 'We had a lot of potential applications for our technology because the TLO and the faculty member tell you the technology can be applied to everything.' And the founder of another MIT software spinoff says, 'Selecting an application has been a problem since the day we started. I've been struggling with it because it's not an easy decision.'

Despite the difficulty of selecting a market application for the technology, the founders of most university spinoffs eventually make this choice.[4] In general, they focus on several factors to select an application, including choosing those applications with the potential to achieve a high volume of sales, those applications for which the technology provides the greatest value to the customer, those applications for which the spinoff has the best ability to serve the market, and those applications for which the spinoff is most likely to create a sustainable competitive advantage.

Sales volume

One way that founders of university spinoffs select the market applications for their technologies is to focus on market size. The founders of many of the MIT spinoffs that I interviewed explained that their companies focused on the application with the largest market size. For example, the founder of one MIT biotechnology spinoff explains, 'We looked at five areas, bladder, colon, cervical, breast, and prostate cancer. We chose those five on the basis of market size.'

Choosing an application on the basis of market size is an effective approach because a large market is often necessary to recoup the costs of investing in the development of the technology. An MIT inventor whose patents led to the founding of one of the MIT software spinoffs explains why spinoffs need large markets to recoup the costs of their investment in the development of their technology:

> You're trying to get your product into the market. Starting far down in the technology base, starting with the science base, you see some potential markets and some products. If the market wasn't significant enough to represent a reasonable return on investment, then the effort wasn't worth it. So the question is to identify the potential applications that are really promising from a business point of view.

Value to the customer

A second way that founders of university spinoffs select the market applications for their technologies is by choosing those applications for which the use of the technology provides the most value to the customer. If customers will derive greater productivity benefits from the application of the technology in one area than they will in another area, the founders of the spinoffs can expect to derive greater financial benefit from the former application than from the latter.

Several of the founders of the MIT spinoffs that I interviewed explained that it was best to focus on market applications in which customers derived the greatest gains. For example, the CEO of one of the MIT materials spinoffs explains that his technology would generate much greater value to customers in certain applications than in others, and that he concentrated his company's efforts on the high value applications:

> Take improving your basic supermarket meat tray, your polystyrene dish. The product we have is a little nicer looking and the process whereby it's made is a little more stable, but the whole thing is only worth 5 or 6 percent on some companies' bottom line. So instead we looked at areas where we came to understand that, if we could do it, people would really care.

Similarly, a venture capitalist describes why the MIT spinoffs that he was involved with chose their particular applications for MIT's Three Dimensional Printing technology. He says, '3DP had some unbelievable advantages over all the other free form fabrication technologies. But the making of models for surgeons didn't seem to be one of the strengths over other fabrication technologies that made it worthy of focusing on.'

The founders of the MIT spinoffs identified several different mechanisms for identifying the applications for which customers would derive the most value. First, the founders look at the ease of demonstrating value to customers. Given the difficulty of selling new technology products and services, these founders explain that a demonstration of value to the customer is crucial to making sales, and a demonstration of value is easiest for applications for which the customers derived the most benefit. For example, the founder of one of the MIT optics spinoffs explains,

> We looked at the automotive industry, but we'd have very expensive tools. We were talking about a tool that can range from $375,000 to $700,000. We were concerned that the overall payback on this tool in that industry was questionable. To get a $375,000 tool paid off by simply sampling wouldn't be enough. We chose semiconductor testing because all the testing prior to the introduction of our technology was done destructively. We would have a non-destructive evaluation, and where you do that, there's a huge amount of value added. They also had an overwhelming desire to ramp production volumes up fast because the life of a chip is so limited. In magnetic storage the customer value proposition wasn't nearly as good as with the chips.

Second, the founders look at areas where their technologies offer a distinct performance improvement over existing technology. In these areas, customers derive significant value from switching from the old technology to the new technology. The data that I collected from the MIT spinoffs illustrate this point. For example, an MIT inventor whose patents led to the founding of one of the MIT software spinoffs explains that his spinoff looked for applications 'where the technology provides a distinctive improvement over what's there, such as lower costs. We asked, "Is it going to produce perceptively better performance that would give you a chance of competing with the existing known technology?" '

Ability to serve the market

The founders of university spinoffs also select market applications for university inventions by looking at the spinoff's ability to serve customers. The logic of this approach is that spinoffs have to ensure that they can deliver new products and services that meet customer needs. Because the creation of products and services from university inventions is far from automatic, whether the spinoff could produce one product more easily than another is important in determining the application on which to focus.

Many of the MIT spinoff founders and investors that I interviewed indicated that they choose their market applications on the basis of their ability to serve the market. For instance, a venture capitalist that backed one MIT software spinoff explains that the spinoff's choice of where to focus is determined by 'where they can provide what the customers want'. Similarly, the CEO of one of the MIT biotechnology spinoffs explains that his company's 'choice of application was made on technical grounds. It was a straightforward and obvious thing to first use the gene to protect cells against chemotherapeutic drugs'.

The founders of university spinoffs focus on several parameters to determine which products or services they can produce most easily. One parameter is the stage of development of the technology. Many of the MIT spinoffs focused on the application for which the technology was already most developed. For instance, the founder of one of the MIT biotechnology spinoffs explains, 'You focus on the application which seems to be the most obvious and straightforward to pursue in the laboratory and to demonstrate proof of principle.' Similarly, the founder of one of the MIT medical device spinoffs explains that he focused on the applications 'that had been explored the most in R&D and therefore had the largest amount of data saying, "yes, it will definitely work." ' And the founder of another biotechnology spinoff explains, 'We picked our application on proof of principle, which ones seem to work best from the studies we've done.'

A second parameter that founders used to determine the market application for which they would have the greatest ease in serving customers was the simplicity of producing a product or service. By focusing on the application in which the product or service is easiest to produce, the founders of the spinoff increase the likelihood that they can come up with something that demonstrates the value of the technology to potential customers, thereby making it easier to sell products or services later. Therefore the founders of several MIT spinoffs explain that they selected their applications on the basis of the simplicity of creating new products or services. For instance, the founder of one MIT medical device spinoff says,

> The main reason we chose the application is that it's ideally suited to our particular technology. It was primarily just matching our technology to the market the best because we had such an efficient high speed process for making arrays in that particular market.

A third parameter that founders used to determine the market application for which they would have the greatest ease in serving customers was that of time to market. Focusing on where the technology will work sooner rather than later provides an advantage to new companies because they need to generate something that is valuable to customers to stay alive. Therefore the founder of one MIT materials spinoff explains that his spinoff focused on 'taking the easier technologies and moving them to commercialization first'.

Some of the founders even pointed out that the spinoff has to reach market quickly with an application or it will run out of cash. For instance, the founder of one materials spinoff explains that his venture exploited the 'electronic packaging market rather than the automotive market, where barriers to acceptance are really high, even though the numbers in automotive are great. [In automotive] it'll take us a long time. We would starve before we got there.'

A fourth parameter that founders use is the scalability of the technology. In some cases, the results from proof of principle studies suggest that the founders should choose certain applications because the technology will scale most easily in these applications. For example, the founder of one of the MIT biotechnology spinoffs explains,

> We selected the application on the basis of the likelihood that the patents which are based on laboratory findings with small n's [numbers] will work on ninety plus percent of the people in the real world. It's one thing to show that something works in a controlled laboratory situation and it's quite another to have a million people testing it out there. Then how powerful is the effect? Will the compound only have a minor effect on the disease?

A fifth parameter that founders use is the location of customers. In general, when spinoffs make their decisions about which applications to pursue on the basis of the ease of serving customers, they tend to focus on markets where the customers are geographically proximate. For example, the founder of one optics spinoff explains his company's decision not to go after the flat panel display market. He says,

> We needed to have a domestic rollout first because we didn't want to have international sales first because it would require more equity and we didn't think we could do that on the first round. We rejected flat panel display because the vast majority

of production is in Japan and it would be very hard for us to service the market initially.

Competitive advantage

A fourth way that founders of university spinoffs select market applications for technology is to choose those applications for which the use of the technology provides a competitive advantage. By choosing applications on the basis of competitive advantage, the founders of the spinoffs can increase the likelihood that they will appropriate any financial returns to the successful commercialization of the university inventions.

Several of the founders of the MIT spinoffs that I interviewed indicated that they select market applications on the basis of where they can obtain a competitive advantage. For instance, a venture capitalist that backed one of the MIT software spinoffs explains that his company focused on the market application 'where they would have the most defensible position long term'.

In many cases, the selection of an application where the spinoff could ensure a competitive advantage involves selection of an application in which the company can obtain additional patents. Because university spinoffs do not have many competitive advantages in their earliest days, the ability to obtain intellectual property protection for their technologies is an important source of competitive advantage for these firms. Therefore many of the founders of the MIT spinoffs, particularly those in biotechnology, where patents are particularly effective, indicated that they select their market applications on the basis of the opportunity to obtain additional patents and build a defensible intellectual property position against competitors.

In other cases, selecting an application where the spinoff could ensure a competitive advantage involves figuring out the application in which the spinoff can do something that cannot be done by other firms. The ability to differentiate the spinoff from competitors is an important source of competitive advantage, given that university spinoffs are rarely low-cost producers. Therefore, several of the founders of MIT spinoffs explain that they choose market applications where they would have little, if any, competition. For example, the founder of one MIT biotechnology spinoff explains how that company selected its market application. She says, 'We were looking for things that no one else could do, that couldn't be done another way.'

Selling the Products and Services

A third part of the process of developing the market for university technologies involves selling the products or services that are created from the university inventions. Many of the founders of MIT spinoffs that I interviewed indicated that they found selling their products or services one of the more difficult and time-consuming parts of the process of creating a new company.

Because many of the university spinoffs are founded by or employ the inventors of the technology that led to the founding of the spinoff in the first place, the founders and employees of university spinoffs often underestimate the importance and difficulty of selling the university technology. Having worked on the development of the technology, most of the people employed by the spinoff already believe in the value of the new technology. As a result, they do not realize how hard it is to persuade others of that value.

The founders' belief in the value of the technology that the spinoff is developing leads many of them to believe that customers will buy the technology when it is presented to them without requiring any sales effort. For example, the founder of one of the MIT computer hardware spinoff explains,

> We talked to a lot of people trying to figure out where we would take the technology, what market would really be the best application for it. We really thought that we could show a prototype of this stuff working and people would say, 'Yeah, this is it.'

As a result of their belief that their inventions would 'sell themselves', many of the founders of the MIT spinoffs that I interviewed indicated that they underestimated the importance of selling. For example, the founder of one MIT robotics spinoff explains,

> You think this stuff is the most exciting thing in the world. You are doing research that you believe is cutting edge and that you would pay anything to get your hands on. But only a few people in the world would feel that way because only a few people in the world were presented with the same problems and opportunities that we had. Just a few labs were doing that type of work. I didn't realize how small that world was.

However, in reality, the founders of spinoff companies need to convince customers of the value of their technologies. This process involves effective selling. For instance, the founder of one of the MIT medical device spinoffs explains,

> When you sell something that's completely new, a novel analytical technology, you have to do a lot of missionary work and education work in the field because people say, 'I've never heard of this before. I don't know if it works or not.' So you really have to do a lot to prove that it works.

Moreover, selling the products and services developed by a university spinoff is particularly difficult, for several reasons. First, in most cases, customers of new technology products and services have problems or issues that require the development of a unique approach to selling to them. Therefore convincing customers of the value of a technology often requires different activities for each segment of the market.

Several of the founders of the MIT spinoffs that I interviewed indicated that they had to develop unique approaches to convince each customer of the value of their technology products and services. For instance, one inventor–entrepreneur describes the problems that his spinoff had in persuading customers:

> For each application, special concerns came up that required some consulting time, and each of those led to improvements in the method and new ways to do it. When you have a product that needs to be customized to be effective, the delivery is slow. People were needed on every application. I don't think that there were any sales that didn't have a whole lot of development time.

Second, the founders of the university spinoffs need to persuade customers to purchase enough units of the new product or service for the company to generate enough revenues to survive. With university inventions, often customers are interested in purchasing one or two units to learn about the new technology, but are unwilling or unable to adopt the products or service in large volume. Thus, even when a few early adopters purchase initial versions of the product or service, the founders of many university spinoffs have trouble finding willing customers to purchase a large enough volume of products or services for the spinoff to survive.

Several of the founders of the MIT spinoffs that I interviewed described the problem of achieving a large volume of sales for products and services made to exploit university inventions. For example, the founder of one MIT robotics spinoff explains,

> As I was exiting MIT, [my advisor] directed me to a lead from NASA to sell the first of these robot arms. I was pretty excited about that because I was about to charge 150K, which was enough for one year's salary plus materials and supplies. As it turned out, it took longer than a year and it ended up costing me money to make the arms. I was doing pure technology push, but because of that initial sale, I had the thought that everyone would beat a path to my door. So when people said, 'You need to market, market, market' I had a hard time putting that into context.

Third, selling products and services based on university technology is difficult because most companies will not purchase new products and services unless the seller of those products and services can convince them that they will benefit substantially from the new technology. Customers are reluctant to change suppliers because changing suppliers is disruptive to the operations of an organization. As a result, selling new products and services based on university inventions requires the founders of university spinoffs to demonstrate the value of the products and services to the customer's bottom line. This process is difficult if that level of value is not very large.

Several of the founders of the MIT spinoffs that I interviewed described the problem of trying to sell to customers that would not derive a major benefit from purchasing the spinoff's products or services. For example, the founder of one MIT semiconductor spinoff explains,

> The hardest part of selling this product is not that the technology doesn't work or that there's a use for it, but that using it requires a change in the way semiconductors are manufactured. Our technology is a real time test while it's being processed and the old way is after the fact. That can be a big benefit but it requires that they change some things. And the payback is a million dollars in a fab. In a fab where they talk about billions of dollars, that's not much. It's not that they're completely uninterested, but it's a hard sell because it's not a huge benefit.

SUMMARY

This chapter has discussed the process by which university spinoffs develop their technologies, and identify and satisfy customer demand. The first part of this process usually involves further development of the technology. At the time that an entrepreneur makes the decision to found a spinoff, university technologies are typically very early stage inventions that require additional development. Some university spinoffs are based on such early stage technology that the company needs to establish proof of principle before any other activity can take place. After proof of principle has been achieved, a university spinoff has to develop a prototype and then must turn the university invention into a product or service.

Creating a product involves additional technical development, for a variety of reasons. First, most customers do not generally buy raw technology, but buy products or services. Second, university technology needs to be changed into a form that fits the expectations of the commercial world and makes external stakeholders comfortable. Third, customer feedback reveals problems or provides information about customer needs that necessitate changes to the product or service. Fourth, product development creates new intellectual property that can be protected by patents or other forms of protection.

Many of the founders of university spinoffs underestimate the importance of product development because they do not know what product development is or how the process works. However, the founders of successful university spinoffs typically need to learn about product development because they need to make changes to their new technologies to transform them into products and services. These changes include such things as improving performance, enhancing robustness, adding supporting technology, scaling up for manufacturing, increasing ease of use and changing mechanisms and architecture.

Because the founders of spinoffs must often change university technologies to make them appropriate for the commercial environment, many university spinoffs face considerable technical uncertainty even after they have developed prototypes. No one knows if the changes that would be required are physically possible because no one knows if the founders are capable of making these changes, and because the transformation of the university inventions requires the development of other technologies beyond the control of the founders.

When university spinoffs are established, they often face significant market uncertainty because no one knows if the spinoff can provide a product or service that customers want or need, what the level of demand for the product or service will be, whether that demand can be satisfied in a cost-effective manner or whether the spinoff can provide a better alternative than that provided by competitors. To overcome market uncertainty, the founders of university spinoffs need to evaluate the markets for their technologies. In general, this involves figuring out if there is a customer need.

The founders of university spinoffs need to interact with customers to obtain feedback on their technologies because the type of information that is necessary for the spinoff to develop a valuable product or service is not available in the university environment. Moreover, it is very difficult for the founders of university spinoffs to decide what market applications to pursue in the absence of information from customers. Customer feedback provides the spinoff with information about how to integrate the new technology with existing technologies that are already being employed by customers. Finally, this feedback provides information about the customers' future technology plans.

The process of obtaining feedback from potential customers is very difficult for the founders of university spinoffs. Customers often cannot give accurate feedback until the spinoff has invested in the development of the technology, yet the founders of the spinoffs often cannot develop anything useful for potential customers without some customer feedback. As a result, the founders of university spinoffs often have to create a product in the absence of feedback, test it with customers, and then iterate toward meeting customer needs.

The founders of university spinoffs often have to choose a market application in which to employ their technology. Because the technologies that they use are often at a very early stage and are introduced via technology push, the 'right' market applications for the technology are not always apparent to the founders of university spinoffs. To select which market applications to pursue, the founders of university spinoffs focus on several factors, including sales volume, value to the customer, ability to serve the market and the ability to create a sustainable competitive advantage.

The founders of university spinoffs also need to sell their products or services. Although they generally believe that customers will buy technology when it is presented to them, they soon learn that they need to convince customers of the value of their products and services.

Having described the process of spinoff development, I now turn to the financing of university spinoffs, the subject of Chapter 11.

NOTES

1. In some cases, the inventors had only undertaken simulations and prototype development was necessary to provide evidence of the value of the technology that went beyond the basic proof of principle. For instance, a venture capitalist that invested in one of the MIT software spin-offs describes the situation with that company at the time of founding: 'At the time they started, there were some simulations so there were things done that showed it would work. It was not just theory, but simulations of what was going to be done that verified the key aspects of it. But we didn't have a prototype.'
2. In some cases, the time horizon is even longer. In the case of Integra Life Sciences, an MIT spinoff that created artificial skin, the technology took 20 years to develop and 5 years to achieve FDA approval (*Boston Globe*, 1998).
3. Even when customers are willing to buy prototypes of university technologies, the founders of spinoffs do not necessarily know the customer need that the technology is filling. For example, the CEO of one MIT robotics spinoff explains, 'It was unclear what business oppor-tunity we were going to pursue. There was this fabulous technology that was patented and came out of MIT and people were buying it. But it wasn't clear exactly what they were buying it for and what the market was. It was a solution looking for a problem. But it seemed to be solving someone's problem because people were buying and that's what we tried to ascertain. You know so many MIT companies turn out to be technology in search of a problem and we had to work hard to make sure we were solving a real problem.'
4. The CEO of one of the MIT materials spinoffs explains why selecting a market application is important. He says, 'We basically tried the technology in a lot of applications. After a while I realized that we had a very small chance of randomly picking an application and having the application work.'

11. The financing of university spinoffs

This chapter explains how the founders of university spinoffs acquire the capital that they need to exploit their new technologies. As the previous chapter explained, most university spinoffs need to engage in both technical and market development before they can sell new technology products or services. As a result, they need to finance the development of their companies. While the entrepreneur can provide this financing from his or her own savings, the cost of developing university spinoffs can reach many millions of dollars, making self-financing difficult for many entrepreneurs to undertake. As a result, in many cases, the entrepreneur acquires capital from external sources, including business angels, venture capitalists and government agencies.

When the entrepreneur seeks capital from an external source, two important factors – uncertainty and information asymmetry – influence the process. The founders of university spinoffs often have much more information than other parties about the technical and market potential of their technologies, particularly at the very early stages when the companies are first founded. Moreover, the spinoffs that exploit these technologies face considerable uncertainty because no one knows for certain whether a market for them exists or if the technologies can be converted into commercializable products or services. Because of this uncertainty and information asymmetry, the financing of university spinoffs demands specific actions by entrepreneurs and their investors.

The first section of the chapter explains the importance of capital acquisition for university spinoffs. The second discusses the financing gap that many spinoffs face, and explains why public sector funding is important to spinoff company development. The third section explains why uncertainty and information asymmetry make capital acquisition difficult for the founders of university spinoffs, and discusses how entrepreneurs and investors cope with these problems. The final section describes the different sources of capital used to finance university spinoffs.

THE IMPORTANCE OF RESOURCE ACQUISITION

In general, university spinoffs require significant amounts of capital. The need for spinoffs to conduct significant technical and market development after founding makes them capital-intensive start-ups. While no data exist on the amount of capital raised by the average university spinoff, some data exist on the amount of capital raised by MIT spinoffs founded between 1980 and 1996. The mean level of capital raised by these companies was $5 271 935 (Shane and Stuart, 2002). By way of comparison, Aldrich (1999) reports that less than one percent of all start-ups founded in the United States raise more than $1 000 000 in financing.

Obtaining adequate capital facilitates the development of university spinoffs for several reasons. First, capital provides slack that allows new companies to adapt to adverse environmental conditions, thereby allowing entrepreneurs to consider a wider range of potential alternatives and enhancing external perceptions of the stability, acceptability and dependability of new ventures (Shane, 2003). Second, obtaining adequate amounts of capital enhances the performance of university spinoffs. As Chapter 12 will explain in greater detail, the single greatest reason for people to abandon efforts to spin off companies is their inability to obtain capital, and the amount of capital raised by a spinoff is positively associated with the likelihood of desirable outcomes like acquisition and initial public offering, and negatively associated with undesirable outcomes like venture failure (Shane and Stuart, 2002).

Because of the importance to university spinoffs of raising external capital, the entrepreneur typically seeks funding from investors after founding a spinoff. The process of obtaining capital from private sources usually requires issuing equity to investors and going through several investment rounds (Roberts and Malone, 1996). However, university spinoffs in areas other than biotechnology can rarely obtain private funding in their earliest days. Private sector investors are often not interested in university spinoffs at their earliest stages of development because the risks facing these ventures are quite high. Moreover, entrepreneurs often use public funds to develop their new ventures first to avoid giving up the large amounts of equity that they would need to relinquish to obtain adequate financing of high risk, early stage ventures.

THE PUBLIC SECTOR AND THE FINANCING GAP

The initial capital obtained by university spinoffs in areas other than biotechnology generally does not come from private investors, creating a funding gap in the development of university spinoffs. Private sector investors generally want to invest in spinoff companies that have reached later stages of development. Although the ability to raise private capital at the time of spinoff company formation varies across institutions (with spinoffs from the more prestigious institutions being more likely to raise external capital from private sources immediately upon formation), investors generally do not invest in university spinoffs when they are first founded. Even spinoffs from the most prestigious academic institutions, like MIT, often need to obtain public sector capital before they can obtain private financing because of investor preferences. For instance, one of the investors in an MIT biotechnology spinoff explained, 'Before I invest, I would probably want to see the assay development move farther along to the point where you can make an assay, which may or may not be funded from the normal sources of funding in an academic environment.'

This problem is most severe in areas other than biotechnology. While investors in biotechnology spinoffs are often willing to invest in those companies at very early stages in their development, many of the investors in spinoffs exploiting other types of technology believe that the appropriate time to invest in a university spinoff is not in the beginning, when the spinoff is seeking to prove the principle of its technology, but later on, when the company has a prototype and is engaged in product development. Because private sector investors need to consider the financial returns that they will achieve in making their investment decisions, and these returns are very much influenced by the length of time it takes a company to develop a product, investors in nonbiotechnology spinoffs are often unable to earn sufficient financial returns to justify investment until a university spinoff is close to the development of a product or service.[1] For example, an angel investor in one of the MIT software spinoffs explains that his investment in that company was a mistake because he invested in the company too early in its life. He says, 'Most of the money was spent on very rudimentary things that we started to do. I should have gotten involved in 1995 when the technology was farther along, when they had a product.'

The bias of private investors in university spinoffs toward later stage investing means that the founders of university spinoffs often have trouble raising seed stage capital from private sector sources. My interviews with the founders of MIT spinoffs reveal the difficulty that the founders of these companies had in raising money from seed stage investors. For instance, the founder of one of the mechanical device spinoffs recounts his firm's experience raising funds. He says, 'We talked to venture capitalists. Usually there was no interest. They'd say "You're too early for us." '

Other researchers report similar findings. For example, Lowe (2002:22) quotes one entrepreneur who founded a spinoff from the University of California as saying, 'Our technology was early-stage. We could only describe where we were going, but we didn't have any prototype to show [venture capitalists]. They want to see that you're going to have a product soon.'

Because the founders of university spinoffs often have trouble financing their initial operations from private sector sources, they often turn to government grants and contracts (Lerner, 1998). Although many government agencies provide the capital that university spinoffs use to develop their new technologies, the Advanced Technology Program (ATP) at the National Institute of Standards and Technology, and the Small Business Innovation Research Program (SBIR) are the most important. My interviews with the founders of MIT spinoffs revealed that many of these companies were funded initially through Phase I and Phase II Small Business Innovation Research Grants from a variety of government agencies, including the US Air Force, The National Science Foundation and the National Institutes of Health.

In particular, government grants and contracts are often the major source of revenue for university spinoffs during the initial period of technology development and allow those companies to develop their technology to the point where the spinoffs can achieve private sector financing.[2] For instance, research by Lowe (2002) showed that many spinoffs from the University of California obtained substantial government research grants and contracts to develop their technologies before they reached a stage at which they could interest private investors, and that the receipt of these grants and contracts allowed the new companies to reach a stage of development that was appropriate for private sector financing.

Some researchers have even shown that government funding is necessary for spinoffs to be founded and to survive. For example, Audretsch *et al.* (2000) examined the formation and survival of biotechnology firms and found that many of them would not have been formed and would not have survived their early years in the absence of the SBIR program.

My interviews with the founders of MIT spinoffs also provide support for the proposition that the SBIR program enhances the formation and survival of university spinoffs. For instance, the founder of one MIT mechanical device spinoff explains that the receipt of an SBIR grant was central to the formation of his company: 'I joined Arthur D. Little after graduating, but wrote an SBIR grant [proposal]. After I'd been at Arthur D. Little for a month or so, I won the SBIR. Within a month I left Arthur D. Little and started [the company] in a spare room in my apartment.' Similarly, the founder of one of the MIT biotechnology spinoffs explains that the receipt of SBIR was were central to the survival of her company. She says, 'If we didn't do as well as we did with the SBIR program, we would have ended up having less cash than expenses.'

The relationship between the receipt of government funding and the development of university spinoffs has also been observed in other countries. For instance, Blair and Hitchens (1998) report on 17 companies that were spun out of Queen's University in Northern Ireland. They found that government grants were central to the development of those companies. Similarly, the UK Department of Trade and Industry (2002) argues that proof of concept funds, University Challenge Funds and University Seed Corn Funds are all responsible for the growth in spinoff companies from UK universities in recent years. And Mustar (1997) found that 70 percent of French spinoffs relied on public financial support for their initial development, through either direct innovation grants, research contracts or tax credits.

The founders of university spinoffs offer a variety of reasons why public sector financing fills the financing gap and allows these companies to develop to a stage at which private sector financing is possible. First, government grants and contracts pay for further development of university technologies, which is necessary to achieve proof of principle, to develop prototypes and to transform inventions into new products or services. For instance, MIT spinoff Jentek Sensors used SBIR grants to prove the principle behind its sensor technology and further advance its development (Hsu and Bernstein, 1997). Similarly, the founder of one MIT software spinoff explains that government funding paid for his firm's product development: 'I got some SBIR funding from NASA and from NSF and we used it to develop the product. We made advances and improvements to it and that really made a big difference.'

In some cases, government funding allows the founders of university spinoffs to figure out how to use specific materials and components, uses that were unknown at the time of invention of the technology and founding of the spinoff. As a result, government funding allows the spinoffs to develop products or services that are appropriate for a valuable market application. For example, the founder of one MIT materials spinoff explains why he sought an SBIR grant for his spinoff:

> Government R&D programs will . . . provide [us] with a controlled test case for the design and manufacturing of specific components and will give us a vehicle for optimization of components through feedback from the customer. . . . [It will also] greatly increase our ability to select alloys for specific composite applications utilizing some of the MIT technology that we are licensing as well as establish a base cash flow to the company.

In other cases, government funding allows the founders of university spinoffs to figure out how to assemble and package its products, something that many of them do not know how to do at the time that the spinoffs are established. As a result, the government funding allows the founders of the spinoffs to complete the product development process. For instance, the founder of one MIT semiconductor spinoff explains,

> A very important part of the funding of the company has come from technology development sources, namely government agencies. In the case of [our company], none of the venture capitalists could help us with the issue we were most concerned with, which was the semiconductor technology. We knew how to make the semiconductor devices, but we didn't know how to package them.

Second, government grants and contracts allow the founders of university spinoffs to find commercial uses for their technologies. As Chapter 10 explained, many university spinoffs are created to exploit technologies for which the founders have not yet identified a commercial use. As a result, the founders of the spinoffs undertake significant effort to evaluate markets, estimate potential demand, assess customer needs, obtain feedback on their ideas for products and services, and choose market applications. All of these activities are costly, and government funding provides a useful source of funding to pay for this effort.

My interviews with the founders of MIT spinoffs provide empirical support for this proposition. For instance, one MIT inventor whose patents led to the founding of a software spinoff explains how government funding allowed that company to find a commercial use for inventions. He says, 'We had a three year government contract which was essentially a hunting license to see what mathematics could be used for. We explored interactive design and process CAD/CAM. We even modeled the manufacturing process so that you'd get an entire system.'

Third, government grants and contracts facilitate the acquisition of private sector financing. Often government funding of university spinoffs is complementary to private sector funding because the government spurs private sector investment by serving as a catalyst for further investment and by providing a subsidy to reduce private sector financing costs.

In some cases, the government serves as a catalyst for private sector financing by paying for the initial test that proves the value of a technology and so motivates private investors to make subsequent investments. The financing of the MIT spinoffs provides evidence of this effect. For example, a venture capitalist who backed an MIT semiconductor spinoff explains this process in the context of superconducting technology. He says, 'Venture capitalists are looking for an aggressive commitment by the government. The problem is going to be who will pay for the one-mile test cable when we think we can build a superconducting cable' (Feder, 1987: D6).

In other cases, government funding provides a direct subsidy that lowers the investment cost of private sector investors and so spurs them to make investments. My interviews with MIT spinoff investors and founders support this argument. Take, for instance, the story of one MIT mechanical device spinoff. The founder of the company explains that the venture capitalist 'made an investment of $250 000 during the development period contingent on us getting the phase two SBIR grant and agreed to put in more money once the phase two SBIR was over'. The venture capitalist that financed this spinoff adds, 'We invested, in part, because the money we put in got us a $600 000 development program.'

Other MIT spinoffs provide additional examples of this subsidy effect. For instance, the venture capitalists that invested in an MIT software spinoff explained that they looked very favorably upon the $500 000 ARPA grant that the company received because it increased the capital in the venture without them increasing the size of their investment.

Fourth, government funding provides a way to manage the high risk inherent in developing products or services from university technologies. Because much of the university technology that spinoffs develop is cutting edge, these companies face significant technical and market risk, as Chapter 10 described. Many private sector investors find this level of risk to be too high to justify investment in early stage university spinoffs. As a result, the founders of the spinoffs turn to government agencies as a source of funding to overcome initial technical and market risks so that the level of risk that the ventures face at the time that they seek private sector financing has been reduced significantly.

My interviews with the founders of MIT spinoffs provide evidence that government funding is used to reduce the risk of developing high technology products and services. For instance, the founders of one MIT biotechnology spinoff described their strategy of using government funds to develop their new venture and reduce risk. In their business plan, they state,

> Due to the significantly high risk in the development of this product, the Company is relying on the SBIR grant . . . to partially finance the research and feasibility studies of various product and product concepts (phase I SBIR proposal), as well as to provide capital to support the preclinical evaluation of the products (phase II SBIR proposals). Specifically, the SBIR grants will provide the company . . . with the seed money to pursue high-risk product concept projects which otherwise may not be justified to pursue.

The use of federal funds to reduce the risk of developing products and services from their university inventions was not limited to the MIT biotechnology spinoffs. The founders of spinoffs based on other technologies described similar strategies. For instance, the founder of an MIT materials spinoff explains,

> I took all the technical uncertainties and converted them into government projects. For example, we've developed a connecting rod for a two-cycle engine as a result of the SBIR program. Once we've gotten through the proof and the field tests, then we'll get a bit more energetic in pursuit of the market. But right now we have federal funds that keep our development going.

THE DIFFICULTY OF CAPITAL ACQUISITION UNDER UNCERTAINTY AND INFORMATION ASYMMETRY

Obtaining capital from private sector sources is not easy for university spinoffs, even at later stages of venture development, because the information asymmetry and uncertainty that these ventures face create important problems in the financing process. Specifically, information asymmetry creates four problems in financing university spinoffs. First, the entrepreneur wants to keep his or her superior information about an opportunity secret because this information provides the basis of the new venture's competitive advantage (Shane, 2003). As a result, the entrepreneur will not disclose everything to potential investors (Casson, 1995) and investors must make decisions with limited information. Second, the entrepreneur can use his or her information advantage to extract resources that fully informed investors would not provide (Shane and Cable, 2002). Third, the entrepreneur can exploit this information asymmetry and the limits on investor monitoring that it imposes to expose investors' capital to excessive risk (Shane, 2003). Fourth, information asymmetry creates the potential for adverse selection because it makes it difficult for investors to distinguish between talented entrepreneurs pursuing valuable opportunities and untalented entrepreneurs pursuing opportunities of limited value (Sahlman, 1990).

Uncertainty makes financing spinoff companies difficult in three ways. First, it makes the evaluation of opportunities by investors difficult (Shane and Stuart, 2002). Second, it creates bargaining problems between entrepreneurs and investors by leading the entrepreneurs and investors to disagree about the profitability of the opportunity (Wu, 1989). Third, it leads investors to seek collateral to minimize the magnitude of investors' loss in the event of failure (Casson, 1982).

The MIT spinoffs provide good examples of the difficulty of financing university spinoffs. For example, Sherri Oberg, founder of MIT biotechnology spinoff Acusphere, explains why raising money for that company was problematic: 'We couldn't tell a venture capitalist much about the company or its competences at this [the initial] stage. We could show them an opportunity, but this was basically a bet that if Bob, Harry, and I were put in a room, we'd come up with something interesting' (Hansen and Anderson, 1996:9).

Given the problems engendered by the pursuit of uncertain opportunities by entrepreneurs with asymmetric information, the acquisition of capital involves two very important processes: efforts by the founders of spinoffs to demonstrate the value of their ventures to potential investors and the exploitation of social ties between entrepreneurs and investors.

Demonstrating the Value of the Ventures

Investors often look to factors that the founders of university spinoffs do not directly control as a way to obtain signals of the value of their ventures (Shane, 2003). These signals include such things as evidence of a large market, the presence of a proprietary technology, the existence of a platform technology and an indication of entrepreneurial talent among members of the founding team (Low and Abrahamson, 1997; Carter and Van Auken, 1990; Kaplan and Stromberg, 2001; Amit *et al.*, 1990). The subsections below explain how the founders of university spinoffs use these signals to obtain financing for their new ventures under conditions of information asymmetry and uncertainty.

Large markets

Private sector investors favor university spinoffs that are developing products or services for a large market. The standard venture capital model of investing holds that private investors should favor ventures that operate in large markets, which can provide greater financial returns if the company successfully introduces its product, given a relatively high cost and uncertainty of technology and market development by spinoff firms. Therefore most private sector investors that finance university spinoffs prefer spinoff companies that are aiming at large markets.

The MIT spinoffs that I investigated provide good examples of the preference of private sector investors for those spinoffs that exploit large markets. Take, for example, the approach of one venture capital firm to an investment in an MIT medical device spinoff. The investor's internal memorandum recommended funding the spinoff in large part because of the 'huge market opportunities' that the company faced for its blood glucose monitor technology. This focus is notable particularly because the venture capital firm decided against investing in other MIT spinoffs because the potential markets for the technologies of those companies were relatively small.

Proprietary technology

Private sector investors in university spinoffs also favor those spinoffs with strong patent protection on their technologies. In general, investors in high technology companies prefer to finance new companies that possess patented technologies because patents provide externally verifiable evidence of a competitive advantage (Bhide, 2000). As a result, investors can have some confidence that a spinoff that they finance would, in fact, be able to appropriate the returns to innovation, should it succeed in commercializing its technology.

Several observers have shown that patents enhance the ability of university spinoffs to raise money. For instance, judging by her experience running the technology-licensing office at Stanford University, Kathy Ku (Ku, 2001) reports that university spinoffs with exclusive rights to patents raise money more easily than other university spinoffs.

My interviews with the founders of MIT spinoffs also support the proposition that strong patent protection facilitates the acquisition of capital by spinoff companies. For example, the founder of one MIT biotechnology spinoff explains that potential investors focused very heavily on his spinoff's intellectual property position when deciding whether or not to fund it. He says, 'One of the first questions that any venture capitalist asked is what the property rights were and if we had license to them.' Similarly, one of the venture capital investors in an MIT medical device spinoff decided to finance that company in part because the company's 'I/P position is very strong with broad claims in place. . . . [It has] breakthrough and proprietary technology with strong I/P position.'

Some evidence from the MIT spinoffs even supported the proposition, suggested by Kathy Ku, that the possession of an exclusive license to patented technology facilitates the acquisition of capital by the founders of university spinoffs. For instance, in a letter to MIT in January 1982, the president of one MIT materials spinoff requested that MIT provide specific milestones that his firm needed to achieve to receive an exclusive license to an MIT patent, saying 'It could make a significant difference to our ability to attract both people and capital, and, therefore, could affect the speed with which the successful commercialization of this technology can be realized.'

One large sample statistical study of university spinoffs also supports the proposition that strong patent protection facilitates the financing of spinoff companies. Focusing on variation in the effectiveness of patents across different industries, Shane and Stuart (2002) examined the performance of the 134 spinoffs from MIT from 1980 to 1996 and found that, the more effective patents were at preventing imitation of a technology in an industry, the more likely a spinoff was to raise venture capital.

General-purpose technologies

Private sector investors in university spinoffs also favor those spinoffs that possess general-purpose technologies that can be applied in a variety of different markets. The possession of a general-purpose technology facilitates the financing of university spinoffs because university spinoffs face significant technical, market and competitive uncertainty. Entrepreneurs cannot know with certainty whether they will be able to produce new technology products or services, whether there is a market for those products or services, or whether the firm or its competitors will capture the returns from the introduction of those new products and services. Consequently, the founders of university spinoffs need to be flexible and adapt to changing circumstances. As Chapter 6 explained, general-purpose technologies offer the founders of university spinoffs greater flexibility and adaptability in the development of their companies.

In the interviews that I conducted, several people involved with the formation and financing of MIT spinoffs pointed out the preference of investors for those spinoffs that have general-purpose technologies. For instance, one investor explains that he invests in those MIT spinoffs that have a general-purpose technology. As he says, 'You look around at what the company is doing. Does it have more than one product?' Similarly, a partner in a venture capital firm that invested in several MIT spinoffs reported that his firm invested in those spinoffs that had a 'platform technology with multiple applications' and did not invest in those spinoffs without a general-purpose technology.

Moreover, the founders of MIT spinoffs that are not pursuing the development of a general-purpose technology explain that they have a very hard time obtaining private sector financing for their new companies. For example, the founder of one biotechnology spinoff explains that his company had trouble obtaining capital because its technology had one major application. After that company learned that it could no longer pursue that application, its founders were unable to find the financing that they needed to continue operations.

Founder attributes

Private sector investors in university spinoffs also favor those spinoffs that are founded by people who fit the profile of successful entrepreneurs. While much research has examined the preferences of investors for certain attributes of entrepreneurs, very little research has explored the effect of founder attributes on the financing of university spinoffs. Nevertheless, the limited research that has been conducted suggests that investors prefer founders with the industry and management experience to identify and exploit successfully entrepreneurial opportunities in new technology. As a result, prior research suggests that founders of university spinoffs with more management and industry experience are more likely to obtain financing than those without that experience (Vohora *et al.*, 2002b).

For instance, many venture capital funds that invest in university spinoffs look to invest in spinoffs in which the founders have both marketing and management expertise (Roberts and Malone, 1996). As a result, investors tend to favor entrepreneur-founded university spinoffs or inventor-founded spinoffs where the inventors work with managers with significant amounts of industry experience. At a minimum, observers explain that investors seek entrepreneurs with a sufficient level of business skills to allow them to work effectively with business people, preferring those founders with significant research funding from industry, which investors believe demonstrates sensitivity to the demands of industry personnel.

My interviews with the investors who financed the MIT spinoffs indicate that investors prefer spinoffs with founding team members that have industry experience. For example, a venture capitalist whose firm funded one of the MIT software spinoffs explains,

> At the end of the day, you don't just want an average smart person to come along and take something and try to make something of it. You want somebody who really knows the market that it might be pointed at. It's got to be somebody who is intimately familiar with the market from a product technology point of view.

Moreover, private investors favor companies whose founders have knowledge of customer needs. While the founders of university spinoffs often have little knowledge of whether customers are interested in their technologies (Vohora *et al.*, 2002b), private investors tend to select those spinoffs whose founders have greater knowledge of markets and customers.

My investigation of the MIT spinoffs provides support for this proposition. For instance, one of the MIT technology-licensing officers explains,

> The major asset to put in front of investors were people who had talked to the customers and who understood who the customers were going to be for the product, what customers were currently doing in the area, how they were doing it, how much it cost, where this technology would fit into that market space, and why it was compelling. The best were those that had one or two examples of 'Here, call this guy at XYZ Company.'

The investors in the MIT spinoffs also pointed out that evidence of founder knowledge of customer needs increased the likelihood that they would finance a university spinoff. For example, a venture capitalist that invested in one of the MIT software spinoffs explains why his firm invested in that company:

> We invested because of the references that [the founder] provided. These were people he had called on. They weren't customers yet. These were companies he presented to before [the company] was started. They said, 'Yeah, we could use a tool like this and we might use it across 3000 desktops.'

In short, the evidence of customer interest in the company's products led the venture capital firm to invest in the spinoff.

Social ties

When the founders of university spinoffs seek external financing, uncertainty and information asymmetry complicate their ability to obtain funding. Because new firms have limited performance histories, investors face significant uncertainty about their value. This uncertainty is compounded by the uncertainty of new technologies (Aldrich and Fiol, 1994) for which technical development and market acceptance are unsure (Tushman and Rosenkopf, 1992). New firms also face significant information asymmetry because founders of new companies know more than other people about their abilities and commitment, as well as the intricate details of their ventures.

As a result, social ties facilitate the financing of university spinoffs (Venkataraman, 1997). Social ties mitigate information asymmetry and uncertainty problems in venture finance in four ways. First, social relationships reduce the likelihood that either party will act opportunistically towards the other by leading people to consider social obligation, generosity, fairness and equity in their dealings with others (Marsden, 1981; Uzzi, 1996; Granovetter, 1985). Second, social ties create an incentive to preserve that relationship for future interactions, by sanctioning those who violate implicit contracts (Gulati, 1995). Third, social ties transfer information about people and opportunities (Burt, 1992). Fourth, social ties lead people to make more positive attributions about others (Podolny, 1994; Stuart *et al.*, 1999).

Several pieces of evidence support the proposition that social ties between founders of university spinoffs and the investment community facilitate the financing of university spinoffs. First, my interviews with the founders of MIT spinoffs point to the role of social ties. For instance, several of the founders of spinoffs recounted the difficulty that they faced in raising capital because they lacked adequate social ties to investors. As the founder of one of the medical device spinoffs explains, 'We didn't have the contacts in the VC community so it was very difficult for us to raise money with the large VCs.'

Second, my interviews with founders of MIT spinoffs indicated that technology-licensing officers often served as brokers who helped the founders of university spinoffs to obtain financing. For example, the founder of one of the biotechnology spinoffs explains that, if the director of the Technology-Licensing Office 'makes phone calls, that helps to raise money'. Similarly, the founder of one MIT software spinoff explains, 'The MIT network enabled me to get my seed capital. At the end of the day it was [the venture capitalist] going to Lita Nelsen.'

Some large sample statistical evidence also supports the proposition that social ties facilitate the financing of university spinoffs. For instance, Shane and Stuart (2002) examined the performance of 134 spinoffs from MIT from 1980 to 1996 and found that those spinoffs whose founders had a pre-existing relationship with a third party who can refer a founder to sources of financing were 2.8 times as likely as other spinoffs to receive venture capital. In addition, these authors showed that those spinoffs whose founders had direct ties to venture capitalists or business angels prior to founding their firms were also more likely to receive venture capital financing.

THE SOURCES OF CAPITAL

University spinoffs raise capital from different sources, depending, in large part, on the goals of the founders and the attributes of the spinoff companies.

Some observers have divided university spinoffs into two categories, based on their needs and sources of financing. The first category includes spinoffs, like many software companies, that need minimal amounts of cash (less than $100 000). These companies are often self-financed or bootstrapped. The second category includes those spinoffs, like many biotechnology companies, that need several million dollars before they are able to produce a valuable product or service. These companies are typically financed by venture capital if they have large upside potential and are pursuing a large market, and are generally financed by angel investors or customers if they have limited upside potential and are pursuing a relatively smaller market.

Some large sample empirical evidence supports the proposition that spinoffs can be divided into different categories based on how they are financed. In particular, the evidence shows that some spinoffs obtain external capital to finance their development, while others finance their development through the cash flow from their existing operations. For instance, Shane and Stuart (2002) examined the performance of the 134 spinoffs from MIT from 1980 to 1996 and found that the log of cumulative sales had a negative effect on the hazard of external financing, suggesting that those ventures that achieved greater sales needed to obtain less external financing than those ventures that achieved lesser sales.

The diversity of funding sources for university spinoffs is quite large, reflecting the diversity in funding needs among spinoffs and the uncertainty and information asymmetry inherent in the venture finance process. For instance, of the MIT spinoffs started between 1980 and 1996, 30 percent received financing from venture capitalists and formal angel investor groups, with 91 different organizations providing financing to 134 companies. Moreover, only 17 of the investors funded more than one MIT spinoff, with the most frequent investors being Bessemer Venture Partners and Advent International Group, which each invested in five spinoffs.

Although the data from MIT indicate that many spinoffs receive venture capital funding, particularly in comparison to the proportion of high technology companies in general that receive venture capital funding, they also indicate that many university spinoffs receive angel financing instead of, or in addition to, venture capital financing. For example, among the MIT spinoffs founded between 1980 and 1996, 45 percent received financing from angel investors.

Angel investors are popular with the founders of university spinoffs because they provide several important advantages over venture capitalists. First, business angels are more patient investors than venture capitalists, who demand rapid development of spinoffs and their products. Rapid development allows venture capitalists to liquidate their investments and distribute the proceeds to limited partners during the lifetime of their funds, which is important to venture capitalists who raise money from institutional investors through funds that last approximately ten years.

Patient investors are important to the founders of university spinoffs because they often face significant uncertainty about when they will be able to commercialize their technologies. In many cases, venture capitalists are too impatient to deal with this uncertainty. For instance, Lowe (2002:39) quotes the founder of a University of California spinoff called Nitres as saying,

> We didn't want VC money initially because they want to see a prototype too soon, and the technology was still too fragile. If they don't see a product coming up soon in the process, VCs get worried and can put unreasonable pressure on the company.

Second, business angels make investments at an earlier stage of technological development than venture capitalists. The willingness to make early stage investments is important for university spinoffs, which require financing before a market application is known. Evidence from the MIT spinoffs provides support for the proposition that business angels are desirable investors for university spinoffs because they are willing to make investments before a market application is known. For example, an angel investor in one of the MIT optics spinoffs explains,

> I realized that if [the company] went to the formal venture capital industry to fund the company, no one would fund it. With venture capitalists, you have this model of developing the product, making ten different versions and selling it. You figure out what you can make, and how big the market is and then you get money. With this technology, we didn't know what the application would be: automobiles, flat panel displays, or semiconductors. That situation does not lend itself to a venture capitalist style of investing.

Third, business angels do not require as high a rate of return on their investments as venture capitalists because they often invest to become involved in the technology company creation process. Because university inventions are often very early stage technologies, and require many years of development and significant amounts of capital, university spinoffs often run into trouble when obtaining venture capital. To achieve the rates of return that venture capitalists demand, the founders of university spinoffs often have to give up more capital than investors would like them to relinquish, given the moral hazard problems generated by low levels of founder stock ownership. As a result, the founders of university spinoffs are often better off with angel financing, with its relatively low required rate of return.

SUMMARY

This chapter has explained how the founders of university spinoffs acquire the capital that they need to develop their new ventures. University spinoffs often require large amounts of capital, given the significant technical and market development that these companies need to undertake after founding, and because the amount of capital acquired by the spinoff is positively related to the performance of those new firms.

Outside biotechnology, the initial capital obtained by university spinoffs generally does not come from private investors because private investors want to invest in later stage companies. Because the founders of university spinoffs outside biotechnology usually cannot finance their initial activities from private sources, they turn to government grants, which provide a major source of revenue for many university spinoffs during the initial period of technology development. Public funding permits the transformation of university inventions into new products and services, allows founders of spinoffs to find a commercial use for their technologies, serves as a catalyst or subsidy for private investment and provides a way to have government agencies bear high-risk development.

Even at later stages of venture development, obtaining capital from private sector sources is not easy for the founders of university spinoffs because the information asymmetry and uncertainty that these ventures face create important problems in the financing process. Consequently, the acquisition of capital involves two important processes: efforts by the founders of university spinoffs to demonstrate the value of their ventures to potential investors, such as providing evidence of a large market, a proprietary technology, a general-purpose technology and founder experience, as well as the exploitation of social ties between entrepreneurs and investors.

University spinoffs raise capital from different sources, depending on the goals of the founders and the attributes of the spinoff companies. In fact, the diversity of funding sources for university spinoffs is quite large. Many university spinoffs receive angel financing rather than, or in addition to, venture capital financing because angel investors tend to be more patient than venture capitalists, make earlier stage investments and do not require as high rates of return.

Having described the financing of university spinoffs, I now turn to a discussion of the performance of these companies, the subject of Chapter 12.

NOTES

1. One reason why investors can earn sufficient returns from the investment in biotechnology spinoffs well before the stage when those companies will have products or services is that

these companies can go public before they have developed new products or services, allowing the investors to liquidate their investments. The Internet bubble not withstanding, university spinoffs in areas other than biotechnology often need to have developed products or services to go public.

2. It is important to note that the more successful university spinoffs appear to use public financing to attract private sector capital and develop products and services; the less successful spinoffs do not seem to use public financing for either of these purposes.

12. The performance of university spinoffs

For both the universities that spawn spinoff companies and the entrepreneurs that found them, the creation of high-performing companies is an important goal of the spinoff effort. In general, this effort is quite successful. As Chapter 2 explained, university spinoffs perform better than typical start-up companies. However, not all university spinoffs perform well. This chapter explores the factors that enhance the performance of university spinoff companies and differentiate more successful firms from less successful ones.

The findings of this chapter are by no means comprehensive. The set of factors that influence the performance of new companies is broad, but has not been the subject of extensive research by scholars. This is due to the fact that relatively few data are available to test, on university spinoffs, the effects of those factors that prior research has shown to influence the performance of new companies in general. Therefore the ability to draw strong conclusions from scholarly investigation of the performance of university spinoffs is limited.

Nevertheless, several important patterns emerge. The performance of university spinoffs is influenced by the human capital of the founders, the financial resources of the new ventures, the efforts of the founders of university spinoffs to overcome the technology push problem and develop products and services that meet customer needs, the nature of the spinoff's technology and strategy, and the support provided by the universities that spawn the spinoffs. Each of these factors is discussed in a separate subsection of the chapter. I begin with human capital.

THE EFFECT OF HUMAN CAPITAL

Research on the performance of university spinoffs suggests that the human capital of the venture team affects the performance of the spinoff company. University spinoffs are founded with little more than the technology that the new company will exploit and the attributes of the founders who create the companies. Moreover, prior research in entrepreneurship indicates that founder human capital enhances the performance of new ventures in general (see Shane, 2003, for a review). More motivated and committed firm founders, with better knowledge of management, firm formation and the industry in which they plan to operate, are more likely than other firm founders to create companies that survive and grow. In the particular context of university spinoffs, researchers have shown the performance implications of two aspects of human capital: complementary venture teams and the commitment of the entrepreneurs to the ventures.

Complementary Teams

In his seminal study of spinoffs from MIT, Roberts (1991a) found that companies with multiple founders tended to perform better on a variety of performance measures than companies with a single founder. He explained this result by arguing that ventures created by multiple founders are more likely than single founder ventures to have a founding team composed of people with expertise in all functional areas of the firm, and ventures with a more complementary team of founders perform better than those with a less complementary team.

Other observers have built upon Roberts' (1991a) argument, positing that university spinoffs founded by a team that involves both the inventor and people with significant industry experience tend to perform better than other university spinoffs (Doutriaux and Barker, 1995; Chrisman *et al.*, 1995). Preston (1997) explains that complementary teams perform better than non-complementary teams because the specialization of labor between business and technical professionals enhances the performance of spinoff companies. For instance, a venture founded by a technology expert and a business expert will have a higher probability of success than a venture founded by a technologist alone because each expert can focus more of his or her time and attention on those areas in which he or she has the more expertise. In addition, spinoffs with complementary teams that include people who come from both academia and industry perform better than other spinoffs because successful university spinoffs need people who have knowledge of the segment of industry in which the new company will operate, as well as people with knowledge of the technology who can continue to develop it. The subsections below discuss the advantages that people with business knowledge and inventors provide for university spinoffs.

Business knowledge
Building a successful technology company demands three types of business knowledge: knowledge of how to develop and manage a new company, knowledge of the processes of product development and production, and

knowledge of the particular market in which the new company will operate. These types of knowledge are important because they represent key aspects of creating and developing a new technology company. In general, most academic inventors do not possess business knowledge because their careers have been spent developing expertise in scholarly research and teaching. Therefore spinoffs are more successful when their management teams incorporate people from industry than when they do not.

Management knowledge   One aspect of business knowledge that is important to the performance of university spinoffs is management knowledge, or knowledge of how to run companies. Management knowledge is often learned by experience, leading people's stock of management knowledge to increase with the time they spend in management positions (Shane, 2003). Through management experience, people learn about many of the aspects of business that are relevant to creating a spinoff company, such as finance, sales, technology, logistics, marketing and organization (Romanelli and Schoonhoven, 2001; Klepper and Sleeper, 2001). Moreover, management experience provides training in many of the skills needed for starting a spinoff company, including selling, negotiating, leading, planning, decision making, problem solving, organizing and communicating (Shane, 2003).

The founders of successful spinoffs are more likely than the founders of the average spinoff to involve people with significant management experience on their venture teams when they start their firms. Specifically, successful inventor–founders understand that they lack management expertise and seek people of equal caliber to them in the business world. As Lita Nelsen, the Director of the MIT Technology-Licensing Office put it, 'The successful inventors have enough common sense and respect for the fact that they need people as good as they are in the business function when they start companies.'

My interviews with the founders of MIT spinoffs indicated that the entrepreneurs who started successful MIT spinoffs followed the logic of specialization that was described above. For instance, the founder of several successful MIT biotechnology spinoffs explains,

> I've always taken the attitude that I'm not a businessman. If we're going to be successful, I'd better find people who are good businessmen. Sometimes when things don't work, you haven't had good people at the company. I think a really good CEO is important.

In contrast, the founders of MIT spinoffs that were not as successful often pointed out that they learned the hard way the importance of having people with significant management knowledge involved with the companies that they founded. For instance, the founder of one MIT biotechnology spinoff explains, 'One important lesson I learned from starting a spinoff was to make sure you have a good management team in place.' Similarly, the founder of one MIT materials spinoff says, 'The most important lesson I learned from starting this company was that we did not make sound business decisions. We hired someone as CEO who was really good, but he had no management experience.'

The founders of the unsuccessful MIT spinoffs identified several specific problems that they experienced by founding companies without experienced managers on the team. The first problem was the cost of on-the-job training. Spinoffs without experienced managers faced significant costs in time and money as the senior managers of these companies tried to learn how to operate a company in real time. As the founder of one software spinoff explains,

> I learned an important lesson. In retrospect, it would have been better to have more seasoned corporate leadership at the start. There was a lot of training on the job going along and we paid for that directly or indirectly in time and money that was eaten up.

The second problem was a lack of leadership. Spinoffs without experienced managers suffered because they lacked someone who could lead and coordinate the efforts of the new venture. For example, the CEO of one MIT biotechnology spinoff explains,

> It is important to hire the right leadership right from the very beginning and if you have to spend a little more money to do that to hire people with particular experience, it's worth that investment. You've got to know what to do to make an impact.

The third problem was a lack of management problem solving ability. Many of the issues that university spinoffs face are managerial issues, and having someone with management knowledge is important to resolving these issues. For instance, one MIT technology-licensing officer explained that one of the biotechnology spinoffs had problems 'because the hiring was done by professors who didn't want to understand that different experience was needed to develop products and that academic criteria were not appropriate'.

The fourth problem was that people have limited time and attention. As a result, a firm founder does not have enough time to develop both the business and the technical sides of the business simultaneously. Consequently, spinoffs without sufficient management expertise suffered from slow development of the organization, the technology, or both. For instance, the founder of one of the MIT computer hardware spinoffs explains,

> You need to cover both sides of the spectrum. You need somebody who can make the technology work and he has to focus on that. The problem I got into was that I had to sell the company and make it interesting to people. I had to recruit people. I had to invent the physics. I needed somebody early on to focus on running the business.

This problem is exacerbated by the fact that scientists and engineers tend to play down the importance of business knowledge. As a result, founders of university spinoffs who lack partners with significant amounts of management experience generally do not give sufficient attention to the business activities that will make the new company successful, hindering its performance. As the founder of one of the MIT biotechnology spinoffs explains,

> Scientists tend to think of business people as a bunch of dummies. In the case of [our company], we should have found a business head sooner rather than later because [the inventor–founder] was just getting way ahead of what people antici-pated could be done. In the end the business leadership is the thing that's going to get you there. You can do the best science in the world, but it's not going to go anywhere unless you've got a brilliant strategic thinker and implementer.

The inventor–founder of that spinoff concurs with her co-founder's state-ments, explaining that the company would have been better off if it had included a business founder with significant management experience. She says,

> A very important lesson I learned was that scientists, technical people, are not the best people to run the business. They are very passionate about science. I've learned how to save this passion and how to modify it a lot but I still believe that it would have been extremely helpful to have had a business person on board from day one.

Knowledge of product development and production   Another aspect of busi-ness knowledge that is important to the performance of university spinoffs is knowledge of product development and production. As Chapter 10 pointed out, the skills that it takes to conduct academic research are different from those that it takes to develop and produce new products and services. The people with product development and production expertise tend not to reside in universities, which reward people for their cutting edge research. As a result, university spinoffs are more successful when the venture team includes industry people with product development and production expertise than when they do not.

My interviews with the founders of the MIT spinoffs support this proposi-tion. As the founder of one of the biotechnology spinoffs explains, to succeed 'one really must have a multi-disciplinary, talented team, which includes people who have long standing interests and talents in a variety of domains whether that be in regulatory affairs, manufacturing controls, quality assur-ance, etc.'

In particular, several founders of MIT spinoffs point out that their compa-nies experienced problems that hindered performance because their founding teams lacked people with expertise in product development. For instance, the founder of one medical device spinoff explains, 'Our biggest mistakes were caused by an absence of having somebody who'd done a clinical product that involves diagnostic technology that has to be proven.' Similarly, the founder of one of the MIT biotechnology spinoffs explains, 'None of us [inventors] had business experience. When you get into making products, you don't have the insight or credibility to move this along.'

The case of one of the MIT software spinoffs provides insight into why the lack of product development expertise is such a problem for university spinoffs. Product development demands much more specific, practical business knowledge than is the case for research. As a result, spinoffs that do not include people with product development expertise on their teams have a hard time making the transition from the theoretical orientation of basic research to the practical orientation of product development. The MIT inventor whose technology led to the founding of the software spinoff explains, 'There's a point where general analysis has to be much more specific and at that point a team has to be assembled that includes not only the more visionary and abstract people, but the people who actually know how to do things and make products work.'

One of the investors in that spinoff expands on this point. He explains that one of the key obstacles that slowed product development at the company was a lack of knowledge of how to turn cutting edge university research into practical products or services. He says,

> What we didn't do right was to get people with the right kind of experience. Some of the people that developed our technology were very, very smart theoretically, but were highly impractical people. We didn't have the right mix of people to go from the theoretical to the practical. That's very difficult to do. You've met these people.
>
> You have your idiot savants in the world that are really absolute geniuses, but if they don't have a practical, realistic view of what they are really doing or are interested in that nothing happens.
>
> To a certain extent, creative people don't like to finish things. They like to know that they can solve a problem and then they're done with it. But the actual dog work to get from the absolute theoretical into something that's practical is worrying to them. It almost requires a whole different mind set and we only had the one mind set really in the company.

This problem was not limited to this example. The investor in the software company also explains that an MIT computer hardware spinoff that he invested in suffered from similar problems. He explains that, lacking expertise in product development, the founding team had trouble creating a commercial product:

> That company would have done better if the people involved had a more practical and deeper understanding of markets in general. Then they could really have hit home runs. [The inventor] also suffered from the fact that he didn't have a lot of

practical experience. If they had had a couple more traditional business people in there in the mix with those people, they would of hit upon a few things. A guy like [one of the technologists] has a tremendous gift in one area, but he still needs the guys with the business experience and he still needs the practical engineers rather than the developmental engineers to get all of these things to where they make money. If you just have all of one kind for the whole time, you might as well work for the government.

Knowledge of markets   A third aspect of business knowledge that is important to the performance of university spinoffs is knowledge of the company's industry. New ventures face uncertainty about customer needs and market demand for the products and services that they intend to provide. People with industry experience, whether as a producer, customer or supplier, often have a better understanding of how to satisfy customer needs and meet market demand than other people (Knight, 1921; Von Mises, 1949). As a result, spinoffs perform better if they include people with industry experience on the founding team.

My interviews with the founders of the MIT spinoffs provide evidence that supports the proposition that spinoffs perform better if they have founders with industry knowledge on the venture team.[1] For example, the founder of one of the MIT biotechnology spinoffs explains that, to succeed, 'We needed someone who had knowledge in the industry, who thoroughly understands how the business you're trying to get into works.' Similarly, the founder of one of the MIT software spinoffs explains, 'I knew that I had to go out and hire a CEO that knew this industry, that knew this market. So right away we went out and did that.'

Some large sample statistical analysis also supports the proposition that spinoffs with founding teams that have more industry experience perform better than other spinoff companies. Shane and Stuart (2002) examined the performance of 134 MIT spinoffs established between 1980 and 1996 and found that spinoffs in which at least one founder had industry experience was more likely than other spinoffs to experience an initial public offering. Similarly, Nerkar and Shane (forthcoming) examined the survival of MIT spinoffs established between 1980 and 1996 and found that, the greater the industry experience of the spinoff's founding team, the less likely the ventures were to fail.

Prior research has identified several reasons why university spinoffs that have founders with industry knowledge perform better than other university spinoffs. First, most marketing activities demand tacit knowledge of the industry in which the new company will operate (Shane and Stuart, 2002). In particular, tacit knowledge of customer needs helps a firm founder to identify specific products and services that are likely to meet these customer needs.

The data collected on the MIT spinoffs provide empirical support for this proposition. For instance, the inventor of a technology that led to the founding of one of the successful MIT software spinoffs explains, 'The best marketing is done by people who are already working in a particular field and who have general knowledge of what's going on.'

Several of the founders of MIT spinoffs explained that a failure to include someone on their venture team that had significant industry experience made it difficult for the spinoff to understand customer needs and hindered performance. For instance, the founder of another of the MIT software spinoffs explains,

> The initial employees for the company were my own students. They were really technology driven and idea driven. That was a big mistake. I thought all it took was a bunch of technical people who were smart and go and do the product. But we didn't have a clear product spec. We didn't know what the customer really wanted. So if there was something we made that nobody really wanted then we had to change it to do what somebody really wanted. If we had a real marketing person up front that knew about customer service and could figure out what people really wanted, what people would really pay money for, we would have been better off.

The founder of one of the MIT computer hardware spinoffs echoes these sentiments, saying,

> One of the mistakes we made was waiting to bring in the real industry focused team. Our team really didn't have the vertical experience. As a result, we ended up with our first pass at the product being a 0.7 release when we were told it was a solid 1.0. And our pricing was off a lot in the early days.

Second, successful marketing requires ties to customers. On average, people with more industry experience have better social ties with customers in their industry than do people with less industry experience. The founders of the MIT spinoffs that I interviewed provide support for this argument. For instance, the founder of one of the MIT semiconductor spinoffs explains why finding a partner with semiconductor industry experience enhanced the performance of his spinoff:

> My disadvantage was that I did not know the customers on a first name basis. In fact, I didn't even know who the movers and shakers were in the various companies. To make a lot of money in the semiconductor business, I felt that it was absolutely crucial to have somebody who was plugged in very, very well. I found that person, who was a senior vice president at a semiconductor company, which at that point was a $600 million company.

Inventor involvement

While the preceding section points out the importance of having founding team members with business knowledge to the success of university spinoffs, this alone is not enough. As Chapter 6 explained, a successful university spin-off also needs inventor involvement. As Chapter 10 explained, the founders of university spinoffs engage in a substantial amount of technology development after these companies are formed. Much of the knowledge necessary to under-take this development is tacit, making the inventor crucial to further technical advance (Jensen and Thursby, 2001).

My interviews with the founders of the MIT spinoffs provide support for the proposition that spinoffs perform better if they have inventor involvement. For example, the founder of one MIT software spinoff explains,

> I think one of the elements that you might glean from our experience was the neces-sary involvement of the MIT participants. If you're dealing in knowledge-based industry such as software, what's in the person's head is often far more important than the tangible thing.

The investors in the MIT spinoffs also indicate that inventor involvement enhances the performance of university spinoffs. Discussing his firm's best success at financing a university spinoff, a company that had experienced an initial public offering and was acquired for $360 million, one venture capital-ist explains that spinoffs require a management team that understands how to overcome the technical problems that the spinoff would inevitably experience. He says,

> We had the key guy as part of the bundle. Having access to the people is almost crucial. At the same time as we funded this company, we backed another equally promising company that didn't do well. We had clear title to the intellectual prop-erty but we didn't hire anyone from the lab. We had some people who were very capable, but we just had a consulting relationship with the lab. We had technologi-cal glitches along the way, we had false starts in scaling it up and a number of things that were of a technical nature that perhaps would have been more successful if we had one of the bodies from the lab as part of our team instead of an arm's length arrangement.

Several researchers have also shown that inventor involvement improves the performance of university spinoffs in large sample statistical studies. For example, Lowe (2002) examined the spinoffs from the University of California system and discovered that inventor-founded university spinoffs were much more likely than other licensees to continue development work on university inventions after licensing them. Lowe's (2002) data showed that, while established firms terminated 80 percent of the licenses to inventions undertaken by both inventor-founded spinoffs and established firms, inventor-founded spinoffs terminated only 6 percent of the licenses, suggesting that inventor-founded spinoffs are more likely than established firms to conduct additional technical development on university inventions. Moreover, Nerkar and Shane (forthcoming) examined the survival of MIT spinoffs established between 1980 and 1996 and followed through 1997. They found that, when the entrepreneur that founded the firm was an inventor, the spinoff was less likely to fail than when the entrepreneur was not an inventor.

Full-time Entrepreneurs

A second important dimension of the human capital that enhances the performance of university spinoffs is the presence of a full-time entrepreneur. Blair and Hitchens (1998) offer two explanations for this. First, by working full time, the founders of university spinoffs signal their personal commitment to the new company, which is important in generating support among potential stakeholders (Shane, 2003). Second, as university spinoffs grow, the demands on the founders' time escalate, making it difficult for them to accomplish the necessary firm development tasks without making a full-time commitment. In fact, in their empirical research on spinoffs in the United Kingdom and Ireland, Blair and Hitchens (1998) could identify no examples of a spinoff company that had developed beyond the initial formation stage in which the founder served as a part-time managing director or general manager.[2]

My interviews with the founders of MIT spinoffs also indicated that spinoffs led by part-time founders underperformed other spinoffs. For example, the CEO of one MIT biotechnology spinoff explained that his venture's problems could be attributed to the lack of a full-time commitment from its founders. He says, 'We didn't even have someone who left the university to commit themselves to the company and who was putting their career and their life and their future on the line. I mean these guys where doing this as a part-time avocation.'

Similarly, the inventor of the technology that led to one of the MIT software spinoffs explains that the failure of that venture is best explained by the lack of a full-time commitment by any of the founders. He says, 'The major lesson I learned from founding this company is that you need to find a way to put your entire soul into it. It certainly reaffirmed the notion that if you don't do it full time, it goes slowly – that's exactly what happened.'

OVERCOMING THE TECHNOLOGY PUSH PROBLEM

University spinoffs succeed because they have products or services that customers want, not because they have the best technology.[3] However, as I have explained in earlier chapters, academics create new technologies as a byproduct of their research activities, not because they are asked to come up with technical solutions to specific customer problems. Consequently, after establishing their companies, the founders of successful university spinoffs need to identify specific customer problems that their new technologies can be used to solve and need to turn their technologies into products and services that solve those problems.

Several of the founders of MIT spinoffs that I interviewed explained that the creation of products and services that meet customer needs is crucial to spinoff company performance. For instance, the founder of one MIT biotechnology spinoff explains,

> The biggest lesson I take away from [my company] for people starting technology companies out of university is that it's all about customers that need some products to satisfy their needs. The technology may be interesting, but if you don't get the products, it's a waste of time.

The positive performance effect of efforts to create products and services that meet customer needs also holds for spinoffs in computer software. For instance, an investor in one of the MIT software spinoffs explains, 'It's not the beauty of the software or the elegance of its implementation or the wonderful code underneath, or any of that other stuff. It's really the commercial viability of the software that determines the success.'

The founders of successful university spinoffs undertake several activities to overcome the technology push problem: creating products, identifying market applications and assessing markets. In the subsections below, each of these activities is discussed in turn.

Creating Products

Research has shown that successful university spinoffs develop products and services; whereas unsuccessful spinoffs do not.[4] My interviews with the founders of MIT spinoffs also illustrate that university spinoffs perform poorly when they do not transform their technologies into products and services. In particular, university spinoffs perform poorly when their founders try to sell their technology in raw form. For instance, as the founder of one of the MIT software spinoffs explains,

> We first tried to license the technology directly to companies who wanted to embed it. In the early days, [the company] did not feel like it needed to commercialize a product. It hoped that direct relicensing of the technology would be sufficient. Making the technology commercial quality was perceived as being a relatively unimportant task. If the appropriate outside company came along, they would see the amazing potential of the technology and want to pay us a lot of money for the rights to use it in their products. [The company] did make a couple of deals to license the technology, but not in the way I think we had originally conceived of it. We resisted picking particular product areas to focus on. We just said we can focus

on the technology in the abstract and when a customer expresses a particular product idea, we'll then try to redirect our energies in that direction. That ultimately did not prove to be a very successful strategy.

Identifying a Market Application

The success of a spinoff company also depends on the identification of a market application. Successful spinoffs figure out specific applications in which their technologies are useful to potential customers, whereas unsuccessful spinoffs fail to identify appropriate market applications.

The data that I collected on the MIT spinoffs indicated that successful spinoffs were more likely than unsuccessful spinoffs to identify an appropriate market application for their technology.[5] For example, one of the MIT technology-licensing officers explains that one of the MIT optics spinoffs experienced problems because 'the inventors were unable to articulate a market for the technology'. Similarly, she explains that one of the MIT semiconductor spinoffs had trouble because 'it didn't have a clear application for the technology'.

The founders of many of the MIT spinoffs explained that they learned from experience the importance of identifying a market in which they could develop products and services from their technology. For instance, the founder of one MIT software spinoff explains, 'It's wrong to have just a technology which is cool, and everyone tells you is cool. That's not enough, by far not enough, to make a successful company. It's much better to identify a market and a product.'

Moreover, for a spinoff to be successful, the market application that the founders identify needs to be large enough to support the founding of a new company. In some cases, the founders of university spinoffs identify a market for their companies' technologies, but these markets are to small to support the development of the spinoff. For instance, the founder of one of the failed MIT mechanical device spinoffs explains,

> We thought the MRI market had a lot of potential. Right from the start, the project was to see if we could develop a new refrigeration system for this product. It was a definite market. It was an established market, but it was small because it was only 1000 units a year and we were looking at $25,000 for the price of this refrigeration system.

A venture capitalist that invested in the spinoff corroborates the founder's observation. He says, 'If I had it to do over again, I wouldn't have made the investment. I'm not sure the company could ever have been successful, that there was really a big enough market for that.'

In other cases, the founders of university spinoffs deliberately choose not to pursue the largest market for their company's technology, hindering the performance of the spinoff. A venture capitalist that invested in one of the MIT computer hardware spinoffs explains how that company suffered from the founder's choice not to pursue the largest market application for the technology:

> The company went from a very broad market base to a very narrow market base. When the narrow market base collapsed and there was no market for this type of machine, their market dwindled to zero. They took a very very large market and concentrated on a very small market, selling to very, very sophisticated users in defense or the intelligence community. The take away lesson is to look at whether or not there's a market for the product. It doesn't really make any difference what the technology is as long as there is a market and the market can be created.

One large sample statistical study also supports the proposition that identifying a market application large enough to support a new company is important to the success of a spinoff. Shane and Stuart (2002) examined the performance of 134 MIT spinoffs founded between 1980 and 1996 and found that the size of the industry at founding had a positive effect on the likelihood of initial public offering, offering at least indirect support for this proposition.

Assessing and Satisfying Customer Needs

The success of a spinoff company also depends on assessing and satisfying customer needs. The founders of successful spinoffs assess the market for their technologies and figure out which customers will purchase a product or service that uses the technology and why they will make that purchase. Unsuccessful spinoffs fail to make this assessment.

My interviews with the founders of MIT spinoffs illustrate that university spinoffs perform poorly when they do not figure out which customers will purchase a product or service that uses the technology, and why customers will make that purchase. For example, the founder of a failed MIT software spinoff explains,

> The major uncertainty at the time we started was who was going to buy the product and how are we going to convince people to purchase it. The major lesson I learned in starting a university spinoff was the mistake I made in relying too much on a pure technology play rather than assessing the marketing hurdles carefully beforehand.

To assess and satisfy customer needs, the founders of university spinoffs need to demonstrate the value to the customer of buying the spinoff's product or service. By demonstrating the value of the product or service to the customer, the spinoff founder can be sure that the product or service meets customer needs. My interviews with the founders of the MIT spinoffs revealed that this process was a problem for the founders of many of the unsuccessful companies. Take, for instance, the following explanation by the founder of an unsuccessful MIT mechanical device spinoff:

> What's the business value that our ignition system creates? Good question. I've been grappling with that for eight years. The value that we have is our ability to create bigger sparks that do a better job of igniting the fuel in a combustion chamber of an engine and thereby providing better fuel economy and lower emissions. Unfortunately, I can't quantify that value for the auto companies.

In contrast, the founders of the successful MIT spinoffs were able to articulate the direct financial benefit to customers of the spinoff's product or service. For instance, the founder of a successful MIT software spinoff explains,

> The savings we provide customers depends on how many phone calls they do, how many operators they have. By way of example, if you look at directory assistance, for every second that the phone company can shave off a director assistance call, it would save a million dollars. Now that's a very high quality call center business. So if we're shaving 30 seconds off an airline's phone call, its definitely seven figures of savings.

To assess and satisfy customer needs, founders of university spinoffs also need to listen to customer feedback. Because the founders of the spinoffs do not seek to commercialize technologies that are invented to solve specific customer problems or meet specific customer needs, they must listen very carefully to the feedback provided by customers if they are to be successful. The founder of one successful MIT computer hardware spinoff explains that this was an important lesson that he learned. He says,

> The biggest mistake we made in starting the company was that we should have been more market driven. When we were doing the product development we did not put as much emphasis on listening to our customers, as we should have because we believed that the technology was ready to do anything. We thought that people would want anything that we put out there. But that's not entirely true.

In particular, the founders of the MIT spinoffs explained that the product development process was quite ineffective if they did not listen to customers. In the absence of feedback from customers, the founders of spinoffs have to conduct product development without an understanding of what the customers want. Efforts to conduct product development in this type of vacuum tend to fail. For example, the founder of one MIT semiconductor spinoff explains,

> A lesson we learned was to listen very, very intently to everything we were told by our customers. You couldn't possibly succeed without understanding in great depth

everything that's going on in their minds. If you can't understand everything that's going on in their mind, then you can't go anywhere because you can't do things in a vacuum.

By talking to customers about their needs, the founders of the MIT spinoffs were able to develop an understanding of the problems and issues that customers faced. This understanding made it much easier for the founders of the spinoffs to anticipate how they could use their technology to solve real customer problems and avoid making assumptions that the customers did not believe were correct. For instance, the founder of one of the MIT mechanical device spinoffs explains,

> If I had to do it over again I would have talked to more customers. Now that I've talked to 1000 potential customers I have a mind share with them. I understand where they're coming from in a way that I didn't really when we started the business. When I think back on the part quality that I would have found acceptable, it's probably lower than what would have allowed us to be successful.

Not only did many of the unsuccessful MIT spinoffs fail to gather sufficient information from customers to assess and satisfy their needs, but also many of them ignored the customer feedback that they received, choosing instead to focus on developing the best possible technology that they could, even when customers were not interested in better technology. Failed MIT spinoff Thinking Machines Corporation provides a case in point. Taubes (1995) explains that Thinking Machines Corporation failed because founders Danny Hillis and Cheryl Handler wanted to create a tool for artificial intelligence research, rather than provide a product that was useful for scientific computing applications. The result was a $5 million computer that few artificial intelligence laboratories could afford and no one else wanted to buy. The product was not useful for scientific computing because it could not run FORTRAN, the standard computer language, requiring customers to learn new programming techniques to use it. Moreover, it could not accommodate floating-point calculations, creating a significant disadvantage in the 'database mining' segment of the supercomputer market.

OBTAINING ADEQUATE FINANCIAL CAPITAL

A third factor that is associated with the success of university spinoffs is the acquisition of adequate capital.[6] Obtaining adequate capital is important to the performance of university spinoffs because technological development is close to impossible without it. Not only does having adequate capital increase the pace at which technical development can occur, but also, without sufficient capital, spinoffs face the obstacle of being unable to hire the personnel or obtain the equipment that they need to undertake technical development. Moreover, the development of university spinoffs is highly uncertain. Given this uncertainty, slack financial resources are valuable because they allow the founders of a spinoff to change direction if they learn information about the market or technology that indicates that the pursuit of a different market application or approach to development would be a superior option. Furthermore, obtaining adequate capital is important to the performance of university spinoffs because raising money is time consuming. If a spinoff does not raise sufficient capital each time it seeks financing, the founders will spend too much time raising money relative to developing their products, hindering the development of their ventures. Finally, obtaining adequate capital enhances the performance of university spinoffs because many stakeholders of new firms view the amount of capital that the new venture has raised as a signal of its quality and legitimacy. As a result, raising adequate capital makes the new venture look more appealing to external stakeholders, thereby enhancing the venture's performance.

Two large sample statistical studies support the proposition that the amount of capital raised by university spinoffs is positively associated with their performance. First, Shane and Stuart (2002) examined the performance of 134 MIT spinoffs founded between 1980 and 1996 and found that the cumulative amount of venture capital raised by the spinoffs increased the probability of initial public offering and lowered the probability of firm failure. In fact, their analysis indicated that each $2 million of venture capital raised by a university spinoff doubles the likelihood of initial public offering. Second, Nerkar and Shane (forthcoming) provide less direct evidence of the effect of the amount of capital raised on the performance of university spinoffs. These authors examined the survival of MIT spinoffs established between 1980 and 1996, and found that, the more venture capital that was available in a venture's industry, the more likely that the venture was to survive over time.

Practitioners also report observations that are consistent with this large sample statistical analysis. For instance, the founder of one of the MIT biotechnology spinoffs explains that one of the lessons he learned from founding a spinoff is that 'more cash is better than less cash' because adequate capitalization is a necessary condition for new venture survival and positive performance. Similarly, when asked to identify the factors associated with the successful performance of MIT spinoffs, Lita Nelsen, the Director of the MIT Technology-Licensing Office, explains, 'All the successes that come to mind have been well financed. I can't think of major successes that were completely bootstrapped, nor founded and financed with SBIR or other government grants.'

SECURING UNIVERSITY SUPPORT

Obtaining adequate support from the university that spawns the spinoff is also important to the success of university spinoffs. Because most university technology is at a very early stage, additional work in the university environment where the inventors reside is valuable for the development of the spinoff and its technology.

The university support that enhances the performance of spinoffs can take a variety of forms. First, researchers have shown that a continuing relationship between the spinoff and the university laboratory that generated the spinoff's technology enhances the new company's performance. As Wilson and Szygenda (1991) explain, by using university resources the founders of university spinoffs can keep their costs low, which is important to the performance of new ventures.

Several studies provide evidence of the value of a continuing relationship between a spinoff and the university laboratory that generated it. For instance, Mustar (1997) examined the performance of university spinoffs in France, and found that those spinoffs that maintained cooperative relationships with the laboratories that spawned them performed better than those spinoffs that did not maintain such relationships. Steffensen *et al.* (1999) examined case studies of six spinoffs from laboratories at the University of New Mexico and discovered that the development of spinoffs was enhanced when the university research unit allowed the spinoff to continue to use its laboratory facilities and equipment after the company was created. Lowe (2002) examined the formation of spinoffs from the University of California system and found that the development of those spinoffs was enhanced by allowing them access to laboratories to conduct research, either at no cost or on an hourly basis, thereby dramatically reducing the investment needed to develop a company.

Second, researchers have shown that a flexible approach of the university to its relationship with the spinoffs enhances the performance of university spinoffs because such an approach allows the relationship to adapt to changing environmental circumstances. Lita Nelsen explains that such flexibility is a goal of universities, like MIT, that seek to create a large number of spinoffs. She says,

> The structure of the agreement between MIT and the startups influences performance. It's our truism that every company that succeeds will have renegotiated its license agreement with us in some way over the first four years. The way the university used to do it was to take unrealistic milestones and then hold the entrepreneurs to them. What does that do? It drives the company out of business. We don't want to do that. We want to help craft and recraft realistic agreements and realistic sublicensing agreements.

The data that I collected on the MIT spinoffs provide evidence in support of the argument that a flexible approach of the university to its relationship with spinoffs enhances the performance of the latter. For example, MIT's flexibility in renegotiating the terms of one semiconductor spinoff's licensing contract helped that company survive an early cash flow crisis and subsequently grow into a billion-dollar company. Similarly, MIT's flexibility toward the timing of payment for the use of university resources helped an MIT software spinoff survive its early years and subsequently grow into a public company. One of the early employees at the software spinoff recalls, 'I remember that MIT helped us out by not insisting that we pay our computer time bills even though we were about a year behind.' This flexibility towards payment to MIT allowed the software spinoff to pay its other creditors on time and conserve its limited cash.

Third, the presence of external liaison organizations that transform university research and technology into products and services facilitates the performance of university spinoffs (Mustar, 1997). Because most university technology is at the pre-prototype stage when university spinoffs are founded, external liaison organizations, such as scale-up facilities, incubators and testing laboratories facilitate the development of university spinoffs and their technologies. In fact, in a large sample statistical study, Doutriaux and Barker (1995) found that the performance of university spinoffs was superior if they came from institutions that have these organizations than if they did not.

THE EFFECT OF THE TECHNOLOGY

Just as the nature of technological inventions influences the founding of university spinoffs, it also influences their performance subsequent to founding. Research has shown that two aspects of technology influence the performance of university spinoffs: the strength of patent protection and the degree to which a technology is general-purpose.[7] In the subsections below, the effects of the nature of technology on the performance of university spinoffs are discussed.

Intellectual Property Protection

The amount and strength of a spinoff's intellectual property protection enhance its performance. As Chapter 6 explained, strong intellectual property protection is the only competitive advantage available to a new firm when the company is first created. Therefore a strong intellectual property position is important to allowing a spinoff company to compete successfully in its early days.

One large sample study provides empirical support for this proposition. Shane and Stuart (2002) examined the 134 MIT spinoffs founded from 1980 to 1996 and found that the number of patents held by the spinoff at the time of founding reduced the likelihood of company failure. My interviews with the founders of MIT spinoffs also provide empirical support for the proposition that the possession of strong patents enhances the performance of university spinoffs.[8] For example, the founder of one of the successful MIT biotechnology spinoffs explains,

> It's critical to develop a defendable intellectual property position. If you don't have that, it doesn't make any difference how good your management is, how good your scientists are, how wonderful your drug is, you're not going to succeed or even survive unless you've nailed down your intellectual property.

The founders of several MIT spinoffs explained that a strong patent portfolio provides a sustainable competitive advantage for a university spinoff. For example, the founder of another successful MIT biotechnology spinoff explains, 'the MIT intellectual property is very important to us from a barrier to entry perspective'. The founder of a successful MIT software spinoff explains this same concept in greater detail:

> There is always the chance that somebody's going to invent something that will wipe you out. But I felt with the combination of the MIT code and our ability to understand the market and define a product that had features that nobody else's product had would provide a winning combination.

In contrast, several observers explain that a weak patent portfolio leaves a university spinoff without a sustainable competitive advantage. For instance, one of the MIT technology-licensing officers explains that one of the MIT optics spinoffs had no competitive advantage because 'the patent position was weak. All they had was a manufacturing ability advantage, they didn't have a performance advantage'.

A strong patent position is particularly useful in protecting a university spinoff against competition from established companies. These companies often have sufficient expertise and resources to imitate the technologies developed by university spinoffs. For example, the founder of one successful MIT mechanical device spinoff explains, 'If there is a bigger player sitting out there and you didn't have good patent protection as soon as you do the market entry work, somebody else can pounce on it.'

Moreover, a strong patent position leads established companies to work with the spinoff as a partner instead of developing the technology on their own. Preston (1997) explains that, when a spinoff has developed a technology that will enhance the performance of a large company, the spinoff's negotiating position is much stronger if it has a strong patent position because the large company is going to prefer to develop the technology on its own rather than by becoming a partner of the spinoff. If the spinoff has a weak patent position, the large company will respond to any information about the new technology disclosed by the spinoff and imitate it. However, if the spinoff has a strong patent position, the large company will have to be a partner of the spinoff to gain access to the technology.

My interviews with the founders of the MIT spinoffs provide empirical support for the proposition that a spinoff's strong patent position will encourage large companies to become its partner.[9] For example, the founder of one MIT medical device spinoff explains,

> Motorola took a very keen interest in the company. They'd been doing some fairly serious due diligence in trying to determine who had some key intellectual property in the area. After 13 months of investigating, they claimed that we had some of the strongest IP of any company. Also, Kleiner Perkins, a VC group that was interested in backing another company in the area, did some investigation. They realized that our patents that were filed about 18 months before their patents had the key core technology to the things that they were doing, so they became interested in acquiring us.

Several of the founders of the MIT spinoffs also explained that weak patent protection hinders the performance of a spinoff company because it does not allow the company sufficient room to develop a broad technology that is applicable to a wide portion of the market. For instance, an executive at one of the MIT biotechnology spinoffs explains, 'In some of the biotech areas, there's always lots of good ideas, but when the patent claims get hammered out, they bump up on each other. It takes real aggressive, competitive intellectual property management if you're going to succeed.'

For this reason, the founders of university spinoffs believe that only those companies that are founded on strong university patents will perform well. Spinoffs founded on weak university patents will be unable to protect themselves against competitors. For instance, the CEO of one MIT biotechnology spinoff, explains,

> The major risk is that there's someone else out there that you don't know about and later a patent emerges and gets in your way. A large patent estate allows you to defend yourself. I think it's important to obtain a technology position from a university in which the patent position is well established.

One of the most important characteristics of an effective patent is a strong set of claims. Patent claims define the actual property right to a university invention. If a patent's claims protect many aspects of a technology effectively, the patent provides a strong competitive advantage to the patent holder.

However, if the patent claims do not protect a technology effectively, they provide no such advantage.

The MIT spinoffs that I studied provide good examples of the effect of patent claims on the performance of university spinoffs. The founders of several spinoffs explained that weak patent claims meant limited competitive advantage for their new companies. For instance, after founding his company, the founder of one MIT medical device spinoff found out that other patent holders held claims on the intellectual property he licensed from MIT, forcing him to license other patents to compete, thereby raising his company's costs and hindering its performance.

In an even more extreme example, one of the MIT semiconductor spinoffs was actually terminated when its investors determined that the pursuit of a patent was no longer justified because patent claims would be insufficient to protect the spinoff. As the inventor of the company's technology explained in a letter to the MIT Technology-Licensing Office in January 1990,

> What I have learned in working over the past three years with various attorneys and what I did not appreciate at the time of the original filing by MIT in January of 1987 is that even if the other claimants did not understand the role of the materials they are claiming and, indeed, even if such materials are selected on the basis of erroneous assumptions, a patent is a patent, and many of the materials I would like to claim now constitute prior art. What this means is that the broad applicability of the selection criteria enunciated therein is seriously impaired because some of the materials called out by these selection criteria are already in the prior art. It seems virtually certain at this point that further attempts to secure a patent on the basis of all previous applications, including that filed in July of 1989, will prove to be futile. Accordingly, I am asking that you suspend efforts to obtain a patent for the technology as it is presently disclosed.

Sometimes a weak patent position does not come from weak claims, but rather from a spinoff's lack of exclusive rights to a patent. Because university spinoffs do not have any competitive advantages in their earliest days, other than those based in intellectual property, the founders of university spinoffs need to ensure that potential competitors will not gain access to the technology that they are using to start their companies. Exclusive licensees are important to the achievement of this goal.

My interviews with the founders of the MIT spinoffs provide empirical support for this proposition. For example, the founder of one MIT software spinoff explains how a lack of an exclusive license hindered the performance of his spinoff. He says,

> The problem I have always faced is that I have the knowledge to enhance and develop the software interfaces necessary to make this work but the patent itself is held by three different entities, all of whom have the right to operate independent of each other: MIT, myself and a large telecommunications company. The only one of

those three with the interest in this has been myself. But in any really large deployment where someone may wish to obtain full rights to the technology, it's not possible to grant exclusivity and there will always be other sources of the technology in terms of patent sublicensing.

The founder of one of the MIT robotics spinoffs explains that his company faced a similar problem. Lack of exclusive rights to the MIT invention on which the company was founded hindered the performance of his company. He says,

> When I left MIT, my key advisor wanted to have some control over the technology. He was thinking of starting a company. So he didn't want to let go of the technology. So he and I ended up being co-exclusive controllers of the technology. The problem is that any time I went to someone with a business plan and they saw co-exclusive it created this question mark. They would say, 'Wait a minute. If we invest in you, you're saying that there's this other company out there that has no restriction on competing with you.'

While the limits on exclusivity sometimes result from competing interests of different inventors, as was the case with the spinoff described above, they are more often the result of conditions imposed by private firms that finance the university research that leads to the technology. For instance, many of the spinoffs from MIT's Media Lab were hindered by their inability to obtain exclusive rights to Media Lab Technology because the companies that fund the lab have non-exclusive rights to all of the technology produced there. In a more specific example of the problems created by conditions imposed by industry funders of university research, the MIT Technology-Licensing Office determined that the development of one of its software spinoffs was hindered by a condition on the restriction of exclusive use established by one of the sources of research funds, limiting the spinoff to small niches of the market and hindering the development of that company.

General-purpose Technology

Successful university spinoffs exploit general-purpose technologies that can be applied in multiple applications. First, general-purpose technologies offer multiple market applications to exploit, allowing entrepreneurs to change direction if one application fails to perform or cannot generate a large enough market to support the new firm. Second, established companies have trouble identifying how to exploit general-purpose technologies, given the variety of market applications and stages of the value chain at which they can be applied. As a result, established companies tend to cede general-purpose technologies to new firms, allowing spinoffs to enter markets without facing immediate competition.

The MIT spinoffs that I studied provide evidence of the value of general-purpose technologies to the success of university spinoffs. For example, the success of one MIT medical device spinoff depended on the general-purpose nature of its underlying technology because the founders of that company originally thought that they would apply their technology to cardiac imaging, but later shifted to cardiac arrhythmia when they found that they could not provide effective cardiac imaging with their invention. Had the founders of this company been exploiting a single purpose technology, they would have been unable to shift applications, and the spinoff would likely have failed.

One of the MIT mechanical device spinoffs provides a good example of an MIT spinoff that had a single purpose technology and failed when its application proved to be insufficient to support the spinoff. One of the MIT technology-licensing officers explains that this spinoff's technology 'was not a platform technology. They had few places to apply it. It was difficult to put anywhere other than an MRI machine. If the MRI market didn't work, where are you?'

The founder of the spinoff confirms that the single purpose to which his company's technology could be put led to its demise:

> The technology that we licensed from MIT for this MRI application turned out to be very specific for this very low temperature. Everything we did was focused on this one market and this one type of product for that one temperature. We looked at different sizes of the same type of product, but it was all the same product aimed at this low temperature superconductivity application. We tried to find other applications for it, but there just weren't any.

Some observers also explain that general-purpose technologies enhance the performance of university spinoffs for cash flow reasons. Because a general-purpose technology has multiple uses, the founder of a spinoff can exploit one application for early cash flow and then another target application in a larger market once that first application has been exploited successfully.

My interviews with the founders of MIT spinoffs also support this proposition. For instance, the founder of one of the MIT biotechnology spinoffs says,

> You need platform technologies. People want platform technologies that have short-term commercialization paths and might also have some sort of revenue through research contracts early on. Our technology was a broad platform. From a research standpoint, for early cash flows, the cells serve as an assay to search for other proteins. The only ones that are fairly well known are for bone, muscle and cartilage. There are no isolated proteins yet for ligaments, tendon heart muscle and all the other tissues that you could think of. To be able to screen for it and potentially find and isolate each of those types of tissues is a great tool and ultimately worth a lot to the company.

THE EFFECT OF FIRM STRATEGY

The performance of university spinoffs is also affected by the strategies adopted by the founders of these companies. In particular, research has shown that, when founders adopt a two-part strategy of focus and adaptive flexibility, their spinoffs perform better than when they do not adopt this type of strategy. The subsections below explain why strategic focus and adaptive flexibility enhance the performance of university spinoffs.

Strategic Focus

University spinoffs that adopt a focus strategy perform better than other university spinoffs, for several reasons.[10] First, a focus strategy allows the founders of the spinoffs to make more effective use of the resources available to them. Second, a focus strategy minimizes the costly process of raising capital for the new venture. Third, a focus strategy is appealing to the investors that finance university spinoffs. Fourth, a focus strategy enhances the ability of spinoff company founders to gather information from their customers.

My interviews with the founders of the MIT spinoffs provide empirical support for the proposition that focusing enhances the performance of university spinoffs by allowing them to make more effective use of the resources available to them. For example, a business angel that invested in one of the MIT software spinoffs explains, 'We had to focus, given the lack of resources.' Similarly, the founder of one of the MIT medical device spinoffs explains that his company adopted a focus strategy because it 'didn't have the resources for more than one product'. Moreover, the founder of one of the MIT optics spinoffs explains, 'Unless you have unlimited funding and you were able to staff each one of the application groups with a full component of staffing, you have to focus.'

One important limited resource that leads the founders of university spinoffs to develop a focus strategy is the human resources that are necessary to develop the new technology. Given the uncertainty inherent in the development of university spinoffs, the founders of these companies find it difficult to attract large numbers of employees in the earliest period of the new companies' lives. As a result, university spinoffs generally start small, and do not have sufficient human resources to pursue more than one application of their technology at a time.

A number of the founders of MIT spinoffs explained that human resource constraints led them to focus on one product application for their technology. For example, the founder of one of the MIT semiconductor spinoffs explains, 'In the semiconductor industry, each product takes an enormous effort to develop and when you're small, you don't have the people to do more than one.' Similarly, the founder of one of the MIT medical device spinoffs explains, 'We focused on one product. It's a function of how much resource you can put into it. In a two-man company, what can you do in the course of a year?'

The founders of several of the MIT spinoffs indicated that the human resource constraint was not just the physical limit of too few people. Many of the founders did not believe that they could manage the complexity of a multiple application organizing effort. For example, the founder of one of the MIT computer hardware spinoffs explains,

> We focused on one product at a time. It's the best use of management. Within each product there were two efforts: the hardware effort and the operating system effort. We just didn't have the bandwidth to do more. It's trying just to get the hardware done and then get the operating system done.

Similarly, the founder of one of the MIT mechanical device spinoffs explains, 'We couldn't go off and build a recipe portfolio for everything out there. We weren't physically able to conceive of doing that so we looked at the auto industry and focused down on that.'

Given the limited human resources that spinoff companies have, any effort to pursue multiple applications simultaneously comes at the expense of the depth of development in any one area. Thus strategic focus makes it easier for spinoffs to do a high quality job of developing their technologies and exploiting their markets.

Several founders of the MIT spinoffs articulated this point in the interviews. For instance, the founder of one of the MIT materials spinoffs explains, 'We focused because we could do four things in a sub-optimal way or we could do one thing in a world class way and we chose to do one thing in a world class way.' Similarly, the founder of one of the MIT software spinoffs explains, 'You have to focus because if you're trying to do too many things in too many markets then you have the risk of spreading yourself too thin. If you try to do it in several areas, you may not be able to do as careful and as good a job in all those areas.'

The problem of spreading the venture too thin is particularly great on the marketing side of the equation. The process of product development and introduction takes a tremendous effort by organizations. This level of effort necessitates a strategic focus. Thus those spinoffs that do not focus on developing and marketing one product at a time tend to perform worse than other spinoffs.

My interviews with the founders of the MIT spinoffs provide empirical support for this proposition. For example, the founder of one of the MIT computer hardware spinoffs explains, 'To bring a product out takes a lot of energy and resources. If you pursue too many at a time, you can't do a good job.' Similarly, the founder of one of the MIT software spinoffs explains, 'You build up a sales and marketing team and they're willing to sell people pink elephants, anything that people want. We can't do it. We're resource constrained. Our policy is to focus on things we know we can sell.'

Another limited resource that leads the founders of university spinoffs to adopt a focus strategy is capital. Given the uncertainty and information asymmetry present with new technology, university spinoffs pay a high price to obtain the capital that they need to develop and exploit their technologies. Most private investors expect internal rates of return of 70 percent per year or more to invest in early stage spinoff companies. To generate high rates of return for potential investors, the founders of spinoffs must give up equity to investors. This leads the founders of university spinoffs to focus the activities of their spinoffs to minimize the expenditure of capital. For example, the founder of one of the MIT mechanical device spinoff explains, 'We could never have raised the money to do more than one application. There's a tremendous amount of work just to make a dense object using this technology.' Similarly, the founder of several MIT biotechnology spinoffs explains, 'It's very hard for a company to develop all aspects of a technology. It would be great if they could, but it's an expensive proposition. It's hard enough to develop one, as they found out.'

Moreover, even if investors were willing to provide the founders of university spinoffs with large amounts of capital, the effort to raise that capital is not costless to entrepreneurs. If the founders of university spinoffs devote their time to raising money, they have limited time available to develop their technology and sell their new products to their customers. Thus founders of university spinoffs often believe that it is better to raise a small amount of capital and focus their activities rather than to raise a large amount of capital to pursue multiple activities simultaneously.

The founders of the MIT spinoffs that I interviewed confirm this proposition. For example, the founder of one of the MIT medical device spinoffs explains, 'Even if you try to raise the resources, you are going to spend a significant amount of time trying to raise capital.'

University spinoffs also adopt a focus strategy because that strategy is appealing to investors. The investor preference for spinoffs that focus is explained by their ability to diversify their investments across a variety of new companies. Spinoff company investors, such as venture capitalists, can invest their money simultaneously in several new companies, each pursuing a different application for a given technology. Because they can diversify across firms, investors are better off if each new company in which they invest focuses on its highest value application, rather than if each new company diversifies across its own alternatives. The greater variance in the value of technology opportunities across companies means that cross-company diversification yields higher expected returns than does within-company diversification, while still managing risks.

My interviews with the founders of and investors in the MIT spinoffs support the proposition that many of them also adopt a focus strategy because that strategy is appealing to investors. For instance, a venture capitalist that funded one of the MIT software spinoffs explains the investor preference for spinoffs that engage in strategic focus:

> If a company does its homework it should be able to pick which is the best of the applications and really focus on that one. As soon as the company starts to focus on three products, you end up tripling the size of development teams, which are 18 to 25 people. You're burn rate goes way up. You always want to put all your wood behind the product that you think has the best chance. Doing a second and third product would just defocus.

Similarly, the founder of one of the MIT biotechnology spinoffs explains how the preference of investors for spinoffs that focus on a single application influenced his company's decision to focus on a single application for its technology. He says,

> We learned in the early stage to focus on what we thought were high value applications of the technology and we dropped more commodity type applications. We learned quickly that we couldn't do everything at the same time because of resources. Our ability to attract funding was directly related to focusing on high value medical applications. Venture capitalists were not interested in commodity applications for the chemical industry or things like that. So we focused on a smaller group of applications and tried to get them as far as we could. So [our company] has focused 85 percent of its resources on one product. In clinical developing and human testing, the R&D costs just escalate dramatically. They almost go up exponentially. So in order to keep up with progressing our product, we had to focus on one.

Investors also favor spinoffs that focus because they use real options reasoning to manage their investments. When spinoffs raise money from external sources, investors provide additional funding only if the spinoff meets agreed upon milestones in a given amount of time. Strategic focus facilitates the ability to achieve milestones in a limited amount of time because it concentrates the efforts of the spinoff's personnel on the achievement of those milestones.

The founders of the MIT spinoffs that I interviewed confirmed that investor use of real options led them to adopt focus strategies. For example, the founder of one of the MIT biotechnology spinoffs explains, 'You focus on one market application at a time because of the availability of the funds from investors who want to see that you've got something that's going to support other research going forward.'

A final reason for the founders of university spinoffs adopting focus strategies is that these strategies facilitate information gathering from customers.

Pursuing multiple applications simultaneously makes it difficult for the founders of spinoffs to listen to their customers and understand their needs. A multiple application approach creates too much variance in the information that customers are communicating to the spinoff for the founders of the spinoff to make effective use of it.

Moreover, successfully satisfying customer needs involves understanding customer needs and communicating back to customers that the spinoff has developed solutions that meet those needs. University spinoffs lack the ability to overcome customer objections to new technology and to communicate back to customers the value of their technology in meeting those needs if that communication needs to occur across multiple applications simultaneously.

The interviews that I conducted with the founders of the MIT spinoffs provide empirical support for this proposition. For example, the founder of one of the MIT optics spinoffs explains how the need to understand customer needs led his company to adopt a strategic focus:

> If we tried to understand our customers' needs in a multiple series of applications, undoubtedly we would have gotten crushed. You have to listen to what your customer is saying on a daily basis and he's changing his needs on a daily basis. If we hadn't been listening, we would have delivered a product at the end of two years that would have answered a question that was moot two years ago. If you're trying to do that five different times, you're going to miss the boat. We can just barely keep up with the semiconductor industry. Also, there's a huge evangelical role in technology startups. You have to go out and educate the world about why your technology is the new solution and to do that requires a huge amount of time. Everybody's rooted in the old technology. So to get the new technology in front of these guys, you've got to be out there banging the drum and tambourine. And you can only bang in so many places.

The interviews that I conducted with the founders of MIT spinoffs also provided many examples of spinoffs that ran into performance problems because they did not focus on a single market application at a time. For example, an executive with one of the MIT biotechnology spinoffs explains that his firm suffered in its early days because it did not focus, pursuing five different technologies including a cholera vaccine, HIV gene therapy and an HIV vaccine in its first 18 months and making little progress in any area. Similarly, one of the executives at another MIT biotechnology spinoff explains the problems created by a lack of strategic focus:

> We pursued multiple opportunities for too long. We literally duplicated work forces to the point where the company grew to over a hundred employees by the second full year of operation. The burn rate was phenomenal. In fact, I would have to fault the company in retrospect. Their horizons were way too broad. The company had very little focus. In contrast to most small biotech companies, [the founder] wanted to develop everything from A to Z, including a marketing strategy and, in fact, had

developed a sales force for this test skin product which is very expensive for a company to do. I think you're duplicating the efforts of large pharmaceutical companies. I think that type of all encompassing attitude is one which severely restricts and limits, and probably is not appropriate for most small biotech companies.

The adverse effect of a lack of focus on the performance of MIT spinoffs was not limited to the biotechnology companies. Similar patterns existed with the electronics, computer and mechanical device spinoffs. For instance, an MIT inventor whose technology led to the founding of one of the software spinoffs explains that a lack of strategic focus was a big mistake of that company. He says, 'From the beginning we had this problem of having too many different application areas for the technology and being unable to decide which one. We never really did make a choice. It was a big mistake.' Similarly, the founder of another MIT software spinoff explains that his firm suffered from failing to focus in its earliest years:

We shouldn't have wasted time and effort on an add in to Lotus 123. We should have stayed focused. The cost of development for what we ultimately decided to do is quite high. We had a lot to accomplish, a lot to deliver this complete platform.

Some of the founders of MIT spinoffs even argue that the adverse performance effects of not focusing are so severe that the act of focusing may even be more important than where a university spinoff focuses. For example, the founder of one of the MIT software spinoffs explains,

It was very, very hard to make a choice about the application of the technology. One of the mistakes that we made is that we tried to grow all of them a little bit as opposed to doing any of them really well. If I had it to do over again, I'd focus. I think it's extremely important to have a focus for the company and stick with it. I think it is more important to do whatever you decided to do well than to pick the right direction.

Adaptability

A second important dimension of the strategy of successful university spinoffs is adaptability. Given the technological and market uncertainties facing university spinoffs, success over time requires the organizations to make changes to their technologies and shift market applications as outcomes are revealed. Those spinoffs whose founders adapt their strategic direction perform better than those spinoffs whose founders do not.

My interviews with the founders of MIT spinoffs support the proposition that strategic adaptation influences the performance of university spinoffs. For example, the founder of one of the MIT semiconductor spinoffs explains,

'Your success doesn't come from well executed plans you had in advance. Your success comes from being able to adapt to all the things that happen to you because there are just endless things that you never anticipated.'

Two types of adaptation appear to be particularly important to the development of successful spinoffs: adaptation of the technology and adaptation to market needs. The subsections below discuss further both types.

Adaptation of the technology

The founders of university spinoffs often have to adapt their technologies to be successful. Most university inventions face significant technical risk at the time that they are licensed. The scientific principles behind the inventions often have to be proven, prototypes need to be created, and products and services need to be developed and made appropriate for the commercial environment. As a result, those spinoffs whose founders change the company's technology to overcome these technical risks perform better than those spinoffs whose founders do not.

In fact, one important aspect of technology adaptation by successful university spinoffs is to try new technologies if the original technology proves to be ineffective. Because the original technologies that university spinoffs are founded to exploit rarely work as the inventors had hoped, without substantial modification and adaptation, Stankiewicz (1994) argues that many successful university spinoffs adopt new technologies after founding.

Several of the MIT companies that I studied provide excellent examples of the way successful spinoffs evolve from an initial technology that led to the company's founding, but ultimately did not provide commercial value, to a different technology that provided commercial value to the new company. For instance, MIT spinoff Aware Inc. did not ultimately use the Howard Resnikoff wavelet patents that led to the formation of the company, but became a successful company on the basis of a communication technology (Schonfeld, 1998).

In most cases, the evolution of a university spinoff's technology occurs because the technology does not work effectively. For example, the founder of one MIT materials spinoff explains how he changed his spinoff's technology because of problems he had with his original technology. He says, 'One aspect of our patent wasn't working. So we went outside of our original patent and came up with a better way and patented it.'

My interviews with the founders of the MIT spinoffs support the proposition that spinoffs whose founders adapt their technologies perform better than spinoffs whose founders do not. Several MIT spinoffs failed because the technologies that led to their founding ultimately did not work, but the founders of those spinoffs did not change to a new technology. For example, the founder of one MIT biotechnology spinoff explains this problem:

The founders weren't prepared to be flexible enough to look for alternatives to what they initially put into the company as technology assets when those assets began to tell us that they weren't going to deliver in a reasonable time frame. They weren't prepared to provide alternative ideas.

Adaptation to the market

Successful university spinoffs also involve flexibility and adaptation to the needs of the market. My interviews with the founders of MIT spinoffs revealed two different ways that university spinoffs need to adapt to the market to be successful: changing products and services to meet customer needs, and shifting markets when the initial market proves to be insufficient.

Changing products and services to meet customer needs   Those spinoffs where the founders change their products or services to meet customer needs are more successful than those where the founders do not. Because university spinoffs are founded to exploit technologies that are invented as a byproduct of academic research, it is not surprising that the customer needs that they meet are not always apparent at the time that the spinoff is founded. In many cases, for the spinoff to achieve market acceptance, the products or services that are created from the technology must change as the founders of the spinoffs learn about the needs of customers.

The interviews that I conducted with the founders of the MIT spinoffs provide empirical support for this proposition. For instance, the inventor of a technology that led to the founding of one of the successful MIT software spinoffs explains how adaptation was important to the success of the spinoff:

> You could print terrific quality pictures with amateurs on the controls of the product that [the company] developed from my invention. It got a lot of attention and won prizes at World Com; however, it had only minor sales. What was limiting about this product was that it handled only one aspect of the color printing process – the part about getting the colors right – but it didn't do page layout, for example. So you would have to combine it with some other software to meet customer needs. It was not a complete solution. So [the company] developed other products that met the needs of customers better. The lesson here is to look at the market.

In many cases, the founders of successful spinoffs initially launched products or services based on their technologies that did not meet customer needs. The failure to satisfy customers led the founders to change the products and services according to the feedback that they received from the market place. For instance, the founder of one of the MIT computer hardware spinoffs explains that the failure of his company to meet customer needs initially led to an evolution of his product:

Originally, it was a technology push driven by an invention. It evolved when I couldn't fund that kind of business. We learned why it was so hard to make a business like that work. We built custom hardware for a super computer. However, the customer was not going to buy a super computer from a start-up. On the other hand, they had an SGI workstation anyway and you could get the customer to buy a board that slides in there and you can scale that thing up. The technology evolved into something that served a customer need and was a viable business – a board that went into an SGI workstation.

Shifting markets   Those spinoffs where the founders change their products or services because the market they are aiming at dies or never emerges are more successful than those spinoffs where the founders do not make changes to their product or services to find a viable market. Because the cost of establishing a new company is relatively large, university spinoffs need to have a market of reasonable size to recoup the cost of investing in the creation of a new technology product or service and a new company to support that effort. If a spinoff's initial target market is not large enough to recoup this cost, then the spinoff needs to change to other markets to survive and grow.

My interviews with the founders of the MIT spinoffs provide empirical support for this proposition. For example, the founder of one of the MIT medical device spinoffs explains, 'We changed from the blood glucose monitor that we started with to another product because the market place was going in the wrong direction.' One of the MIT technology-licensing officers adds, '[the company] was agile and flexible. They saw the market shift and changed products from a glucose monitor to something for carpel tunnel syndrome'.

In some cases, the initial market targeted by the founders of the university spinoff is too small to support the spinoff because the spinoff is founded too early in the life of the market. Most technologies develop in an evolutionary fashion with adoption rates that are initially slow, and then accelerating as the product becomes appropriate for mainstream customers. When spinoffs are founded too early in the life of the market, the level of demand for their product or service is too low to support the new company, requiring the founder of the spinoff to adjust to products or services that are appropriate for the spinoff's stage of market evolution. Otherwise the spinoff will not be successful.

My interviews with the founders of the MIT spinoffs revealed the performance implications of the failure to change products or services when the spinoff was established too early in the evolution of a market. For example, the inventor whose patents led to the founding of one MIT software spinoff explains,

One of the problems that new technology companies have is that often they lead the market. For a period of time when the market is being built, a small company will need to redefine the product to be less innovative to match what present interests are and hope to survive while the market is being built. That was certainly our case.

Some of the mathematical results that I came up with and am very impressed with are likely to have applications, but not now. So it's the recognition that something is potentially of use, but that technology is not too different from what the market wants in terms of product and function. For instance, an early application was in the commercial aircraft industry. However, because the risks of design were so great, it would take too long. They review and get the bugs out of their codes in a period of 10 to 15 years. That means it's not a business for a start-up. That's a business for NASA or the Defense Department to support.

One way that the founders of university spinoffs overcome the problem of mistiming the evolution of the market is to keep their technologies in the laboratory until the market is ready for them. Several of the founders of the MIT spinoffs explained that they adopted this approach to market timing. For instance, the founder of one of the MIT medical device spinoffs explains how she used this strategy with her spinoff:

In 1985, I realized that the technology I developed for chips could have many different applications. But, in the 1980s, the market was not that big; it wasn't ready yet. So I started thinking about it until 1995 when I started my company. Then the technology could be used for video bandwidth compression.

Unfortunately, the founders of many spinoffs are unable to time the market for their technologies. Rather than keep their technologies in the laboratory until the market has taken off, these founders establish their companies when the market for products that use their technologies is too small. If the founders of these spinoffs are unable to adapt their technologies to meet the needs of a wider portion of the market, these spinoffs fail.

My interviews with the founders of the MIT spinoffs revealed numerous examples of spinoffs that failed because they could never find a market for their technologies large enough to support their new companies. For example, the founder of one of the MIT software spinoffs explains,

There was no single market segment large enough to sustain a business so we had to sell to someone who wanted the technology. When we started in 1990, we were probably about six years ahead of the curve in terms of there being a true market opportunity. Education was probably the only real market, yet it wasn't big enough. There were probably six independent variables that needed to be solved for a real opportunity to exist. There was the software, which we controlled, but there was also the cost of computing hardware, the speed of the CPU, compression technology, bandwidth, and hard disk storage. All these pieces needed to be in place for there to be a real market and we couldn't control any of these things. [We] had no way of reducing the cost or improving the speed and the performance of compression or hard disk storage or anything like that.

Many of the founders of the MIT spinoffs explained that the rate of growth of complementary technologies was the most important factor limiting their ability to time the founding of the spinoff to match the growth of the market. In the absence of appropriate complementary technologies, the market for the spinoff's technology will not materialize, hindering the spinoff's performance. For instance, the founder of one of the MIT software spinoffs explains,

> The main thing holding us back was the technology at the time. A 486PC was about as fast as you could get. But it was just not adequate to run our technology because it requires floating point processors and pretty fast graphics boards. So everything we did back then was fairly simple and kind of unappealing. Only just now are computers able to keep up with the technology. We were ahead of our time in terms of machine power, and because people really couldn't understand why you couldn't just do regular animation.

SUMMARY

This chapter has explored the factors that enhance the performance of university spinoffs. It showed that the human capital of the founders, the financial resources of the new ventures, the efforts of the new ventures to meet the needs of customers, the new technology, the firm strategy and university support all differentiate successful from unsuccessful spinoffs.

Two aspects of human capital enhance the performance of university spinoffs. First, spinoffs founded by complementary venture teams perform better than spinoffs not founded by complementary teams. Involving business founders provides the spinoffs with management knowledge, expertise in product development and production, and industry knowledge, all of which university inventors tend to lack. On the other hand, inventor involvement provides a mechanism to transfer the inventor's tacit knowledge of technology development to the new venture, which enhances performance. Second, spinoffs founded by full-time entrepreneurs perform better than spinoffs founded by part-time entrepreneurs. By working full time, founders signal their personal commitment to the new company, which is important to generate support among potential stakeholders. Moreover, as university spinoffs grow and develop, the demands on the founders' time escalate, making it very difficult for them to accomplish necessary activities without a full-time commitment.

University spinoffs also succeed because they have products or services that meet customer needs, not because they have the best technology. However, most university spinoffs employ 'technology push' rather than 'market pull'. The founders of successful university spinoffs overcome the problems of technology push by creating products or services rather than by trying to sell technology in raw form. In addition, they identify markets that are large enough to support spinoffs, and assess and satisfy customer needs.

A third factor that enhances the success of university spinoffs is the acquisition of adequate capital. Adequate capital facilitates technological development, allows the spinoff to change strategic direction if need be, minimizes the time that founders have to spend raising money rather than developing products and services, and signals the quality and legitimacy of the spinoff.

Having adequate university support is also important to the success of university spinoffs. Because most university technology is at a very early stage at the time spinoffs are founded, the opportunity to conduct additional work in the university environment where the inventors reside is valuable. In addition, a flexible approach of the university to the relationship with the spinoffs enhances performance by allowing the spinoff to renegotiate the terms of its agreement if it needs to do so to survive. Furthermore, external liaison organizations that transform university research and technology into products and services enhance the performance of university spinoffs by minimizing the cost, and simplifying the process, of transforming university inventions into products and services.

Just as the nature of technological inventions influences the founding of university spinoffs, it also influences the performance of those spinoffs after they are founded. Two characteristics of university technology affect the performance of university spinoffs. First, a strong intellectual property position enhances the performance of university spinoffs because intellectual property protection is the only competitive advantage available to a new firm at the time when the company is first created. Second, a general-purpose technology enhances the performance of university spinoffs both because these technologies allow entrepreneurs to change directions if information reveals better alternative applications, and because established companies have trouble exploiting general-purpose technologies.

The strategies adopted by the founders of university spinoffs also affect the performance of these companies. Research has shown that when founders adopt a focus strategy, their spinoffs perform better than when they do not adopt this type of strategy because spinoffs have limited human and financial resources available to them, because investors prefer spinoffs to have this strategy and because a focus strategy facilitates the process of gathering information from customers.

Research has also shown that university spinoffs are more successful when they are more adaptive than when they are less adaptive. Given the technological and market uncertainties facing university spinoffs, success often requires their founders to make changes to their technologies and market applications. One aspect of adaptation to the market involves changing products and services to meet customer needs, as those needs are revealed. Another aspect is adapting to a target market of sufficient size to support the new venture.

Having described the factors that influence the performance of university spinoffs, I now turn to a discussion of the problems that university spinoffs generate for the universities that spawn them, the subject of Chapter 13.

NOTES

1. Some of the founders of the MIT spinoffs even believe that the CEO of the spinoff company should have strong industry experience, leaving the inventor to perform other roles in the new organization. For example, an MIT inventor whose technology led to the founding of one of the MIT software spinoffs explains how his experience with that company would lead him to approach a spinoff differently the next time around. He says, 'I have a better idea of what kind of characteristics the CEO should have – a marketing background. The person we had was technically very good, but in a different area. You know market connections, knowing people, that's very important.'

2. Moreover, a full-time commitment on the part of the founder is important because many universities want their faculty to create spinoff companies as well as continue their academic work. The pressure from universities to try to pursue both activities simultaneously might be as great a source of the problems that come from a part-time commitment to spinoffs as the decisions of faculty members themselves.

3. The CEO of one MIT software spinoff explains that succeeding with a spinoff 'is more a marketing battle than it is a technical battle'.

4. One of the executives in an MIT biotechnology spinoff explains that, to be successful, 'You need to have a real clear understanding validated with market studies that show a plan for developing the technology into something that's going to make money for somebody as a product or service.'

5. As the founder of one MIT materials spinoff explains, 'Just because you have an interesting technology doesn't necessarily mean that you have a market.'

6. Some researchers have also argued that obtaining capital from the right financing sources also enhances the performance of university spinoffs (Shane and Stuart, 2002). This argument suggests that university spinoffs funded by high status investors, such as prestigious venture capital firms, should perform better than other university spinoffs. Practitioners of university spinoff activity provide qualitative evidence consistent with this argument. Preston (1997) explains that one of the factors that enhanced the performance of Genentech, an early biotechnology university spinoff, was the assistance that its venture capital firms, Mayfield Ventures and Kleiner Perkins, provided in helping the company gain access to key stakeholders. Moreover, my interviews with founders of MIT spinoffs also support this proposition. For example, one founder of several MIT biotechnology spinoffs explains, 'A good VC is important. A lot of places, their track record is so good that everybody wants to co-invest with them. If a venture capital firm is one that noone has heard of, you have a higher hurdle to reach in raising money.'

7. Some research also indicates that university spinoffs with radical technology perform better in fragmented markets than in concentrated markets. For instance, Nerkar and Shane (forthcoming) examined the survival of MIT spinoffs established between 1980 and 1996 and followed through 1997, and found that firms with more radical technology were more likely to survive if they operated in fragmented industries.

8. The founder of one of the MIT biotechnology spinoffs explains that having a strong intellectual property position was one of the lessons he learned in the process of creating a spinoff company. He says, 'Never be complacent about how much intellectual property you have, always have more.'

9. Even if strong patents do not motivate large firms to be partners with spinoff companies, they provide the spinoff with an option to use the court system to enforce its property rights. Strong patents provide a better basis for a court case to enforce the spinoff's property rights because they provide evidence of the spinoff's intellectual property right that the imitator is

accused of violating. For example, Lowe (2002:29) quotes the CEO of University of California spinoff Xenometrix as saying, 'You want the IP there since it's the only tangible evidence you have in court.'

10. For example, Roger Salquist, CEO of AxyS Pharmaceuticals explains, 'You have to have the broadest commercial technology platform and marry that with sharp commercial focus' (Calkins and Pierce, 1998:1). Similarly, the founder of several MIT biotechnology spinoffs explains, 'Focusing is really important. Lack of focus is a reason why a lot of the biotech spinoffs fail.'

13. The problems with university spinoffs

Although the first 12 chapters of this book presented a very positive view of university spinoffs, the creation of these companies is not without drawbacks. This chapter discusses some of the problems created by university spinoffs. Although previous researchers have identified several different problems that spinoffs impose, the drawbacks of university spinoffs can be divided into two broad categories: problems of integration into the traditional model of the university, and problems of earning financial returns from technology licensing to spinoff companies. The subsections of this chapter discuss each of these broad categories of problems in turn.

THE PROBLEMS OF INTEGRATING FIRM FORMATION WITH THE UNIVERSITY MODEL

Universities differ significantly from private firms in their goals and mode of governance. The primary mission of academic institutions is the creation and dissemination of knowledge through research and teaching. To achieve this mission, most universities are governed by faculty committees, which make collective decisions about the direction of their institutions. University spinoffs generate several problems for the achievement of the traditional academic goal of the creation and dissemination of knowledge, as well as for faculty governance. Specifically, observers of university spinoff activity have identified three central problems: the lack of widespread faculty support for spinoff activity, the adverse effect of the commercial model on traditional university goals, and conflict of interest problems.

Lack of Faculty Support

The committee form of university governance means that, to institute policies and procedures effectively at an academic institution, the majority of faculty members must support those policies and procedures. University spinoffs are a problem because most university faculty do not support university involvement with spinoff companies. For instance, in a survey of faculty across a wide variety of institutions and in a wide range of fields, Lee (1996) found that only

44.1 percent of faculty members agreed with the policy of offering start-up assistance to new technology companies that emerge from universities, and only 26.5 percent agreed with the policy of taking equity in return for the intellectual property licensed to companies founded to exploit university research. In fact, many university faculty expressed the belief that spinoff activity conflicts with academic values about knowledge dissemination, conflict of interest, long-term research and scholarly freedom (Lee, 1996).

Because the average faculty member at most universities does not support the creation of spinoffs, this activity must be driven by actions of the central administration that are counter to the wishes of faculty. This, of course, creates conflict between the central administration and faculty over university governance. Moreover, even if a university administration can institute spinoff-friendly policies in an institution, university spinoffs do not meet with the general support of academics, making spinoffs uneasy participants in the university environment.

University spinoffs also exacerbate the conflict between academic units, particularly that which exists on many university campuses between applied and commercially oriented fields, like engineering and business, and less commercially oriented fields, like the arts and humanities. Universities are plagued by a silo orientation in which separate schools, and even departments within schools, operate with goals of enhancing their own positions, even if the goals of separate units conflict with each other and hinder the development of the institution. University spinoffs play into this conflict because they enhance the goals of engineering and science faculty, but do very little to help social science and humanities faculty.

As a result, university spinoffs often become a point of contention between science and engineering faculty, who want one set of policies to encourage spinoffs, and humanities and social science faculty, who want another set of policies to limit spinoffs. Studies of faculty attitudes toward university spinoffs and technology commercialization indicate a wide divergence of beliefs in the value of technology commercialization between engineering, science and medical faculty, on the one hand, and arts and humanities faculty, on the other. For instance, Lee's (1996) survey of faculty showed that faculty with the lowest level of linkage to industry had the most negative view of campus entrepreneurship and university spinoffs. In particular, Lee found that engineering faculty were more likely than science faculty, who were more likely than social science faculty, to support policies to take equity in university spinoffs or to offer assistance to people to start new technology companies from university research. Because of these divergent views toward university spinoffs and institutional assistance for these organizations across campus units, university spinoffs often lead to conflict between university units over what constitutes desired activity on the part of the university administration and faculty members toward spinoff companies. The end result is often a set of political battles over conflict of interest policies, rules about equity holdings, royalty distribution plans or the use of university funds for the development of new companies.

The effect of this difference in attitudes across academic units toward university policies for spinoffs and technology commercialization is exacerbated by the different rates of spinoff activity across different parts of the university. For instance, in an investigation at the University of Calgary, Chrisman *et al.* (1995) found that approximately 19 percent of the faculty in the sciences and 24 percent of the faculty in medicine had founded companies, as compared to 2 percent of the faculty in the humanities.

The data that I collected at MIT shows patterns similar to those described by Chrisman *et al.* (1995). Table 13.1 shows the distribution of MIT spinoffs from 1980 to 1996 by academic department, and demonstrates the concentration of spinoff activity.

Table 13.1   The departmental distribution of MIT spinoffs from 1980 to 1996

Department	Percentage of spinoffs
Aeronautics and Astronautics	3
Architecture	1
Artificial Intelligence Lab	3
Biology	18
Biomedical Engineering	5
Brain and Cognitive Science	3
Center for Advanced Educational Services	1
Chemical Engineering	9
Chemistry	3
Computer Science/Electrical Engineering	14
Lincoln Laboratory	11
Materials Science	4
Mechanical Engineering	15
Media Lab	4
Nuclear Engineering	2
Physics	5
Sloan School of Management	1

Source: Data collected from the records of the MIT Technology Licensing Office.

Because the views of many faculty are directly related to their own self-interest, it is not surprising that faculty from academic units where spinoffs tend to be created are the most supportive of spinoff activity and university policies to support it. Universities typically adopt policies that allow the inventor's department to obtain a share of royalties from licensed inventions and returns from equity holdings in spinoffs. Consequently, those units of the university that generate more spinoff companies benefit more financially from the formation of spinoffs than other units. As a result, it is not surprising that engineering, science and medical faculty see the support of technology transfer and spinoff activity as much more in the interest of their academic units, while arts and humanities faculties do not (Nelson, 2001).

The Adverse Effects of a Commercial Orientation

Critics charge that university spinoffs bring to university campuses a commercial orientation that has adverse effects: in particular, that spinoffs reorient university activity toward commercial goals, and away from scholarly goals of knowledge creation and dissemination. Because universities have a unique purpose – creating and disseminating knowledge for the benefit of society – critics believe that spinoff activities undermine the unique role of universities in society. Derek Bok, former president of Harvard University, perhaps best articulated this position. In an article written in 1981, he explained,

> [The concerns] stem from an uneasy sense that programs to exploit technological development are likely to confuse the university's central commitment to the pursuit of knowledge and learning by introducing into the heart of the academic enterprise a new and powerful motive – the search for commercial utility and financial gain. (Bok, 1981:26)

To the critics of university spinoffs, in a capitalist system, private firms provide the role of spurring innovation through the search for financial gain. Introducing this search for private gain onto university campuses might not be desirable. This problem, critics charge, does not generally lie with university technology transfer officers, who are not solely motivated by financial gain in supporting the creation of university spinoffs, and, in fact, are often driven as much by the desire to see technology commercialized as to generate revenues for the university. Rather, the problem lies with the university spinoffs that license university technology. These organizations are private firms, and are motivated by the same search for financial gain as other private companies. Consequently, in their interactions with university administrators, these companies introduce private sector goals that conflict with the academic goals of universities, and keep educational institutions from achieving their primary and unique societal role. In particular, the search for private gain undermines the open creation and dissemination of knowledge, research freedom and the education of students.

Spinoffs hinder open dissemination of knowledge

Critics of university spinoffs charge that spinoffs make universities less willing to engage in the open dissemination of knowledge, one of the hallmarks of academia. Several researchers have shown that the formation of spinoff companies reduces the level of knowledge dissemination coming out of academic laboratories. For example, Boly (1982:174) quotes a post-doctoral researcher in Herbert Boyer's laboratory describing changes that occurred in the laboratory after biotechnology spinoff Genentech was founded. The researcher says,

> I remember that first day. . . . There were only twelve of us in Boyer's lab, and one guy was singled out to have a confidential meeting with Herb and Bob Swanson. We all wondered what was going on, and he came back out and couldn't tell us. Right then, that very moment, things changed in the lab, and it sort of fell apart from that point.

Large sample survey data corroborate this qualitative evidence. For instance, Louis *et al.* (2001) conducted a survey of researchers in the biological sciences and found that those academics that were also entrepreneurs (they held equity in a start-up company) were significantly more likely than other academics to withhold their research results from other academics. This result suggests that involvement with spinoff companies reduces the willingness of academics to disseminate knowledge for the benefit of society.

Another way in which spinoff activity hinders the dissemination of knowledge created by universities is seen when the founders of university spinoffs delay publication or distribution of their research results until they have patented their inventions and transferred their academic patents to private firms intent on profiting from them (Golub, 2003). Because the patent system requires inventors to file for patents before they make their research results public, spinoff companies that seek to benefit financially from exploiting university inventions typically need to wait to make scientific discoveries public until after they have obtained patent protection. The desire of spinoff companies to patent their academic inventions before they are disclosed to the scientific community slows the dissemination of academic knowledge.

Some researchers report that the founders of spinoff companies have slowed the dissemination of their research results until after they have obtained patent protection on those findings. For instance, Hsu and Bernstein (1997) explain that MIT delayed publication of Neil Goldfine's PhD thesis until after patents could be filed on the results of his research so that foreign patent protection could be established before the research was released into the public domain.[1]

The desire of spinoffs to obtain exclusive rights to university inventions also slows the dissemination of potentially valuable commercial technology by limiting the distribution of that knowledge. While exclusive licensing motivates spinoff companies to undertake the risk of commercializing university technology, thereby enhancing the likelihood of commercialization, it also reduces the probability of transmitting the technology to a party that might be better able to commercialize it. As a result, the reliance on exclusive licensing to spinoffs imposes potential costs on society if the spinoff is not the entity best able to commercialize the technology and dissemination of knowledge to those best able to make use of it is hindered (Shane, 2000).

This problem is exacerbated by the fact that a significant minority of university spinoffs are 'living dead' firms. Unable to commercialize a piece of technology, but holding an exclusive license, these firms keep others from using the technology (Nelsen, 1991). While university technology-licensing offices can write contracts to exclusive licenses with performance milestones to mitigate this problem, the early stage at which university technologies tend to be licensed makes it difficult to write contracts with effective performance clauses that avoid this problem. As a result, the use of exclusive licensing to spinoffs likely hinders the dissemination of academic knowledge to potential users.

Spinoffs influence the subject matter of faculty research

Critics of university spinoffs also argue that the opportunity for researchers to create new companies and benefit personally from the wealth generated from these enterprises influences the subject matter of faculty research. Specifically, the opportunity to found spinoff companies leads faculty to focus on more applied research topics at the expense of basic science (for example, emphasizing product design) (Kenney, 1986; Etzkowitz, 2003) or to avoid research areas with limited commercial potential (for example, not studying tropical diseases) (Miner *et al.*, 2001).

While scholars of university spinoffs and technology transfer have not found any direct evidence to support the proposition that the opportunity to found university spinoffs leads researchers to focus on more applied research at the expense of basic science or to avoid research areas with limited commercial potential, they have found indirect evidence of these effects. In particular, the opportunity to create spinoffs has led researchers to focus their attention on those areas in which commercial gains can be more easily appropriated by new firms. Feller (1990) argues that spinoffs lead university researchers to shift their research toward questions whose answers are more likely to be patentable. To test this argument, Shane (forthcoming) examined university patenting from 1969 to 1996 and found that, over time, universities have shifted their patenting towards lines of business in which patents are more effective. He explains that this result does not mean that the direction of the research necessarily changed. Over the past three decades, universities simply may have focused their attention on patenting those inventions that they were most likely to sell. Nevertheless, the fact that the dramatic rise in university technology transfer and spinoff activity over the past 30 years is correlated with an increased concentration of university patenting in fields where patenting activity is more effective at protecting intellectual property raises the question of why that shift has occurred.

Education of students

Critics of spinoffs also argue that these companies divert universities' attention away from their primary mission of educating students. Although this topic has not been the subject of serious scholarly inquiry, anecdotal evidence suggests the existence of this problem. At several state institutions, critics have charged that taxpayer funds, allocated for the education of students, have been used to support the creation of spinoff companies. For example, when Penn State University invested in a spinoff called Diamond Materials Corporation, which was established to commercialize research undertaken at the university, one Pennsylvania state legislator responded, 'Where did Penn State get the money that it spun off? . . . We give them $200 million in state appropriations and we give it to them primarily to keep tuition down, not to use it as venture capital' (McDade, 1988:A4).

Despite this anecdotal evidence that spinoffs divert resources and attention away from the education of undergraduate and masters students, the greatest potential for the problems of diversion of resources by spinoffs lies in doctoral education. In particular, critics of university spinoffs argue that these organizations generate the potential for faculty exploitation of graduate students for commercial gain, undermining the doctoral education process. For example, Leonard (2001) has pointed out that strong rifts exist in many universities over doctoral student mentoring, between those academics who have started companies to exploit their research and those who have not. Faculty members who have started spinoff companies are much more willing than other faculty to believe that it is acceptable for doctoral students to be assigned work that benefits the spinoff company.

This problem leads to faculty sensitivity toward the role of doctoral students in university spinoffs. Many of the founders of MIT university spinoffs that I interviewed pointed out their concern over the potential for the abuse of doctoral students by faculty who found spinoffs. For example, one MIT inventor who founded several biotechnology companies explains,

> I would be very uncomfortable setting up a company based on work that we did in my lab. I'm much more comfortable licensing that out. I don't want people to say that I'm taking the work of graduate students. I want to keep my business and academic work separate and not worry about ethics and conflict of interest.

However, this issue appears not to be one solely of appearances. Several observers have documented examples of improper treatment of doctoral students by faculty motivated by the desire to commercialize inventions through spinoffs. The most common problem appears to be assignment of doctoral students to work on applied projects for faculty spinoff companies (Miner *et al.*, 2001). For instance, Jonathan King testified before a congressional committee looking into this matter, saying, 'Graduate students . . . and post doctoral fellows . . . are very often changed to something that has to be done for the marketability of that project' (King, 1981:73). Moreover, the University of Colorado microbiology department actually censured three of its faculty members who founded a spinoff called Syrengen for using graduate student research to further develop the company's products (Matkin, 1990).

A more severe type of improper treatment of doctoral students is the improper patenting of doctoral student research by faculty to assemble the intellectual property to found companies. Although no systematic evidence of this problem has been documented, several examples of lawsuits over it can be found. For instance, Joany Chou sued her advisor Bernard Roizman and his spinoff company, Aviron, for patenting, without her knowledge, and then licensing from the University of Chicago, a new gene based on 14 years of her research (Stephan, 2001). Although Chou lost the case, it raises the question of whether other faculty members have improperly patented research based on doctoral student research to assemble the intellectual property for spinoff companies.

Conflict of Interest

Another problem spinoffs create for university goals and mission is that of conflict of interest. Critics charge that the potential for commercial gain from spinoff activity leads faculty entrepreneurs to neglect their academic duties to further their personal gains from entrepreneurial activity. Several observers have pointed out that spinoffs create conflict with academic duties. In a study of professors who founded biotechnology companies, Powell and Owen-Smith (1998) found that the academics shifted some of their effort and creativity away from their academic work toward their companies. Moreover, Kenney (1986) explains that spinoffs create an opportunity cost for academic work because inventor–entrepreneurs channel their energy toward raising capital for their companies rather than toward pursuing grant money. Similarly, Leonard (2001), speaking about the Howard Hughes Medical Institute's experience with university spinoffs, stated that the Institute was concerned that spinoff activity leads faculty members to reduce their scientific activity because their time is spread too thinly across many activities when they work on founding and running spinoffs.

While less common than the basic shifting of time and attention, critics charge that more insidious forms of conflict of interest also exist when academics become entrepreneurs. Most notably, the potential for financial abuse exists when faculty members hold equity in companies for whom they are doing research. For example, Blumenthal (1992) provides the example of a research fellow at Massachusetts Eye and Ear Infirmary who sold his stock in a small company just before his research results showed that the company's new drug was ineffective. Similarly, Samson and Gurdon (1993) report that Werner Baumgartner, who founded Psychemedics Corporation to commercialize his diagnostic testing technology, was criticized for his failure to do peer reviewed studies on his technology.

Blumenthal (1992) points out that the potential for problems exists even if faculty members do not hold equity in spinoffs, but the university and its administrators do. He provides the example of Boston University, which invested $85 million of its endowment in its spinoff, Seragen, which lost $150 million over a six-year period (Press and Washburn, 2000). Because members of the board of trustees and the university president also invested in the spinoff, their objectivity in making additional rounds of investment with university funds was questioned (Blumenthal, 1992). Similarly, questions were raised about the conflict of interest of the University of Pennsylvania Medical School, which was a major investor in a company conducting a gene therapy study that resulted in the death of a patient because of the financial gain that the university would have received if the therapy were successful (Bok, 2003).

To avoid conflict of interest problems, many universities preclude the founders of spinoff companies from working on the same projects at the university as their companies undertake. However, this solution creates suboptimal efforts to create companies.

The founders of several MIT spinoffs that I interviewed provided examples of the way conflict of interest rules make company creation efforts suboptimal. MIT rules preclude the inventor of a technology from holding equity in the spinoff that is conducting additional research for the company at MIT. Consequently, in the case of one MIT semiconductor spinoff, the inventor was retained as consultant to the spinoff. However, as Jensen and Thursby (2001) explain, this type of consulting arrangement is insufficient to develop a university spinoff, because the early stage and tacit nature of university technologies exploited by spinoffs means that strong ties between the inventors and the spinoff are necessary for successful technology development. As a result, the inventor did not have strong enough ties to the spinoff company to develop the technology into a commercial product. Moreover, when the initial technology failed to work as expected, the inventor had limited incentive to work with the spinoff to develop an alternative technology, leading the company to fail.

A final area of conflict of interest facing spinoff companies lies in the possibility of the founders of successful spinoff companies achieving personal financial gain from taxpayer-funded research. Because the federal government funds most university research, but universities can license inventions that were developed from that research without compensating the government for its investment, many observers see spinoffs as creating a conflict of interest between faculty's role as generators of new knowledge for the good of society and the faculty members' desire to make money. To the critics, taxpayers funded research that faculty members then use to become rich without compensating the taxpayers for their contribution to the wealth created by the technology that they funded.

For universities, the problem is not that university technology transfer officers or faculty entrepreneurs are doing anything wrong (the Bayh–Dole Act specifically encourages this type of entrepreneurial activity) but that critics discount the contributions made by the entrepreneurs who bear considerable risk to commercialize valuable technology, generate jobs and pay taxes. As a result, the creation of spinoffs often creates a perception of universities in the popular media as commercially oriented entities, using public resources for private gain, something that is at odds with the perception of universities as entities whose primary goal, most people believe, should be the betterment of society.

A *Boston Globe* article (1998:A25) illustrates the problem as critics see it. The article explains that MIT spinoff,

> Integra Life Sciences has no obligation to repay the taxpayers who made [the inventor-founder] Yannas' work possible. Federal records show Yannas has received more than $3 million in grants from the National Institutes of Health since 1972. And while taxpayers receive no financial return on that investment, such as royalties or licensing fees, Yannas certainly has. In addition to his MIT salary, Yannas in 1992 signed a consulting deal with Integra. . . . In return, Yannas receives options for 240,000 shares of Integra stock, vested over the life of the contract. The option price was 26.5 cents a share, compared with a current Integra stock price of roughly $4 a share. . . . Among other MIT millionaires is Professor Richard J. Cohen who received more than $1.5 million in government support leading to the development of noninvasive ways to diagnose heart disease. Cohen controls roughly $12 million worth of stock in Cambridge Heart. . . . Then there is professor Richard Wurtman who received more than $1 million in public support for his work on, among other topics, ways to control overeating. Wurtman controls shares of Lexington based Interneuron Pharmaceuticals worth roughly $10 million.

To many observers, the system of making the founders of university spinoffs wealthy from taxpayer-funded research without compensating the taxpayers for their investment in the technology that led to the spinoff suggests a fundamental unfairness with spinoff companies that make them problematic.

THE PROBLEMS OF MANAGING TECHNOLOGY TRANSFER TO SPINOFFS

Even in the absence of the problems that university spinoffs create for university goals and objectives, creating spinoff companies generates problems for the management of technology transfer in universities interested in reaping financial returns from this activity. First, spinoff companies are costly. Second, spinoff companies impose significant risks on universities. In the subsections below, each of these problems is discussed in turn.

The Cost and Difficulty of Developing Spinoff Companies

Critics charge that spinoff companies are a very costly mechanism for technology transfer. In fact, developing the typical university spinoff is an expensive undertaking, with each spinoff created in the United States costing approximately $141 million in research money to create (Pressman, 2002). Moreover, research has shown that creating spinoffs is more costly and time-consuming in terms of licensing office resources than is licensing to established firms because the creation of spinoffs imposes a variety of additional costs (Tornatzky *et al.*, 1995). To create spinoffs, university technology transfer officers often require additional training to understand how to work with start-up companies (Golub, 2003). For instance, the licensing officers must learn how venture capital operates and how to develop effective business plans. To create spinoffs, universities must also incur the cost of building technology-licensing officer ties to investors who can finance spinoffs, a networking process that takes time away from other activities (Feller, 1990). The cost of creating spinoffs is also high because spinoffs require more assistance than established firm licensees in negotiating agreements and defending their patents in lawsuits, and because universities often have to bear patent fees to create spinoffs (Golub, 2003). In an era of tightening university budgets, it is questionable whether investment in the development of spinoffs is financially a worthwhile activity for universities.

Establishing spinoffs is also more difficult than licensing to established companies. As Roberts and Malone (1996) explain, valuing the equity in a spinoff is more difficult than establishing a royalty rate on a license, and demands expertise that is rare among university personnel. For instance, most university technology transfer officers lack the expertise to identify high potential spinoffs or to facilitate their development (Matkin, 1990). Venture capitalists develop this expertise in selecting and developing spinoffs by specializing in the development of new technology companies. However, university licensing officers are unable to specialize in many of the value-added activities that venture capitalists engage in to facilitate the development of their portfolio companies, such as building ties to investment bankers, creating relationships with suppliers and customers, and arranging for management talent. As a result, most university technology-licensing officers have trouble figuring out how to help to create successful university spinoffs.

Risk of Creating New Firms

Creating university spinoffs is a risky activity. Creating new companies adds organizing and financing risks to the already high technical and market risks of commercializing university technologies. Moreover, the magnitude of the downside risk for creating spinoffs is very large, particularly if universities invest in their own spinoffs. For instance, Boston University ended up losing $50 million of its $166 million endowment by investing in its biotechnology spinoff Seragen (Matkin, 1990). Given that many universities lack the expertise to organize and finance new companies, it is questionable whether they should incur these types of risks.[2] This problem could be averted if universities did not invest their endowments in spinoff companies, but simply limited their ownership of spinoff companies to the equity that they receive in return for providing intellectual property. However, the desire among many university administrators to generate revenue to cover the ever-increasing costs of higher education makes it difficult for many universities to hold back from investing in their own spinoffs, imposing significant investment risk on universities.

Another type of financial risk that universities face in managing spinoffs lies in timing their exit from spinoff companies. To profit successfully from equity holdings in spinoff companies, universities must time the sale of equity correctly. This requires figuring out movements of the stock market. While many universities, like Stanford University, have a policy of getting out of equity investment at the first liquidatable event (Ku, 2001) making market timing impossible, other institutions allow administrators to decide when to liquidate their investments. This latitude means that administrators risk picking the wrong time to sell their equity in spinoff companies. For example, the University of California at Berkeley capitalized a software license in one of its spinoffs, Inktomi, in 1996, and obtained 6667 shares in return. That investment was worth $870 000 in July of 1990, but only $19 000 by April of 2002 (Kenney and Goe, forthcoming). Similarly, Carnegie Mellon's equity position in Lycos was worth $500 million in September of 2000, (Kenney and Goe, forthcoming), but to date has not come close to that value again.

Another risk that university spinoffs impose on universities is not the financial risk from losing capital invested in university spinoffs, but risk of loss from legal exposure created by university spinoffs. Powell and Owen-Smith (1998:270) ask, 'Who is the fiduciary when universities convert a professor's discovery into equity ownership in a company and that company is subsequently sued for patent infringement?' Birley (2002) addresses a similar issue when she discusses the role of universities in providing warranties to the ownership of the intellectual property that is licensed to spinoff companies. She points out that universities are the entities that will be sued if one of the inventors is left out of the patent, or if an inventor who originally worked on the project comes up with a competing invention. Because proven patent infringement results in treble damages, this question is important. If universities are the fiduciaries and a spinoff infringes a patent, universities can lose far more money from a problematic spinoff than they ever earned from it.

An even more subtle risk is the risk to university reputations if the founders of university spinoffs act in inappropriate ways. Because universities are perceived as institutions designed to benefit all of society, they are expected to maintain strong ethics and avoid all manner of impropriety. As a result, any improprieties that the founders of university spinoff companies engage in can reverberate quite loudly. For instance, Matkin (1990) explains that McGill University invested in a faculty spinoff called DeVoe-Holbein, in which the researchers who founded the company violated conflict of interest policies, tarnishing McGill University's reputation in the Montreal community and requiring the university to invest significant amounts of time and resource into rebuilding its reputation.

The problem of risking the university's reputation may be greatest in the life sciences, where university faculty conduct scientific investigations of drugs and medical devices. Life science faculty are in a position to damage university reputations because the structure of biotechnology firms often involves faculty members sitting on scientific advisory boards and holding equity in spinoff companies for which they conduct research. Moreover, both the government and society at large hold medical research to a particularly high ethical standard. As a result, problematic behavior on the part of life scientists can be a major risk to university reputations. As Blumenthal (1992: 3348) explains,

> When investigators have financial relationships (usually through consulting or equity holding) with companies that may benefit from their clinical research, the resulting conflicts of interest, real or apparent, are particularly troublesome for academic institutions. The problem lies in the potential damage to the credibility and public reputation of the life sciences that could flow from real or apparent misconduct associated with academia–industry relationships (AIRs) involving research on humans.

A final type of risk that universities incur in promoting spinoff activity is the real or perceived risk of 'pipelining'. This is a term used to explain collusion by university administrators and faculty members to use university resources and federal government funds to enrich themselves by funneling technology to particular licensees, rather than engaging in an arm's length activity of technology transfer.

My investigation of the MIT spinoffs indicates the importance of the pipelining issue. For example, the founding of one semiconductor spinoff demonstrates the concern that university administrators have for the problem of pipelining. At the time that this company was founded, the responsible licensing officer wrote a letter to venture capitalists who were funding an MIT spinoff, explaining that the MIT Technology-Licensing Office was willing to allow the venture capitalists to set up a project to fund research in the laboratory of the inventor whose invention led to the spinoff only if it was clear from the outset that the venture capital firm was willing to set up a new company to exploit any additional technology that came out of the research. Otherwise, the university would be concerned that any licensing arrangement would be perceived as pipelining. As the licensing officer wrote in her memo,

> MIT has been deeply concerned with any appearance of channeling new technology to [the first spinoff]. . . . MIT is also concerned about the appearance to the outside world – the *New York Times* front-page article test – that it is pipelining valuable research technology to companies in which it owns an interest. Thus, any involvement of the new company with ASC would need to come as the result of an indisputable 'level playing field' proposal.

SUMMARY

This chapter has discussed the problems created by university spinoff activity. The drawbacks of university spinoffs can be divided into two categories: problems of achieving university goals and objectives, and problems of managing technology transfer.

One of the problems for university goals and objectives that spinoffs create is the fact that most university faculty do not support spinoff activity, making spinoffs at odds with the goals of the faculty that govern most universities. Moreover, university spinoffs exacerbate the conflict that exists between academic units, particularly that between applied and commercially oriented fields, like engineering and business, and less commercially oriented fields like the arts and humanities.

Critics also charge that university spinoffs adversely affect university goals because they reorient university activity toward commercial goals and away from scholarly goals. According to critics, spinoffs make universities less willing to engage in the open dissemination of knowledge, lead faculty to focus on more applied topics at the expense of basic science, avoid research areas with limited commercial potential, lead researchers to conduct research for which commercial gains can be more easily appropriated and divert the university's attention away from its primary mission of educating students.

Another problem that spinoffs create for university goals and mission is that of conflict of interest. Critics charge that the potential for commercial gain from spinoff activity leads faculty entrepreneurs to neglect their academic duties to further their personal gains from entrepreneurial activity. In addition, the potential for financial abuse exists when faculty members hold equity in companies for which they are conducting research.

To avoid conflict of interest problems, many universities preclude the founders of spinoff companies from working on the same projects at the university that their companies undertake. However, this solution creates suboptimal efforts to create companies, a cost that many university administrators believe is necessary to retain the university's independence.

A final aspect of conflict of interest is that spinoff companies often appear to be mechanisms for professors to achieve personal financial gain from taxpayer-funded research. Because the federal government funds most university research, but universities can license the inventions that were developed from that research without compensating the government for its investment, many observers see spinoffs as creating a conflict of interest between faculty's role as generators of new knowledge for the good of society and the faculty members' desire to make money, hindering the positive perception of universities in society.

Even in the absence of the problems that university spinoffs create for university norms and values, creating spinoff companies generates two problems for the management of technology transfer in universities interested in using spinoffs to reap financial returns: the cost and difficulty of developing spinoff companies and the risks that spinoffs impose.

Research has shown that creating spinoffs is more costly and time consuming than licensing to established firms because the creation of spinoffs generates a variety of additional costs for technology-licensing offices. Moreover, establishing successful spinoffs is more difficult than establishing successful licenses to established companies because it demands licensing officer expertise and specialization in many of the value-added activities of venture capitalists.

Creating university spinoffs is also a risky activity. Creating companies adds organizing risk and financing risk to the already high technical and market risk of commercializing university technologies. Moreover, to profit successfully from holding equity in spinoff companies, universities must time their exits correctly. Creating spinoffs also imposes risk to university reputations if the founders of university spinoffs act in inappropriate ways and there is also the real or perceived risk of 'pipelining'.

Having described the drawbacks of university spinoffs, I now turn to some concluding comments in the final chapter.

NOTES

1. The evidence of efforts by universities to delay publication of research to enhance the development of spinoff companies is anecdotal and spotty at best. Moreover, the length of the delays reported by previous observers are not very long (a few weeks or a few months) and would likely have a substantive effect on scientific advance in a very small number of cases.
2. Many university administrators agree. At the University of California at Berkeley, the university's investment of $1 million in a failed 1969 faculty software start-up called Berkeley Computer Corporation led to a policy of not making investments in start-ups except through venture capital funds until the mid-1990s (Kenney and Goe, forthcoming).

14. Conclusions

As explained in Chapter 1, university spinoffs are an important, but little investigated, topic. Several important technology companies, including Cirrus Logic, Lycos, Google and Genentech, were founded to exploit technological inventions made by faculty, staff or students of American universities. Moreover, on average, university spinoffs are very high-performing companies. From 1980 to 1986, 18 percent of the spinoffs from MIT's Technology-Licensing Office experienced an initial public offering, a rate 257 times higher than the IPO rate of the average start-up firm.

The economic importance of university spinoffs has generated significant interest in these companies among university administrators and public policy makers. As a result of this interest, many, if not all, universities have created technology transfer operations designed to exploit university-assigned intellectual property. Most universities also have incubators, venture capital funds and business plan competitions to help inventors and other entrepreneurs start new companies to commercialize university inventions and, it is hoped, revolutionize industries, generate wealth for the founders and the university, and spur local economic development.

Topping all of this off is the community of practitioners who help people to found university spinoffs. Not only has the number of universities with technology licensing offices grown rapidly over the past 20 years, but also the volume of spinoff activity and employment at these offices has also grown significantly. Moreover, the Association of University Technology Managers (Pressman, 2002) reports that the proportion of university technology that is exploited through the creation of university spinoffs has grown in every year that data have been collected.

Given the level of interest in university spinoff activity, one would expect university spinoffs to be the subject of significant academic inquiry. However, scholarly investigation of this topic is virtually non-existent. Only a handful of books and scholarly articles that even touch on the topic of university spinoffs have ever been written. Moreover, the subject matter of these books and articles is often not comprehensive, making our knowledge of university spinoffs fragmentary, without a general explanation to link the pieces of the puzzle together.

As a result, a systematic understanding of university spinoffs is quite limited. To date, we have limited evidence of the economic importance of spinoffs, the historical evolution of spinoff activity, the factors that explain their formation, the process of spinoff creation and development, the factors that explain the performance of university spinoffs or the effect of spinoffs on the universities that create them. Simply put, we have very little information about most aspects of spinoff activity and no systematic effort to assemble in one place the fragmentary pieces of knowledge that we do have.

This book's purpose was to describe university spinoffs, explain their formation and account for their role in the commercialization of university technology and wealth creation in the United States and elsewhere. Specifically, this book had four goals. First, it sought to explain why university spinoff activity is important both historically and at present. Second, the book sought to explain how four major factors – the university and societal environment, the technology developed at universities, the industries in which spinoffs operate and the people involved in the spinoff process – jointly influence the formation of university spinoffs. Third, the book sought to describe the process of spinoff company creation, focusing on the development of the technology into new products and services, the identification and exploitation of markets for these new products and services, and the acquisition of resources for these organizations. Fourth, the book sought to identify the factors that enhance the performance of university spinoffs, as well as account for the effect of university spinoffs on the institutions that spawn them.

The book also outlined the relationships between the different parts of the university spinoff story so that readers could see the phenomenon as a related whole, rather than as unrelated pieces of information. As a result, the book sought to present university spinoffs in such a way that an educated reader could understand the totality of the topic. Moreover, the book provided both the conceptual arguments for particular empirical patterns and the empirical evidence collected to date about those aspects of university spinoffs. As a result, this book has shown both where we have arguments for, and evidence of, particular propositions about university spinoffs, and where future research is needed to provide answers to important questions.

Because my goal was to explain university spinoffs rather than to test particular theories, I took an interdisciplinary approach in this book. I drew upon the work of economists, psychologists, sociologists, entrepreneurship scholars, students of strategic management, management of technology researchers and public policy scholars with equal abandon. I used whatever tools and frameworks brought me closer to the goal of understanding university spinoffs. Although I tried to adhere to the same assumptions throughout the book, my willingness to cross perspectives may require readers to have an understanding of topics or issues that are unusual for readers from a particular disciplinary perspective.

However, I believe that this approach has led to a clearer understanding of the actual phenomenon of university spinoffs. Take, for example, the decision of an inventor to found a spinoff. That decision might very well be explained by a rational economic motive to generate the greatest financial returns from an invention, as well as a psychological desire to be independent. This book has provided a framework for scholars truly interested in university spinoffs to develop explanations (and empirical tests of those explanations) that include all of the relevant factors that influence the phenomenon, whether a particular discipline focuses on those factors or not.

A REVIEW OF THE CHAPTERS

Each of the chapters of this book provided the explanation behind, and empirical evidence in support of, different dimensions of university spinoffs. Chapter 1 provided an introduction to university spinoffs, explaining the importance of the topic, defining university spinoffs, and explaining the goals and structure of the book.

Chapter 2 identified several important examples of university spinoffs, including Google in Internet search engines, Cirrus Logic in semiconductors and Genentech in biotechnology, by way of demonstrating that university spinoffs, though small in number, tend to be economically important high technology firms. The chapter also offered several different explanations for university spinoffs being valuable companies: they enhance economic development, are high performing companies, enhance the commercialization of university technologies that would otherwise go undeveloped and help universities with their primary missions of research and teaching.

Chapter 3 explained that universities have been involved in the commercialization of technology and the formation of spinoff companies from the earliest days of the modern university through to the present day. In the United States, universities began to experiment for the first time with spinning off companies as a way to use university inventions to develop local economies in the early 20th century. World War II transformed the American research university by increasing both the total amount of university research funding and the federal government's share of that research, leading to the creation of a generation of spinoff companies to commercialize the outputs of research from universities that received a large amount of federal funding during World War II and the Cold War. The 1970s were a period of profound change in university technology commercialization, as university patenting began to increase, universities began to develop policies to support spinoffs and the biotechnology industry was born. In 1980, the US Congress passed the Bayh–Dole Act, which gave universities the property rights to federally funded inventions, marking a watershed in the development of university spin-offs and dramatically increasing university invention disclosures, patent production, patent productivity, licensing office creation, licensing activity and spinoff company foundings.

Researchers have offered several explanations for the dramatic growth in spinoff activity over the past two decades: the growth of biomedical research at universities, the passage of the Bayh–Dole Act, changes in patent laws, a contagion effect, shortened product life cycles in key areas of science, changes in the financing system, and growth in the use of equity as an investment tool.

Chapter 4 examined the variation in spinoff activity across academic institutions. Research has shown that allowing exclusive licensing, permitting the university to take equity in spinoffs, offering leaves of absence for inventors who wish to found companies, permitting spinoffs to use university resources to develop technology, allocating a lower share of royalties to inventors, and providing spinoffs with access to pre-seed stage capital are all policies that enhance the rate of spinoff formation at universities. Moreover, the characteristics of the university's technology-licensing office also influence its rate of spinoff creation, with universities that provide their licensing offices with more resources, whose licensing officers have more expertise in firm formation and which embed their licensing officers in a network of start-up company stakeholders generating more spinoffs. Furthermore, several other university characteristics also influence the rate of spinoff activity, including cultures that reinforce entrepreneurial activities, the possession of more entrepreneurial role models, greater prestige, and more industry funding.

Chapter 5 examined the effects of environmental forces on the rate of spinoff company formation across geographic locations. Spinoff activity varies significantly across countries, with Canadian educational institutions being much more likely than US educational institutions to generate spinoff companies and UK universities producing more spinoffs per dollar of research funding than American and Canadian universities. Research has shown that four factors influence the level of spinoff activity in a particular geographic location: access to capital, the locus of property rights, rigidity of the academic labor market and the industrial composition of the geographic area.

Chapter 6 examined the types of technologies that lead to the formation of university spinoffs. Because established firms have a variety of advantages in commercializing technology, only a small proportion of university inventions are appropriate for creating spinoffs. Research shows that radical, tacit, early stage and general-purpose technologies, which provide significant value to customers, represent major technical advances and have strong intellectual property protection are more likely to provide the basis for spinoffs than other technologies.

Chapter 7 discussed the variation across industries in the creation of university spinoffs. A variety of studies have shown that university spinoffs are most common in biomedical industries because of the collapsed discovery process in biotechnology, the longer commercialization time horizon in the life sciences, the locus of expertise in the life sciences in universities, the preference of customers for products that are most efficacious regardless of cost, and the discreteness of biomedical inventions.

In addition to trying to explain why biomedical inventions are more likely than physical science inventions to lead to spinoffs, researchers have explored specific industry characteristics that encourage the formation of university spinoffs. Spinoffs are more common in industries in which patents are more effective, in industries that require a smaller amount of complementary assets in manufacturing, marketing and distribution, in industries with a younger technology base, in markets that are more segmented and in industries with smaller average firm size.

Some research has also explored the conditions under which spinoffs are better than established firms at commercializing university inventions. Spinoffs are better at commercializing university inventions in industries with more firms, in industries in which less of the value-added comes from manufacturing, and in smaller markets. Non-inventor-founded spinoffs are better at commercializing university inventions in industries in which patents are relatively effective.

Chapter 8 explored the role of people in the university spinoff process. The chapter explained that spinoffs occur more often when inventors are interested in the formation of new companies as a way to develop their inventions than when they are not interested in spinoff companies. While university inventors exert an important influence on the formation of university spinoffs, inventor–entrepreneurs do not always lead the efforts to found these companies. External entrepreneurs interested in founding companies that license university inventions through technology-licensing offices, and investors who bring together technology and entrepreneurs, also lead efforts to found university spinoffs.

Although very little research has explored the difference between inventor-led spinoffs, external entrepreneur-led spinoffs and investor-led spinoffs, researchers have shown that inventor-led spinoffs are more common when intellectual property protection is not very effective, that inventor-led spinoffs are more likely to be established near the universities that generate them, that investor- and external entrepreneur-led spinoffs are more common in major cities and technology centers, that inventor-led spinoffs are more likely than other types of spinoffs to be founded before patents issue and that inventor-led spinoffs are more likely than other types of spinoffs to be founded by part-time entrepreneurs.

Some evidence suggests that university inventors found spinoffs because they are people who have always wanted to start companies and who use their university inventions as a way to achieve their entrepreneurial goals. Anecdotal evidence suggests the effect of three psychological attributes on the formation of inventor-led spinoffs: a desire to bring technology into practice, a desire for wealth and a desire for independence.

Other research suggests career-oriented explanations for spinoff company formation. Academics are more likely to found companies later in their careers after they have invested in the development of their human capital, if they have achieved a higher university rank, if they are the leading researchers in their fields and if they have more entrepreneurial experience.

Chapter 9 discussed the creation of university spinoffs from the initial scholarly research that results in university inventions to the discovery of entrepreneurial opportunities and the founding of spinoff companies. The process begins when university researchers use funding from companies, foundations and government agencies to obtain human and physical resources for the research effort. When university inventors believe that they have come up with technological inventions, they are generally expected to disclose those discoveries to their universities. University technology-licensing offices evaluate these invention disclosures to determine whether patents or copyrights can protect the inventions and whether the expected return from licensing the inventions exceeds the cost of protecting them. In some institutions, the licensing officers also determine whether the inventors made 'material use' of university resources in creating the invention. If these conditions are met, university technology-licensing offices seek to protect the inventions.

University technology transfer offices then market the technologies to entities interested in licensing and commercializing them. Because this process of marketing university technology is difficult, only about half of all patented university inventions are licensed, and most licensed inventions have only one interested licensee.

While established companies license most university intellectual property, approximately 14 percent of all university inventions lead to spinoff company formation. When universities license technology to spinoff companies, the founders of those companies often option the technology first as a way to mitigate technological and market uncertainty. In addition, many spinoff companies take exclusive licenses to university inventions as a way to mitigate competitive uncertainty. Given the uncertainty and early stage of most university inventions at the time that spinoffs are founded, the entrepreneurs that found these companies typically have prior knowledge of markets that allow them to see entrepreneurial opportunities inherent in the technologies.

Chapter 10 discussed the process by which university spinoffs develop their technologies, and identify and satisfy customer demand. The first part of this process usually involves further technical development, leading to proof of principle, prototype development and the creation of a product or service.

The second part of this process involves market development. This process involves interacting with customers to obtain feedback on products and services, choosing a market application in which to employ the technology and selling the products or services to interested customers.

Chapter 11 explained how the founders of university spinoffs acquire the large amounts of capital that they need to develop their new ventures. Except in biotechnology, the initial capital obtained by university spinoffs generally does not come from private investors, but from public sources. The use of public sources of financing permits the transformation of university inventions into new products and services, allows founders of spinoffs to find a commercial use for their technologies, serves as a catalyst or subsidy for private investment and provides a way to have government agencies bear high-risk technology development.

Even at later stages of venture development, obtaining capital from private sector sources is not easy. Consequently, the acquisition of capital involves two important processes: efforts by the founders of university spinoffs to demonstrate the value of their ventures to potential investors, and the exploitation of social ties between entrepreneurs and investors.

University spinoffs raise capital from different sources, depending on the goals of the founders and the attributes of the spinoff companies. In fact, the diversity of funding sources for university spinoffs is quite large. Moreover, many university spinoffs receive angel financing rather than, or in addition to, venture capital financing because of the advantages that such financing provides.

Chapter 12 explored the factors that enhance the performance of university spinoffs. First, founder human capital enhances the performance of university spinoffs. Spinoffs founded by complementary venture teams perform better than spinoffs not founded by complementary teams, and spinoffs founded by full-time entrepreneurs perform better than spinoffs founded by part-time entrepreneurs. Second, the performance of university spinoffs is enhanced if they develop products or services that meet customer needs, even if they do not have the best technology. Third, adequate capital enhances the performance of university spinoffs. Fourth, having adequate university support increases the success rate of university spinoffs. Fifth, the spinoff's technology influences its performance. In particular, performance is enhanced by a strong intellectual property position and the possession of a general-purpose technology. Sixth, the strategy adopted by the founders of university spinoffs also affects firm performance. When founders adopt a focus strategy and when they are more adaptive, the performance of university spinoffs is enhanced.

Chapter 13 discussed the problems created by university spinoff activity.

Critics argue that university spinoffs create a number of problems for the achievement of university goals and objectives, including challenging the faculty governance model, exacerbating the conflict between more and less commercially oriented fields, reorienting university activity away from scholarly goals and generating conflicts of interest. Even in the absence of the problems that university spinoffs create for university norms and values, creating spinoff companies generates two problems for the management of technology transfer in universities interested in using spinoffs to reap financial returns: first, creating spinoffs is more costly and time-consuming than licensing to established firms; second, creating companies imposes a variety of risks on universities, including organizing risk, financing risk, risk from legal exposure, risk to university reputations and the real or perceived risk of 'pipelining'.

ISSUES FOR THE FUTURE

Because this book is an invitation to other scholars to investigate university spinoffs and further advance our knowledge of this important topic, I would like to accomplish more than just provide a summary of the previous chapters in this conclusion. Instead, I would like to make an argument for further scholarly investigation of several important aspects of university spinoffs. As astute readers no doubt noticed, some parts of the discussion of university spinoffs in the chapters that preceded were based on a greater base of empirical evidence than others. In this section, I would like to highlight areas that are most in need of additional scholarly inquiry.

Chapter 2 explained why university spinoffs are important economic entities. While this chapter provides a great deal of valuable evidence about why spinoffs matter, much more research could be done. To date, we have relatively little information about the population of university spinoffs. Because patents are more readily documented than other types of university intellectual property, most studies of university spinoffs examine new companies created to exploit patented university inventions. However, spinoffs could be formed to exploit non-patented university inventions, and about this we know almost nothing. Therefore one important unanswered empirical question is this: how often are spinoffs formed to exploit university intellectual property other than patents? Are spinoffs founded to exploit software copyrights or trade secrets different from those founded to exploit patents? If so, how are they different?

We also know very little about the population of university spinoffs. Only in the United States do we even have a count of university spinoffs, and even there we have had this information for only the past 15 years. Moreover, even in the United States, we have little more than a count of these companies. We lack information about the names of spinoff companies or information about what happened to them. For instance, we do not know how many spinoff companies have experienced an initial public offering, were acquired or have declared bankruptcy. Further research is clearly needed to provide more demographic information about university spinoffs so that we can develop explanations of the factors that influence their formation and performance.

Chapter 2 also provides some information about how university spinoffs differ from other technology start-up firms. However, much of this information is based on small ad hoc samples studied by a few researchers in the United Kingdom. While it seems that university spinoffs are different from other high technology firms, we need additional studies that carefully compare matched samples of university spinoffs and other high technology start-ups so that we can identify the dimensions on which these firms are similar to and different from each other.

The chapter indicates that university spinoffs have a positive economic impact. While this is true, the evidence is so thin that it begs for more precise studies. For instance, what are the economic returns to the creation of university spinoffs relative to the economic returns to licensing inventions to established firms? Because we do not know how much economic value spinoffs create relative to their cost of creation, nor do we have the same information for technology licensing to established companies, we have no way of knowing if creating spinoffs is a better strategy for universities or for society at large than licensing to established companies. Moreover, Chapter 2 suggested that spinoffs are beneficial because they resolve a market failure, commercializing technology that would not otherwise be licensed. However, all of the evidence presented in the chapter on this question is qualitative. We lack large sample statistical evidence which indicates that entrepreneurs actually found companies to exploit technology that otherwise would have gone unlicensed.

We also know very little about the distribution of the economic benefit from university spinoffs. For example, we do not know how much economic benefit from university spinoffs accrues in different geographic locations. Are the benefits of spinoffs equal in all locations or are there location-related factors that interact with the presence of spinoffs? How geographically localized is the effect of university spinoffs? Does the economic benefit occur within a one-mile, ten-mile, hundred-mile or thousand-mile radius of the spinoff's location? Furthermore, we know very little about the form that the benefits from university spinoffs take. For instance, we do not know how much of the benefit of university spinoffs takes the form of job creation, or the types of jobs that spinoffs tend to create.

Chapter 2 also provided some evidence that university spinoffs perform better than the typical start-up company. However, this evidence is incomplete at best. First, we lack information on how well the average spinoff performs.

For instance, we do not know what the likelihood of spinoff failure is as a function of age. Nor do we know the average level of sales, employment and profits that spinoffs generate. Second, we do not know how spinoffs compare to other types of start-ups most similar to them. For instance, are university spinoffs more or less likely to receive venture capital financing, experience an initial public offering or be acquired than other high technology companies founded in the same industries at the same time as spinoffs?

Chapter 3 summarizes some of the history of university spinoffs. While it provides examples of some of the spinoff companies founded prior to 1980, we lack a detailed history of spinoffs that systematically documents the university spinoffs that were founded prior to the passage of the Bayh–Dole Act in 1980. In fact, much of our understanding of pre-1980 spinoff activity in the United States comes from studies of MIT, which is hardly representative of the typical American university. We clearly need more research that documents the history of university spinoff companies.

Chapter 3 also provides several explanations for the dramatic growth in spinoff activity over the past two decades: the birth and growth of biotechnology, the passage of the Bayh–Dole Act, changes in patent laws, the reduction of product cycles in several science-based industries, contagion effects, the adoption of equity investment policies at a variety of institutions and changes in the system of financing spinoff companies. However, no large sample statistical studies have sought to determine which, if any, of these explanations is dominant. Future research would do well to determine which, if any, of these explanations is the true driver of the growth of spinoff activity. Such an investigation is essential for the development of a parsimonious explanation for the growth of university spinoffs in the United States over time. Moreover, other research is needed to determine the factors that influence the growth of university spinoffs in other countries. While it seems unlikely that exactly the same factors explain the growth of spinoffs in other countries as explain the growth of spinoffs in the United States, no research has sought to explain the patterns of growth in spinoff activity outside the United States.

Chapter 4 examined the variation in spinoff activity across academic institutions. While this chapter provided evidence that differences in university policies, licensing office strategies and other university characteristics account for this variation, several important questions remain. First, large sample statistical evidence has shown that permitting equity holdings and giving inventors a smaller share of royalties increase the rate of spinoff activity out of universities. However, only qualitative evidence supports the propositions that allowing exclusive licensing, offering leaves of absence for inventors who wish to found companies, permitting spinoffs to use university resources to develop technology and providing access to pre-seed stage capital increase spinoff rates across universities. Further research is clearly needed to evaluate the importance of these other factors. When compared with each other in a multivariate design, these additional factors may have no statistical effect on the spinoff rate.

Second, many of the factors that prior research has shown to influence the rate of spinoff out of universities are clearly endogenous. For example, prior research has shown that universities that have licensing offices with more expertise in firm formation, that embed their licensing officers in a network of start-up company stakeholders, have more entrepreneurial role models and a culture that supports spinoff companies have more spinoffs than other universities. But these relationships do not mean that these factors are causally related to spinoff company formation. Universities that have more spinoff companies may also have these other attributes because they had more spinoff companies historically. More research is clearly needed to identify the causal factors that drive the rate of spinoff activity. In the absence of such research, policy makers will be unable to identify the levers necessary to increase or decrease the rate of spinoff company formation out of universities.

Third, we do not yet know the relative magnitudes of the effects of the factors that increase the rate of spinoff company creation or the relative cost of generating effects of those magnitudes. In the absence of such information, it is difficult for researchers to offer policy makers normative recommendations on how to increase the rate of spinoff company formation. For instance, does a policy of allowing equity holdings in university spinoffs increase the rate of spinoff activity more than establishing an institutional culture that is supportive of university spinoffs? Even if we knew that the magnitude of the effects of these changes were the same (which we do not yet know), we do not know the cost of adopting a policy of allowing equity holdings in university spinoffs relative to the cost of establishing an institutional culture that is supportive of university spinoffs. In the absence of this information on costs and benefits, it will be difficult for policy makers to ascertain which policies are the best for generating spinoff companies.

Chapter 5 examined the effects of environmental forces on the rate of spinoff company formation across geographic locations and found that four factors influence the level of spinoff activity in a particular location: access to capital, locus of property rights, rigidity of the academic labor market and the industrial composition of the area. However, the empirical evidence that supports the arguments in this chapter is quite thin in two respects. First, data on the cost of creating university spinoffs are available only from three countries, the United States, the United Kingdom and Canada. As a result, there are not enough data to conduct large sample studies of the factors that account for variance in the cost of creating spinoff companies across geographic locations. Therefore we cannot yet determine which, if any, of these four factors has the greatest effect on spinoff company formation. Second, much of the evidence of the effect of environmental forces on the creation of spinoffs comes from qualitative comparisons of two-country dyads. Because many unobserved differences exist between any pair of countries, it is entirely possible that the factors identified in the literature to date are merely proxying for the key explanatory variables that have not yet been identified. Clearly, more research is needed to provide robust evidence of the effect of environmental factors on the formation of university spinoffs.

Chapter 6 examined the types of technologies that lead to the formation of university spinoffs and showed that radical, tacit, early stage and general-purpose technologies, which provide significant value to customers, represent major technical advances and have strong intellectual property protection, are more likely to provide the basis for spinoffs than other technologies. While the findings presented in this chapter are valuable, they are limited in several ways that suggest a need for further research. First, while large sample statistical evidence indicates the effects of certain aspects of technology on the likelihood of firm formation (for example, radical technologies that are major technical advances), the only evidence for the effects of other dimensions of technology (for example, tacit and general-purpose technologies) is qualitative and univariate. Therefore, more large sample statistical evidence is needed before researchers and policy makers can conclude that certain types of technology clearly lead to firm formation.

Second, the evidence of the effects of different aspects of technology on the formation of university spinoffs presented in Chapter 6 is based on the assumption that the different dimensions of technology are uncorrelated. However, many of the aspects of university technology are likely correlated (for example, early stage technology is likely to be more tacit than late stage technology). As a result, a smaller number of dimensions of university technology might drive firm formation than is discussed in Chapter 6. More research is needed to determine what might be a smaller cluster of dimensions that make a technology appropriate for the formation of a spinoff.

Chapter 7 discussed the variation across industries in the creation of university spinoffs. The chapter explains that university spinoffs are more common in biomedical industries than in other industries, and provides six possible explanations for this result. While informative about the possible factors that lead to the greater frequency of spinoffs in biomedical industries, the evidence and arguments presented in Chapter 7 beg the following question: are all of these factors equally important in explaining the greater frequency of university spinoffs in biomedical industries? To date we do not know the answer to this question because no research has compared these different explanatory factors.

In addition, the results presented in Chapter 7 show that certain industry characteristics make spinoffs more likely to be founded and more likely to bring university inventions to market. However, astute readers will recognize that the basis for this evidence is quite thin. All of the results about the effects of industry differences on rates of firm formation reported in the chapter are based on data from one university for one time period – the Massachusetts Institute of Technology from 1980 to 1996. Therefore additional research is necessary to determine whether these results are generalizable.

Chapter 8 explored the role of people in the university spinoff process. While interesting, the results presented in this chapter are also shocking in that they show how little we really know about this topic. First, prior research has documented that three sets of entrepreneurs tend to lead efforts to found university spinoffs (inventors, external entrepreneurs shopping at universities, and investors) but insufficient large sample statistical evidence has been amassed to compare these three types of entrepreneurs. Not only do we lack knowledge of how these three groups of entrepreneurs differ, we have little information about the relative frequencies with which the three groups lead efforts to found firms and what factors influence the formation of firms by one group rather than by another.

Second, very little research has examined the factors that lead individuals to found university spinoffs. In comparison to the mainstream entrepreneurship literature, which has examined a wide variety of psychological and demographic factors that lead entrepreneurs to found companies, the literature on university spinoffs has only examined a handful of characteristics, and even the evidence for these characteristics has been largely anecdotal. Clearly, large sample statistical surveys that use well validated psychological measures to compare the founders of university spinoffs with appropriate control groups are needed to provide individual-level data on the decision to create spinoff companies that would be robust enough for researchers to draw firm conclusions.

Third, the models used to explain the decisions of individuals to found spinoff companies are incomplete. To date, the empirical research on the role of people in the creation of university spinoffs has examined the affect of career stage and three psychological factors: the desire for independence, the desire for wealth and the desire to build something. Even a cursory investigation of the firm formation decision indicates a variety of individual-level factors missing from such a model, including the knowledge, skills and abilities of the potential founders, the circumstances under which they are making the decision of whether or not to found a firm, and their alternative activities and the opportunity cost associated with them. Future research needs to develop and test more comprehensive models of the individual-level decisions to found university spinoffs.

Chapter 9 describes how university spinoffs are founded. Although this chapter provides useful description not available elsewhere, it also demonstrates the importance of additional research. First, the description of the spinoff company formation process presented in this book is based on qualitative evidence collected from MIT. Because the process of company formation likely differs across more and less prestigious institutions, institutions that generate smaller and larger numbers of spinoffs, and state and private institutions, researchers need to gather additional data before we can have strong confidence that the process of spinoff company formation described in Chapter 9 accurately describes the process at all institutions.

Second, more research is clearly needed to explain the process by which technology-licensing officers evaluate invention disclosures and market technologies. To date we have very thin descriptions of these processes. We lack models to explain which invention disclosures result in patents and which patents are licensed. Moreover, to be able to explain which university disclosures are likely to lead to patents and which patents will become licensed, we need to develop a richer understanding of the evaluation and marketing processes. Specifically, we need to document the standard operating procedures used by technology licensing offices in these processes.

Third, Chapter 9 explains that prior knowledge is important to the identification of entrepreneurial opportunities in new technology. However, recent research in the entrepreneurship literature (see Shane, 2003) indicates that the identification of opportunities depends on factors that affect the flow of information (search processes, social networks and so on) as well as cognitive factors, such as prior knowledge. Future research is necessary to consider the flow of information in the process of discovering entrepreneurial opportunities in university technology, as well as the recognition process described in the chapter. Moreover, prior knowledge is only one factor that influences the recognition of opportunity. Future research would do well to explore other factors, such as intelligence and cognitive factors that prior entrepreneurship research has shown to be important in the opportunity identification process. Furthermore, future research based on larger sample studies is needed to confirm the finding that prior knowledge influences the discovery of entrepreneurial opportunity in new technology, as the main evidence provided in Chapter 9 is based on a single case study of an MIT technology.

While Chapter 10 provides valuable evidence on a topic that suffers from a paucity of empirical data, the processes by which spinoffs undertake technology and market development, it also suffers from several important limitations. First, virtually all of the evidence is drawn from a sample of spinoff companies from MIT, making the sample largely unrepresentative of the typical university spinoff. Additional research is needed to differentiate the factors that might be MIT-specific from those that are more general influences. Second, the data presented in this chapter are largely qualitative. Clearly, quantitative studies that examine the effects of different factors, while controlling for others, on samples that better represent the total population of university spinoffs would help to determine more precisely the effect of different factors on the development of the spinoff's technology and market.

Chapter 11 provides useful information about capital acquisition in university spinoffs, but much more could be known about this topic. For instance, do investors use other mechanisms than those described in Chapter 11 to overcome the problems engendered by information asymmetry and uncertainty when financing university spinoffs?

We also need to know about the different types of investors who are targets of the founders of spinoffs. To date, we have only anecdotal evidence about the choice between venture capitalists and business angels in funding university spinoffs. Clearly, we need more large sample evidence of the choice that spinoff company founders make between these investors. For instance, why do both types of resource providers fund university spinoffs? Are the different sources of financing for university spinoffs complements or substitutes? Do the two types of investors make decisions and manage their investments in spinoffs in the same way?

Furthermore, we lack even anecdotal evidence to explain why the founders of spinoffs sometimes raise external capital for their new ventures and sometimes bootstrap them. Future research would do well to provide empirical evidence in support of arguments to explain the choice between raising external capital and bootstrapping new ventures.

Chapter 11 also provides evidence of the important role of government funding in the development of university spinoffs. While this qualitative evidence is quite suggestive, it begs research to answer several questions. First, would the private sector fail to finance early stage university spinoffs in the absence of government funding? Or does the private sector allow the public sector to invest first to minimize the risk involved in financing university spinoffs? Second, why do private sector investors finance the development of early stage spinoffs in biotechnology much more readily than early stage spinoffs in other technologies? Third, why does public funding help spinoffs to develop? Chapter 11 suggests three alternative mechanisms for the way public funding benefits spinoffs but does not determine which one is dominant. Future research would do well to determine whether public funding (a) allows for the development of the spinoff's technology to a point where the private sector becomes interested, (b) subsidizes private sector investors, improving the risk–return tradeoff for investing in a spinoff, or (c) serves as a catalyst that encourages private firms to become involved in financing a technology.

Chapter 12 explained that the human capital of the founders, the financial resources of the new ventures, the efforts of the founders of the new ventures to meet customer needs, the venture's technology, its strategy and the support provided by the university from which the spinoff emerges influence performance of university spinoffs. This chapter suggests several important avenues for future research. First, it shows that founder industry experience and inventor involvement both enhance the performance of university spinoffs, but the evidence presented does not say what conditions might make one of these characteristics more important than the other. For instance, when technologies are radical and destroy existing competence in an industry, is industry experience less important for spinoff company performance than when the new technologies are incremental?

Moreover, inventors lead the efforts to found some university spinoffs and external entrepreneurs lead other efforts. This observation begs the question: is the effect of human capital different for inventor-led and external entrepreneur-led spinoffs? Does the effect of human capital vary, depending on the role that the inventor plays in the spinoff (for instance, chief executive officer rather than chief technology officer)?

The issue of entry and exit from spinoff teams as they develop is also an open and important one. Future research would do well to examine this question. For instance, do university spinoffs perform better if they begin with founding teams made up largely of inventors and then replace them with people with more industry experience as the technology develops and market and competitive risk become relatively more important to the new venture than technical risk?

Second, Chapter 12 explained that university spinoffs perform better if they raise more capital. However, is the acquisition of capital endogenous? The research summarized in the chapter cannot tell us whether university spinoffs that raise more capital perform better because the additional capital enhances performance or because better university spinoffs both raise more external capital and perform better. Future research is needed to determine whether the provision of additional capital to university spinoffs would enhance performance.

Third, research to date has only explored the effect of two aspects of spinoff company strategy on performance – focus and adaptability. However, many aspects of firm strategy other than focus and adaptive flexibility might influence the performance of university spinoffs. More research is needed to identify the aspects of strategy that influence the performance of university spinoffs. For instance, is the creation and patenting of technology additional to that licensed from the university important to spinoff performance? Alternatively, is the design of the organization that exploits university technology important to spinoff company performance?

Fourth, data collection constraints have limited the evidence on the performance of university spinoffs to correlations between firm policies and discrete outcomes such as the likelihood of initial public offering and firm failure. The effect of the factors discussed in Chapter 12 on the sales or profits of university spinoffs is largely unexplored, and the factors might not be the same as those that influence the likelihood of initial public offerings or bankruptcy. Future research would do well to explore the effect of these factors on measures of spinoff company performance other than just the likelihood of initial public offering and firm failure.

Fifth, we have no evidence of contingent relationships between the factors that affect spinoff company performance and the technology opportunity being exploited or the attributes of firm founders. However, it seems plausible that interactions between different factors influence the performance of university spinoffs. For example, certain strategies, such as focusing on a particular market application, might be more effective with certain types of technology than with others.

Sixth, Chapter 12 explains that having adequate university support is also important to the success of university spinoffs. However, this observation raises many unanswered questions. What is the most important mechanism by which university support enhances spinoff performance: the opportunity to conduct additional work in the university environment where the inventors reside, a flexible approach of the university to the contractual relationship with the spinoffs, the presence of external liaison organizations that help to transform university research and technology into products and services, or all of the above? The evidence that supports the effects of university support on the performance of university spinoffs is largely anecdotal. More large sample, controlled studies are needed to provide robust measures of the magnitude of such effects.

Chapter 13 discussed some of the problems created by university spinoffs both for the societal role of universities and for the process of managing technology transfer. While this chapter provides important examples of problems created by spinoffs, it raises many unanswered questions. First, Chapter 2 explained that university spinoffs provide many benefits to university research and teaching, whereas Chapter 13 explained that university spinoffs impose many costs on research and teaching. A comparison of these two arguments begs the following empirical question: on average, do the benefits of spinoffs for university research and teaching outweigh the costs?

Second, almost all the evidence of the problems created by university spinoffs is anecdotal. Therefore we do not really know if spinoff activity is as problematic as some critics suggest. Large sample statistical evidence of the prevalence of many of the problems described by the critics (conflicts of interest, changing research agendas, abuse of the doctoral student relationship and so on) is needed before we can know whether the issues identified in Chapter 13 are rare examples or common problems.

Third, the chapter argues that the cost and the risk of spinoffs are high. However, these are not absolute concepts, but must be considered relative to the next best alternative use of the university's resources. We do not yet know how much more costly it is for universities to create spinoffs than to license to established companies. Similarly, we do not know how much more risky the creation of spinoffs is than licensing to established firms. In the absence of data on the cost and risk of creating spinoffs relative to licensing to established firms, it is impossible for policy makers to know whether the spinoff companies generate large enough returns to justify investment in them.

A FINAL COMMENT

This book has sought to explain the formation of university spinoff companies and their role in the commercialization of university technology and wealth creation in the United States and elsewhere. Specifically, the book explained why university spinoff activity is important and traced the historical development of university spinoff activity. It described how four major factors – the university and societal environment, the technology developed at universities, the industries in which spinoffs would operate and the people involved in the spinoff process – jointly influence spinoff activity. It documented the process of spinoff company creation, focusing on the formation of spinoff companies, the transformation of the spinoff's technology into new products and services, the identification and exploitation of a market for these new products and services, and the acquisition of financial resources for these organizations. The book described the factors that enhance and inhibit the performance of university spinoffs, as well as the effect that university spinoffs have on the institutions that spawn them. For all of these topics, both logical arguments and empirical evidence were provided in support of those arguments. Given the early stage of our collective understanding of university spinoffs, much of this evidence is limited and therefore I have suggested many areas for future research. I hope that this book stimulates other researchers to join the effort to explain the important phenomenon of university spinoffs.

References

Aldrich, H. (1999), *Organizations Evolving*, London: Sage.

Aldrich, H. and M. Fiol (1994), 'Fools rush in? The institutional context of industry creation', *Academy of Management Review*, **19** (4), 645–70.

Allen, D. and F. Norling (1991), 'Exploring perceived threats in faculty commercialization of research', in A. Brett, D. Gibson and R. Smilor (eds), *University Spin-off Companies*, Savage, MD: Rowman and Littlefield Publishers, pp.85–102.

Amit, R., J. Brander and C. Zott (1998), 'Why do venture capital firms exist? Theory and Canadian evidence', *Journal of Business Venturing*, **13**, 441–66.

Amit, R., L. Glosten and E. Muller (1990), 'Entrepreneurial ability, venture investments, and risk sharing', *Management Science*, **38** (10), 1232–45.

Amit, R., E. Muller and I. Cockburn (1995), 'Opportunity costs and entrepreneurial activity', *Journal of Business Venturing*, **10**(2), 95–106.

Anonymous (2001), 'Supplement to University Research Council Final Report' (dated 4 November).

Arrow, K. (1962), 'Economic welfare and the allocation of resources for inventions', in R. Nelson (ed.), *The Rate and Direction of Inventive Activity*, Princeton, NJ: Princeton University Press, pp.609–25.

Association of University Technology Managers (1996), *AUTM Licensing Survey: FY 1991–1995*, Norwalk, CT: Association of University Technology Managers.

Audretsch, D. (1995), *Innovation and Industry Evolution*, Cambridge, MA: MIT Press.

Audretsch, D. (2000), 'Is university entrepreneurship different?', working paper, University of Indiana.

Audretsch, D. and P. Stephan (1996), 'Company–scientist locational links: The case of biotechnology', *American Economic Review*, **86** (3), 641–52.

Audretsch, D. and P. Stephan (1998), 'How and why does knowledge spill over? The case of biotechnology', working paper, University of Indiana.

Audretsch, D., J. Weigand and C. Weigand (2000), 'Does the small business innovation research program foster entrepreneurial behavior? Evidence from Indiana', in C. Wessner (ed.), *The Small Business Innovation Research Program*, Washington, DC: National Academy Press, pp.160–93.

Bagby, R., J. Stevens and M. Sewell (1995), 'Applied Research Laboratory Technology Transfer and Intellectual Property Project: A Benchmark Study', 15 August.

Bank of England (2002), *Finance for small firms – a ninth report*, Bank of England Domestic Finance Division, London: Bank of England.

Barnes, S. (2002). 'The Renovo story (A): Venture capital at the cutting edge', The Management School Imperial College, case 802-030-1.

Bauer, E. (2001), 'Effects of patenting and licensing on research', presentation to the National Academies Board on Science, Technology, and Economic Policy Committee on Intellectual Property Rights in the Knowledge-Based Economy, 17 April.

Bee, E. (2002), 'Turning community inventions into sustainable technology clusters: Finding the right strategy', *The IEDC Economic Development Journal*, **1** (2), 1–19.

Bhide, A. (2000), *The Origin and Evolution of New Businesses*, New York: Oxford University Press.

Birley, S. (2002), 'Universities, academics, and spinout companies: Lessons from Imperial', *International Journal of Entrepreneurship Education*, **1** (1), 133–53.

Blair, D. and D. Hitchens (1998), *Campus Companies – UK and Ireland*, Aldershot, UK: Ashgate.

Blumenthal, D. (1992), 'Academic–industry relationships in the life sciences', *Journal of the American Medical Association*, **268** (23), 3344–9.

Blumenthal, D., E. Campbell, N. Causino and K. Louis (1996), 'Participation of life science faculty in research relationships with industry', *The New England Journal of Medicine*, **335** (23), 1734–9.

Bok, D. (1981), 'Business and the Academy', *Harvard Magazine*, **83**, 23–5.

Bok, D. (2003), *Universities in the Marketplace: The Commercialization of Higher Education*, Princeton, NJ: Princeton University Press.

Boly, W. (1982), 'Strained relations', *California Magazine*, **7**, 78.

Boston Globe (1998) 'MIT unrivaled in reaping rewards of its inventions', *Boston Globe*, 7 April, A25.

Bray, M. and J. Lee (2000), 'University revenues from technology transfer: Licensing fees vs. equity positions', *Journal of Business Venturing*, **15** (5/6), 385–92.

Bruderl, J., P. Preisendorfer and R. Ziegler (1992), 'Survival chances of newly founded business organizations', *American Sociological Review*, 57, 227–302.

Burt, R. (1992), *Structural Holes: The Social Structure of Competition*, Boston, MA: Harvard University Press.

Busenitz, L. and C. Lau (1996), 'A cross-cultural cognitive model of new venture creation', *Entrepreneurship Theory and Practice*, **20** (4), 25–39.

Calkins, K. and E. Pierce (1998), 'New shoots for old roots', *Biocentury*, 1 June, 1.

Campbell, C. (1992), 'A decision theory model for entrepreneurial acts', *Entrepreneurship Theory and Practice*, **17** (1), 21–7.

Campbell, E., K. Louis and D. Blumenthal (1998), 'Looking a gift horse in the mouth: Corporate gifts supporting life sciences research', *Journal of the American Medical Association*, **279** (13), 995–9.

Carter, R. and H. Van Auken (1990), 'Personal equity investment and small business financial difficulties', *Entrepreneurship Theory and Practice*, **15** (2), 51–60.

Casson, M. (1982), *The Entrepreneur*, Totowa, NJ: Barnes and Noble Books.

Casson, M. (1995), *Entrepreneurship and Business Culture*, Aldershot, UK and Brookfield, US: Edward Elgar.

Charles, D. and C. Conway (2001), *Higher Education–Business Interaction Survey*, Newcastle upon Tyne: Centre for Urban and Regional Development Studies, University of Newcastle upon Tyne.

Chrisman, J., T. Hynes and S. Fraser (1995), 'Faculty entrepreneurship and economic development: The case of the University of Calgary', *Journal of Business Venturing*, **10**, 267–81.

Christiansen, C. and J. Bower (1996), 'Customer power, strategic investment and the failure of leading firms', *Strategic Management Journal*, **17**, 197–218.

Cohen, W. (2000), 'Taking care of business', *ASEE Prism Online*, January, 1–5.

Cohen, W. and S. Klepper (1992), 'The tradeoff between firm size and diversity in the pursuit of technological progress', *Small Business Economics*, **4**, 1–14.

Cohen, W. and D. Levinthal (1990), 'Absorptive capacity: A new perspective on learning and innovation', *Administrative Science Quarterly*, **35** (1), 128–53.

Cohen, W., R. Florida and W. Goe (1994), 'University–industry research centers in the United States', Center for Economic Development, Carnegie Mellon University.

Cornie, J. (1997), 'Welcome', *MMCC Compositions*, Fall, 1–2.

Dahlstrand, A. (1997), 'Entrepreneurial spinoff enterprises in Goteborg, Sweden', *European Planning Studies*, **5** (5), 659–74.

Dahlstrand, A. (1999), 'Technology-based SMEs in the Goteborg Region: Their origins and interaction with universities and large firms', *Regional Studies*, **33** (4), 379–89.

Darby, M. and L. Zucker (1997), 'Local academic science driving organizational change: The adoption of biotechnology by Japanese firms', NBER working paper, no. 7248.

Darby, M. and L. Zucker (2001), 'Change or die: The adoption of biotechnology in the Japanese and U.S. pharmaceuticals industries', *Research in Technology Innovation Management and Policy*, **7**, 85–125.

Davies, R. (1981), 'Advent of Aspen', *Reports on Research*, **9** (1), 1–2.

Davis, C. (2003), 'EU retreat to give spinoffs cash bonanza', *The Times Higher Education Supplement*, 2 May, 1.

Dechenaux, E., B. Goldfarb, S. Shane and M. Thursby (2003), 'Appropriability and the timing of innovation: Evidence from MIT inventions', working paper, Purdue University.

Del Campo, A., A. Sparks, R. Hill and R. Keller (1999), 'The transfer and commercialization of university-developed medical imaging technology: opportunities and problems', *IEEE Transactions on Engineering Management*, **46** (3), 289–98.

Department of Trade and Industry (2002), *Excellence and Opportunity – A Science and Innovation Policy for the 21st Century*, London: Department of Trade and Industry.

DiGregorio, D. and S. Shane (2003), 'Why do some universities generate more start-ups than others?', *Research Policy*, **32** (2), 209–27.

Doutriaux, J. and M. Barker (1995), 'The university–industry relationship in science and technology', *Industry Canada Occasional Papers*, Ottawa: Industry Canada, 11.

Duchesneau, D. and W. Gartner (1990), 'A profile of new venture success and failure in an emerging industry', *Journal of Business Venturing*, **5** (5), 297–312.

Dueker, K. (1997), 'Biobusiness on campus: Commercialization of university-developed biomedical technologies', *Food and Drug Law Journal*, **52**, 453–509.

Etzkowitz, H. (1989), 'Entrepreneurial science in the academy: A case of the transformation of norms', *Social Problems*, **36** (1), 14–29.

Etzkowitz, H. (1998), 'The norms of entrepreneurial science: Cognitive effects of the new university–industry linkages', *Research Policy*, **27**, 823–33.

Etzkowitz, H. (2003), 'Research groups and "quasi-firms": the invention of the entrepreneurial university', *Research Policy*, **32**, 109–21.

Feder, B. (1987), 'The rich promise of superconductors', *The New York Times*, 17 June, D6.

Feldman, M. (1994), 'The university and economic development: The case of Johns Hopkins University and Baltimore', *Economic Development Quarterly*, **8** (1), 67–76.

Feldman, M. (1999), 'The new economics of innovation, spillovers and agglomeration: A review of empirical studies', *Economics of Innovation and New Technology*, **8**, 5–25.

Feldman, M. (2001), 'Trends in patenting, licensing and the role of equity at selected U.S. universities', presentation to the National Academies Board on Science, Technology, and Economic Policy Committee on Intellectual Property Rights in the Knowledge-Based Economy, 17 April.

Feldman, M., I. Feller, J. Bercovitz and R. Burton (2000), 'Understanding evolving university–industry relationships', working paper, Johns Hopkins University.

Feller, I. (1990), 'Universities as engines of R&D-based economic growth: They think they can', *Research Policy*, **19**, 335–48.

Florida, R. and M. Kenney (1988), 'Venture capital financed innovation and technological change in the United States', *Research Policy*, **17**, 119–37.

Foster, R. (1986), *Innovation: The Attacker's Advantage*, New York: Summit Books.

Franklin, S., M. Wright and A. Lockett (2001), 'Academic and surrogate entrepreneurs in university spin-out companies', *Journal of Technology Transfer*, **26**, 127–41.

Gittelman, M. (2001), 'The institutional origins of national innovation performance: Careers, organization and patents in biotechnology in the United States and France', working paper, New York University.

Gogan, J. and L. Applegate (1996), 'Open Market, Inc.: Managing in a turbulent environment', Harvard Business School, case no. 9-196-097.

Goldfarb, B. and M. Henrekson (2003), 'Bottom-up versus top-down policies towards the commercialization of university intellectual property', *Research Policy*, **32** (4), 639–58.

Goldman, M. (1984), 'Building a mecca for high technology', *Technology Review*, May–June, **86**, 6–8.

Golub, E. (2003), 'Generating Spin-offs from University-Based Research: The Potential of Technology Transfer', PhD dissertation, Columbia University.

Gompers, P. and J. Lerner (1999), *The Venture Capital Cycle*, Cambridge, MA: MIT Press.

Gort, M., and S. Klepper (1982), 'Time paths in the diffusion of product innovations', *Economic Journal*, **92**, 630–53.

Granovetter, M. (1985), 'Economic action and social structure: The problem of embeddedness', *American Journal of Sociology*, **91**, 481–510.

Gregory, W. and T. Sheahen (1991), 'Technology transfer by spin-off companies versus licensing', in A. Brett, D. Gibson and R. Smilor (eds), *University Spin-off Companies*, Savage, MD: Rowman and Littlefield, pp.133–52.

Gulati, R. (1995), 'Does familiarity breed trust? The implications of repeated ties for contractual choice in alliances', *Academy of Management Journal*, **38** (1), 85–112.

Gupta, A. and H. Sapienza, (1992), 'Determinants of venture capital firms' preferences regarding the industry diversity and geographic scope of their investments', *Journal of Business Venturing*, **7**, 342–62.

Gustin, B. (1975), 'The Emergence of the German Chemical Profession, 1790–1867', PhD dissertation, University of Chicago.

Hannan, M. and J. Freeman (1984), 'Structural inertia and organizational change', *American Sociological Review*, **49**, 149–64.

Hansen, B. and P. Anderson (1996), 'Acusphere', The Amos Tuck School, Dartmouth College.

Harhoff, D., F. Narin, F. Scherer and K. Vopel (1999), 'Citation frequency and the value of patented inventions', *Review of Economics and Statistics*, **81** (3), 511–15.

Hayek, F. (1945), 'The use of knowledge in society', *American Economic Review*, **35** (4), 519–30.

Hebert, R. and A. Link (1988), *The Entrepreneur: Mainstream Views and Radical Critiques*, New York: Praeger.

Henderson, R. (1993), 'Underinvestment and incompetence as responses to radical innovation: Evidence from the photolithographic alignment equipment industry', *Rand Journal of Economics*, **24** (2), 248–70.

Henrekson, M. and N. Rosenberg (2001), 'Designing efficient institutions for science-based entrepreneurship: Lessons from the US and Sweden', *Journal of Technology Transfer*, **26** (3), 207–31.

Hsu, D. and T. Bernstein (1997), 'Managing the university technology licensing process', *Journal of the Association of University Technology Managers*, **9**, 1–33.

Jansen, C. and H. Dillon (1999), 'Where do leads for licenses come from? Source data from six institutions', *Journal of the Association of University Technology Managers*, **11**, 51–66.

Jensen, R. and M. Thursby (2001), 'Proofs and prototypes for sale: The tale of university licensing', *American Economic Review*, **91**, 240–59.

Jovanovic, B. (1982), 'Selection and the evolution of industry', *Econometrica*, **50** (3), 649–70.

Kaplan, S. and P. Stromberg (2001), 'Venture capitalists as principals: Contracting, screening and monitoring', *American Economic Review Papers and Proceedings*, **91** (2), 426–30.

Keck, O. (1993), 'The national system for technical innovation in Germany', in R. Nelson (ed.), *National Innovation Systems: A Comparative Analysis*, Oxford: Oxford University Press, pp.115–57.

Kelleher, N. (1995), 'For metal company, the lighter the better', *Boston Herald*, 27 June, 24.

Kenney, M. (1986), *Biotechnology: The University–Industrial Complex*, New Haven: Yale University Press.

Kenney, M. and W. Goe (forthcoming), 'A tale of two universities: Entrepreneurship in the departments of electrical engineering and computer science at UC Berkeley and Stanford', *Research Policy*.

Khilstrom, R. and J. Laffont (1979), 'A general equilibrium entrepreneurial theory of firm formation based on risk aversion', *Journal of Political Economy*, **87** (4), 719–48.

King, J. (1981), 'Prepared statement and testimony of Jonathan King at a hearing before the Subcommittee on Investigations and Oversight and the Subcommittee on Science, Research and Technology, U.S. House of Representatives, 8–9 June, 1981', *Commercialization of Academic Biomedical Research*, Washington, DC: US Government Printing Office, pp.61–76.

Kirzner, I. (1973), *Competition and Entrepreneurship*, Chicago: University of Chicago Press.

Klepper, S. and S. Sleeper (2001), 'Entry by spinoffs', working paper, Carnegie Mellon University.

Klofsten, M. and D. Jones-Evans (2000), 'Comparing academic entrepreneurship in Europe – The case of Sweden and Ireland', *Small Business Economics*, **14**, 299–309.

Knight, F. (1921), *Risk, Uncertainty, and Profit*, New York: Augustus Kelley.

Kobus, J. (1992), 'Universities and the creation of spin-off companies', *Industry and Higher Education*, **6** (3), 136–42.

Ku, K. (2001), 'Effects of patenting and technology transfer on commercialization', presentation to the National Academies Board on Science, Technology, and Economic Policy Committee on Intellectual Property Rights in the Knowledge-Based Economy, 17 April.

Latour, B. (1987), *Science in Action*, Cambridge, MA: Harvard University Press.

Lee, Y. (1996), '"Technology transfer" and the research university: A search for the boundaries of university–industry collaboration', *Research Policy*, **25**, 843–63.

Leonard, J. (2001), 'Effects of patenting and licensing on research', presentation to the National Academies Board on Science, Technology, and Economic Policy Committee on Intellectual Property Rights in the Knowledge-Based Economy, 17 April.

Lerner, J. (1994), 'The importance of patent scope: An empirical analysis', *RAND Journal of Economics*, **25** (2), 319–33.

Lerner, J. (1995), 'Venture capitalists and the oversight of private firms', *Journal of Finance*, **50** (1), 301–18.

Lerner, J. (1998), 'Venture capital and the commercialization of academic technology: Symbiosis and paradox', working paper, Harvard Business School.

Lerner, J. (1999), 'The government as venture capitalist: The long run impact of the SBIR program', *Journal of Business*, **72** (3), 285–318.

Leslie, S. (1993), *The Cold War and American Science: The Military–Industrial–Academic Complex at MIT and Stanford*, New York: Columbia University Press.

Levin, R., A. Klevorick, R. Nelson and S. Winter (1987), 'Appropriating the returns from industrial research and development', *Brookings Papers on Economic Activity*, **3**, 783–832.

Lockett, A., M. Wright and S. Franklin (2002), 'Technology transfer and universities' spin-out strategies', working paper, Nottingham Business School.

Louis, K., D. Blumenthal, M. Gluck and M. Stoto (1989), 'Entrepreneurs in academe: An exploration of behaviors among life scientists', *Administrative Science Quarterly*, **34**, 110–31.

Louis, K., L. Jones, M. Anderson, D. Blumenthal and E. Campbell (2001), 'Entrepreneurship, secrecy, and productivity: A comparison of clinical and non-clinical faculty', *Journal of Technology Transfer*, **26** (3), 233–45.

Low, M. and E. Abrahamson (1997), 'Movements, bandwagons, and clones: Industry evolution and the entrepreneurial process', *Journal of Business Venturing*, **12** (6), 435–58.

Lowe, R. (2002), 'Invention, Innovation and Entrepreneurship: The Commercialization of University Research by Inventor-Founded Firms', PhD dissertation, University of California at Berkeley.

Marsden, P. (1981), 'Introducing influence processes into a system of collective decisions', *American Journal of Sociology*, **86**, 1203–35.

Matkin, G. (1990), *Technology Transfer and the University*, New York: Macmillan.

McDade, P. (1988), 'Unprecedented investment raises question of ethics', *Centre Daily Times*, 31 January, A4.

McQueen, D. and J. Wallmark (1982), 'Spinoff companies from Chalmers University of Technology', *Technovation*, **1**, 305–15.

McQueen, D. and J. Wallmark (1991), 'University technical innovation: Spin-offs and patents in Goteborg, Sweden', in A. Brett, D. Gibson and R. Smilor (eds), *University Spin-off Companies*, Savage, MD: Rowman and Littlefield Publishers, pp.103–15.

Merges, R. and R. Nelson (1990), 'On the complex economics of patent scope', *Columbia Law Review*, **90** (4), 839–916.

Merton, R. (1973), 'The Mathew effect in science', in N. Storer (ed.), *The Sociology of Science*, Chicago: University of Chicago Press.

Miner, A., D. Eesley, M. Devaughn and T. Rura (2001), 'The magic beanstalk vision: Commercializing university inventions and research', in C. Schoonhoven and E. Romanelli (eds), *The Entrepreneurship Dynamic*, Palo Alto: Stanford University Press.

Mowery, D. (2001), 'Trends in patenting, licensing, and the role of equity at selected U.S. universities', presentation to the National Academies Board on Science, Technology, and Economic Policy Committee on Intellectual Property Rights in the Knowledge-Based Economy, 17 April.

Mowery, D. and B. Sampat (2001a), 'Patenting and licensing university inventions: Lessons from the history of the research corporation', *Industrial and Corporate Change*, **10** (2), 317–55.

Mowery, D. and B. Sampat (2001b), 'University patents and patent policy debates in the USA, 1925–1980', *Industrial and Corporate Change*, **10** (3), 781–814.

Mowery, D. and A. Ziedonis (2001), 'The commercialization of national laboratory technology through the formation of "spin-off" firms: evidence from Lawrence Livermore National Laboratory', *International Journal of Manufacturing Technology and Management*, **3** (1/2), 106–19.

Mowery, D., R. Nelson, B. Sampat and A. Ziedonis (2001), 'The growth of patenting and licensing by U.S. universities: an assessment of the effects of the Bayh–Dole Act of 1980', *Research Policy*, **30**, 99–119.

Mustar, P. (1997), 'Spin-off enterprises. How French academics create high-tech companies: conditions for success or failure', *Science and Public Policy*, **24** (1), 37–43.

National Science Foundation (2002), *Science and Engineering Indicators*, Washington, DC: United States Government Printing Office.

Nelsen, L. (1991), 'The lifeblood of biotechnology: University–industry technology transfer', in R. Ono (ed.), *The Business of Biotechnology*, Boston: Butterworth–Heinemann.

Nelson, R. (1995), 'Recent evolutionary theorizing about economic change', *Journal of Economic Literature*, **33**, 48–90.

Nelson, R. (2001), 'Observations on the post-Bayh–Dole rise of patenting at American universities', *Journal of Technology Transfer*, **26**, 13–19.

Nelson, R. and S. Winter (1982), *An Evolutionary Theory of Economic Change*, Cambridge, MA: Belknap Press.

Nerkar, A. and S. Shane (forthcoming), 'When do startups that exploit academic knowledge survive?', *International Journal of Industrial Organization*.

New York Times (1980), 'Profit – and losses – at Harvard', *New York Times*, 13 November, A34.

Nicolaou, N. and S. Birley (2003), 'Academic networks in a trichotomous categorisation of university spinouts', *Journal of Business Venturing*, **18** (3), 333–60.

Olofsson, C. and C. Wahlbin (1992), 'Firms started by university researchers in Sweden – roots, roles, relations, and growth patterns', in N. Churchill, S. Birley, W. Bygrave, D. Muzyka, C. Wahlbin and W. Wetzel (eds), *Frontiers of Entrepreneurship Research*, Babson Park, US: Babson College, pp.610–20.

Parker, D. and D. Zilberman (1993), 'University technology transfers: Impacts on local and U.S. economies', *Economic Inquiry*, **11**, 87–99.

Pavitt, K. and S. Wald (1971), *The Conditions for Success in Technological Innovation*, Paris: OECD.

Pisano, G. (1991), 'Using equity participation to support exchange: Evidence from the biotechnology industry', *Journal of Law, Economics, and Organization*, **5** (1), 109–26.

Podolny, J. (1994), 'Market uncertainty and the social character of economic exchange', *Administrative Science Quarterly*, **39**, 458–83.

Podolny, J. and T. Stuart (1995), 'A role-based ecology of technical change', *American Journal of Sociology*, **100** (5), 1224–60.

Powell, W. and J. Owen-Smith (1998), 'Universities and the market for intellectual property in the life sciences', *Journal of Policy Analysis and Management*, **17** (2), 253–77.

Press, E. and J. Washburn (2000), 'The kept university', *Atlantic Monthly*, March, 39–54.

Pressman, L. (ed.) (2000), *AUTM Licensing Survey: FY 1999*, Northbrook, IL: Association of University Technology Managers.

Pressman, L. (ed.) (2001), *AUTM Licensing Survey: FY 2000*, Northbrook, IL: Association of University Technology Managers.

Pressman, L. (ed.) (2002), *AUTM Licensing Survey: FY 2001*, Northbrook, IL: Association of University Technology Managers.

Pressman, L., S. Guterman, S. Abrams, D. Geist and L. Nelsen (1995), 'Pre-production investment and jobs induced by MIT exclusive patent licenses: A preliminary model to measure the economic impact of university licensing', *Journal of Association of University Technology Managers*, **7**, 49–81.

Preston, J. (1997), 'Success Factors in Technology-Based Entrepreneurship', presentation to the MIT Club of Tokyo, 26 February.

Reid, R. (1997), *Architects of the Web*, New York: John Wiley and Sons.

Richter, M. (1986), 'University scientists as entrepreneurs', *Society*, July/August, 80–83.

Roberts, E. (1991a), *Entrepreneurs in High Technology*, New York: Oxford University Press.

Roberts, E. (1991b), 'The technological base of the new enterprise', *Research Policy*, **20**, 283–98.

Roberts, E. and R. Malone (1996), 'Policies and structures for spinning off new companies from research and development organizations', *R&D Management*, **26** (1), 17–48.

Roberts, E. and H. Wainer (1971), 'Some characteristics of technical entrepreneurship', *IEEE Transactions on Engineering Management*, **18** (3), 100–109.

Romanelli, E. (1989), 'Environments and strategies of organization start-up: Effects on early survival', *Administrative Science Quarterly*, **34**, 369–87.

Romanelli, E. and K. Schoonhoven (2001), 'The local origins of new firms', in K. Schoonhoven and E. Romanelli (eds), *The Entrepreneurial Dynamic*, Stanford, CA: Stanford University Press, pp.40–67.

Rosenberg, N. and R. Nelson (1994), 'American universities and technical advances in industry', *Research Policy*, **23** (3), 323–48.

Rosenbloom, R. and C. Christiansen (1994), 'Technological discontinuities, organizational capabilities, and strategic commitments', *Industrial and Corporate Change*, **3**, 655–85.

Sahlman, W. (1990), 'The structure and governance of venture capital organizations', *Journal of Financial Economics*, **27**, 473–521.

Samson, K. and M. Gurdon (1993), 'University scientists as entrepreneurs: A special case of technology transfer and high-tech venturing', *Technovation*, **13** (2), 63–71.

Saxenian, A. (1994), *Regional Advantage: Culture and Competition in Silicon Valley and Route 128*, Cambridge, MA: Harvard University Press.

Schonfeld, E. (1998), 'Aware', *Fortune*, 6 July, 82.

Shane, S. (2000), 'Prior knowledge and the discovery of entrepreneurial opportunities', *Organization Science*, **11** (4), 448–69.

Shane, S. (2001a), 'Technology opportunities and new firm creation', *Management Science*, **47** (2), 205–20.

Shane, S. (2001b), 'Technology regimes and new firm formation', *Management Science*, **47** (9), 1173–90.

Shane, S. (2002), 'Selling university technology: Patterns from MIT', *Management Science*, **48** (1), 122–37.

Shane, S. (2003), *A General Theory of Entrepreneurship: The Individual Opportunity Nexus*, Cheltenham, UK and Northampton, MA, USA: Edward Elgar.

Shane, S. (forthcoming), 'Encouraging university entrepreneurship? The effect of the Bayh–Dole Act on university patenting in the United States', *Journal of Business Venturing*.

Shane, S. and D. Cable (2002), 'Network ties, reputation, and the financing of new ventures', *Management Science*, **48** (3), 364–81.

Shane, S. and R. Katila (2003), 'When are new firms more innovative than established firms?', working paper, University of Maryland.

Shane, S. and R. Khurana (2003), 'Bringing individuals back in: The effects of career experience on new firm founding', *Industrial and Corporate Change*, **12** (3), 519–43.

Shane, S. and T. Stuart (2002), 'Organizational endowments and the performance of university start-ups', *Management Science*, **48** (1), 154–70.

Shane, S. and S. Venkataraman (2000), 'The promise of entrepreneurship as a field of research', *Academy of Management Review*, **26** (1), 13–17.

Siegel, D., D. Waldman, L. Atwater and A. Link (2002), 'Commercial knowledge transfer from universities to firms: Improving the effectiveness of university–industry collaboration', working paper, Rensselaer Polytechnic Institute.

Smilor, R., D. Gibson and G. Dietrich (1990), 'University spin-out companies: Technology start-ups from UT-Austin', *Journal of Business Venturing*, **5**, 63–76.

Sobocinski, P. (1999), *Creating Hi-Tech Business Growth in Wisconsin: University of Wisconsin–Madison Technology Transfer and Entrepreneurship*, Madison, WI: University of Wisconsin System Board of Regents.

Sorenson, O. and T. Stuart (2001), 'Syndication networks and the spatial distribution of venture capital', *American Journal of Sociology*, **106** (6), 1546–88.

Stankiewicz, R. (1986), *Academics and Entrepreneurs: Developing University–Industry Relations*, London: Frances Pinter.

Stankiewicz, R. (1994), 'Spin-off companies from universities', *Science and Public Policy*, **21** (2), 99–107.

Steffensen, M., E. Rogers and K. Speakman (1999), 'Spinoffs from research centers at a research university', *Journal of Business Venturing*, **15**, 93–111.

Stephan, P. (2001), 'Educational implications of university–industry technology transfer', *Journal of Technology Transfer*, **26**, 199–205.

Stephan, P. and S. Levin (1996), 'Property rights and entrepreneurship in science', *Small Business Economics*, **8**, 177–88.

Stipp, D. (1987), 'Venture capitalists are plugging into superconductors', *The Wall Street Journal*, 29 July, 6.

Stuart, T., H. Huang and R. Hybels (1999), 'Interorganizational endorsements and the performance of entrepreneurial ventures', *Administrative Science Quarterly*, **44**, 315–49.

Taubes, G. (1995), 'The rise and fall of Thinking Machines', *Inc. Technology*, **3**, 61.

Teece, D. (1987), 'Profiting from technological innovation: Implications for integration, collaboration, licensing and public policy', in D. Teece (ed.), *The Competitive Challenge*, Cambridge, MA: Ballinger.

Teece, D. (1998), 'Capturing value from knowledge assets: The new economy, markets for know-how and intangible assets', *California Management Review*, **40** (3), 55–78.

Teece, D. and G. Pisano (1994), 'The dynamic capabilities of firms: An introduction', *Industrial and Corporate Change*, **3**, 537–56.

Thursby, J. and M. Thursby (2000), 'Industry perspectives on licensing university technologies: Sources and problems', *Journal of the Association of University Technology Managers*, **12**, 9–21.

Thursby, J., R. Jensen and M. Thursby (2001), 'Objectives, characteristics and outcomes of university licensing: A survey of major U.S. universities', *Journal of Technology Transfer*, **26**, 59–72.

Torero, M., M. Darby and L. Zucker (2001), 'The importance of intellectual human capital in the birth of the semiconductor industry', working paper, UCLA.

Tornatzky, L., P. Waugaman and J. Bauman (1997), 'Benchmarking university–industry technology transfer in the South: 1995–1996 data', *A Report of the Southern Technology Council*, Atlanta: Southern Technology Council.

Tornatzky, L., P. Waugaman and D. Gray (1999), 'Industry–university technology transfer: Models of alternative practice, policy, and program', *A Report of the Southern Technology Council*, Atlanta: Southern Technology Council.

Tornatzky, L., P. Waugaman, L. Casson, S. Crowell, C. Spahr and F. Wong (1995), 'Benchmarking best practices for university–industry technology transfer: Working with start-up companies', *A Report of the Southern Technology Council*, Atlanta: Southern Technology Council.

Tushman, M. and L. Rosenkopf (1992), 'Organizational determinants of technological change: Toward a sociology of technological evolution', *Research in Organizational Behavior*, **14**, 311–47.

Utterback, J. (1994), *Mastering the Dynamics of Innovation*, Boston, MA: Harvard Business School Press.

Utterback, J. and L. Kim (1984), 'Invasion of a stable business by radical innovation', in P. Kleindorfer (ed.), *The Management of Productivity and Technology in Manufacturing*, New York: Plenum Press, pp.113–51.

Uzzi, B. (1996), 'The sources and consequences of embeddedness for the economic performance of organizations: The network effect', *American Sociological Review*, **61**, 674–98.

Venkataraman, S. (1997), 'The distinctive domain of entrepreneurship research: An editor's perspective', in J. Katz and R. Brockhaus (eds), *Advances in Entrepreneurship, Firm Emergence and Growth*, vol. 3, Greenwich, CT: JAI Press, pp.119–38.

Vohora, A., M. Wright and A. Lockett (2002a), 'The formation of high-tech university spinouts: The role of joint ventures and venture capital investors', working paper, Nottingham Business School, Nottingham, United Kingdom.

Vohora, A., M. Wright and A. Lockett (2002b), 'Critical junctures in the growth of university high technology spinout companies', working paper, Nottingham Business School.

Von Mises, L. (1949), *Human Action: A Treatise on Economics*, New Haven, CT: Yale University Press.

Wainer, H. (1965), 'The Spinoff Technology from Government-Sponsored Research Laboratories: Lincoln Laboratory', unpublished Master's thesis, Massachusetts Institute of Technology.

Wallmark, J. (1997), 'Inventions and patents at universities: The case of Chalmers University of Technology', *Technovation*, **17** (3), 127–39.

Wickstead, S. (1985), *The Cambridge Phenomenon*, Thetford, UK: Thetford Press.

Williamson, O. (1985), *The Economic Institutions of Capitalism*, New York: The Free Press.

Wilson, M. and S. Szygenda (1991), 'University technical innovation: Spin-offs and patents in Goteborg, Sweden', in A. Brett, D. Gibson and R. Smilor (eds), *University Spin-off Companies*, Savage, MD: Rowman and Littlefield, pp.153–64.

Wright, M., A. Vohora and A. Lockett (2002), *Annual UNICO–NUBS Survey on University Commercialisation Activities: Financial Year 2001*, Nottingham: Nottingham University Business School.

Wu, S. (1989), *Production, Entrepreneurship and Profit*, Cambridge, MA: Basil Blackwell.

Yu, T. (2001), 'Entrepreneurial alertness and discovery', *The Review of Austrian Economics*, **14** (1), 47–63.

Zucker, L., M. Darby and J. Armstrong (1998a), 'Geographically localized knowledge: Spillovers or markets?', *Economic Inquiry*, **36**, 65–86.

Zucker, L., M. Darby and M. Brewer (1998b), 'Intellectual human capital and the birth of U.S. biotechnology enterprises', *American Economic Review*, **88** (1), 290–305.

Zuckoff, M. (1998), 'Tax dollars fuel university spinoffs', *Boston Globe Online*, 7 April, 1–10.

Index